Program Authors

Peter Afflerbach

Camille Blachowicz

Candy Dawson Boyd

Wendy Cheyney

Connie Juel

Edward Kame'enui

Donald Leu

Jeanne Paratore

P. David Pearson

Sam Sebesta

Deborah Simmons

Sharon Vaughn

Susan Watts-Taffe

Karen Kring Wixson

PEARSON

Scott
Foresman

Editorial Offices: Glenview, Illinois • Parsippany, New Jersey • New York, New York
Sales Offices: Needham, Massachusetts • Duluth, Georgia • Glenview, Illinois
Coppell, Texas • Sacramento, California • Mesa, Arizona

About the Cover Artist

Tim Jessell draws and paints in Stillwater, Oklahoma. He and his wife are raising three great children, whom he coaches in many sports. When not playing catch or illustrating, Tim trains falcons for the sport of falconry. Occasionally, he can still be found making a racket behind his drum set, with kids dancing around.

ISBN: 0-328-10837-5

2 3 4 5 6 7 8 9 10 V057 14 13 12 11 10 09 08 07 06 05

Dear Reader,

A new school year is beginning. Are you ready? You are about to take a trip along a famous street—*Scott Foresman Reading Street.* During this trip you will meet exciting people, such as Lewis and Clark, a girl who understood the music of whales, an astronaut who actually saw the "invisible" side of the moon, and the great magician Houdini. You will visit exotic places, such as Antarctica and Machu Picchu.

As you read selections about the rain forests in the Amazon, pink dolphins, the person who learned to decode hieroglyphics, and people who chase storms for a living, you will gain exciting new information that will help you in science and social studies.

While you're enjoying these exciting pieces of literature, you'll find that something else is going on—you are becoming a better reader, gaining new skills and polishing old ones.

Have a great trip—and send us a postcard!

Sincerely,
The Authors

UNIT 1 Contents

This Land Is Your Land

How do the diverse regions and peoples of the United States reflect its greatness?

4

5

Work & Play

What is the value of work and play?

6

PATTERNS in NATURE

What are some patterns in nature?

Read It ONLINE
sfsuccessnet.com

8

9

UNIT 4 Contents

PUZZLES AND MYSTERIES

IS THERE AN EXPLANATION FOR EVERYTHING?

11

ADVENTURES BY LAND, AIR, AND WATER

Read It ONLINE
sfsuccessnet.com

WHAT MAKES AN ADVENTURE?

12

UNIT
6
Contents

Reaching for Goals

What does it take to achieve our goals and dreams?

Read It
ONLINE
sfsuccessnet.com

14

UNIT 1

This Land Is Your Land

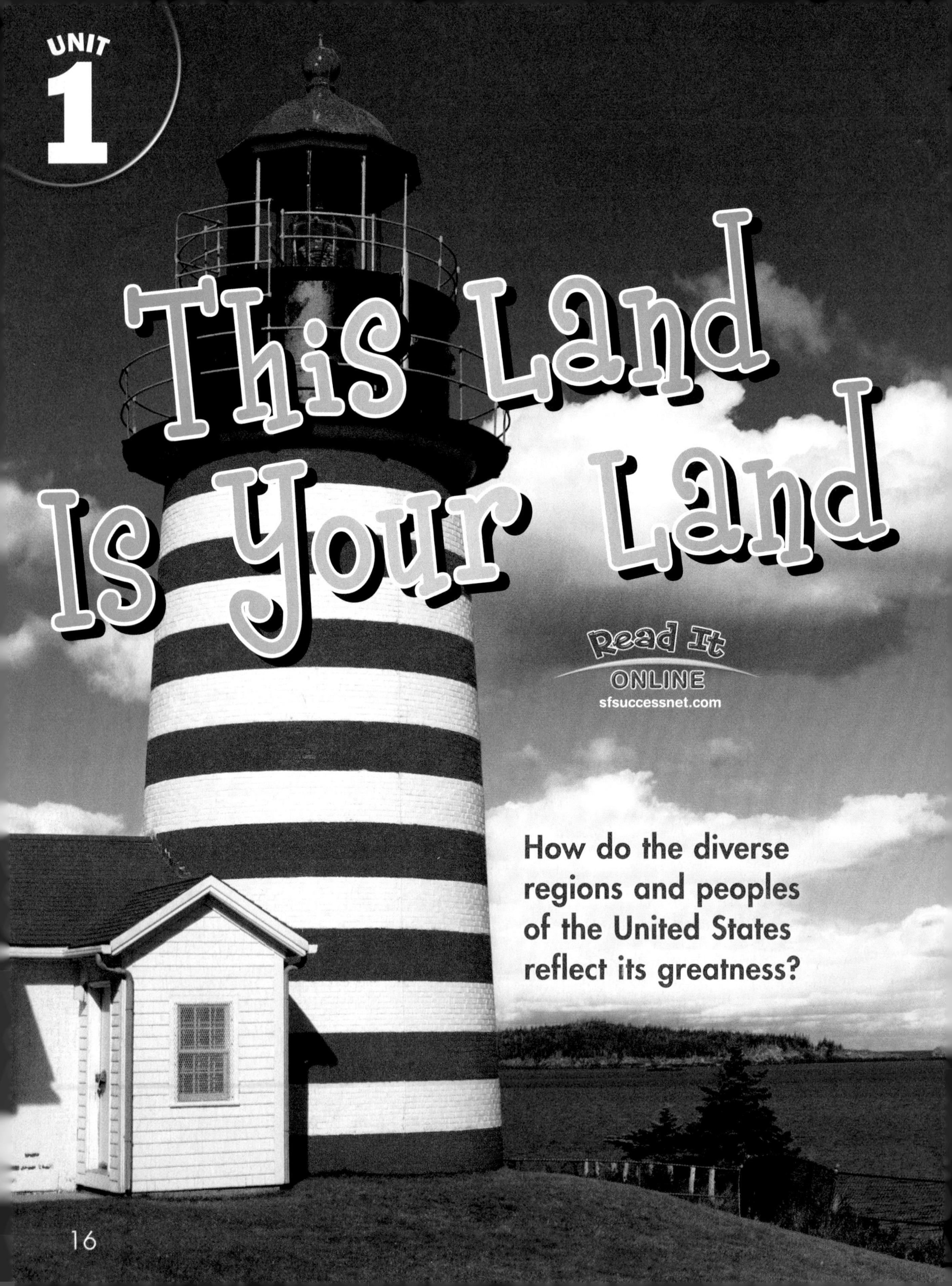

Read It ONLINE
sfsuccessnet.com

How do the diverse regions and peoples of the United States reflect its greatness?

Because of Winn-Dixie

A dog brings two people together in a Florida library.

Realistic Fiction

Lewis and Clark and Me

A group of men and their dog explore the Midwest.

Historical Fantasy

Grandfather's Journey

A Japanese man makes his home in California.

Historical Fiction

The Horned Toad Prince

A girl strikes a bargain on the Texas prairie.

Modern Fairy Tale

Letters Home from Yosemite

A traveler to Yosemite National Park recalls her trip.

Narrative Nonfiction

Skill
Sequence

Strategy
Summarize

Sequence

- Events in a story occur in a certain order, or sequence. The sequence of events can be important to understanding a story.

- Sometimes events in a story are told out of sequence. Something that happened earlier might be told after something that happened later.

Main Event   **Main Event**

Main Event   **Main Event**

Strategy: Summarize

Good readers summarize. As they read, they pause to sum up the important ideas or events. This helps them remember the information. As you read a story, note the main events. After you read, ask yourself what the main events were and in what order they occurred.

1. Read "Going Batty." Make a graphic organizer like the one above to put the main events in order. Start with "Kindergarten class goes to Story Hour."

2. Use your graphic organizer to write a summary of the story. Include only the main events.

Going Batty

Mrs. Koch's fourth-grade class walked down the hall to the library, just as they did every afternoon. At the door, their mouths dropped open. Hanging everywhere were bats—upside-down, little black bats. It took a few seconds before they realized the bats were paper. "What's with all the bats?" they asked Mr. Egan, the librarian.

Mr. Egan laughed. "We had some excitement this morning." He went on to explain.

"The day started quietly enough. I checked in some books and shelved new ones. Then a kindergarten class arrived for Story Hour. They sat in a circle while I began reading *Stellaluna*. You remember that story, don't you? It's about a little fruit bat. Well, suddenly the children yelled, 'Stellaluna! It's Stellaluna!' I love it when kids get excited about a story, but this was ridiculous! Then I saw they were pointing up. Somehow a little bat had gotten into the library! It was darting all over. Luckily, I was able to trap it in a box and take it outside. The kids all made paper bats to take its place."

The fourth graders looked around the room hopefully. But there were no bats—no real ones, anyway. They all sighed. Sometimes little kids have all the luck.

Skill Which grade is mentioned first in the story? Why do you suppose it is not the first event on your graphic organizer?

Skill What time word clues tell you that Mr. Egan is going to tell about events that happened earlier in the day?

Strategy See if you can summarize what Mr. Egan told the fourth graders. Be sure to give the events in order.

Strategy Now summarize the day's events in the library, not in the order in which you read about them but in the order in which they actually happened.

memorial

prideful

recalls

peculiar

grand

positive

selecting

Remember

Try the strategy. Then, if you need more help, use your glossary or a dictionary.

Vocabulary Strategy
for Suffixes

Word Structure Suppose you are reading and you come to a word you don't know. Does the word have *-ful* or *-al* at the end? You can use the suffix to help you figure out the word's meaning. The suffix *-ful* can make a word mean "full of ____," as in *careful*. The suffix *-al* can make a word mean "of or like ____," as in *fictional*.

1. Put your finger over the *-ful* or *-al* suffix.

2. Look at the base word. (That's the word without the suffix.) Put the base word in the phrase "full of ____" or "of or like ____."

3. Try that meaning in the sentence. Does it make sense?

As you read "The Storyteller," look for words that end with *-ful* or *-al*. Use the suffixes to help you figure out the meanings of the words.

The Storyteller

Thursday mornings at the James P. Guthrie Memorial Library are magical. That's because every Thursday morning Ms. Ada Landry tells stories to anyone who wants to listen. But she does not just tell the stories. She acts them out. She makes them come alive.

When Ms. Ada describes what she calls "a prideful person," she puffs out her chest and looks down her nose. She talks in a loud, boastful voice. When she tells about a sly person, she narrows her eyes and pulls up her shoulders. She talks in a shady kind of voice. When she recalls things that happened long ago, she gets a faraway look in her eyes, and she talks in a quiet, dreamy voice.

Ms. Ada's stories are entertaining, but they nearly always have a lesson in them too. A person whom everyone thinks is a bit peculiar turns out to be kind or brave. A person whom everyone thinks is grand proves to be cowardly or mean. A mistake or disaster ends up having a positive effect.

When it comes to selecting and telling stories, Ms. Ada is the best.

Write

Write about what you like best about the library. Give reasons for your choice. Use some words from the Words to Know list.

Because of Winn-Dixie

by Kate DiCamillo
illustrated by Kevin Hawkes

Genre

Realistic fiction has characters and events that are like people and events in real life. As you read, think about how the people and events in your life are similar to or different from the characters and events in this story.

What happens in a library because of Winn-Dixie?

India Opal Buloni, known best as Opal, has recently moved to Naomi, Florida, with her preacher father. Shortly after her arrival, Opal rescues a scrappy dog that she names Winn-Dixie, after the store in which she finds him. She convinces her father, who often preaches about caring for the needy, that this dog is certainly in need. Thus a summer of adventures begins.

I spent a lot of time that summer at the Herman W. Block Memorial Library. The Herman W. Block Memorial Library sounds like it would be a big fancy place, but it's not. It's just a little old house full of books, and Miss Franny Block is in charge of them all. She is a very small, very old woman with short gray hair, and she was the first friend I made in Naomi.

It all started with Winn-Dixie not liking it when I went into the library, because he couldn't go inside, too. But I showed him how he could stand up on his hind legs and look in the window and see me in there, selecting my books; and he was okay, as long as he could see me. But the thing was, the first time Miss Franny Block saw Winn-Dixie standing up on his hind legs like that, looking in the window, she didn't think he was a dog. She thought he was a bear.

This is what happened: I was picking out my books and kind of humming to myself, and all of a sudden, there was this loud and scary scream. I went running up to the front of the library, and there was Miss Franny Block, sitting on the floor behind her desk.

"Miss Franny?" I said. "Are you all right?"

"A bear," she said.

"A bear?" I asked.

"He has come back," she said.

"He has?" I asked. "Where is he?"

"Out there," she said and raised a finger and pointed at Winn-Dixie standing up on his hind legs, looking in the window for me.

"Miss Franny Block," I said, "that's not a bear. That's a dog. That's my dog. Winn-Dixie."

"Are you positive?" she asked.

"Yes ma'am," I told her. "I'm positive. He's my dog. I would know him anywhere."

Miss Franny sat there trembling and shaking.

"Come on," I said. "Let me help you up. It's okay." I stuck out my hand and Miss Franny took hold of it, and I pulled her up off the floor. She didn't weigh hardly anything at all. Once she was standing on her feet, she started acting all embarrassed, saying how I must think she was a silly old lady, mistaking a dog for a bear, but that she had a bad experience with a bear coming into the Herman W. Block Memorial Library a long time ago, and she never had quite gotten over it.

"When did that happen?" I asked her.

"Well," said Miss Franny, "it is a very long story."

"That's okay," I told her. "I am like my mama in that I like to be told stories. But before you start telling it, can Winn-Dixie come in and listen, too? He gets lonely without me."

"Well, I don't know," said Miss Franny. "Dogs are not allowed in the Herman W. Block Memorial Library."

"He'll be good," I told her. "He's a dog who goes to church." And before she could say yes or no, I went outside and got Winn-Dixie, and he came in and lay down with a *"huummmppff"* and a sigh, right at Miss Franny's feet.

She looked down at him and said, "He most certainly is a large dog."

"Yes ma'am," I told her. "He has a large heart, too."

"Well," Miss Franny said. She bent over and gave Winn-Dixie a pat on the head, and Winn-Dixie wagged his tail back and forth and snuffled his nose on her little old-lady feet. "Let me get a chair and sit down so I can tell this story properly."

"Back when Florida was wild, when it consisted of nothing but palmetto trees and mosquitoes so big they could fly away with you," Miss Franny Block started in, "and I was just a little girl no bigger than you, my father, Herman W. Block, told me that I could have anything I wanted for my birthday. Anything at all."

Miss Franny looked around the library. She leaned in close to me. "I don't want to appear prideful," she said, "but my daddy was a very rich man. A very rich man." She nodded and then leaned back and said, "And I was a little girl who loved to read. So I told him, I said, 'Daddy, I would most certainly love to have a library for my birthday, a small little library would be wonderful.'"

"You asked for a whole library?"

"A small one," Miss Franny nodded. "I wanted a little house full of nothing but books and I wanted to share them, too. And I got my wish. My father built me this house, the very one we are sitting in now. And at a very young age, I became a librarian. Yes ma'am."

"What about the bear?" I said.

"Did I mention that Florida was wild in those days?" Miss Franny Block said.

"Uh-huh, you did."

"It was wild. There were wild men and wild women and wild animals."

"Like bears!"

"Yes ma'am. That's right. Now, I have to tell you, I was a little-miss-know-it-all. I was a miss-smarty-pants with my library full of books. Oh, yes ma'am, I thought I knew the answers to everything. Well, one hot Thursday, I was sitting in my library with all the doors and windows open and my nose stuck in a book, when a shadow crossed the desk. And without looking up, yes ma'am, without even looking up, I said, 'Is there a book I can help you find?'

"Well, there was no answer. And I thought it might have been a wild man or a wild woman, scared of all these books and afraid to speak up. But then I became aware of a very peculiar smell, a very strong smell. I raised my eyes slowly. And standing right in front of me was a bear. Yes ma'am. A very large bear."

"How big?" I asked.

"Oh, well," said Miss Franny, "perhaps three times the size of your dog."

"Then what happened?" I asked her.

"Well," said Miss Franny, "I looked at him and he looked at me. He put his big nose up in the air and sniffed and sniffed as if he was trying to decide if a little-miss-know-it-all librarian was what he was in the mood to eat. And I sat there. And then I thought, 'Well, if this bear intends to eat me, I am not going to let it happen without a fight. No ma'am.' So very slowly and very carefully, I raised up the book I was reading."

"What book was that?" I asked.

"Why, it was *War and Peace,* a very large book. I raised it up slowly and then I aimed it carefully and I threw it right at that bear and screamed, 'Be gone!' And do you know what?"

"No ma'am," I said.

"He went. But this is what I will never forget. He took the book with him."

"Nuh-uh," I said.

"Yes ma'am," said Miss Franny. "He snatched it up and ran."

"Did he come back?" I asked.

"No, I never saw him again. Well, the men in town used to tease me about it. They used to say, 'Miss Franny, we saw that bear of yours out in the woods today. He was reading that book and he said it sure was good and would it be all right if he kept it for just another week.' Yes ma'am. They did tease me about it." She sighed. "I imagine I'm the only one left from those days. I imagine I'm the only one that even recalls that bear. All my friends, everyone I knew when I was young, they are all dead and gone."

She sighed again. She looked sad and old and wrinkled. It was the same way I felt sometimes, being friendless in a new town and not having a mama to comfort me. I sighed, too.

Winn-Dixie raised his head off his paws and looked back and forth between me and Miss Franny. He sat up then and showed Miss Franny his teeth.

"Well now, look at that," she said. "That dog is smiling at me."

"It's a talent of his," I told her.

"It is a fine talent," Miss Franny said. "A very fine talent." And she smiled back at Winn-Dixie.

"We could be friends," I said to Miss Franny. "I mean you and me and Winn-Dixie, we could all be friends."

Miss Franny smiled even bigger. "Why, that would be grand," she said, "just grand."

And right at that minute, right when the three of us had decided to be friends, who should come marching into the

Herman W. Block Memorial Library but old pinch-faced Amanda Wilkinson. She walked right up to Miss Franny's desk and said, "I finished *Johnny Tremain* and I enjoyed it very much. I would like something even more difficult to read now, because I am an advanced reader."

"Yes dear, I know," said Miss Franny. She got up out of her chair.

Amanda pretended like I wasn't there. She stared right past me. "Are dogs allowed in the library?" she asked Miss Franny as they walked away.

"Certain ones," said Miss Franny, "a select few." And then she turned around and winked at me. I smiled back. I had just made my first friend in Naomi, and nobody was going to mess that up for me, not even old pinch-faced Amanda Wilkinson.

Reader Response

Open for Discussion In your mind's eye, see the Herman W. Block Memorial Library. Tell about that place and what happened there.

1. This author has won prizes for her books. Why? Find a part of this story that could win a prize.

2. Think about the sequence. What happens to Miss Franny's feelings about Winn-Dixie from the beginning of the story to the end? Why do her feelings change?

3. When summarizing a story, you only include important details. Which two of the following statements would you leave out of a summary of the story? Why?

   a. The Herman W. Block Memorial Library is a little old house full of books.

   b. Miss Franny Block is afraid of Winn-Dixie because she thinks he is a bear.

   c. Amanda Wilkinson returns a book to the library.

4. Miss Franny Block describes the bear as having a *peculiar* smell. What other words might she have used in place of *peculiar*? Use a thesaurus. Remember that some synonyms will not be appropriate to describe the bear's smell.

Look Back and Write Winn-Dixie is a dog with talent. What is that talent? Look back at page 32 and then write about Winn-Dixie's talent.

34

Read these books by Kate DiCamillo.

As a child, Kate DiCamillo was often sick. When Kate was five, a doctor said warm weather would be better for her health. She and her mother moved to a small town in Florida. The people were friendly, and Kate loved the way they talked. "I also had a dog I loved. I spent a lot of time dressing Nanette up—in a green ballet tutu and then later as a disco dancer."

After college, Ms. DiCamillo moved to Minneapolis and got a job at a bookstore. She lived in a tiny apartment and never had enough money. "I wrote *Because of Winn-Dixie* because I was homesick for Florida. Also, my apartment building didn't allow dogs. So I made up one to keep me company." She got up at 4:00 every morning to write before going to work.

Since then, Ms. DiCamillo's life has really changed. She has now written three award-winning books. She bought a new home and a new car. And she no longer has to work at the bookstore. "I couldn't have imagined in my wildest dreams what's happened to me!"

The Tiger Rising

The Tale of Despereaux

Science
in Reading

Expository Nonfiction

Genre
- Expository nonfiction provides information about people, places, animals, and other things in the real world.

- Expository nonfiction may give a few facts or it may describe a subject in depth with many facts.

Text Features
- A head above each paragraph tells you what the paragraph will be about.

- The map is important because it gives visual information to go along with the text.

Link to Science
Choose a favorite animal to research. Use the library or the Internet to find a complete description of that animal—where it lives, what it looks like, what it eats. Make a "Fast Facts" poster about your animal.

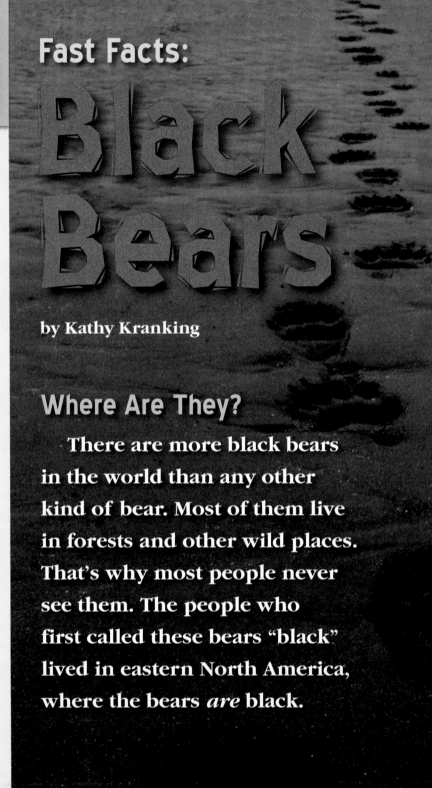

Fast Facts:

Black Bears

by Kathy Kranking

Where Are They?

There are more black bears in the world than any other kind of bear. Most of them live in forests and other wild places. That's why most people never see them. The people who first called these bears "black" lived in eastern North America, where the bears *are* black.

Take a Stand

Like other bears, black bears can stand upright as humans do. They may stand to see over tall grass or to sniff an odor in the breeze. Or they may stand to get to food that's hard to reach.

Long, Sharp Claws

Black bears have sharp claws that grow up to 2.5 inches (6.25 cm) long. The bears use their claws to climb, tear apart prey, dig for food, and make dens.

Trees Are a Breeze

Adult black bears are good at climbing trees. They usually go up to get food such as acorns or cherries.

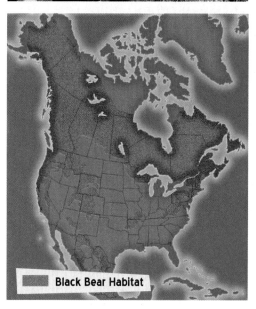

Black Bear Habitat

Body Length: 4-6 feet (1.2-1.8 m)
Weight: 100-900 pounds (45-400 kg)
Life Span: About 30 years
Habitat: Woods, meadows, and swamps
Range: See orange areas on map.

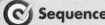 **Sequence** Is sequence always important in what you read?

Bear Bodies

🐾 Bears of Many Colors

Black bears can be white, light brown, dark brown, cinnamon, blond, or blue-black. Most of the black bears that aren't black live in western North America. Sometimes western cubs from the same family are different colors.

🐾 Working Out

Even though they're big and bulky, black bears can really move. They can run 30 miles (48 km) per hour and swim as far as 2 miles (3.2 km) at a time. And they can leap short distances when they want to.

🐾 Heading Home

Even after wandering far off, black bears can find their way home. They use all of their senses to find the way back, especially their keen sense of smell. They may be the best "sniffers" of all the mammals in North America.

🐾 Tricky Tongues and Paws

Black bears have very long tongues. Their tongues come in handy for slurping food, such as insects, from hard-to-reach places.

They're also very good at using their paws. They can even unscrew jar lids to get at goodies that were left behind by careless campers!

Chow Time

Hairy Neighbors

More and more people have been moving into areas that once were "bear country." Soon the bears start looking for food near people, and *that* causes problems.

Black Bear Menu

Black bears aren't picky eaters—they'll eat almost anything. Nuts, fruits, seeds, roots, grasses, and honey are all on a bear's menu. They'll also eat animals such as insects, fish, and rodents.

Bears Are Back

Black bears usually would rather run from people than hurt them. Even so, for many years some people shot or poisoned the bears until their numbers went way down. Today there are strict laws about when and where bears may be hunted, so they're making a big comeback. Hooray for black bears!

Reading Across Texts

Which facts about black bears could Miss Franny Block verify from her experience?

Writing Across Texts List the facts about black bears that Miss Block could verify.

 Summarize What general statements summarize these facts?

Comprehension

Skill
Author's Purpose

Strategy
Answer Questions

 Skill

Author's Purpose

- The author's purpose is the reason or reasons the author has for writing.

- An author may write to persuade, to inform, to entertain, or to express ideas and feelings.

	Author's Purpose	Why do you think so?
Before you read: What do you think it will be?		
As you read: What do you think it is?		

 Strategy

Strategy: Answer Questions

Good readers know where to look for the answers to questions. They know that sometimes the answer to a question is in one place. Other times it is in several places. They know that sometimes they must use what they've read plus what they know to answer a question. That is what you usually have to do to answer a question about the author's purpose.

1. Read "Jefferson's Bargain." Make a graphic organizer like the one above to keep track of the author's purpose.

2. After you read the article, answer these questions: Do you think the author met his or her purpose? Why or why not?

40

Jefferson's BARGAIN

About 200 years ago, when the United States was still new, our third President, Thomas Jefferson, had a big idea. He wanted to discover what lay west of the Mississippi River. This land was known as Louisiana.

Today one of our southern states is called Louisiana. But at that time, "Louisiana" was all of the land between the Mississippi River in the east and the Rocky Mountains in the west. This was an area of more than 800,000 square miles!

France said it owned this land. However, it was at war with England. It didn't want to fight another war with the United States over Louisiana. So France agreed to sell the land. President Jefferson got it for— are you ready?—less than 3 cents an acre!

The land became known as the Louisiana Purchase. In time it would become all or part of 13 states. But when Jefferson sent Lewis and Clark to explore this area in May of 1804, the two men and their group would enter a far-reaching wilderness.

Skill Preview the article. Do you think the author's purpose is to persuade, to inform, to entertain, or to express?

Strategy To answer the skill question, look at the title and skim the text. Do you see numbers and dates? What purpose do they suggest?

Skill Is the author's purpose what you thought it would be when you previewed the article? Why or why not?

Strategy Why did the author ask "are you ready?" in this paragraph?

Words to Know

yearned

wharf

docks

scan

migrating

scent

Remember

Try the strategy. Then, if you need more help, use your glossary or a dictionary.

Vocabulary Strategy
for Endings

Word Structure Sometimes when you are reading, you may come across a word you don't know. Look at the end of the word. Does it have *-ed* or *-ing*? The ending *-ed* is added to a verb to make it past tense, or tell about past actions. The ending *-ing* is added to a verb to make it tell about present or ongoing actions. You may be able to use the ending to help you figure out the meaning of the word.

1. Put your finger over the *-ed* or *-ing* ending.

2. Look at the base word. Do you know what the base word means?

3. Try your meaning in the sentence. Does it make sense?

As you read "Westward Ho!" look for words that have the *-ed* or *-ing* ending. Use the ending to help you figure out the meanings of the words.

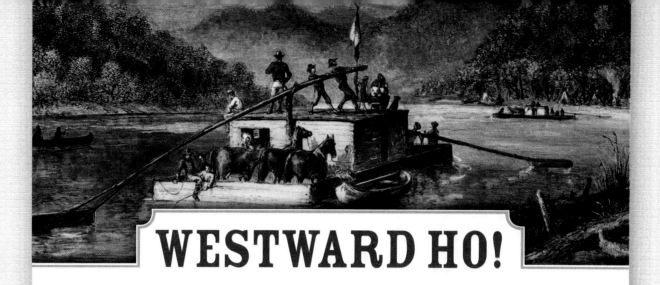

WESTWARD HO!

In the 1800s, America grew ever larger as land in the West was bought. As it grew, men and women of a certain kind yearned to travel west into the unknown. They had pioneer spirit.

There were no roads, of course. However, rivers made good highways for boats. In my mind I can see the pioneers with all their goods, waiting on the wharf in St. Louis. Sailors are busy loading and unloading ships. The pioneers load their belongings onto flatboats tied to the docks.

As they traveled, pioneers would scan the country for food and Indians. There were no grocery stores. And they never knew how the Indians would receive them. If the Indians were friendly, they might talk and trade. If a trapper were present, they were lucky. Trappers knew the country and the Indians well.

It must have been exciting to see this country for the first time. Pioneers saw endless herds and flocks of animals migrating. They breathed pure air full of the scent of tall grasses and wildflowers.

Imagine you are starting a trip to explore an unknown river. Describe your first day on the water. Use words from the Words to Know list.

Lewis and Clark and Me

A DOG'S TALE

by Laurie Myers   illustrations by Michael Dooling

Genre

Historical fantasy is based on real events in history, but it is a story that could never really happen—in this case, because a dog can't write. As you read, look for the facts on which this story is based.

Who will join Lewis and Clark on their journey of exploration?

Note to readers: The extracts from Meriwether Lewis's journal published in this excerpt retain their original spelling.

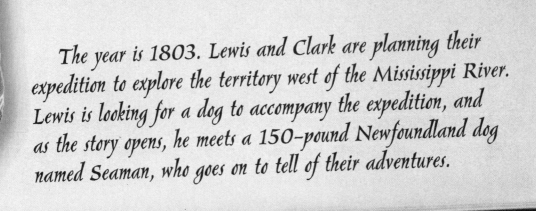

The year is 1803. Lewis and Clark are planning their expedition to explore the territory west of the Mississippi River. Lewis is looking for a dog to accompany the expedition, and as the story opens, he meets a 150-pound Newfoundland dog named Seaman, who goes on to tell of their adventures.

"Seaman!"

I glance at the man beside me.

"Look alive. Here's buyers."

Something caught my attention beyond him, down the wharf—a group of men, but I saw only one. It was Lewis. He was a full head taller than the other men I had known on the docks. And he was dressed in a different way—white breeches and a short blue coat with buttons that shone in the sun. A tall pointed hat with a feather made him look even taller.

Lewis walked along the dock with a large stride. There was a purpose about him. My life on the wharves was good, but I was a young dog and yearned for more. At the time I didn't know exactly what. I sensed that this man was part of what I wanted. I sat straighter as he approached. The man who owned me stood straighter, too. Lewis slowed.

"Need a dog, sir?" my man asked.

"I'm lookin'," Lewis replied. He stooped down and looked me right in the eye. I wagged my tail and stepped forward. I wanted to sniff this strange man. He extended his hand for me. He didn't smell like any I had ever smelled, and it made me want to sniff him all over.

Lewis scratched the back of my neck, where I liked to be scratched.

"I'm headed out west, up the Missouri River," Lewis said.

My man's face brightened.

"This dog be perfect, sir. These dogs can swim. Newfoundlands, they call them. Rescue a drowning man in rough water or in a storm. Look at these paws. You won't find another dog with paws like that. They's webbed." He spread my toes to show the webbing.

"So they are," Lewis replied. Lewis began feeling my chest and hindquarters. His hands were large and muscular.

"Water rolls off this coat," my man added. He pulled up a handful of my thick, dense double coat.

Lewis examined my coat and nodded.

"I know the Mississippi, sir, but I don't know the Meesori," my man said.

"It's off the Mississippi, headin' northwest."

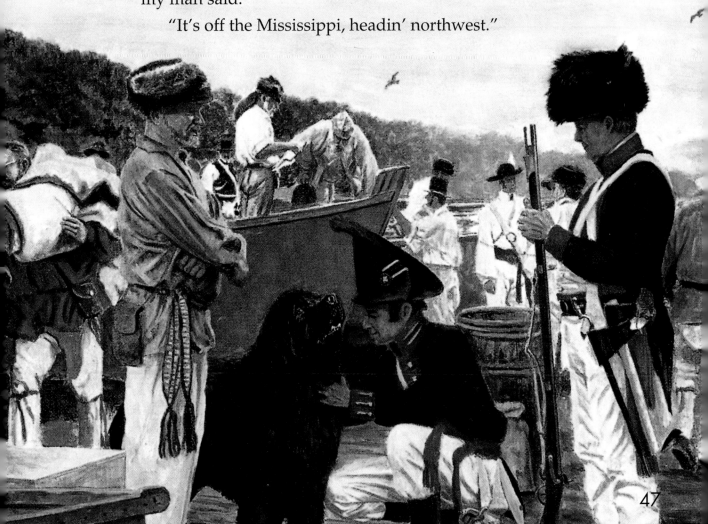

"North, you say. Ah. It'll be cold up that river. Won't bother this one, though." He patted me firmly on the back.

Lewis stood and looked around. He found a piece of wood that had broken off a crate. He showed it to me, then threw it.

"Go," he said.

I wanted to go. I wanted to do whatever this man asked. But I belonged to another. I looked at my man.

"Go on," he said.

I ran for the stick and returned it to Lewis.

"How much?" Lewis asked.

"Twenty dollars. And a bargain at that."

Lewis looked down at me. I lifted my head proudly.

"Won't find a better dog than this. Perfect for your trip," my man said, trying to convince Lewis.

It wasn't necessary. Lewis wanted me. I could tell. He had liked me the minute he saw me. The feeling was mutual. Lewis paid my man twenty dollars.

"Does he have a name?" Lewis asked.

"I been callin' him Seaman, but you can name him anything you like."

"Come, Seaman," Lewis called.

As we walked away, my rope in his hand, he put his other hand on my head. After that, he didn't need a rope. I would follow this man to the ends of the Earth.

...the dog was of the newfoundland breed one that I prised much for his docility and qualifications generally for my journey....

Meriwether Lewis   November 16, 1803

Squirrels

I caught fish off the docks. I chased animals in the woods. But hunting came alive for me on the river—the Ohio, Lewis called it.

I have always loved the water, so the day we boarded the boat and pushed out onto the Ohio River was just about the happiest day of my life. Lewis was excited, too. I could tell by the way he walked. And his voice was louder than usual.

The men were also excited. I could hear it in their voices. They didn't complain when they loaded the boat. Lewis was telling them what to load and how to load it. Anyway, that afternoon, Lewis and I and some men started down the river.

I rode in the back of the boat. It was the highest place and gave me the best view. From there I could scan both banks and the water with just a glance. The first two weeks I couldn't get enough of it. There were animals I had not seen before. Smells I had not smelled. My skin tingled with excitement.

The river was low, and the men had to pole much
of the way. When they weren't poling, they were digging
channels for our boat or hiring oxen to pull the boat from
the shore.

We were only a couple of weeks down the river when
I had my first great day of hunting. The river wasn't quite
as shallow and the current not too strong, so the crew
rowed along leisurely.

I was lying on the back deck of the boat. I had just
scanned the shore—nothing of interest, just a few beaver
and a deer. I decided to close my eyes for a nap. I blinked
a few times and was ready to lay my head on my paws
when something on the water up ahead caught my eye.

I stuck my nose in the air and sniffed. I recognized the scent immediately. Squirrel.

A squirrel on water? That was unusual. I had seen plenty of squirrels, but I had never seen one swim. There was something else strange. The smell of squirrel was especially strong. I had never known one squirrel to project so powerful a scent.

I stood to take a look. Right away I spotted a squirrel off the starboard side. He was swimming across the river. Another squirrel followed close behind. Without a second thought, I leaned over the side of the boat to get a better look.

I saw another squirrel. And another. I could not believe my eyes; hundreds of squirrels were crossing the river. The water up ahead was almost black with them. Every muscle in my body tightened to full alert.

Lewis was on the other side of the boat, talking to two of the men. I turned to him and barked.

"What is it?" he asked.

It is impossible to describe the urge I felt. It was as strong as anything I had ever known. I had to get those squirrels.

I barked again. Lewis scanned the water ahead.

"Look at that," he said to the men. "Squirrels crossing the river. Now why would they do that?"

"Food?" one man suggested.

Lewis paused for a moment. "There are hickory nuts on both banks."

"Migrating?" suggested the other.

Lewis nodded. "Maybe. Or perhaps they're—"

I barked again. They were wasting time wondering why the squirrels were crossing. It didn't matter. The squirrels were there. Hundreds of them, right in front of us. Sometimes men spend too much time thinking. They miss the fun of life.

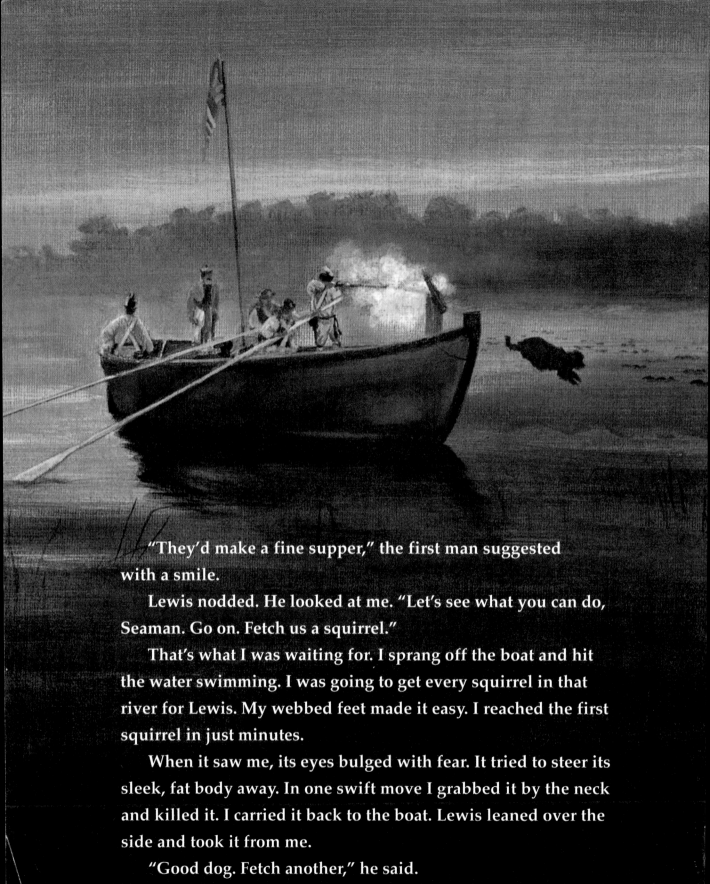

"They'd make a fine supper," the first man suggested with a smile.

Lewis nodded. He looked at me. "Let's see what you can do, Seaman. Go on. Fetch us a squirrel."

That's what I was waiting for. I sprang off the boat and hit the water swimming. I was going to get every squirrel in that river for Lewis. My webbed feet made it easy. I reached the first squirrel in just minutes.

When it saw me, its eyes bulged with fear. It tried to steer its sleek, fat body away. In one swift move I grabbed it by the neck and killed it. I carried it back to the boat. Lewis leaned over the side and took it from me.

"Good dog. Fetch another," he said.

The crew had stopped rowing, and the boat drifted slowly toward the mass of squirrels.

"Look at Captain Lewis's dog!" yelled one of the rowers.

I turned and started swimming again. I could hear the men cheering me on. In two strokes I was on another squirrel.

"Good dog!" Lewis yelled. "Go!"

"Go," the crew echoed. "Go, Seaman, go!"

I went. And went. Over and over, I went. I went until I was exhausted. I don't know how long it lasted. Maybe one hour. Maybe four.

All I know is that when I finished, there was a pile of squirrels in the boat. Lewis and the crew were laughing and cheering. All the rest of the day the men were patting me and saying, "Good dog" and "Good boy" and "We'll be eatin' good tonight." The admiration of the crew was great, but the look of pride on Lewis's face was better than all the men's praise added together.

That night the men fried the squirrels, and we ate well.

In the three years that followed, I hunted almost every day. But the squirrels on the Ohio were my favorite.

...observed a number of squirrels swiming the Ohio... they appear to be making to the south;... I made my dog take as many each day as I had occation for, they wer fat and I thought them when fryed a pleasent food... he would take the squirel in the water kill them and swiming bring them in his mouth to the boat....

Meriwether Lewis September 11, 1803

Bear-Dog

"Indians."

We had not been on the shore very long before I heard Lewis say the word.

Lewis and Clark and I had crossed the river to make some observations. That's when these Indians appeared. They were different from other people I had known—the boatmen and city folk.

I didn't sense that Lewis or Clark were concerned, so I wasn't. The Indians seemed friendly enough. Lewis talked to them. It wasn't until later that I realized Lewis gave the same talk to every group of Indians we met. He talked about the "great white father" in Washington.

The Indians listened patiently as one of the English-speaking Indians translated. Lewis used hand motions to help. As he talked on, it became obvious to me that the Indians were not interested in Lewis or what he was saying. They were staring at me. Finally, Lewis realized what was going on, and he invited the Indians to take a closer look.

They gathered around. They touched me. They whispered about me. They acted like they had never seen a dog before. Then I noticed an Indian dog standing to the side. I took one look at that animal and realized why they were so interested in me.

That dog could not have been more than twenty pounds. Newfoundlands can weigh up to 150 pounds, and I'm a large Newfoundland. If that scrawny dog was the only dog they had seen, then I was a strange sight indeed.

"Bear," one of the English-speaking Indians said.

I looked up. He was pointing at me.

"Dog," Lewis replied patiently.

The Indian looked at his own dog. He looked back at me.

"Bear," he said again.

Lewis looked at me and smiled. Clark was smiling, too.

I lifted my head.

"I guess he does look like a bear," Lewis said.

Lewis picked up a stick and threw it.

"Fetch," he said.

I fetched.

"Stay," he said.

I stayed.

"Sit," he said.

I sat.

The Indians were impressed.

"Dog," Lewis said politely. Lewis was always nice.

The Indian who had called me "bear" turned to consult with his friends.

Finally, he turned.

"Bear-dog," he said with satisfaction.

Lewis smiled.

"Yes, I guess you could call him bear-dog."

Later, George Drouillard explained to us that the Indians don't have a separate word for *horse*. They call a horse "elk-dog." I guess it made sense for them to call me a bear-dog.

The Indian suddenly turned and walked through the crowd to his horse. He pulled out three beaver skins. He held them out to Lewis.

"For bear-dog," he said.

It wasn't often that I saw Lewis surprised. He was then.

I took a step closer to Lewis.

Lewis looked the Indian square in the eye and said, "No trade. Bear-dog special."

As we rode back to camp in the boat, Lewis said to me, "Three beaver skins! Can you believe that?"

No, I could not. The idea that Lewis and I would ever separate was unthinkable. Not many dogs and men fit together like Lewis and I. If you have ever experienced it, then you know what I'm talking about. And if you haven't, well, it's hard to explain. All I can tell you is that when a dog and a man fit like Lewis and I did, nothing can separate them. Lewis said it best.

"No trade."

...one of the Shawnees a respectable looking Indian offered me three beverskins for my dog with which he appeared much pleased... of course there was no bargan, I had given 20$ for this dogg myself—

Meriwether Lewis   November 16, 1803

57

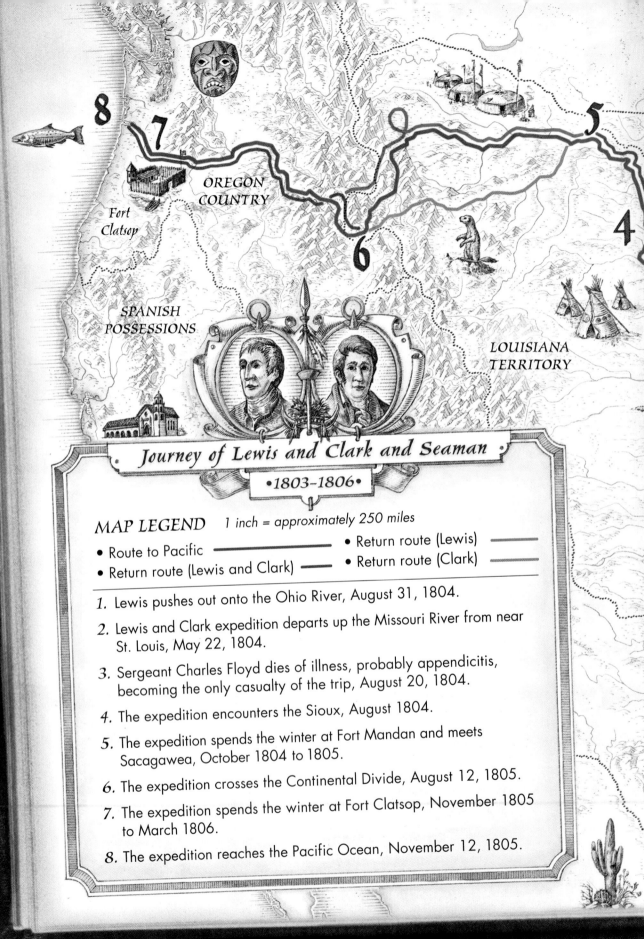

OREGON
COUNTRY

Fort
Clatsop

SPANISH
POSSESSIONS

LOUISIANA
TERRITORY

Journey of Lewis and Clark and Seaman

•1803–1806•

MAP LEGEND   1 inch = approximately 250 miles

- Route to Pacific —————
- Return route (Lewis and Clark) ——
- Return route (Lewis) —————
- Return route (Clark) —————

1. Lewis pushes out onto the Ohio River, August 31, 1804.

2. Lewis and Clark expedition departs up the Missouri River from near St. Louis, May 22, 1804.

3. Sergeant Charles Floyd dies of illness, probably appendicitis, becoming the only casualty of the trip, August 20, 1804.

4. The expedition encounters the Sioux, August 1804.

5. The expedition spends the winter at Fort Mandan and meets Sacagawea, October 1804 to 1805.

6. The expedition crosses the Continental Divide, August 12, 1805.

7. The expedition spends the winter at Fort Clatsop, November 1805 to March 1806.

8. The expedition reaches the Pacific Ocean, November 12, 1805.

BRITISH
POSSESSIONS

N

INDIANA
TERRITORY

3

2

St. Louis

MISSISSIPPI
TERRITORY

1

Reader Response

Open for Discussion A dog couldn't write
a journal, could he? So how did the author,
Laurie Myers, seem to get Seaman's words?
Explain this mystery.

1. Reread the parts from Meriwether Lewis's journal. Some
   of the words are misspelled. Why didn't the author
   correct them?

2. An author's purpose can be to help readers visualize a scene.
   Do you think this might have been one of Laurie Myers's
   purposes? Explain.

3. How does Seaman feel about Lewis? How does he express
   these feelings? Use examples from the story to explain
   your answer.

4. What would you include in a newspaper ad for a
   Newfoundland like Seaman? Write an ad, using words
   from the Words to Know list and the selection.

Look Back and Write Seaman was a dog with special
qualities. Reread page 47. List some of the qualities that
made him special.

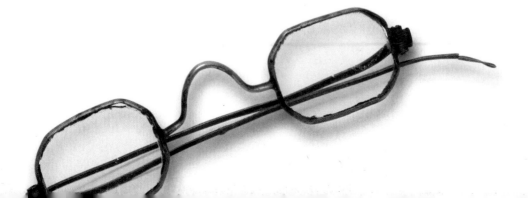

60

Read more books by Laurie Myers and Michael Dooling.

Laurie Myers says she got the idea for *Lewis and Clark and Me* after reading about Meriwether Lewis and his dog. "I've had many dogs over the years and I've been closer to some than others. I saw in Seaman and Lewis a unique closeness that I wanted to express."

To prepare, Ms. Myers read a lot of books about the expedition. "I most enjoyed reading the actual journals by Lewis and Clark. They're filled with great descriptions of wildlife and the adventures they had."

Surviving Brick Johnson
by Laurie Myers

The Amazing Life of Benjamin Franklin
by James Cross Giblin, illustrated by Michael Dooling

Michael Dooling also helped research the book before doing the pictures. He often asks family and friends to pose in historical costumes while he draws or paints.

"Every day at my house is like Halloween!" he says. He also visits schools to teach children about history and art. He comes dressed in a colonial costume and takes children through the steps of making picture books.

Narrative Nonfiction

Genre

- Narrative nonfiction can give facts about a person and tell what he or she did in life.

- Biography and history are kinds of narrative nonfiction.

Text Features

- A short introductory paragraph gives the reader a reason to read on.

- Large, bold-faced subheads identify the historic person to be discussed.

- Realistic pictures give the reader an idea of what the historic person might have looked like.

Link to Social Studies

Do research to find out what places in the West have been named for Sacagawea (sometimes spelled Sacajawea). Write about one of them.

They Traveled with Lewis and Clark

by Elizabeth Massie

Meriwether Lewis and William Clark are known for exploring the vast land between St. Louis and the Pacific Ocean. But they could not have done it without the help of others.

York
African American Explorer

York was a member of Lewis and Clark's Corps of Discovery. He was about the same age as William Clark. The two had grown up together. Both were brave and strong. But there was one difference. Clark was a free man. York was a slave. York belonged to Clark.

Slaves had few rights. They could not vote or carry guns. They were supposed to eat and sleep apart from white people. Yet on the journey west, York proved in many ways that he was equal.

Some of the men could not swim. York could. Clark's journal describes how York swam into a river to gather greens for dinner. York hunted deer, buffalo, and elk. He served as a scout. He cut wood and cooked meals. He even cared for the other men when they were sick.

One day there was a heavy storm. The rain nearly washed Clark and others into the Missouri River. York thought they had been swept away. He ignored his own safety

Author's Purpose Based on your preview, how should this text be read?

and searched through the storm for the missing people. Clark wrote that when they found York he was "greatly agitated," worried that they were gone for good.

Native Americans tribes along the way were amazed at York. They had never seen a man with such dark skin. Some believed he had special powers. Historians think that meeting York made the Indians more willing to let the group move safely across their lands.

York worked hard on the long journey. Yet when it was over he received no pay. Clark did not give York his freedom for another ten years. Some believe York died in Tennessee. Others say he went back west to live with Indians he met on the expedition.

Sacagawea
Native American Guide

Sacagawea was sixteen years old when she joined the Corps of Discovery. She was a Shoshone Indian with a two-month old baby. She was married to a French trader. Warriors from the Hidatsa tribe in North Dakota had kidnapped her when she was twelve. She had been taken hundreds of miles east. There, she learned the language of her new tribe.

Lewis and Clark needed someone who knew Indian languages. They hired Sacagawea's husband. Yet as it turned out, Sacagawea was more helpful than her husband.

Sacagawea interpreted for the explorers. She knew which plants were good to eat. She was familiar with some of the land over which they traveled. When Indians saw her, they knew that the corps was on a peaceful journey. A war party would not travel with a woman and her baby.

Once a storm nearly turned over one of the boats. Many important items fell into the water. While the men shouted and argued in the wind, Sacagawea saved the papers and other goods from the high waves. Lewis thought she was brave. He wrote: "The Indian woman to whom I ascribe equal fortitude and resolution with any person onboard . . . caught and preserved most of the light articles which were washed overboard."

At last the group reached western Montana, Shoshone land. This was the place of Sacagawea's birth. She discovered that her brother had become chief. She talked her brother into trading horses to the explorers. The men needed these horses to get over the Rocky Mountains.

Along with the men, Sacagawea made it to the Pacific Ocean and then back. Most people believe she died at age 25 at Fort Manuel, South Dakota. Some believe she died as a very old woman in 1884, among the Shoshone people in Wyoming.

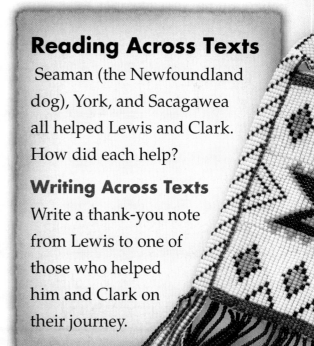

Reading Across Texts

Seaman (the Newfoundland dog), York, and Sacagawea all helped Lewis and Clark. How did each help?

Writing Across Texts

Write a thank-you note from Lewis to one of those who helped him and Clark on their journey.

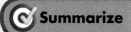 **Summarize** How do the subheads help you summarize?

65

Comprehension

Skill
Sequence

Strategy
Graphic
Organizers

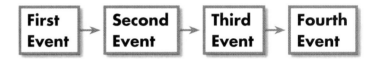

Sequence

- Sequence means the order in which things happen.

- Dates, times, and clue words such as *first, then, next,* and *last* can help you understand the order of events.

- Sometimes two or more events happen at the same time. Words such as *meanwhile* and *during* can show this.

First Event	→	Second Event	→	Third Event	→	Fourth Event

Strategy: Graphic Organizers

Using a graphic organizer can help you understand what you read. Some of these are webs, charts, and diagrams. For example, making a sequence chart like the one above can help you see the sequence. With some articles, you can fill in the organizer as you read. With others, you need to read the entire article before making the organizer.

1. Read "Moving to California." Make a graphic organizer like the one above to identify the sequence of important events in the article.

2. Reread the article, creating a web for "People Who Moved to California." Use your web to write a journal entry that a California resident might have written about the immigrants.

Moving to CALIFORNIA

Over time, many different groups of people have moved to California and made it their home. Because of this, California has a very diverse population today.

In 1542, a man from Spain named Juan Cabrillo entered California. Many people from Spain moved to California after that. Then, starting in 1841, many farmers from the United States moved to California.

After gold was found in California in 1848, thousands of people from Europe, Asia, and other parts of the world moved there. They hoped to become rich. Many of these people came from China.

By 1852, one out of every 10 people who lived in California was from China. But a new law in 1882 said that, for ten years, no one from China was allowed to move to the United States. During that same time, many people from Japan were moving to California.

Today, more people live in California than in any other state in the United States.

Strategy Dates and clue words are important guides to sequence. Put three events from this paragraph on the sequence chart.

Skill Which of the following events took place *first*? How do you know?
(a) People moved to California to become rich.
(b) Juan Cabrillo traveled to California.
(c) Farmers from the United States moved to California.

Skill Sometimes two events happen at the same time. Which event took place while people from Japan were moving to California?

Strategy Why can this information bring an end to the sequence chart?

Grandfather's Journey

Words to Know

homeland

bewildered

amazed

towering

sculptures

longed

still

Vocabulary Strategy
for Multiple-Meaning Words

Dictionary/Glossary Sometimes when you are reading, you may see a word whose meaning you know, but that meaning doesn't make sense in the sentence. It may be a word that has more than one meaning. You can use a dictionary or glossary to help you.

1. Try the meaning that you know. Does it make sense in the sentence?

2. If it doesn't make sense, look up the word in a dictionary or glossary to see what other meanings the word can have.

3. Find the entry for the word. The entries are in alphabetical order.

4. Read all the meanings given for the word. Try each in the sentence.

5. Choose the one that makes the best sense in the sentence.

As you read "Becoming American," look for words that can have more than one meaning. Use a dictionary or glossary to find meanings to try in the sentence. Which meaning makes sense?

Becoming American

People from around the world have been moving to the United States since it began. Full of hope, they left their homeland. They spent weeks crossing the treacherous ocean. Many arrived in strange cities that did not welcome them. The English language and the new mix of customs in America bewildered them. Often they could only get poorly paid jobs that others did not want.

However, they found much that amazed them. There was real freedom for American citizens. There was a feeling that anyone could work hard and have a better life. Towering buildings called skyscrapers soared into the sky. They seemed like sculptures that symbolized the power and promise of the new land.

All around the immigrants were energy and growth. They learned a new language and new customs. They worked tirelessly. They contributed to their new country. Sooner or later, the newcomers were accepted.

The new life did not take away the pain of loss, though. The new Americans longed for the sights and people they had left behind. Having a better life did not still their feelings for their homeland.

Pretend the year is 1900 and you have just come to the United States from another country. Write a letter home describing your new country. Use words from the Words to Know list.

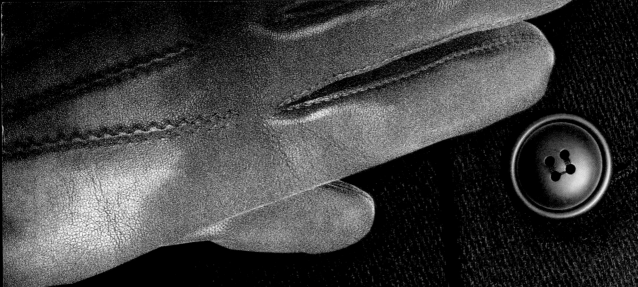

Grandfather's Journey

written and illustrated
by Allen Say

Genre

Historical fiction is set in the past. It is a story in which some of the details are factual but in which others are made up or are loosely based on history. Look for the factual details as you read.

Where does a grandfather's journey take him and what does he learn along the way?

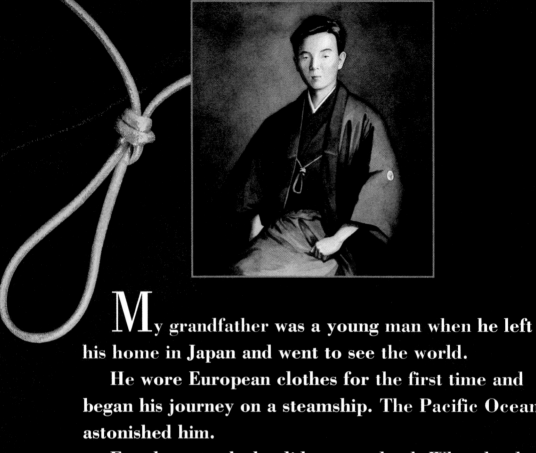

My grandfather was a young man when he left his home in Japan and went to see the world.

He wore European clothes for the first time and began his journey on a steamship. The Pacific Ocean astonished him.

For three weeks he did not see land. When land finally appeared it was the New World.

He explored North America by train and riverboat, and often walked for days on end.

Deserts with rocks like enormous sculptures amazed him.

The endless farm fields reminded him of the ocean he had crossed.

Huge cities of factories and tall buildings bewildered and yet excited him.

He marveled at the towering mountains and rivers as clear as the sky.

He met many people along the way. He shook hands with black men and white men, with yellow men and red men.

The more he traveled, the more he longed to see new places, and never thought of returning home.

Of all the places he visited, he liked California best. He loved the strong sunlight there, the Sierra Mountains, the lonely seacoast.

After a time, he returned to his village in Japan to marry his childhood sweetheart. Then he brought his bride to the new country.

They made their home by the San Francisco Bay and had a baby girl.

As his daughter grew, my grandfather began to think about his own childhood. He thought about his old friends.

He remembered the mountains and rivers of his home. He surrounded himself with songbirds, but he could not forget.

Finally, when his daughter was nearly grown, he could wait no more. He took his family and returned to his homeland.

Once again he saw the mountains and rivers of his childhood. They were just as he had remembered them.

Once again he exchanged stories and laughed with his old friends.

But the village was not a place for a daughter from San Francisco. So my grandfather bought a house in a large city nearby.

There, the young woman fell in love, married, and sometime later I was born.

When I was a small boy, my favorite weekend was a visit to my grandfather's house. He told me many stories about California.

He raised warblers and silvereyes, but he could not forget the mountains and rivers of California. So he planned a trip.

But a war began. Bombs fell from the sky and scattered our lives like leaves in a storm.

When the war ended, there was nothing left of the city and of the house where my grandparents had lived.

So they returned to the village where they had been children. But my grandfather never kept another songbird.

The last time I saw him, my grandfather said that he longed to see California one more time. He never did.

And when I was nearly grown, I left home and went to see California for myself.

After a time, I came to love the land my grandfather had loved, and I stayed on and on until I had a daughter of my own.

But I also miss the mountains and rivers of my childhood. I miss my old friends. So I return now and then, when I cannot still the longing in my heart.

The funny thing is, the moment I am in one country, I am homesick for the other.

I think I know my grandfather now. I miss him very much.

Reader Response

Open for Discussion Suppose Grandfather could tell of his journey. What might he say? Look closely at each picture and tell what Grandfather might be saying.

1. Allen Say's paintings are like photographs, as if people had posed for them. Why do you think Mr. Say made his paintings so lifelike?

2. Summarize what happens in Grandfather's life from the time he arrives in America until he returns to Japan.

3. Create a sequence organizer for the story with boxes for the story's beginning, middle, and end. Briefly describe what happens in each part of the story.

4. Which verbs on the Words to Know list tell how Grandfather felt as he journeyed to and then across North America? Find other verbs in the story to add to the list.

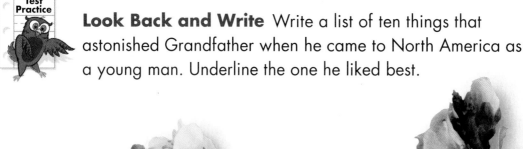

Look Back and Write Write a list of ten things that astonished Grandfather when he came to North America as a young man. Underline the one he liked best.

Meet the Author and Illustrator
Allen Say

Read more books by Allen Say.

Grandfather's Journey is a true story of the author's grandfather. Allen Say, as the story says, was born in Japan and spent his childhood there. When he was 16, he moved to California with his father. Remembering his grandfather's tales, he was excited about the move. But when he arrived, he was lonely and unhappy. He spoke no English. He was the only Japanese student in his school, and no one was very friendly to him.

Mr. Say returned to Japan after high school, planning to stay there. But things had changed a lot in Japan following the end of World War II. After a year, Mr. Say returned to the United States, and he has lived here ever since.

Mr. Say is a talented artist and author who has won a Caldecott Honor Award for his illustrations. He often writes about people who are part of two cultures.

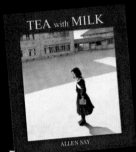

Tea with Milk

The Lost Lake

A Look at Two Lands

Online Reference Sources

Genre

- **You can find reference sources, such as atlases, dictionaries, and encyclopedias, on Internet Web sites.**

- **Some Web sites give you several different reference sources all in one place.**

Text Features

- **Online reference sources look a lot like print sources, and they are organized in the same way.**

- **Instead of turning pages by hand, you use a mouse to click your way through them.**

Link to Social Studies

Think about where you live. How is it like or unlike someplace you've read about? Share your observations.

After reading *Grandfather's Journey*, you wonder what Japan and California are like. "Why did Allen Say's grandfather love both places so much?" you might ask. To find out, you could go to an online reference Web site.

84

Take It to the NET™
ONLINE
more activities sfsuccessnet.com

At the site, you find links to a dictionary, an encyclopedia, and other reference sources. You decide to click on the encyclopedia link.

File   Edit   View   Favorites   Tools   Help

http://www.url.here

ONLINE REFERENCE WEB SITE

Atlas   **Almanac**   **Dictionary**   **Encyclopedia**

File   Edit   View   Favorites   Tools   Help

http://w

Japan   Search

This takes you to the encyclopedia search page, where you type the search term *Japan* into the SEARCH window. A new page opens with your search results.

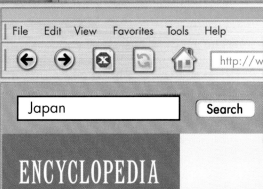

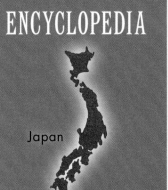

ENCYCLOPEDIA

Japan

Japan [jə pan′] In Japanese, Nihon or Nippon; a country (1995 est. pop. 125,506,000), 145,833 sq mi (377,835 sq km), off the coast of eastern Asia. The capital is Tokyo, which, along with neighboring Yokohama, forms the world's most populous metropolitan region.

Sequence   Why does it make sense to begin with an online encyclopedia?

Now you decide to find out something about California. You find these results in an encyclopedia search.

File   Edit   View   Favorites   Tools   Help

http://www.url.here

California

Search

ENCYCLOPEDIA

California

California   [kal'ə fôr' nyə] California, most populous state in the United States, located in the Far West; bordered by Oregon, Nevada, and, across the Colorado River, by Arizona, Mexico, and the Pacific Ocean.

You want to know exactly where Japan and California are. To find out, you go to an online atlas, which is a collection of maps. On a Web site, you find a world map showing Japan and California.

ew   Favorites   Tools   Help

http://www.url.here

World Map— **JAPAN TO CALIFORNIA**

about 4,500 miles

Japan

California

File   Edit   View   Favorites   Tools

On another Web site, you find these photographs of Japan and California. Now you are beginning to understand why Allen Say's grandfather loved both places so much.

Scenes from
JAPAN

Scenes from
CALIFORNIA

As you have learned from your research, Japan and California are far apart. Yet both contain a beauty that can appeal to many people.

Reading Across Texts

Both *Grandfather's Journey* and this article give information about Japan and California. In which place would you rather live? Choose one and list your reasons.

Writing Across Texts Write about why you would rather live in the place you chose.

Graphic Organizers Which online source might have many lists and charts?

 Skill

Author's Purpose

- An author may write to persuade, inform, entertain, or express ideas or feelings. Often an author has more than one purpose.

- The kinds of ideas and the way the author organizes and states them can help you determine the author's purpose.

Ideas	**Author's Purpose**	**Text**
what they are how they are expressed	→ persuade inform entertain express ←	title and any heads facts and information fictional characters and plot pattern of ideas

 Strategy

Strategy: Story Structure

Active readers note the structure of fictional stories, including the problem or goal, rising action (building up to the climax), climax (where the conflict is confronted), and outcome (where the conflict is resolved). Most stories are told in time order, or sequence, and are written to entertain, but some teach a lesson at the same time they entertain.

 **Write**

1. As you read "The Fox and the Grapes," use a graphic organizer like the one above to figure out the author's purpose.

2. An author can have more than one purpose. Write the lesson about life that "The Fox and the Grapes" teaches.

The Fox and the Grapes

Adapted from Aesop

There once was a hungry fox who came upon a grapevine wound around a high trellis. Hanging from the vine was a bunch of grapes.

"What DEE-LISH-US-looking grapes," the fox said to himself. "I think I'll just step up and grab a few." So he stood up on his hind legs under the trellis, but the grapes were out of reach.

"Hmmm," said the fox. "Those DEE-licious grapes are higher up than I thought." So the fox jumped up as high as he could, but the grapes were still out of reach.

"This is ridiculous," said the fox. "How hard can it be to grab some dee-licious grapes?" So the fox stepped back, took a running leap—and missed. The grapes were still out of reach.

"Humph!" said the fox, walking away with a little toss of his tail. "I thought at first those grapes looked delicious, but now I see they are sour."

Skill What do you think the author's purpose will be? Look at the title, author's byline, and illustrations for clues.

Strategy What is the problem in this story?
a) The grapes look delicious.
b) The fox is stealing the grapes.
c) The fox cannot reach the grapes.

Strategy Think about the way the story develops. Figure out the rising action, climax, and resolution of the story.

Skill In an Aesop's fable, the purpose is usually to teach a lesson about life. How is the fox's behavior an example of how not to act?

Words to Know

prairie

lassoed

riverbed

bargain

favors

offended

shrieked

Remember

Try the strategy. Then, if you need more help, use your glossary or a dictionary.

Vocabulary Strategy
for Synonyms

Context Clues Sometimes when you are reading, you see a word you don't know. The author may give you a synonym for the word. A synonym is a word that has almost the same meaning as another word. Look for a synonym. It can help you understand the meaning of the word you don't know.

1. Look at the sentence in which the unknown word appears. The author may give a synonym in the same sentence.

2. If not, look at the sentences around the sentence with the unknown word. The author may use a synonym there.

3. Try the synonym in place of the word in the sentence. Does it make sense?

As you read "Tall Paul," look for synonyms to help you understand the meanings of the vocabulary words.

Tall Paul

Tall Paul was a cowboy who lived on the plains not so long ago. He was not just any cowboy, though. He was so long legged he could cross a mile of prairie in just one step. And he was so big and strong he lassoed and caught a whole herd of cattle with a single toss of his rope.

Tall Paul had a mighty big appetite too. He ate a mountain of flapjacks for breakfast. One time, out on the range, he got so thirsty he drank a river. The dry riverbed just lay there gasping for water.

Tall Paul felt bad about that so he struck a bargain with the sky.

They agreed to trade favors. The sky would bring a flood of rain. In return, the sky asked this: "I will help you if you do me this service. My servant, Wind, can't blow the clouds over that mountain there. I need you to flatten it a little for me."

Tall Paul said to the mountain, "Now don't be offended. I'll just take a little off the top." The mountain shrieked and screamed, but the deed was done. Tall Paul jumped on that mountain and turned it into a nice little mesa. In an instant, the rains began to fall.

Write

Write your own tale about Tall Paul. Use some words from the Words to Know list.

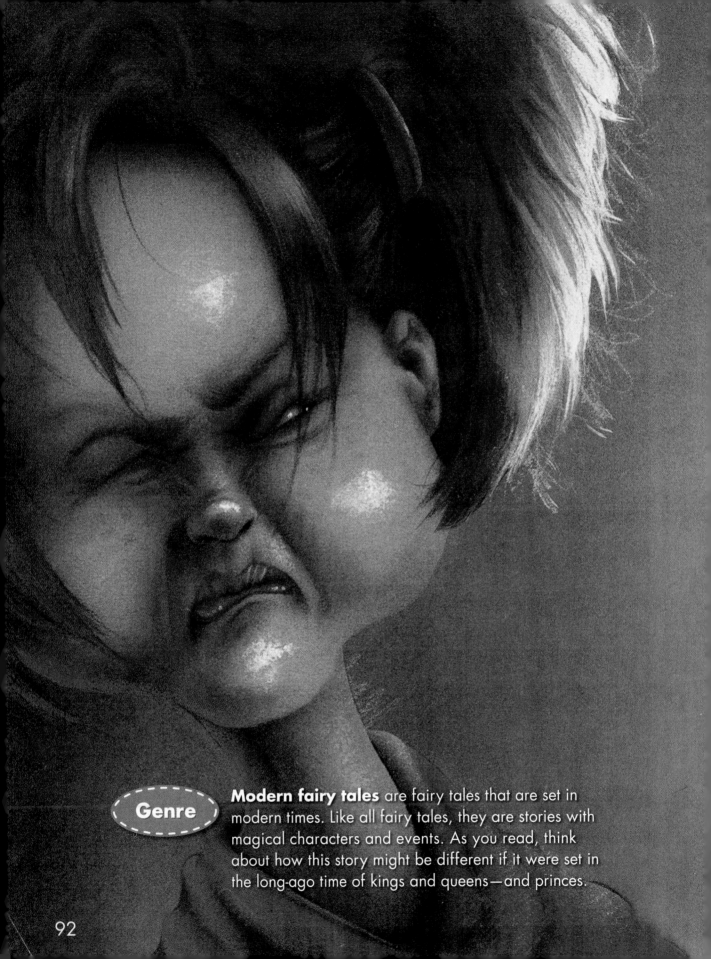

Genre

Modern fairy tales are fairy tales that are set in modern times. Like all fairy tales, they are stories with magical characters and events. As you read, think about how this story might be different if it were set in the long-ago time of kings and queens—and princes.

92

The Horned Toad Prince

by Jackie Mims Hopkins
illustrated by Michael Austin

How could a horned toad
possibly be a prince?

Reba Jo loved to twang her guitar and sing while the prairie wind whistled through the thirsty sagebrush.

Singing with the wind was one of the ways Reba Jo entertained herself on the lonesome prairie. Sometimes she amused herself by racing her horse, Flash, against a tumbleweed cartwheeling across her daddy's land.

But her favorite pastime of all was roping. She lassoed cacti, water buckets, fence posts, and any unlucky critter that crossed her path.

One blustery morning, as she was riding the range looking for something to lasso, Reba Jo came upon a dry riverbed. Her daddy had warned her to stay away from these *arroyos*. He'd told her that a prairie storm could blow in quicker than a rattlesnake's strike, causing a flash flood to rip through the riverbed. The swift water would wash away anything or anyone in its way.

Reba Jo knew she should turn back. But right at the edge of this gully she spied a vulture, all fat and sassy, sitting on top of a dried-up old well, just daring her to toss her spinning rope around his long ugly neck.

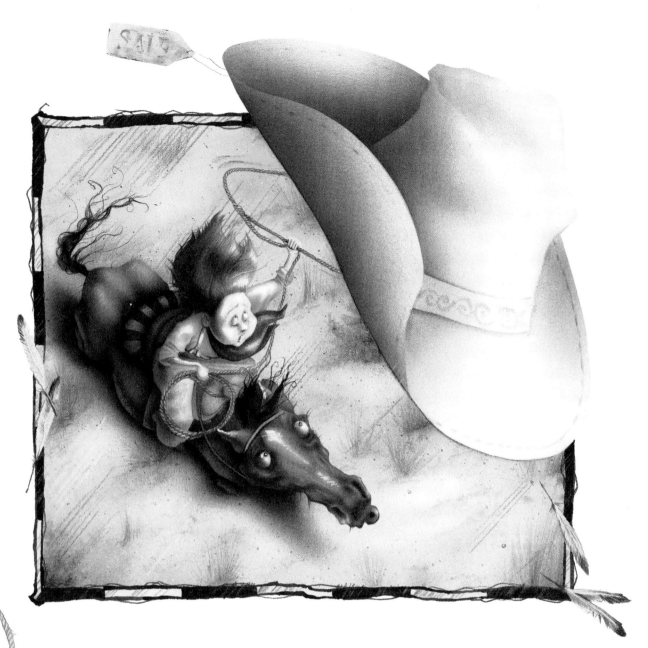

As Reba Jo's lasso whirled into the air, a great gust of wind came whipping through the *arroyo* and blew her new cowgirl hat right off her head and down to the bottom of the dusty old well.

Reba Jo scrambled to the edge of the well. She peered down into the darkness and commenced to crying. Suddenly she heard a small voice say, *"¿Qué pasa, señorita?"*

She looked around and wondered if the wind blowing through the *arroyo* was fooling her ears.

But then, there in the sand, she spotted a big fat horned toad looking up at her. "What's the matter, *señorita?*" he asked again.

"Oh," she cried, "the brand-new hat my daddy bought for me just blew down into this stinkin' old well. I'll never be able to get it out, and I'll be in a peck of trouble when he finds out I've been playin' down here near the *arroyo.*"

The horned toad looked at her slyly and said, "I'll fetch your *sombrero* for you if you will do *tres pequeños* favors for me."

She sniffed and asked, "Three small favors? Like what?"

"All you have to do is feed me some chili, play your *guitarra* for me, and let me take a *siesta* in your *sombrero*."

"Some chili, a song, and a nap in my hat? I don't think so, *amigo*," replied Reba Jo.

"Okay, *señorita*, but do you mind if I follow you home and listen as you explain to your *padre* where your new *sombrero* is, and how it got there?"

"Good point, toad," Reba Jo said. "You've got yourself a deal."

Reba Jo placed the little critter in a splintered wooden bucket and carefully lowered him down the dry well, where he retrieved Reba Jo's hat.

Then, without so much as a *muchas gracias*, Reba Jo snatched her hat from the horned toad and galloped home. As she rode out of sight, she ignored the horned toad's cries of "*¡Espérate!* Wait up, *señorita*, wait up!"

'Long about midday, when Reba Jo had sat down to eat, she heard a tap, tap, tapping at the ranch house door.

Reba Jo opened the door, but when she saw it was the fat horned toad, she slammed the door in his face.

His small voice called, "*Señorita, señorita, por favor.* Please let me come in."

The horned toad rapped on the door again. This time Reba
Jo's father opened it and spotted the little fella on the porch.

"*Hola, señor,*" said the horned toad.

"Well howdy, mister toad. What brings you here?"

"A little deal that I made with your daughter, *señor.*"

"What's this all about, Reba Jo?" her father asked her.

Reba Jo admitted that the horned toad had done her a
favor and in return she had promised to feed him some chili,
play her guitar for him, and let him take a nap in her hat.

"Now, Reba Jo," said her daddy, "if you strike a bargain in these parts, a deal's a deal. Come on in, pardner, you look mighty hungry."

"I am indeed. *Yo tengo mucha hambre,*" said the horned toad. "I hope that is chili I smell." He peeked at Reba Jo's meal.

"Dadburn it!" Reba Jo muttered. She pushed her bowl of chili toward him.

Soon the horned toad's belly was bulging. "Now, for a little *serenata,*" he said.

Reba Jo stomped over, grabbed her guitar, and belted out a lullaby for her guest.

Then the drowsy little horned toad eyed Reba Jo's hat and yawned, saying, "That lovely music has made me *muy soñoliento*. I'm ready for my *siesta*."

"Forget it, Bucko," Reba Jo snapped. "You're not gettin' near my hat. No lizard cooties allowed!"

"Now, señorita, remember what your wise *padre* said about striking a bargain in these parts," said the clever little horned toad.

"I know, I know," grumbled Reba Jo, "a deal's a deal." And with that, she flipped him into her hat.

"Before I take my *siesta*, I have just one more favor to ask," said the horned toad.

"Now what?" asked Reba Jo.

"Would you give me a kiss, *por favor?*" asked the horned toad.

"You've gotta be kiddin'!" shrieked Reba Jo. "You know dang well a kiss wasn't part of this deal, you low-life reptile."

"If you do this one last thing for me, we'll call it even, and I'll be on my way *pronto*," the horned toad said.

"You'll leave right away?" Reba Jo asked suspiciously. "You promise?"

"*Sí, te prometo,*" agreed the horned toad.

Reba Jo thought hard for a minute. She glared at the horned toad. "I can't believe I'm even considerin' this," she said, "but if it means you'll leave right now . . . pucker up, Lizard Lips."

Before Reba Jo could wipe the toad spit
off her lips, a fierce dust devil
spun into the yard, swept the
horned toad off his feet, and whirled him
around in a dizzying cloud of prairie dust.

When the dust cleared, there before Reba Jo
stood a handsome young *caballero*.

"Who are you?" Reba Jo demanded, staring at
the gentleman.

"I am Prince Maximillian José Diego López de España."

"Whoa, how did this happen?" Reba Jo asked in amazement.

"Many, many years ago when I came to this country, I offended the great spirit of the *arroyo*. The spirit put a spell on me and turned me into a horned toad. For many years I've been waiting for a cowgirl like you to break the spell. *Muchas gracias* for my freedom, *señorita*. Now I'll be leaving as I promised."

"Now hold on for just a dadburn minute," said Reba Jo, stepping in front of the nobleman. "I recollect my daddy readin' me a story where somethin' like this happened. Aren't we supposed to get hitched and ride off into the sunset?"

With a twinkle in his eye, the *caballero* replied, *"Lo siento.* So sorry, Reba Jo, when you strike a bargain in these parts, a deal's a deal. *Adiós, señorita!"*

Reader Response

Open for Discussion Did you know what was going to happen in the story or were you surprised? What three questions would you ask Reba Jo if you could?

1. This story is fit for a storyteller. Find a part of the story that could be read the way a storyteller would. Why is that such a good part to read?

2. An author's purpose can be to teach the reader an important lesson. What lesson do you think the author teaches in this story?

3. What was the most important event in the story? Why do you think this?

4. The words *prairie* and *riverbed* on the Words to Know list are clues to the story's setting. Find other words in the story that hint at the Southwest setting.

Look Back and Write At the end of the story, the caballero says, "A deal's a deal." Explain what the deal is. Then tell whether or not you think it is a good deal and why.

Jackie Mims Hopkins wasn't much of a reader as a young girl. "I didn't enjoy reading any book of length. I couldn't sit still long enough to read." Now she is an author and a librarian!

Ms. Hopkins got the idea for *The Horned Toad Prince* when she was researching horned toads for another book. "I realized there weren't many stories about them. I decided it was time to write a story about the little critters," she says. "I started thinking about which fairy tale could be used with a horned toad as the main character. 'The Frog Prince' was a perfect match."

Michael Austin created the art for this story. "*The Horned Toad Prince* stood out to me right away because of its personality and energy," he says. As an artist, Mr. Austin has always had a "strange point of view." He enjoys drawing because it gives him a chance to "draw things my own way, strange or not."

The Three Armadillies Tuff by Jackie Mims Hopkins

Late for School by Mike Reiss, illustrated by Michael Austin

107

Expository Nonfiction

Genre

- Expository nonfiction can tell about animals and where they live.

- The author sometimes organizes the text by explaining a series of events.

Text Features

- The author uses captions to explain photographs.

- The author uses descriptive language to tell about life in the Sonoran Desert.

Link to Science

Use reference materials to find out more about animals that camouflage themselves in the desert. Make a chart describing how these animals camouflage themselves and share it with your class.

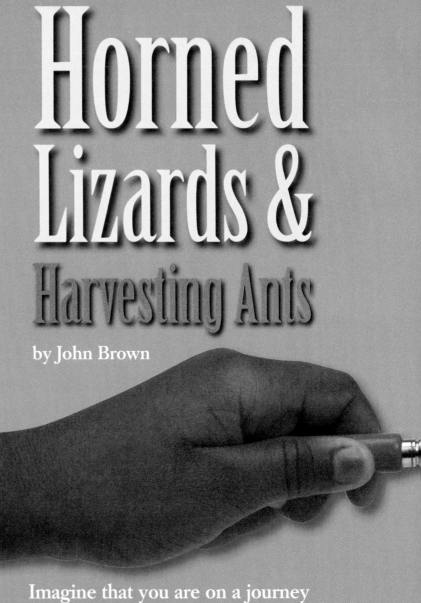

Horned Lizards & Harvesting Ants

by John Brown

Imagine that you are on a journey to the Sonoran Desert, a vast area of flat land and canyons in the southwestern United States and northern Mexico. By day, you explore the many unique plants and animals. At night, you curl up in the safety of your desert home, a tent.

▲ A few clouds remain after last night's storm; the morning air feels cool and clean.

▲ This harvester ant is wrestling to pull a saguaro seed out from the fruit. Imagine trying to pull a football out of a giant-sized sticky gumdrop—with your teeth!

As we are having breakfast, we notice that last night's storm has knocked some of the fruit off the top of a nearby saguaro. This windfall has been discovered by a colony of harvester ants, who are busy pulling the seeds out of the sticky fruit and carrying them back to their hole. They are working very hard to get all the seeds inside their nest before it gets too hot for them to stay out in the sun.

Author's Purpose If the purpose is to inform, how do you read this article?

109

I notice something out of the corner of my eye. It looked like a rock moved! We take a closer look and realize that it isn't a rock but a horned lizard. An amazing little lizard, it is so well camouflaged that you can hardly see it against the pebbles and sand. Up close it looks like a miniature dinosaur.

Resembling a miniature dinosaur, the horned lizard feasts on the ants. Look carefully and you can see an ant valiantly trying to fight back!

Some kinds of horned lizard eat almost nothing but ants, which they gobble up with their sticky tongue. They dart around, and with each quick flick of their tongue another ant disappears. The ants try to fight back, but their strong jaws make no impression on this armored ant-eating machine. We look around and find the lizard's little black droppings.

They crumble as you pick them up–they are made of nothing but the digested remains of dead ants!

These lizards have an amazing trick up their sleeve. Coyotes love to eat lizards, and if a coyote manages to see through a horned lizard's camouflage, the lizard is in big trouble. But if the coyote tries to bite the horned lizard, it squirts blood from its eyes into the coyote's mouth. The lizard's blood must taste disgusting to the coyote, which usually runs off in shock, giving the resourceful little lizard a chance to escape.

We watch the horned lizard having its ant breakfast as we finish ours.

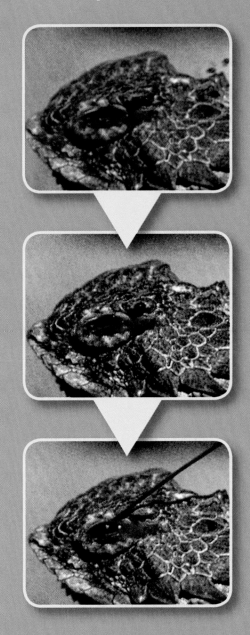

In slow motion we can see the horned lizard squirt blood from its eye.

Reading Across Texts

The "horned toad" in *The Horned Toad Prince* and the "horned lizard" in this article are the same animal. How are the two alike and different?

Writing Across Texts Make a chart showing the ways in which the fictional horned toad was like and unlike a real horned lizard.

 Text Structure How has the author organized this text?

Comprehension

Skill
Main Idea
and Details

Strategy
Graphic
Organizers

 Skill

Main Idea
and Details

- The topic is what a paragraph, part of an article, or a whole article is about.

- The most important thing the author has to say about the topic is the main idea.

- The little pieces of information telling more about the main idea are the supporting details.

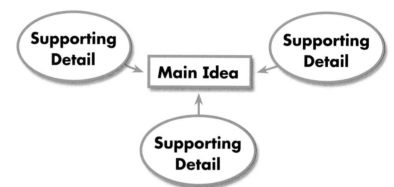

Supporting Detail → Main Idea ← Supporting Detail ← Supporting Detail

 Strategy

Strategy: Graphic Organizers

Active readers often use graphic organizers to help them understand what they read. Graphic organizers can be used before, during, or after reading. You can create a graphic organizer like the one above to help you remember the main idea and details.

1. Read "Send a Ranger!" Make a graphic organizer like the one above to help you understand the article.

2. Use your graphic organizer to help you write about a national park you have visited or would like to visit, and your reasons.

SEND A RANGER!

The job of a ranger is made up of a lot of different jobs. Park rangers are like police officers—they make sure people obey the rules of the park. Park rangers are like teachers—they take people on nature walks and tell them about important places in our history. Park rangers are like scientists—they keep track of information about plants and animals. Park rangers are like firefighters—they keep close watch to help put a stop to forest fires. Park rangers are like rescue workers—they hunt for people who are lost or hurt.

Yes, the job of a park ranger is made up of a lot of different jobs. In fact, Stephen Mather, the first director of the National Parks Service, has said: "If a trail is to be blazed, send a ranger; if an animal is floundering in the snow, send a ranger; if a bear is in a hotel, send a ranger; if a fire threatens a forest, send a ranger; and if someone is to be saved, send a ranger."

Does this sound like fun to you? Maybe you would like to be a park ranger.

Skill The first sentence sounds like a big, overall main idea. Read on to see if this is so or if there is another bigger idea.

Strategy Is each example of a job a supporting detail or a new main idea?

Skill Why do you think the author restated a sentence used earlier? Is this a clue about what the main idea is?

Strategy On the graphic organizer, where would you put these additional jobs?

wilderness

preserve

species

naturalist

slopes

glacier

impressive

Remember

Try the strategy. Then, if you need more help, use your glossary or a dictionary.

Vocabulary Strategy
for Suffixes

Word Structure Suppose you are reading and you come to a word that has *-ist* or *-ive* at the end. You can use the suffix to help you figure out the word's meaning. The suffix *-ist* can make a word mean "one who is an expert in _____," as in *biologist,* an expert in biology. The suffix *-ive* can make a word mean "tending or inclined to _____," as in *active,* which means "tending to act."

1. Put your finger over the *-ist* or *-ive* suffix.

2. Look at the base word. Put the base word in the phrase "one who is an expert in _____" or "tending or inclined to _____."

3. Try that meaning in the sentence. Does it make sense?

As you read "Letter from Denali," look for words that end with *-ist* or *-ive.* Use the suffixes to help you figure out the meanings of the words.

Letter from Denali

Dear Kevin,

Here we are in Denali National Park in Alaska. Denali is a gigantic park. It has more than 6 million acres of wilderness, so we certainly won't be seeing the whole park!

Denali was established to preserve the land and the animals and plants that live here. More than 650 species of flowering plants and 217 species of animals live in Denali! That's what the naturalist on the guided walk told us yesterday. She also said that to live in Denali year-round, a plant or animal species has to be able to survive long, cold winters.

Today we hiked up the lower slopes of Mt. McKinley. It is the highest mountain in North America, and it is part of Denali. We could see a giant glacier looking like a huge field of ice farther up on the mountain. It was a very impressive sight. Mt. McKinley has several glaciers, and some are more than 30 miles long!

I have taken a zillion pictures, but I really think this is a place you have to see in person.

Love,
Lisa

Write a letter to a friend. Describe a park or other natural setting that you have seen. Use some words from the Words to Know list.

115

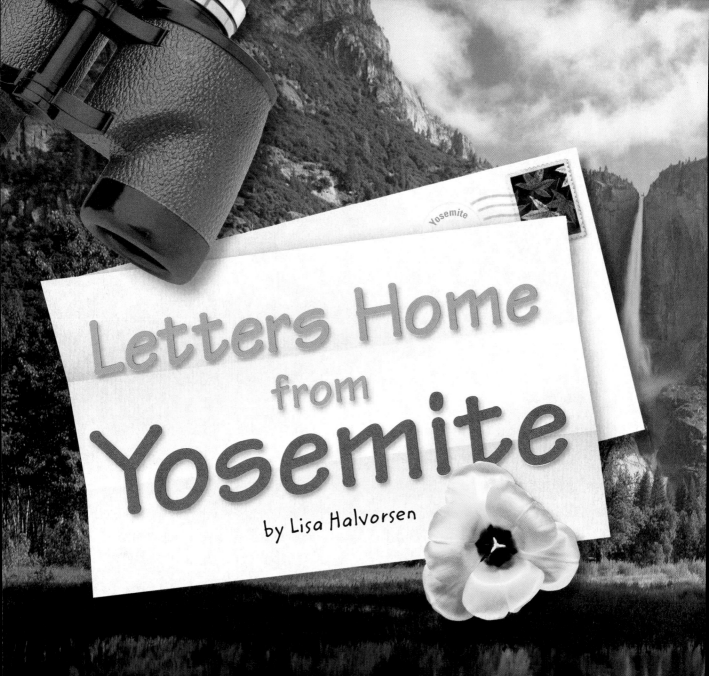

Letters Home from Yosemite

by Lisa Halvorsen

 **Genre**

Narrative nonfiction tells the story of real people, places, or events. The narrator, or teller of the story, presents information in sequence. Notice this sequence as you read about Yosemite National Park.

Why do so many people travel to Yosemite National Park?

Arrival in . . . San Francisco

As our plane touched down in San Francisco, I knew we were in for an exciting vacation. I'd been reading about Yosemite on the plane. I learned that it is America's third national park. Yosemite is known throughout the world for its amazing scenery. It has incredible waterfalls, rock formations, alpine lakes and meadows, and giant sequoia trees. It's located in the east central part of California and covers 1,170 square miles. That's an area about the size of Rhode Island!

Efforts to protect the wilderness around Yosemite began in 1864. That's when President Abraham Lincoln signed the Yosemite Grant deeding the land to California. Yosemite was finally established as a national park on Oct. 1, 1890, by an act of Congress.

Views of **Yosemite**

Yosemite Valley

Topography

Our tour guide said that one of the first people to visit this area was John Muir, a Scottish naturalist. He fought hard to convince the U.S. government to preserve Yosemite as a national park. The name supposedly comes from the Indian name "yo'hem-iteh." That means grizzly bear.

Yosemite is right in the middle of the Sierra Nevada Mountains. These mountains stretch for 430 miles along California's eastern border. The area covers 15.5 million acres, which is about the size of Vermont, New Hampshire, and Connecticut combined! This is the highest and longest single continuous range of mountains in the lower 48 states (not including Alaska and Hawaii).

Native Americans were the first people to live in Yosemite, about 7,000 to 10,000 years ago. When explorers arrived at Yosemite Valley in the 1830s and 1840s, Southern Sierra Miwok Indians were living there. They called the Yosemite Valley "Ahwahnee" (Place of the Gaping Mouth).

Sierra Nevadas from east of Tioga Pass

119

Merced River

Badger Pass

The first tourists arrived in 1855. They traveled on horseback. I wonder if they were as amazed as I am by the first glimpse of this scenic park?

Today, more than 3.5 million people visit the park every year. Most come in the summer months. That's a lot of visitors! And a lot of cars! But what's nice is that 94% of the park has been designated as wilderness. These areas can only be reached by foot or on horseback.

After a four-hour drive from San Francisco, we arrived at the Arch Rock entrance station. This is on the western side of the park, just north of Badger Pass. Badger is a popular ski spot. It opened in 1935 and was California's first ski area. Seven years earlier, the first ski school in the state was started in Yosemite Valley. That's where we'll begin exploring the park.

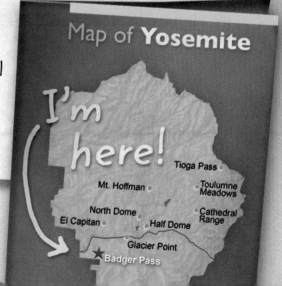
Map of **Yosemite**

I'm here!

Tioga Pass

Mt. Hoffman

Toulumne Meadows

North Dome

Cathedral Range

El Capitan

Half Dome

Glacier Point

Badger Pass

Rafting on the Merced River

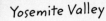

Yosemite Valley

Yosemite Valley is only seven miles long and one mile wide, but it's where the most services are. Our campground is here, and so are many of the park's best natural attractions. It's the most heavily visited part of the park.

Today, we learned about the Miwok and Paiute people, and about the natural history of the park. Then we hopped on the shuttle bus to see famous sights like Yosemite Falls, El Capitan, and Happy Isles. One of my favorite places was Mirror Lake, where we saw Tenaya Canyon reflected in the water.

Bridalveil Creek/Fall

It seems that wherever we look, there's something bigger, higher, or more impressive than before. More than half of America's highest waterfalls are found in Yosemite. One of the prettiest is Bridalveil Fall. It is located near the entrance to Yosemite Valley.

The Ahwahneechee called Bridalveil Fall "Pohono." It means "spirit of the puffing wind." Sometimes hard winds actually blow the falls sideways! I'm glad I brought my raincoat because we got soaked by the spray on the way up! This waterfall is 620 feet high. That's as tall as a 62-story building!

Bridalveil Fall

121

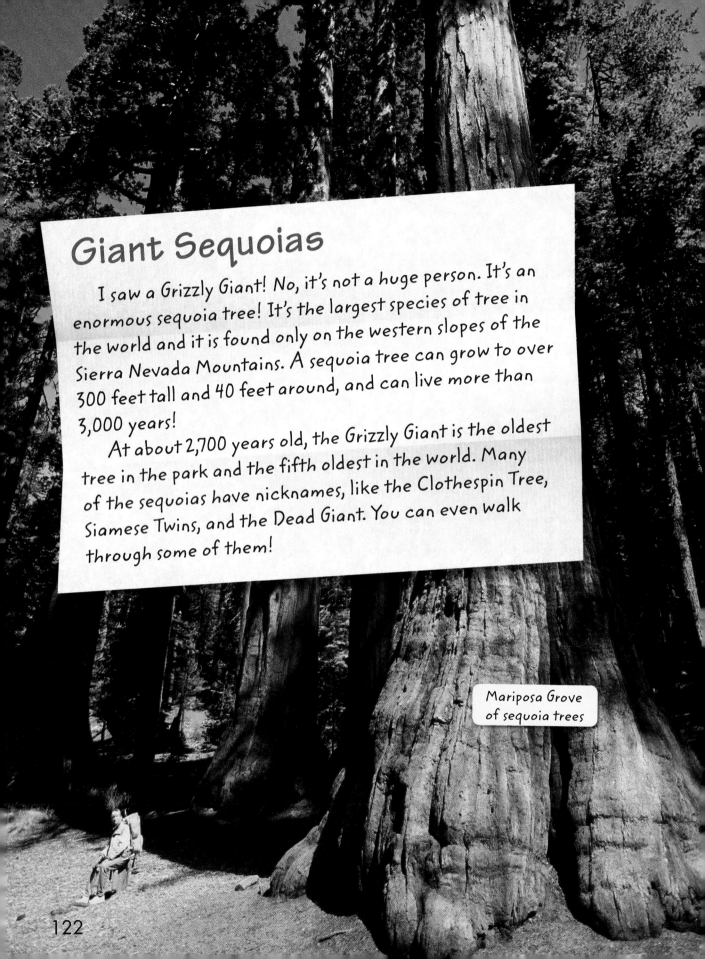

Giant Sequoias

I saw a Grizzly Giant! No, it's not a huge person. It's an enormous sequoia tree! It's the largest species of tree in the world and it is found only on the western slopes of the Sierra Nevada Mountains. A sequoia tree can grow to over 300 feet tall and 40 feet around, and can live more than 3,000 years!

At about 2,700 years old, the Grizzly Giant is the oldest tree in the park and the fifth oldest in the world. Many of the sequoias have nicknames, like the Clothespin Tree, Siamese Twins, and the Dead Giant. You can even walk through some of them!

Mariposa Grove of sequoia trees

Bobcat

Yosemite Wildlife

I'm so excited! This morning on our way to Glacier Point we saw a black bear and her two cubs. The young ones were as cute as teddy bears. The ranger reminded us how dangerous these bears really are. They have a very strong sense of smell and will rip open a tent or even break into a car to get food! That's why we put all our food—and even our toothpaste—in the bear-proof metal box at the campground.

An adult black bear can weigh as much as 500 pounds. The average size is about 300 pounds. Not all of them are black. They may be brown, cinnamon, or sometimes tan. Between 300 to 500 bears live in the park.

We have seen a ton of mule deer since we arrived. They like to graze along the roadsides and in the meadows in the early morning and late afternoon. They can be just as aggressive as bears when approached. Mule deer have long ears like mules. They can run up to 35 miles an hour and can jump 24 feet in a single leap. You'd never know it from looking at them!

The park is also home to mountain lions, bobcats, coyotes, black-tailed jackrabbits, yellow-bellied marmots, rattlesnakes, and California bighorn sheep. Thousands of sheep once roamed the slopes of the Sierra Nevada Mountains. They were nearly wiped out by hunters, disease,

Mule deer

Black bear

Steller's jay

and lack of food. A ranger said they were successfully reintroduced to the park in 1986.

More than 240 species of birds have been spotted in Yosemite. Some of them are endangered, like the willow flycatcher and the great gray owl. Some—like the bald eagle—just spend the winter in the park. My favorite is the Steller's jay, a noisy blue bird with a black crest. It will steal food off your plate if you don't watch out!

I also like to watch bats swooping through the air to catch insects. Did you know that one bat can eat up to 600 mosquito-sized insects in an hour? Yosemite has 15 species of bats. These include the rare spotted bat, which has big ears and three white spots on its back.

Glacier Point

The view from Glacier Point was totally awesome. It made me dizzy to look over the edge. It's 3,200 feet—a little more than a 1/2 mile—straight down to the floor of Yosemite Valley! In the distance I could see Yosemite Falls. I could also see El Capitan and Half Dome. I like the way light reflected off the bare rock surfaces at sunrise and sunset, "painting" them pink, purple, and gold.

The ranger told us that this is a good place to see peregrine falcons in flight. They can dive at speeds up to 200 miles per hour and catch their prey in mid-air. They nest in high places on very narrow rock ledges.

El Capitan

El Capitan

El Capitan is Spanish for "the Captain." This is the biggest single block of granite on Earth. It is more than 3,600 feet from its base to its top. It's a favorite climbing spot for visitors from all over the world. It can take anywhere from several hours to several days to scale this rock. So it's not unusual to see people camped out on the rock ledges.

The highest single waterfall on the North American continent is Ribbon Fall. It plunges 1,612 feet off a cliff on the west side of El Capitan.

Yosemite Falls

Yosemite Falls

All together, Yosemite Falls are the highest waterfalls in North America and rank number five in the world. There are actually three sections of falls, one on top of the other. The total drop is 2,425 feet, which is as high as 13 Niagara Falls!

In late spring and early summer, so much water goes over the falls that you can feel the ground shake! By the end of the summer, the falls may be no more than a trickle. And some years they dry up all together.

Lyell

Lyell Fork

The first person to climb Mt. Lyell was John Tileston in 1871. At 13,114 feet, Mt. Lyell is the park's highest mountain. It also has the largest active glacier, the Lyell Glacier, which clings to the northwest side of the peak. It is about 1/4 mile square. Melting snow from the glacier feeds the Tuolumne River. The river, in turn, provides water to San Francisco by way of a reservoir.

Today the rivers and streams of Yosemite provide places to fish, wade, or raft. But in the past, people flocked to the water to pan for gold! While some gold was found, the area did not yield as much of this precious metal as the foothills to the west of the park did.

Tioga Pass

On our last day we drove over Tioga Pass. It's 9,945 feet above sea level. It's the highest highway pass in the Sierra Nevada range and in all of California.

Because it's so high, many flowers and plants that grow here differ from those in lower elevations such as the Yosemite Valley. The trees are also small and stunted, because it's difficult for them to grow at such high altitudes.

Wherever you go—high in the mountains, or low in the valleys—Yosemite is truly one of the most awesome places on Earth!

Tioga Pass

127

Reader Response

Open for Discussion Make a list of the things you'll do on a future trip to Yosemite. Put the best thing at the top.

1. Why do you think the author chose to use letters and photographs to tell about Yosemite?

2. Reread the letter from Glacier Point on page 100. What sentence states the main idea of the passage? What supporting details can you find?

3. Create a main idea chart for the selection. Draw a box on top of your paper and record the selection's main idea in it. Next, connect boxes to it and fill them in with details that support the main idea.

4. The author uses the word *impressive* to describe many wonders in Yosemite. Tell about some of these wonders. Use words from the Words to Know list.

Test Practice

Look Back and Write At Yosemite, someone says," It all started with Abraham Lincoln." What does this person mean? Reread page 94 and then explain the statement.

Meet the Author
Lisa Halvorsen

Read more books by Lisa Halvorsen.

Lisa Halvorsen has traveled all over the world in her work as a travel writer. She has visited more than 40 countries on six continents. Her favorite trips have been to the Galapagos Islands, Turkey, Ecuador, Kenya, and New Zealand.

Ms. Halvorsen started traveling at an early age. She moved seven times before she started Kindergarten! Today, when she's not on the road, she lives in northern Vermont with her two cats, Dusty Miller and Gina. Her pastimes include hiking, canoeing, sailing, and gardening.

"Writing opens up a lot of doors," says Ms. Halvorsen. "It gives me a chance to travel, learn about places, and meet people I might not meet if I weren't a writer. It gives me a chance to satisfy my curiosity and my sense of adventure."

What is her advice to young writers? "Be curious, be adventurous, and read as much as you can. Write about what you love. Don't be afraid to ask questions and look for answers to what interests you."

Letters Home from the Grand Canyon

Letters Home from Yosemite

Letters Home from Yellowstone

Song

Genre

- Songs are really poems. The lines rhyme and have rhythm so that they can be sung to a melody.

- Since patriotic songs are about a topic important to a whole nation, they are emotional and are widely sung.

- This song begins with the chorus, the part of the song that is repeated after each verse.

- The song's short phrases are easy to sing to the catchy melody.

Link to Social Studies

Make a four-column chart with the heads "Freedom," "Historical Events," "National Symbols," and "Landscape." Write the titles of other songs about the U.S. in the appropriate column(s).

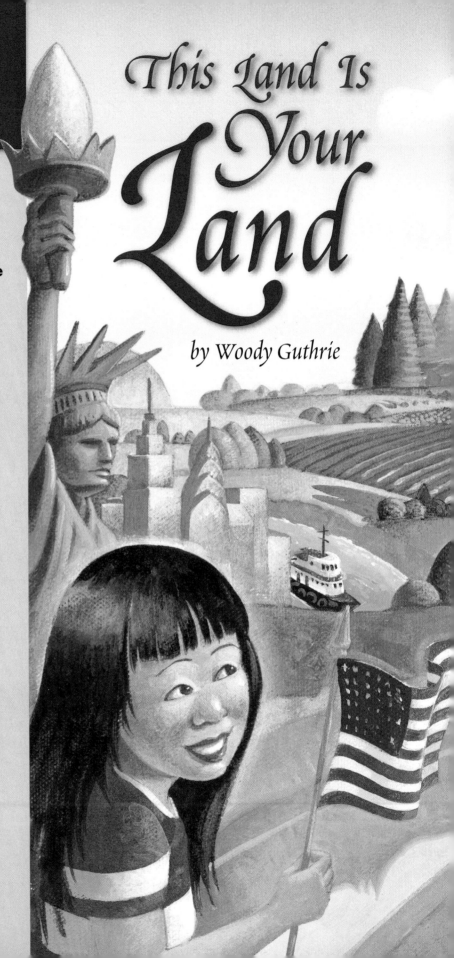

This Land Is Your Land

by Woody Guthrie

CHORUS:

This land is your land, this land is my land,
From California to the New York Island;
From the redwood forest to the Gulf Stream waters,
This land was made for you and me.

✓ Prior Knowledge   Link the song's phrases to what you know about the U.S.

VERSE 1

As I was walking that ribbon of highway,
I saw above me that endless skyway;
I saw below me that golden valley;
This land was made for you and me.

[CHORUS]

VERSE 2

I've roamed and rambled and I followed my footsteps
To the sparkling sands of her diamond deserts;
And all around me a voice was sounding:
This land was made for you and me.

[CHORUS]

Draw Conclusions How does the songwriter feel about the U.S.?

VERSE 3

When the sun came shining, and I was strolling,
And the wheat fields waving and the dust clouds rolling,
As the fog was lifting a voice was chanting:
This land was made for you and me.

[CHORUS]

Reading Across Texts

The song does not mention any of the natural wonders described in *Letters Home from Yosemite*. Which wonder from Yosemite would you like to include in the song?

Writing Across Texts Write a verse for "This Land Is Your Land" that describes the wonder you chose.

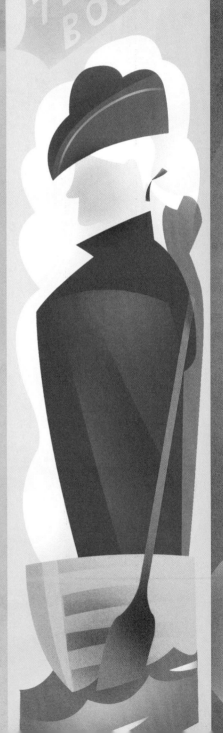

We're All in the Telephone Book

by Langston Hughes

We're all in the telephone book,
Folks from everywhere on earth—
Anderson to Zabowski,
It's a record of America's worth.

We're all in the telephone book.
There's no priority—
A millionaire like Rockefeller
Is likely to be behind me.

For generations men have dreamed
Of nations united as one.
Just look in your telephone book
To see where that dream's begun.

When Washington crossed the Delaware
And the pillars of tyranny shook,
He started the list of democracy
That's America's telephone book.

Speak Up

by Janet S. Wong

You're Korean, aren't you?

Why don't you speak Korean?

Say something Korean.

C'mon. Say something.

Say some other stuff.
Sounds funny.
Sounds strange.

Listen to me?

But I'm American,
can't you see?

But I was born here.

Yes.

Just don't, I guess.

I don't speak it.
I can't.

Halmoni. Grandmother.
Haraboji. Grandfather.
Imo. Aunt.

Hey, let's listen to you
for a change.

Say some foreign words.

Your family came from
somewhere else.
Sometime.

So was I.

CITY I LOVE

by Lee Bennett Hopkins

In the city
I live in—
city I love—
mornings wake
to
swishes, swashes,
sputters
of sweepers
swooshing litter
from gutters.

In the city
I live in—
city I love—
afternoons pulse
with
people hurrying,
scurrying—
races of faces
pacing to
must-get-there
places.

In the city
I live in—
city I love—
nights shimmer
with lights
competing
with stars
above
unknown heights.

In the city
I live in—
city I love—
as dreams
start to creep
my city
of senses
lulls
me
to
sleep.

Midwest Town

by Ruth De Long Peterson

Farther east it wouldn't be on the map—
Too small—but here it rates a dot and a name.
In Europe it would wear a castle cap
Or have a cathedral rising like a flame.

But here it stands where the section roadways meet.
Its houses dignified with trees and lawn;
The stores hold *tête-à-tête* across Main Street;
The red brick school, a church—the town is gone.

America is not all traffic lights,
And beehive homes and shops and factories;
No, there are wide green days and starry nights,
And a great pulse beating strong in towns like these.

Wrap-Up

And the Nominee Is . . .

Suppose that you were asked to nominate someone to receive an award for best representing the greatness of the United States. (It could be a public figure or someone you know.) Whom would you nominate? Write an essay that explains why this person deserves to receive the award.

~ Symbol of ~
Greatness

How do the diverse regions and peoples of the United States reflect its greatness?

Tour Guide

connect to
SOCIAL STUDIES

You are a tour guide in the setting of one of the selections in this unit. What would you tell others about what makes the people or the region special? Make some notes about what you would say. Then in a small group, take turns role-playing a tour guide for the place you chose.

Travel Brochure

connect to
SOCIAL STUDIES

Create a travel brochure for the setting of a selection in this unit or for the region in which you live. (You may need to do a little research.) Organize the information in your brochure to let visitors know about the culture and important sights of the area, especially what makes the area unique. Include some illustrations and a map in your brochure.

139

Work & Play

What is the value
of work and play?

Comprehension

Skill
Cause and Effect

Strategy
Prior Knowledge

Cause and Effect

- An effect is *what* happens. A cause is *why* it happens.

- Clue words such as *because, so,* and *cause* sometimes signal a cause-effect relationship. Sometimes you must figure out for yourself that one thing causes another.

Strategy: Prior Knowledge

Good readers use what they know, their prior knowledge, to help them understand what they read. As they read new information, they try to connect it to what they already know. They think about whether they have ever seen or experienced what they are reading about. This helps them understand the new information. Using what you already know can help you understand causes and effects.

1. Read "Up, Up, and Down." Make a graphic organizer like the one above to describe two cause-effect relationships.

2. Write a sentence about each cause-effect relationship. Use a clue word to show the relationship.

Up, Up, and Down

Did you ever see basketball players leap high into the air to shoot a ball into a basket? Or even higher still to block a shot? How do they jump so high?

The trick is to beat the Earth's gravity. Because of this force, a person is pulled to the ground. To move away from this force, you need energy.

Think of a spring, or better yet, think of a spring in a pogo stick. Your weight on the stick presses the spring down. That stores energy in the spring. When that energy is released, it is enough to lift the stick and you off the ground.

In a similar way, you can build up energy in your legs. If you stand straight and then try to jump up, you can't. You may be able to lift off the ground an inch or so, but that's all. That's why you bend at the knees before jumping up. When you bend, it's as if you are putting a "spring" in your legs. Release that spring, and up you go.

Of course, the energy is not nearly enough to overcome Earth's gravity. That's why the Earth will always pull you back down again.

Skill There is a cause-effect relationship in this paragraph. Look for a clue word.

Strategy Think of what you know about gravity. What effect does this force have on you?

Skill Look for cause-effect relationships in this paragraph. What causes energy to be stored? What effect does releasing it have?

Strategy Have you ever seen or played on a pogo stick? If not, just think of what you know about jumping off the ground as you read the next paragraph.

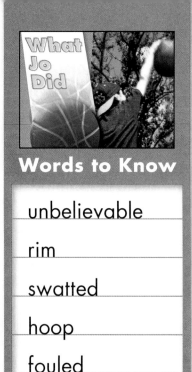
Words to Know

unbelievable

rim

swatted

hoop

fouled

jersey

marveled

speechless

Remember

Try the strategy. Then, if you need more help, use your glossary or a dictionary.

Vocabulary Strategy
for Prefixes and Suffixes

Word Structure Prefixes and suffixes have their own meanings. When they are added to words, they change the meaning of the original word, the base word. The prefix *un-* means "the opposite of ____" or "not ____," as in *unhappy*. The suffix *-able* means "able to be ___ed," as in *enjoyable*. The suffix *-less* means "without ____," as in *painless*. You can use prefixes and suffixes to help you figure out the meanings of words.

1. Look at an unfamiliar word to see if it has a base word you know.

2. Check to see if the prefix *un-* or the suffix *-able* or *-less* has been added to the base word.

3. Think about how the prefix or suffix changes the meaning of the base word.

4. Try the meaning in the sentence.

As you read "At the Game," look for words with the prefix *un-* or the suffix *-able* or *-less*. Use the prefix and suffixes to help you figure out the meanings of the words.

WXXT 6

144

At the Game

"Hello again, sports fans. This is Bud Sherman, WXXT Channel 6, coming to you from the Grandview Center, where the third-place Tigers are battling the second-place Lions in the first round of the HSBA playoffs. Tiger forward Matt Roberts has had a flawless game, scoring 28 points so far. Lion center Darren Jones has been unbelievable under the basket.

"Now Roberts moves in and throws the ball. He's looking for another three-pointer. The ball hits the rim. Maxwell tries a shot, but it's swatted away by Jones.

Grundig has the ball and he's heading for the Tigers' hoop. Oh, my, he's been fouled by Lee, who grabbed Grundig's jersey and arm. I imagine Coach Simmons is unhappy. That's Lee's fourth foul in this half. Grundig, a reliable free-thrower, makes both points. Pfizer throws in to Barton, who passes to—Roberts! You know, I have always marveled at the way Roberts moves around the court, but his performance tonight just leaves me speechless. Roberts shoots from 30 feet out—and he scores! The Tigers win, 87–84."

Write

Imagine that you are playing basketball with a friend. Describe the action. Use words from the Words to Know list.

What Jo Did

text and images by Charles R. Smith Jr.

What can **Jo do** that others cannot?

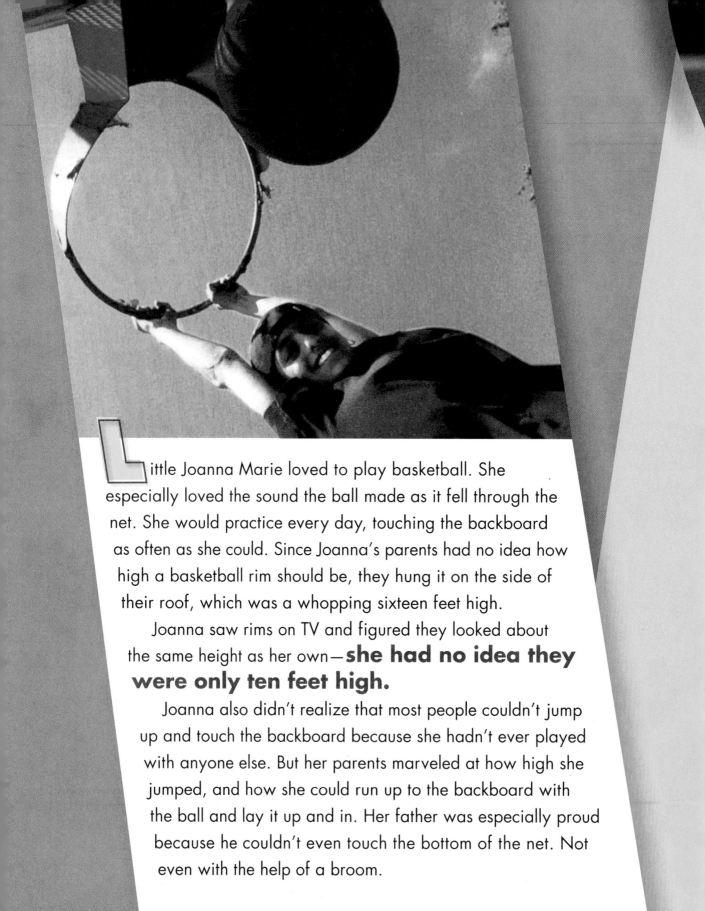

ittle Joanna Marie loved to play basketball. She especially loved the sound the ball made as it fell through the net. She would practice every day, touching the backboard as often as she could. Since Joanna's parents had no idea how high a basketball rim should be, they hung it on the side of their roof, which was a whopping sixteen feet high.

Joanna saw rims on TV and figured they looked about the same height as her own—**she had no idea they were only ten feet high.**

Joanna also didn't realize that most people couldn't jump up and touch the backboard because she hadn't ever played with anyone else. But her parents marveled at how high she jumped, and how she could run up to the backboard with the ball and lay it up and in. Her father was especially proud because he couldn't even touch the bottom of the net. Not even with the help of a broom.

One day Joanna, her hair bundled up under her baseball cap, was dribbling her basketball on the way to the store to get some sugar for her mother. Her mother said that she didn't have to hurry home, as long as she was in by dark. As Joanna moved down the street, a basketball came rolling out of nowhere and bumped her high-tops.

"I'm sorry, man, I didn't mean to hit you with the ball like that," said a young boy dressed in sneakers, shorts, and a Bulls tank top as he picked up the ball.

"Oh, that's okay. I wasn't even paying attention," Joanna said.

"Hey, we need one more to play a game. You in?" he asked her.

"Sure, why not?" she responded.

As Joanna approached the other boys, she remembered that she had her hat on.

They probably think I'm a boy, she thought. Might as well enjoy the ride.

The boys picked teams, and since Joanna was smaller than everyone else, she got picked last. It didn't bother her, though, because she had never played with anyone before and was just happy to be there.

"Hey, kid, what's your name?" asked a freckle-faced kid with red hair.

"Ahhh . . . Jo. My name is Jo," Joanna said nervously.

"All right, Joe, you pick up T.J. over there, see. Make sure he doesn't score a basket. He can jump pretty high, ya know!"

J o moved around, not really touching the ball at first, just trying to get a feel for playing with other people. She had never even passed the ball or received a pass herself. Playing with others took getting used to, but in no time she was passing the ball. The only thing that puzzled her was why the hoop was so low.

Even though the boys passed the ball around a lot, T.J. didn't really touch it much, and when he did, he didn't take a shot. Finally, he was wide open for a jump shot when Jo came out of nowhere, jumped high into the air, **and swatted his shot into the next court.**

"Wow, did you see that?

Did you see how high he jumped?" the freckle-faced kid said, his mouth wide open.

"I've never seen anybody jump that high. Not even Michael Jordan," said the kid with the Bulls jersey on.

"Unbelievable."

"Where'd you learn to do that?"

"Oh, my goodness!!!"

"Poor T.J."

"Hey—I got fouled, and besides, it wasn't that high," said T.J., but his face was so red that he couldn't hide his embarrassment.

"Uh, uh . . . it's just something I picked up. I practice a lot with my dad," Jo added, surprised at how big a deal the boys made of her block.

"Man! You must have some dad," one of the boys said.

The game continued, and Jo was passed the ball more often. Her teammates encouraged her to shoot more, and when she did, they were amazed how the ball arced in the air like a rainbow before falling straight through the hoop, without touching the rim. As the game progressed, Jo felt hot, but she knew she couldn't take her hat off, or else she'd be found out.

Whenever a boy got the ball and Jo came over to play defense, he quickly passed the ball away. Jo blocked a few more shots, which created more *ooooohs* and *aaaaaaahs*, and one of the boys on her team asked her if she could dunk the ball.

"Dunk? What's that?" Jo asked. This was a word she had never heard before.

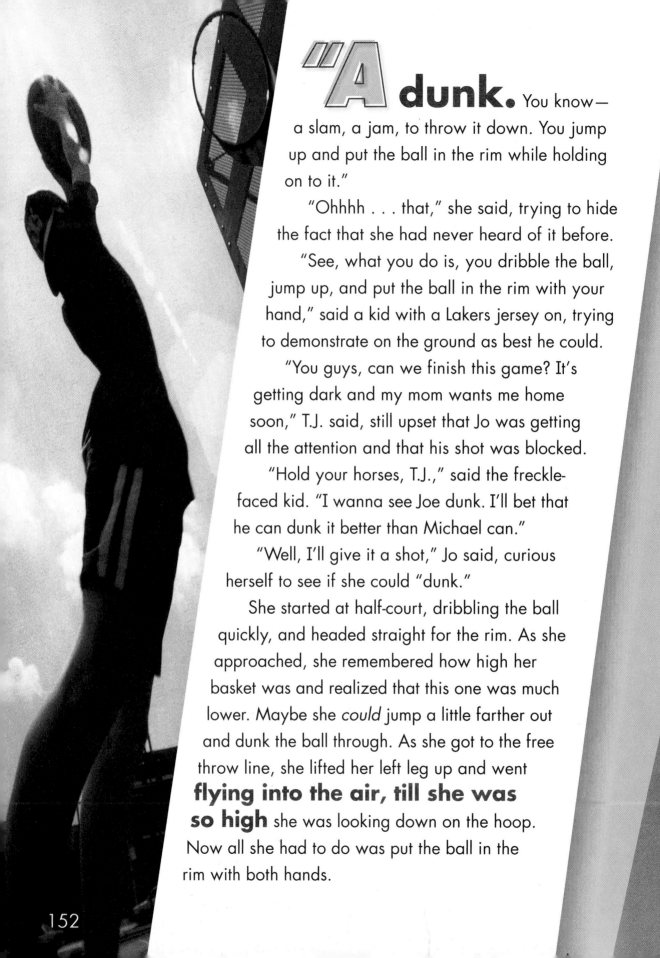

"A dunk.

You know— a slam, a jam, to throw it down. You jump up and put the ball in the rim while holding on to it."

"Ohhhh . . . that," she said, trying to hide the fact that she had never heard of it before.

"See, what you do is, you dribble the ball, jump up, and put the ball in the rim with your hand," said a kid with a Lakers jersey on, trying to demonstrate on the ground as best he could.

"You guys, can we finish this game? It's getting dark and my mom wants me home soon," T.J. said, still upset that Jo was getting all the attention and that his shot was blocked.

"Hold your horses, T.J.," said the freckle-faced kid. "I wanna see Joe dunk. I'll bet that he can dunk it better than Michael can."

"Well, I'll give it a shot," Jo said, curious herself to see if she could "dunk."

She started at half-court, dribbling the ball quickly, and headed straight for the rim. As she approached, she remembered how high her basket was and realized that this one was much lower. Maybe she *could* jump a little farther out and dunk the ball through. As she got to the free throw line, she lifted her left leg up and went **flying into the air, till she was so high** she was looking down on the hoop. Now all she had to do was put the ball in the rim with both hands.

She was up there for a while
before she felt her hands on the rim,
the ball going through, and her feet touching the ground.

When she landed,

all of the boys' mouths were hanging open,

and for a moment they were speechless.

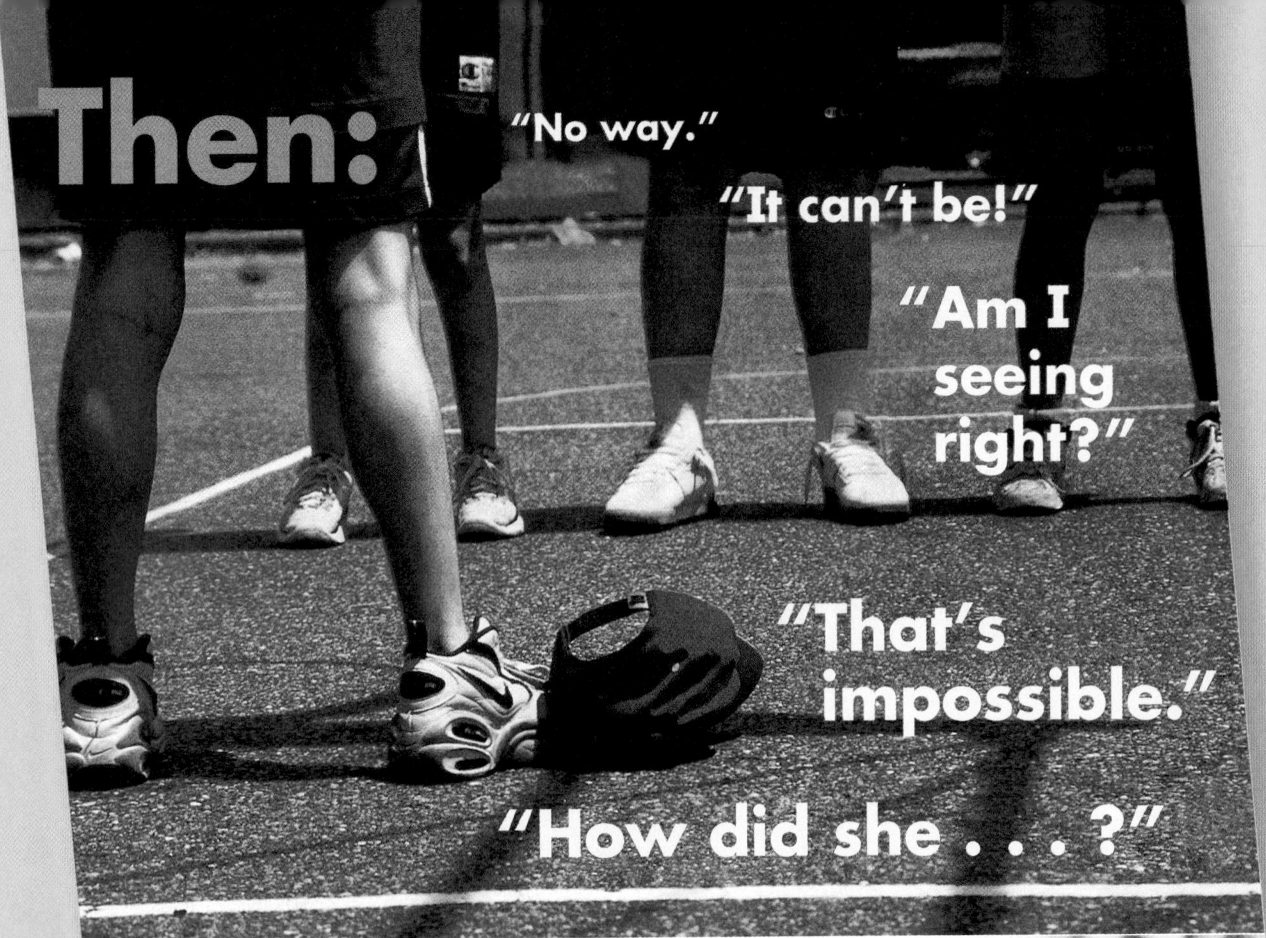

Then:

"No way."

"It can't be!"

"Am I seeing right?"

"That's impossible."

"How did she . . . ?"

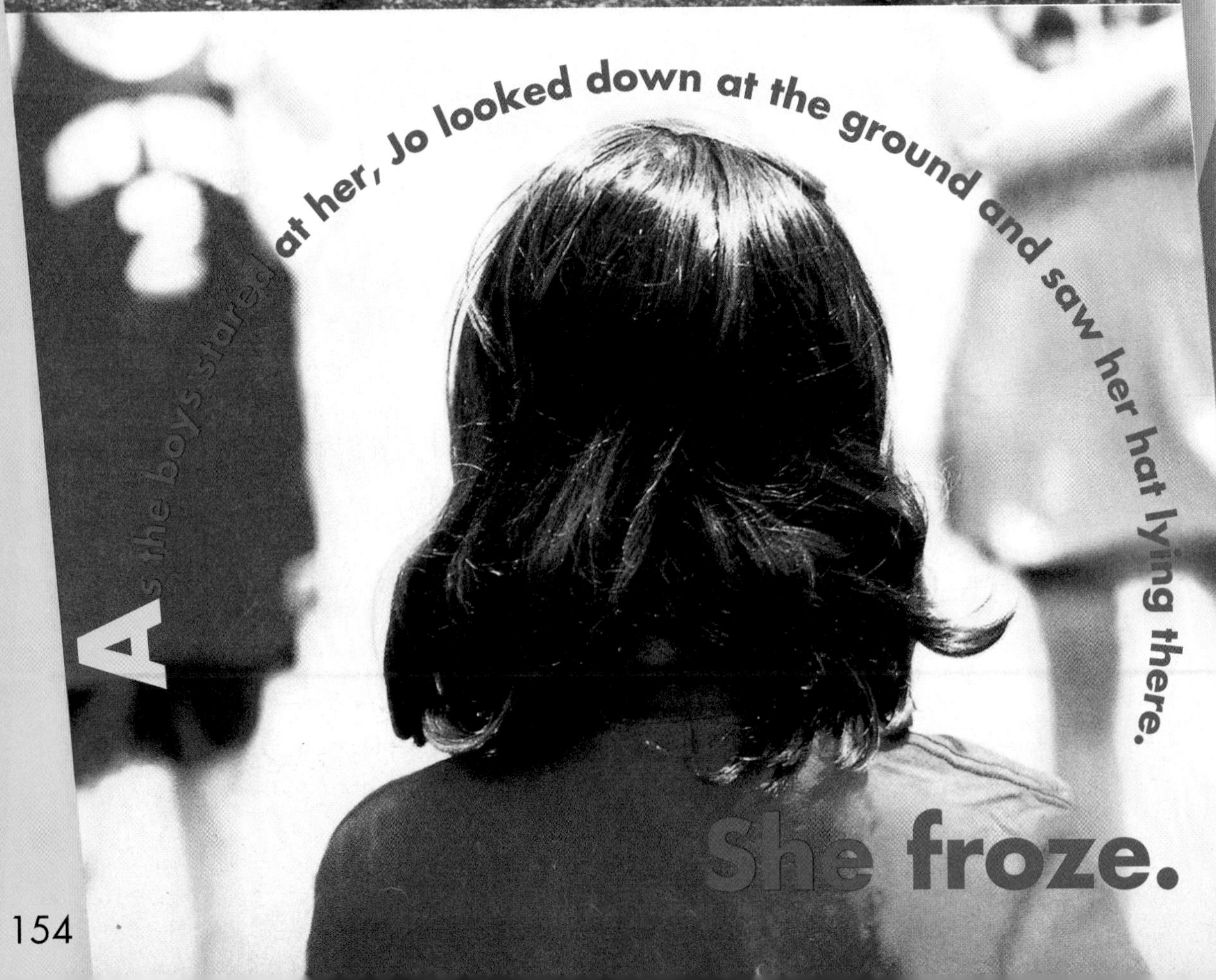

As the boys stared at her, Jo looked down at the ground and saw her hat lying there.

She froze.

154

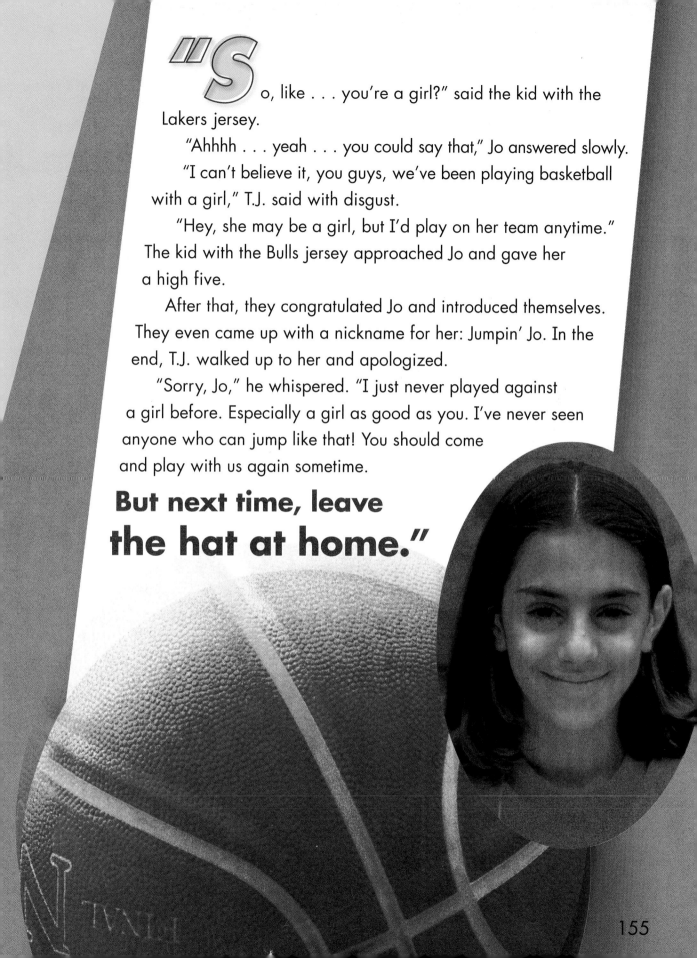

"So, like . . . you're a girl?" said the kid with the Lakers jersey.

"Ahhhh . . . yeah . . . you could say that," Jo answered slowly.

"I can't believe it, you guys, we've been playing basketball with a girl," T.J. said with disgust.

"Hey, she may be a girl, but I'd play on her team anytime." The kid with the Bulls jersey approached Jo and gave her a high five.

After that, they congratulated Jo and introduced themselves. They even came up with a nickname for her: Jumpin' Jo. In the end, T.J. walked up to her and apologized.

"Sorry, Jo," he whispered. "I just never played against a girl before. Especially a girl as good as you. I've never seen anyone who can jump like that! You should come and play with us again sometime.

But next time, leave the hat at home."

Reader Response

Open for Discussion Suppose that Joanna went home and told her parents about the game. Tell what she told, play by play.

1. The author uses basketball terms such as *dunk*. Why? Find five more basketball terms in the story and tell why they are there.

2. What does Joanna do to T.J.'s jump shot? How does he react?

3. Have you ever surprised someone with a skill or talent the person didn't know you had? How did that person react?

4. Three words on the Words to Know list describe people's reactions to Joanna's basketball talent. Write them, along with other words and phrases from the story that people used when they saw her play.

Look Back and Write When the boys discovered that Jo was really Joanna, were they pleased? Reread pages 153–155. Describe how the boys reacted.

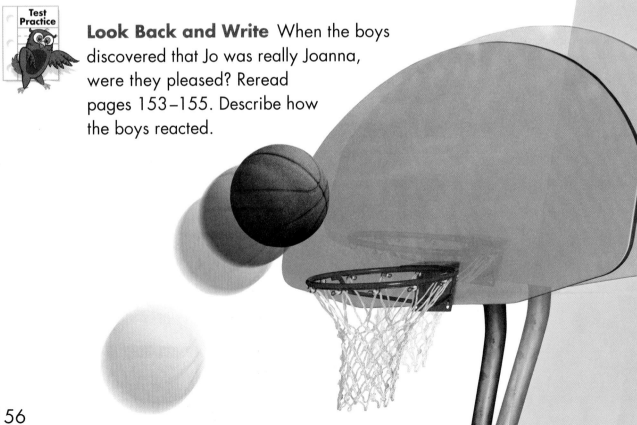

Meet the Author and Photographer

Charles R. Smith Jr.

Read more books by Charles R. Smith Jr.

Tall Tales: Six Amazing Basketball Dreams

Loki & Alex: The Adventures of a Dog & His Best Friend

Charles R. Smith Jr. loves photography, writing, and basketball. These three interests all came together for his book *Tall Tales: Six Amazing Basketball Dreams.* The story "What Jo Did" is just one of the stories in this book.

Before he began writing books, Mr. Smith worked as a photographer In New York City. "The jobs paid the bills but were boring for me. So I decided to begin a series of photos called Street Basketball in New York." A children's book editor saw the photos and suggested Mr. Smith use them for a book. The result was *Rim Shots,* a book of photos, poems, and thoughts about basketball.

For his next book, he decided to used infrared film. The film responds to heat and makes unusual colors. "In my story 'What Jo Did,' you can see the effect in the way the trees look and the colors of the players' clothes."

Mr. Smith knows his stories are "a bit unbelievable." He says that good storytelling begins with some truth. "But realizing you don't have to stick to the truth is even better."

Poetry

Genre

- Poetry is meant to appeal to the senses, emotions, or mind.

- Often poetry gives the reader a fresh, unexpected way of looking at things.

- In many poems the rhyme helps establish the rhythm, or regular beat of stressed syllables.

- Preview the poems. Notice how the author captures the reader's attention with varied text sizes and styles.

Link to Writing

The speaker uses rhyme to describe himself in both poems. Use this style to write a poem about yourself playing a sport or doing some other activity.

FAST BREAK

by Charles R. Smith Jr.

 Prior Knowledge What are some things you know about basketball?

158

Fleet feet
streak
up the concrete
to pull a
sweet treat
for the crowd.
The outlet *pass*—
fast—
as the break
is on
and I'm
gone.
A scene from
The Flash
I *dash*
down**court**
to
meet the pass.
Eyes wide
arms out
a reverse *jam*
is coming
no doubt.
Sky-high
I *fly*
to bring the
silent **crowd**
back
to life.

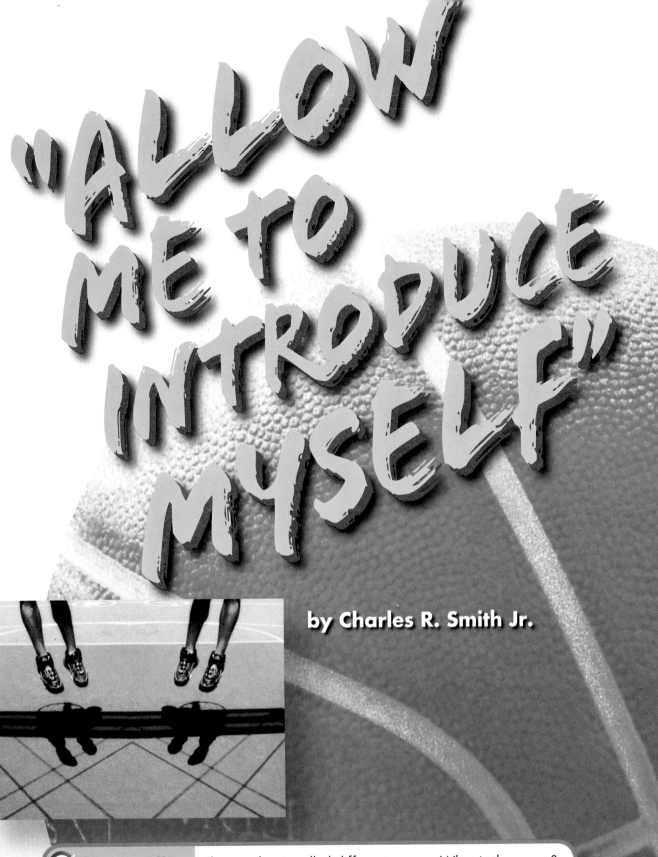

"ALLOW ME TO INTRODUCE MYSELF"

by Charles R. Smith Jr.

Cause & Effect The speaker is called different names. What is the cause?

They call me
the show
stopper
the dime
dropper
the
spin-move-to-the-left
reverse jam **poppa.**
The high
flier
on the high
wire.
The intense
rim-rattlin'
noise
amplifier.
The net-**shaker**
back
board **breaker**
creator
of the funky dunk
hip-**shaker.**
The Man
Sir Slam
The Legend
I be.
That's just
a few of the
names
they call **me.**

Reading Across Texts

The story "What Jo Did" and the poems "Fast Break" and "'Allow Me to Introduce Myself'" are all by Charles R. Smith Jr. How are they alike and different?

Writing Across Texts Write some paragraphs comparing the three selections by Charles R. Smith Jr.

Comprehension

Skill
Draw Conclusions

Strategy
Prior Knowledge

Draw Conclusions

- Drawing a conclusion while you read or after you read is forming an opinion based on what you already know or on the facts and details in a text.

- Check an author's conclusions or your own conclusions by asking: Is this the only logical choice? Are the facts accurate?

Strategy: Prior Knowledge

Active readers bring what they already know to a piece of text to help them understand new information. As you read, think about what you know from your own life, from the world around you, and from other things you've read. Use that knowledge to help you draw conclusions.

1. Make a graphic organizer like the one above to help you find facts and details in "Home, Home on the Range."

2. Would you like to live on a ranch? Use your graphic organizer to draw a conclusion. Write a paragraph with your reasons.

HOME, HOME ON THE RANGE

Skill Draw a conclusion as to why ranches have to be so large. Call on your prior knowledge about cattle and sheep.

A *ranch* is a particular kind of farm where cattle or sheep are raised. Most ranches in the United States are located in the West, in wide open country called the *range,* and most ranches are enormous, consisting of several thousand acres.

Strategy Do you have prior knowledge of what the words *roam* and *graze* mean? If not, can you draw a conclusion about what they mean from the context?

Cattle and sheep need a lot of room to roam and graze. In addition, they must be able to get to streams and ponds for fresh drinking water.

Ranchers today still use horses to get around as cowboys did in the days of the Old West. But they also use vehicles, such as trucks, jeeps, and even helicopters. This is especially important in the winter. When snow covers the ground, the livestock can't graze, so ranchers have to bring hay to them.

Skill Think back to what you know about cattle and how they eat. Then draw a conclusion about how they get food in the winter.

The children of ranchers have to get around too. Because ranches are so large and far apart, most ranch children have to ride a bus a long way to school.

Would you like to live on a ranch?

Strategy Based on what you have seen, read, or experienced, what would this be like?

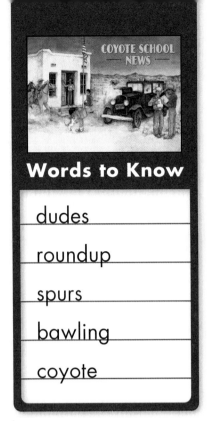

Words to Know

dudes

roundup

spurs

bawling

coyote

Vocabulary Strategy
for Unfamiliar Words

Dictionary/Glossary When you are reading, you may come across a word you don't know. If you can't use the context, or words and sentences around the word, to figure out the word's meaning, you can use a dictionary or glossary to help you.

1. Check the back of your book for a glossary. If there is no glossary, look up the word in a dictionary.

2. Find the entry for the word. The entries are in alphabetical order.

3. Read the pronunciation to yourself. Saying the word may help you recognize it.

4. Read all the meanings given for the word.

5. Choose the one that makes sense in the sentence.

As you read "At a Guest Ranch," use a dictionary or glossary to find the meanings of the vocabulary words. Which meaning makes sense?

AT A GUEST RANCH

Howdy, pardner! That may sound corny, but it's appropriate because my family and I are at a ranch that lets people pay to stay there. This gives them a chance to see what ranch life is like. Guests are called dudes. That's what the cowhands called people from back East. Some dude ranches are just for entertaining visitors, excuse me, dudes. Some are real cattle or sheep ranches that take in a few dudes on the side.

Our ranch, the Double K near Bozeman, Montana, is a working cattle ranch. We went with the cowhands on a roundup. It was exciting to watch. With just a touch of his spurs, a cowhand moves his horse into the herd and cuts out one cow. It was hot, dusty, and noisy too. The cattle were mooing, and the calves were bawling.

We also rode out on a trail and camped out under the stars. Dinner from a chuckwagon, a bedroll by the campfire, and a coyote howling in the distance—I felt as if I were in a Western movie!

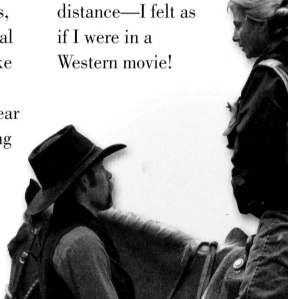

Write

Imagine that you have gone to stay at a dude ranch. Write a journal entry describing a day at the ranch. Use words from the Words to Know list.

Historical fiction is a story that is made up around real events in history. Decide what those real events might have been as you read about children in a southern Arizona country school in 1938–1939.

COYOTE SCHOOL NEWS

by Joan Sandin

What stories make the news at Coyote School?

Rancho San Isidro

My name is Ramón Ernesto Ramírez, but everybody calls me Monchi. I live on a ranch that my great-grandfather built a long time ago when this land was part of Mexico. That was before the United States bought it and moved the line in 1854. My father has a joke about that. He says my great-grandfather was an *americano,* not because he crossed the line, but because the line crossed him.

In my family we are six kids: me, my big brother Junior, my big sister Natalia, my little tattletale brother Victor, my little sister Loli, and the baby Pili. My *tío* Chaco lives with us too. He is the youngest brother of my father.

The real name of our ranch is Rancho San Isidro, after the patron saint of my great-grandfather, but most of the time everybody calls it the Ramírez Ranch.

On our ranch we have chickens and pigs and cattle and horses. The boys in the Ramírez family know

how to ride and rope. We are a family of *vaqueros.* In the fall and spring we have roundup on our ranch. Many people come to help with the cattle and the horses. Those are the most exciting days of the year, even more exciting than Christmas.

The things I don't like about our ranch are always having to get the wood for the fire, and the long and bumpy ride to school.

My tío Chaco drives the school bus.

"It's not fair," I tell him. "We have to get up earlier than all the other kids at Coyote School, and we get home the latest too."

"Don't forget," says my tío, "you get first choice of seats."

Ha, ha. By the time the last kid gets in we are all squeezed together like sardines in a can. And the bus is shaking and bumping like it has a flat tire.

"I wish President Roosevelt would do something about these roads," I tell my tío.

"Hey, you know how to write English," he says. "Write him a letter."

"Maybe I will," I say.

*americano (AH-mair-ee-CAHN-*oh)— American
tío (TEE-oh)—uncle
rancho (RAHN-choe)—ranch
san (sahn)—saint
vaqueros (bah-CARE-rose)—cowboys

Coyote School

"*Mira, mira,* Monchi," Natalia says, pinching my cheek. "There's your little *novia.*"

She means Rosie. I like Rosie, but I hate it when Natalia teases me. Rosie lives at Coyote Ranch, close enough to school that she can walk. Always she waits by the road so she can race the bus.

"*¡Ándale! ¡Ándale!* Hurry up!" we yell at my tío Chaco, but every time he lets her win.

Rosie wasn't first today anyway. Lalo and Frankie were. Their horses are standing in the shade of the big mesquite tree.

Yap! Yap! Yap! Always Chipito barks when he sees us, and Miss Byers says, "Hush, Chipito!" Then she smiles and waves at us.

Miss Byers is new this year. Her ranch is a hundred miles from here, in Rattlesnake Canyon, so five days of the week she and Chipito live in the little room behind the school. All of us like Miss Byers, even the big kids, because she is young and nice and fair. We like that she lives on a ranch, and we like her swell ideas:

1. Baseball at recess,
2. The Perfect Attendance Award,
3. *Coyote News.*

---

mira (MEER-ah)—look
novia (NOVE-ee-ah)—girlfriend
ándale (AHN-dah-lay)—come on; hurry up

Coyote News

All week we have been working on our first *Coyote News*. Natalia made up the name, and Joey drew the coyote. First we looked at some other newspapers: the *Arizona Daily Star, Western Livestock Journal,* and *Little Cowpuncher.* That one we liked best because all the stories and pictures were done by kids.

"Monchi," said Loli, "put me cute."

"What?" I said. Sometimes it's not easy to understand my little sister's English.

"Miss Byers says you have to help me put words to my story," she said.

"Okay," I told her. "But I have my own story to do, so hurry up and learn to write."

Loli's story was *muy tonta,* but one thing was good. She remembered how to write all the words I spelled for her.

Even if Victor is my brother I have to say he is a big tattletale—*chismoso.* When Gilbert was writing his story for *Coyote News,* Victor told on him for writing in Spanish. But Miss Byers did not get mad at Gilbert. She smiled at him! And then she said Spanish is a beautiful language that people around here have been speaking for hundreds of years, and that we should be proud we can speak it too!

Ha ha, Victor, you big chismoso!

When we finished our stories and pictures, Miss Byers cut a stencil for the mimeograph. Then she printed copies of *Coyote News* for us to take home, and we hung them up on the ceiling to dry the ink. My tío Chaco said it looked like laundry day at Coyote School.

muy (MOO-ee)—very
tonta (TONE-tah)—silly
chismoso (cheese-MOE-soe)—tattletale
señor (sin-YORE)—Mr.
grandote (grahn-DOE-tay)—great big, huge

Issue Number One   September 15, 1938

COYOTE NEWS

I am new!

Stories and Pictures by the Students of Coyote School, Pima County, Arizona

Something New at Coyote School

Coyote News was the idea of our teacher, but we write the stories and draw the pictures. The big kids help the little kids...Rosie Garcia, Grade 3

About Coyote School

This year we have 12 kids and all the grades except Grade 5...Billy Mills, Grade 3

We Ride Our Horses to School

The road to Rancho del Cerro is a very big problem for the bus of Mr. Ramirez. For that reason Lalo and I ride our horses to school--16 miles all the days. The year past it was 2,352 miles. We had to put new shoes on the horses 5 times...Frankie Lopez, Grade 6

Ándale Ándale We want to go home

by Lalo Lopez

The Perfect Attendance

Miss Byers will give a prize to anybody who comes to school all the days, no matter what. The prize is called The Perfect Attendance Award and it is a silver dollar! For me perfect attendance is not easy, but oh boy, I would like to win that silver dollar............Monchi Ramirez, Grade 4

Yap! Yap!

by Cynthia

Chipito

The dog of the teacher is called Chipito. He is very cute. He likes Loli best.....story by Loli Ramirez, Grade 1 with help by Monchi Ramirez, Grade 4

Señor Grandote

Our bus driver ran over a big rattlesnake. We took the skin and gave it to our teacher. She measured him with the yardstick. He was 5 feet and 7 inches! She hung him on the wall next to President Roosevelt. We kids call him Señor Grandote because in Spanish it means Mr. Huge................Gilbert Perez, Grade 6

Señor Grandote

by Joey Brown

Chiles

Every day I am asking my father when we will have roundup. He says I am making him *loco* with my nagging and that first we have to pick *todos los chiles*.

All of us kids are tired of picking the chiles. It doesn't matter that we get home late from school, we still have to do it. And then, before the chiles dry out, we have to string them to make the *sartas*.

Last night we were taking about 600 pounds of the chiles to my tío Enrique's ranch. I was in the back of the truck when it hit a big rock. All the heavy sacks fell on me. Oh boy, it hurt so much! But I did not

tell my father. He had told me not to ride in the back of the truck, and I was afraid he would be mad.

My hand was still hurting this morning when Miss Byers did Fingernail Inspection.

"Monchi," she said, "what happened to your wrist? It's all black-and-blue and swollen."

"The chiles fell on him," Victor told her. "My father told him not to ride in the back."

"¡Chismoso!" I hissed at him.

Miss Byers called my tío Chaco over, and they had a long talk.

"Back in the bus, *mi'jo*," my tío said. "I have to take you to Tucson."

"Tucson!" I said. "Why?"

"You got to see the doctor," he said. So we drove all the way to Tucson to my *tía* Lena's house. At first my aunt was surprised and happy to see us, but then my *tío* told her why we were there.

"Monchi!" my *tía* said. "*¡Pobrecito!*" Then she told my *tío* Chaco to go back with the bus and she would take care of me.

My *tía* took me to a doctor. He moved my hand around. It hurt when he did that.

"I'm afraid the wrist is broken," he told my *tía*. "I need to set it and put it in a cast."

So I got a cast of plaster on my arm, and I had to stay in Tucson. But for me that was no problem! My *tía* felt very sorry for me. She cooked my favorite foods, and I got to pick the stations on her radio. That night Miss Byers called on the telephone to ask about me. She said she would come early Monday morning to drive me to school.

On Sunday my *tía* took me to the Tarzan picture show at the Fox Theater. It was swell! After the show we got ice cream and walked around downtown to look in the windows of the stores. I saw many things I liked. The best was a silver buckle with a hole to put a silver dollar. *¡Ay caramba!* I wish I had a buckle like that.

loco (LOW-coe)—crazy
todos (TOE-dose)—all
los (lohs)—the
chiles (CHEE-less)—chile peppers
sartas (SAR-tahs)—strings of chile peppers
mi'jo (MEE-hoe)—my son, sonny
tía (TEE-ah)—aunt
pobrecito (pobe-ray-SEE-toe)—
    poor little thing
¡ay caramba! (EYE car-RAHM-bah)—
    oh boy!

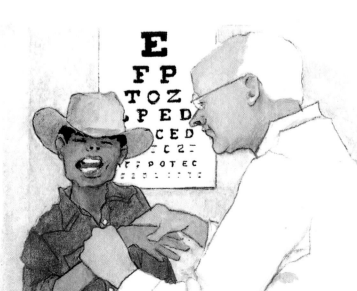

Nochebuena

For *Nochebuena* we are many people. Some are family I see only at Christmas and roundup and weddings and funerals. The day before Nochebuena my cousins from Sonora arrived. Now we could make the *piñata!*

First we cut the strips of red, white, and green paper. Then we paste them on a big *olla.* When the piñata is ready, we give it to my mother to fill with the *dulces* she hides in her secret places.

On Nochebuena, Junior and my tío Chaco hung the piñata between two big mesquite trees and we kids lined up to hit it, the littlest ones first. My mother tied a *mascada* over my little brother Pili's eyes and my tía Lena turned him around and around. She gave him the stick and pointed him toward the piñata. My tío Chaco and Junior made it easy for him. They did not jerk on the rope when he swung.

"*¡Dale! ¡Dale!*" we were yelling, but Pili never came close. None of the little kids could hit it. Then it was Loli's turn.

BAM.

Some peanuts fell out. Gilbert and I dived to get them. One by one, the other kids tried and missed. Then it was Natalia's turn. She took a good swing and—**BAM**.

The piñata broke open, and all the kids were in the dirt, screaming and laughing and picking up gum and nuts and oranges and candies.

Just before midnight we got into my tío Chaco's bus and my father's pickup to go to the Mass at Amado. When we got home my mother and my tías put out *tamales* and *menudo* and *tortillas* and cakes and coffee and other drinks. We had music and dancing. Nobody told us we had to go to bed.

Sometime in the night Santa Claus came and gave us our presents. Junior got a pair of spurs, Victor got a big red top, and Loli got a little toy dog that looks like Chipito. But I got the best present. It was a silver-dollar buckle, the one I had seen with my tía Lena in Tucson. It doesn't have a dollar yet, only a hole, but when I win the Perfect Attendance I will put my silver dollar in that hole.

Nochebuena (NO-chay-BUAY-nah)—
   Christmas Eve
piñata (peen-YAH-tah)—clay pot *(olla)*
   filled with treats
olla (OY-yah)—clay pot
dulces (DOOL-sehss)—sweets, candy
mascada (mas-KAH-dah)—scarf
¡dale! (DAH-lay)—hit it!
tamales (tah-MAH-less)—steamed
   filled dough
menudo (men-OO-doe)—tripe soup
tortillas (tor-TEE-yahs)—flat Mexican bread

Issue Number Five

January 12, 1939

COYOTE NEWS

Happy New Year!

Stories and Pictures by the Students of Coyote School, Pima County, Arizona

Miss Byers' Radio

Miss Byers brought her new radio to school. It has a big battery, so it doesn't matter that Coyote School has no electricity. We got to hear President Roosevelt's speech to the Congress. He told them to be prepared for war. Then he said, "Happy New Year."........Monchi Ramirez, Grade 4

Our President's Voice

None of us kids had heard the President's voice before. When he said "war" it sounded like "waw." We were all laughing because we never heard anybody who talked like that, but Billy said some of the dudes do.............Rosie Garcia, Grade 3

Our President

waw

by Joey Brown

Some Noisy Children

When the President was talking, Loli was noisy. Miss Byers gave her peanuts to make her quiet. I was quiet without the peanuts...Victor, Grade 2

Yap!

By Frankie López

Music on the Radio

We got to listen to the music on Miss Byers' radio. She has many stations, but I liked best to hear the one with the rancheras..........Gilbert Perez, Grade 6

No Earrings for Christmas

Santa Claus didn't bring me any earrings. Loli says it's because he knows that I don't have any holes in my ears like she does......Cynthia Brown, Grade 2

The Perfect Attendance Report

Miss Byers says Santa Claus must have given some of our kids the flu and chicken pox for Christmas. The only kids who still have perfect attendance are Natalia, Monchi, Victor, and me.........Billy Mills, Grade 3

La Fiesta de los Vaqueros Rodeo Parade

We are so excited because Miss Byers just told us something wonderful. Our school gets to be in the Tucson Rodeo Parade!...Natalia Ramirez, Grade 8

Roundup!

The vaqueros were hollering, "¡Ándale! ¡Ándale!" They were cutting through the cattle on their horses, swinging their lassoes in the air to rope out the steers. My tío Chaco threw his saddle up on his horse, Canelo, and joined them. We kids clapped and whistled. Sometimes we helped my father or my tíos. We brought them rope or a fresh horse or something to drink.

That night we boys got to eat with the vaqueros and sit by the fire and listen to them play their guitars and sing their *rancheras.* We got to hear their exciting stories and their bragging and their bad words. When my father came over to Junior and me I thought he was going to tell us to go in to bed, but instead he said, "Tomorrow I want you boys to help with the branding." Junior had helped since he was eleven, but it was the first time my father had ever asked me.

"Tomorrow I have school," I said.

"School!" said Junior. "Monchi, don't you understand? You get to help with the branding!"

"He doesn't want to lose the Perfect Attendance," said Victor.

"The Perfect Attendance!" said Junior. "Monchi, you are crazier than a goat. You are a Ramírez. We are a family of vaqueros. Roundup is more important than the Perfect Attendance."

I knew Junior was right, but I touched the empty hole of my silver-dollar buckle and I sighed. *Adiós,* Perfect Attendance.

rancheras (rahn-CHAIR-ahs)—Mexican folk songs
fiesta (fee-ESS-tah)—party, celebration
de (day)—of
adiós (ah-DYOHSS)—good-bye

For two exciting days Junior and I helped with the roundup. First the vaqueros lassoed the calves and wrestled them down to the ground. Then Junior and I held them while my father and my tío Enrique branded them and cut the ears and gave them the shot.

¡Qué barullo! The red-hot irons were smoking, and the burned hair was stinking. The calves were fighting and bawling like giant babies. They were much heavier than Junior and me. It was hard work and dangerous to hold them down. I got dust in my eyes and in my nose, but I didn't care.

After the work of the roundup was over, we made the fiesta! First was a race for the kids. We had to ride as fast as we could to the chuck wagon, take an orange, and ride back again. Junior won on Pinto. He got a big jar of candies and gave some to all of us. Last came Victor and his little *burro.* All that day we had races and roping contests.

That night we had a big *barbacoa.* The kids got cold soda pops. When the music started, all the vaqueros wanted to dance with Natalia. The one they call Chapo asked her to be his *novia,* but Natalia told him she doesn't want to get married. She wants to go to high school.

Monday morning when we left for school, the vaqueros were packing their bedrolls. We waved and hollered from our bus, "*¡Adiós! ¡Adiós! ¡Hasta la vista!*"

qué (kaye)—what, how
barullo (bah-ROO-yoe)—noise, racket
burro (BOOR-row)—donkey
barbacoa (bar-bah-KOH-ah)—barbecue
hasta la vista (AH-stah lah VEE-stah)—
    see you

Issue Number Nine

May 10, 1939

COYOTE ¡Hasta la vista! NEWS

Stories and Pictures by the Students of Coyote School, Pima County, Arizona

Adios Coyote School!   Lalo Natalia   Good-bye, everybody! Thank you, Miss Byers!

by Lalo Lopez

Eduardo (Lalo) and Natalia Graduate!

Lalo and I have passed the Eighth Grade Standard Achievement Test! I am happy to graduate and I am excited about high school, but I will miss my teacher and all the kids at my dear Coyote School...Natalia Ramirez, Grade 8

I Lose the Perfect Attendance

I was absent from school to help with the roundup. It was very exciting, but now it is over and I am feeling sad. The vaqueros are gone and I will not get a silver dollar for my buckle....Monchi Ramirez, Grade 4

The Perfect Attendance Report

The only one who still has perfect attendance is Victor. Even Miss Byers has been absent, because when it was roundup on her ranch a big calf stepped on her foot. We had Miss Elias for 3 days. Miss Byers had to pay her 5 dollars a day to take her place.....Gilbert Perez, Grade 6

Please forgive me, Miss Byers   300 pounds

By Rosie Garcia

A Visit to the Boston Beans

Mr. and Mrs. Bean invited my family to visit them this summer in Boston. Boston is Back East. It is even bigger than Tucson. No other kid at Coyote School has ever gone that far away!.............Billy Mills, Grade 3

Earrings

My daddy is getting married. Joey and I will get a new mother and 4 new brothers. Laura is nice and she can cook, but the best part is she has pierced ears and now I will get to have them too!....Cynthia Brown, Grade 2

Last Issue for the School Year

This is the last issue before the summer vacation. I am saving all my Coyote News newspapers so that someday I can show my children all the swell and exciting things we did at Coyote School..........Rosie Garcia, Grade 3

181

The Last Day of School

On the last day of school Miss Byers gave us a fiesta with cupcakes and candies and Cracker Jacks and soda pops. We got to listen to Mexican music on her radio. I didn't have to dance with Natalia. I got to dance with Rosie.

Then Miss Byers turned off the radio and stood in the front of the room between President Roosevelt and Señor Grandote. She called Natalia and Lalo up to the front and told them how proud we were that they were graduates of Coyote School, and how much we would miss them. We all clapped and whistled.

Next, Miss Byers gave Edelia a paper and said, "Please read what it says, Edelia."

Edelia read: "Edelia Ortiz has been promoted to Grade Two." Miss Byers had to help her to read "promoted," but we all clapped and cheered anyway. Edelia looked very happy and proud.

Then Miss Byers asked Victor to come to the front of the room, and I knew what that meant. I didn't want to listen when she said how good it was that he had not missed a day of school, and I didn't want to look when she gave him the silver dollar. I knew I should be

"Go up to the front," Natalia said and gave me a push.

Miss Byers smiled and shook my hand. "Congratulations, Monchi," she said, and then she gave me the award.

¡Ay caramba! The *Coyote News* Writing Award was a shiny silver dollar!

"Oh thank you, Miss Byers!" I said. *"¡Gracias!"* I was so surprised and happy. I pushed the silver dollar into the round hole on my buckle. It fit perfectly!

"¡Muy hermosa!" Miss Byers said.

She was right. It was very beautiful.

gracias (GRAHS-see-ahs)—thank you
hermosa (air-MOE-sah)—beautiful

happy that Victor won the Perfect Attendance, but I was not.

"And now, boys and girls," Miss Byers said, "it's time for the next award."

"What next award?" we asked.

"The *Coyote News* Writing Award for the student who has contributed most to *Coyote News* by writing his own stories and by helping others write theirs. The winner of the *Coyote News* Writing Award is Ramón Ernesto Ramírez."

"Me?" I said.

All the kids were clapping and whistling. I just sat there.

183

Reader Response

Open for Discussion Plan a super issue of *Coyote News.* What words will describe life at the Ramirez Ranch and Coyote School? What stories, articles, poems, and drawings will you include?

1. The author helps you get to know Monchi through his words and actions. Find examples of how Monchi's words and actions help you get to know him.

2. How do the members of Monchi's family feel about one another? How do they feel about being a family? Support your answer with details from the story.

3. What surprised you about Coyote School? Why?

4. In this story, the word *coyote* is used most often as part of two compound proper nouns. Write those nouns, and then write the one sentence in which *coyote* is used as a common noun.

Test Practice

Look Back and Write Monchi did not receive the Perfect Attendance Award. Read page 183 again. Write about the award Monchi did get and why he got it.

Joan Sandin

Read books about writing a school newspaper.

Joan Sandin grew up in Tucson, Arizona. "I walked a mile to grade school through the desert, with roadrunners and quail for company," she recalls. As a child, she loved to draw. Art was her favorite subject in school. As an adult, she has written several books and has illustrated many more.

Coyote School News is based on a real school newspaper called *Little Cowpuncher*. Schoolchildren in southern Arizona wrote articles for the paper from 1932 to 1943. Their teacher was Eulalia Bourne. Ms. Sandin explains, "Coyote School is a fictionalized school with fictionalized students, but it was inspired by the *Little Cowpuncher* papers and by conversations with my friend María." María Amado, Ms. Sandin's best friend in high school, lived on a ranch near Tucson when she was young. María attended Sópori School, "a school very much like Coyote School." María's brother, sister, and cousins all wrote articles for the *Little Cowpuncher*.

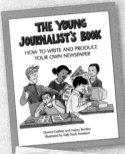

The Young Journalist's Book by Donna Guthrie and Nancy Bentley

Extra! Extra! The Who, What, Where, When, and Why of Newspapers by Linda Granfield

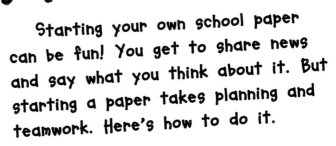

Social Studies
in Reading

How-to Article

Genre

- A how-to article gives step-by-step directions for making or doing something.

- It often includes a list of materials to gather or things to think about before you begin.

Text Features

- Bold-faced type sets off the steps and calls attention to newspaper jobs and kinds of newspaper articles.

- Checkmarks make the text seem like a list that is easy to follow.

Link to Social Studies

Look through a community newspaper. Make a list of the kinds of articles it contains. Share what you learn with your class.

Starting your own school paper can be fun! You get to share news and say what you think about it. But starting a paper takes planning and teamwork. Here's how to do it.

First, pick your team. You'll need to fill these jobs:

✔ The **editor** decides what stories writers will work on. Everybody comes up with ideas, but the editor has the final say.

✔ The **writers** write the stories. They talk to people and dig up facts.

✔ The **copyeditor** checks the writers' work. He or she fixes spelling and other mistakes.

✔ The **photo editor** chooses pictures to go with the stories.

✔ The **designer** decides where the stories and pictures will go on the page. The final result is called a layout.

✔ The **staff adviser** is the adult who guides you. The adviser answers your questions and steers your paper in the right direction.

How to Start a School Newspaper

by Lisa Klobuchar

Next, figure out what to write about. Find out what your classmates want to read about. Ask around, or place an idea box outside your classroom. Here are just a few kinds of writing to put in your paper:

✓ **News** stories tell about what is going on in your school, your town, or even around the world. They must be factual, or true.

✓ In **sports** stories, you can tell when games will be played at your school. You can describe the sports action and list scores, or you can profile a player.

✓ **Arts and entertainment** stories may tell about special school events or introduce readers to a poem, short story, piece of artwork, or movie.

✓ In an **advice column,** students can ask questions about anything, and "Dear So-and-So" will answer them.

Finally, start writing! It feels wonderful to share your ideas and stories with your classmates. And there's no better way to do that than to start a school newspaper.

Reading Across Texts

This article identifies several kinds of writing that can go into a school newspaper. Which kinds of writing appear in *Coyote School News*?

Writing Across Texts Make a list of the stories or features in one issue of *Coyote School News*. Tell what kind of writing each is.

Prior Knowledge What do you already know about newspaper workers?

187

Skill
Draw Conclusions

Strategy
Answer Questions

Draw Conclusions

- Facts and details are the small pieces of information in an article or story.

- Facts and details "add up" to a conclusion, a decision or opinion the author or the reader forms that must make sense.

Facts and Details	+	Facts and Details	=	Conclusion

Strategy: Answer Questions

If you are asked questions about conclusions you draw, you should answer them using the facts and details. Some answers are in the text in one place. Others are in the text but in different places. Some answers combine the text with what you already know. Some answers you just know or can find out.

1. Read "Time Traveler." Make a graphic organizer like the one above to record strange details about Peter's experience.

2. Write a paragraph about how you can conclude that Peter went back in time.

Time Traveler

A storm was approaching, but Peter crawled through the strange little hole in the fence anyway. The last thing he expected to see was a man dressed in peculiar clothes holding a kite.

Surprised, Peter yelled, "Are you going to fly that kite? It could be dangerous! It looks like a storm's coming!"

"Why, my boy, I'm conducting an experiment. I'm trying to demonstrate that lightning is electricity. If I'm correct, when lightning strikes the kite, it will travel down the string. I just don't know how to keep it from giving me a shock."

"That's easy!" said Peter. "We learned about electricity in science. You need to redirect the electricity."

"What genius! I'll tie this key to the kite string," said the man.

"Well, it worked for Ben Franklin, didn't it?" said Peter.

The man was astonished. "My boy, how did you come to know my name?"

Before Peter could reply, he heard his mother calling him as if from very, very far away. "I have to go now," he said. Peter scurried back through the hole in the fence. But when he turned around to wish the strange man good luck, the hole had vanished.

Skill This story seems to be a fantasy. How might you conclude this?

Strategy Who is this strange man? (Hint: Think of the type of story and use your prior knowledge.)

Strategy Would Peter's mother believe him if he told her his story? Why or why not? (Hint: Think about the hole and the strangeness of what happened.)

Skill What conclusion does this story draw about how Ben Franklin came up with his famous experiment?

Words to Know

mechanical

miracle

aboard

awkward

capable

reseats

chant

vehicle

atlas

Remember

Try the strategy. Then, if you need more help, use your glossary or a dictionary.

Vocabulary Strategy
for Prefixes

Word Structure Sometimes when you are reading, you come to a word you do not know. See if the word has a prefix. Prefixes are letters added to the beginning of a word that change its meaning. For example, the prefix *re-* means "again." If you *retie* a knot, you tie it again. The prefix *a-* means "on, in, or at." If you are *abed,* you are in bed.

1. Cover the prefix.

2. Look at the base word. See if you know what it means.

3. Add the meaning of the prefix.

4. Check to see if this meaning makes sense in the sentence.

As you read "Riding into History," look for words that begin with the prefix *re-* or *a-*. Use the prefixes to help you figure out the meanings of the words.

RIDING INTO HISTORY

Inventions have made travel better, safer, and faster in the past 200 years. When each new invention appeared, it seemed like a mechanical miracle. Take the train, for example. The first steam locomotives offered rides in the 1820s. Early riders felt a thrill when they heard "All aboard!" Their hearts raced as they sat on hard, awkward benches and held on for dear life. After all, the train was capable of wild speeds of up to 20 miles per hour!

Put yourself on such a train. Black smoke streams back and coats your hat and gloves. One traveler stands and points at a horse and buggy racing the train. Then he happily reseats himself and waits for the next adventure. Wheels click and engines puff. The sound is like a chant, a travel song with strong rhythm.

In another 150 years, every kind of vehicle will take to the roads. All sizes and shapes of airplanes will fly into the sky. They will bring the farthest countries in the atlas within reach. What is next in transportation? Maybe space buses will take us to the moon!

Write

Pretend you took a ride in one of the first automobiles. Write a letter describing your wild ride. Use words from the Words to Know list.

Grace and the Time Machine

from *Starring Grace* by Mary Hoffman
adapted for Story Theater by Donald Abramson
illustrated by Matthew Faulkner

Genre

A **play** has all the elements of a story—characters, setting, plot, and theme—but it doesn't look like a story because it's written to be performed. As you read, think about how this play might be different as a chapter in a book.

Can a time machine change a person's life?

Characters

AVA Grace's Mother

MRS. MYERSON

MARIA

NANA Grace's Grandmother

GRACE

RAJ

AIMEE

KESTER

ACTOR 1   ACTRESS 1   ACTOR 2   ACTRESS 2

The scene is the kitchen and backyard of the house that GRACE shares with her mother, AVA, and her grandmother, NANA. The time is during summer vacation.

AVA: Grace, I'm off to work at the hospital now.

GRACE: Okay, Ma.

AVA: And what have you got lined up for today?

GRACE: Oh, you know. The kids are coming over. Aimee and Kester and Raj and Maria. I guess we'll find something to do.

AVA: Well, try not to leave the house in a shambles.

GRACE: We won't, Ma.

AVA: And you will help your grandmother? I know she gets around pretty well on her crutches, but it's still awkward for her to do things with that cast on her ankle.

GRACE: Oh, I will, Ma. I bring her the phone or her book—

AVA: Good girl. Nana is in capable hands, then.

NANA *(walking with crutches and favoring one leg):* Nana's in fine hands, thank you. Morning, Ava. Morning, Grace.

AVA: Good morning, Mom. I'd get you some breakfast, but I'm already late.

NANA: Grace can do it. She's been real helpful since I tripped over that silly cat and broke my ankle. You go to work.

AVA: Okay. Bye!

GRACE: Bye, Ma. What can I get for you, Nana?

NANA: Well, Grace, you can bring me a cup of coffee, if you will.

GRACE: Oh, sure.

NANA: Thank you, Honey.

AIMEE *(calling from the yard):* Hello, Grace!

GRACE: It's Aimee. I'm in the kitchen, Aimee! Come on in!

AIMEE *(entering the kitchen):* Hi, Grace. Good morning, Nana.

NANA: Hello, Aimee.

AIMEE: I just saw Kester and Raj. They're on their way over.

GRACE: Good!

KESTER *(calling from the yard):* Hey, Grace!

GRACE: There they are! Are you okay, Nana?

NANA: I'm fine, Grace. I'll just sit here and drink my coffee. Go on out. But take that dangerous cat with you, so I don't fall over him again.

GRACE: Okay. Come on, Paw-Paw.

ACTRESS 1 *(as a cat):* Meowerow!

NANA: I'll call you if I need you.

Grace and Aimee move into the yard.

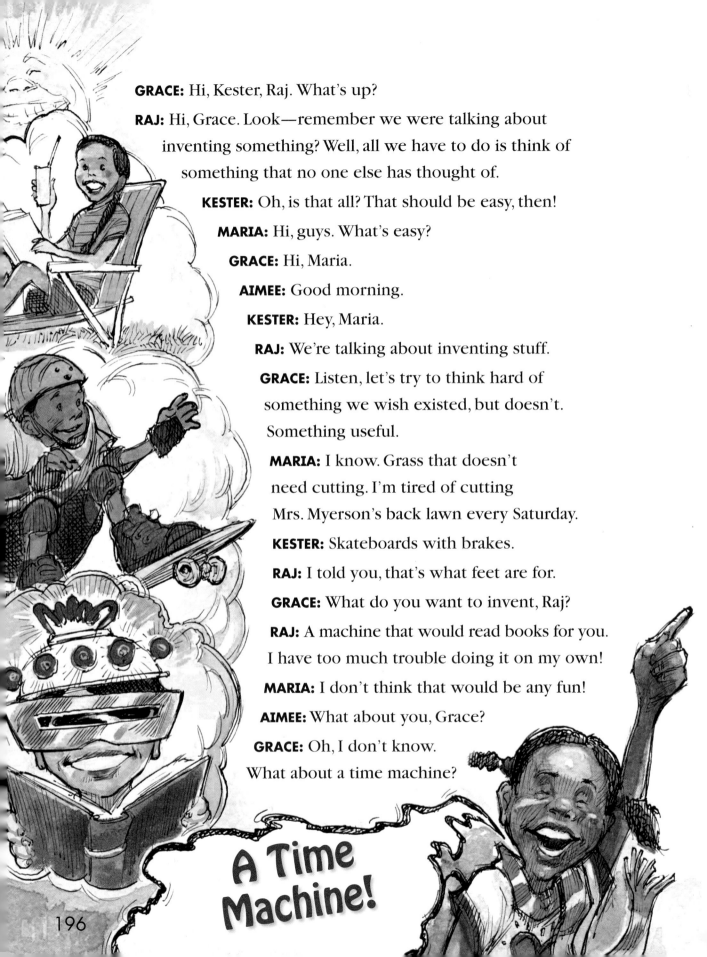

GRACE: Hi, Kester, Raj. What's up?

RAJ: Hi, Grace. Look—remember we were talking about inventing something? Well, all we have to do is think of something that no one else has thought of.

KESTER: Oh, is that all? That should be easy, then!

MARIA: Hi, guys. What's easy?

GRACE: Hi, Maria.

AIMEE: Good morning.

KESTER: Hey, Maria.

RAJ: We're talking about inventing stuff.

GRACE: Listen, let's try to think hard of something we wish existed, but doesn't. Something useful.

MARIA: I know. Grass that doesn't need cutting. I'm tired of cutting Mrs. Myerson's back lawn every Saturday.

KESTER: Skateboards with brakes.

RAJ: I told you, that's what feet are for.

GRACE: What do you want to invent, Raj?

RAJ: A machine that would read books for you. I have too much trouble doing it on my own!

MARIA: I don't think that would be any fun!

AIMEE: What about you, Grace?

GRACE: Oh, I don't know. What about a time machine?

A Time Machine!

KESTER: Hey, that's cheating. You said something useful!

MARIA: That would be useful. You could go forward in time and find out the questions for a math test.

KESTER: Hmmm. Or go back and change things.

AIMEE: Yes, you could go back and pick up your cat, Paw-Paw, so that he didn't trip Nana.

RAJ: So she wouldn't fall and break her ankle.

GRACE: Well, that'd be great.

MARIA: Yeah, I think a time machine would be the best invention of all.

KESTER: That'd be so cool!

MARIA: So, what do we need?

KESTER: Well, let's see what we can find.

They arrange five chairs in the center of the stage and then pantomime adding things to them.

GRACE: We can start with my bike!

AIMEE: Here's an old radio. It's got a dial.

KESTER: Here are a couple of alarm clocks.

GRACE: And here's Nana's kitchen timer, so we know how long we're gone.

RAJ: I'll tape it to your handlebars.

MARIA: Here's a garden rake.

AIMEE: And some garden spinners.

MARIA: Hey, what about this beach umbrella?

KESTER: What's the umbrella for?

MARIA: Well, it looks fancy.

GRACE: And here—I want to bring my atlas, so we can choose places as well as times.

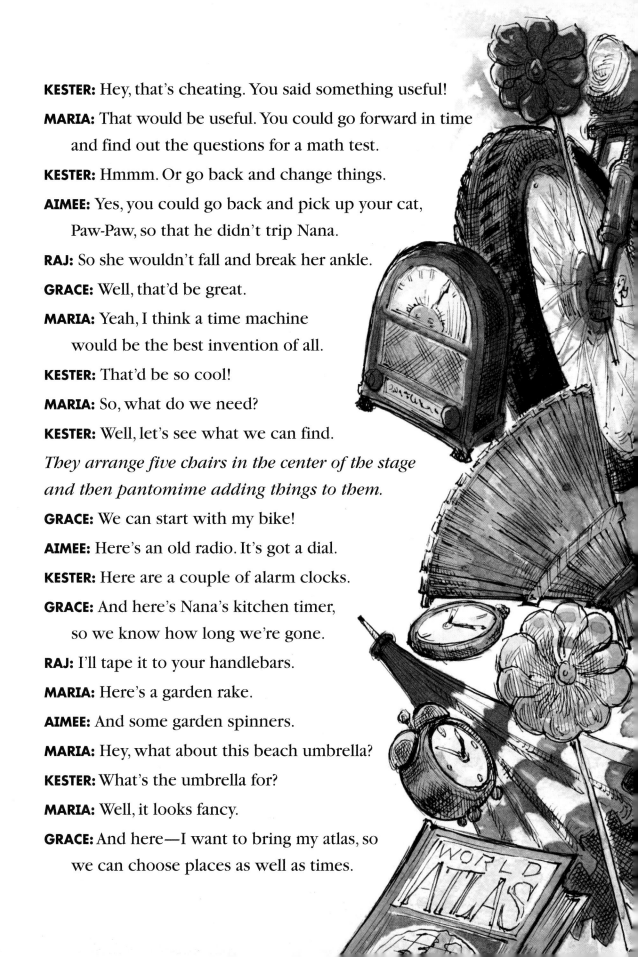

RAJ: Well, that's it, I guess.

AIMEE: It really does look like a mad inventor's been here.

KESTER: But who's going to drive this thing?

AIMEE: It was Grace's idea.

GRACE: Okay, I'll go first, but we can all take turns.

RAJ: That's good.

GRACE: So—all aboard! Where should we go first?

KESTER: I know! Let's go to the future and see what it's like.

GRACE: How far into the future?

KESTER: What do you think? Five hundred years?

GRACE: Okay. We'll just set this clock dial for five hundred years and set the timer. Hold on, everybody—here we go!

They make time-machine noises. Meanwhile, ACTORS and ACTRESSES 1 and 2 come forward and walk about stiffly. Their voices sound very mechanical.

GRACE: And he-e-ere we are!

AIMEE: Well, it doesn't look much different.

MARIA: But check out these people. They look different.

KESTER: Hello—uh, future people.

ACTOR AND ACTRESS 1 *(speaking together):* Hello.

KESTER: What shall we say? Um—is it nice here in the future?

ACTOR AND ACTRESS 2 *(together):* Oh, yes. It is very nice.

MARIA: Tell us about it.

ACTOR AND ACTRESS 1: We have no wars.

ACTOR AND ACTRESS 2: We have no crime.

ACTOR AND ACTRESS 1: No one is ever hungry.

AIMEE: That sounds great.

KESTER: Yeah, but excuse me for asking.
   You're robots, aren't you?

ACTOR AND ACTRESS 2: Yes, we are robots.

AIMEE: Oh, but where are the humans then?

ACTOR AND ACTRESS 1: There are no humans.

ACTOR AND ACTRESS 2: We got rid of humans
   a hundred years ago.

ACTOR AND ACTRESS 1: It is much better this way.

GRACE: Uh—guys! D'you think we'd better go?

KESTER: Yeah. Come on!

GRACE: Raj can drive now.

RAJ: Okay.

MARIA: Where do you want to go, Raj?

RAJ *(busily setting dials):* Well, the future's kind of scary. What about the past?

AIMEE: How far past?

RAJ: Oh—millions of years! Here we go!

They make time-machine noises. ACTORS *and* ACTRESSES 1 *and 2 are now dinosaurs. They prowl around and roar.*

RAJ: And we're here! Now remember, everybody. You can't make any changes here. Otherwise you might change the future.

MARIA: I know—and then we'd never exist.

KESTER: Just look at those trees. They're like ferns—as big as palm trees.

ACTOR 1: Ro-o-oar!

AIMEE: Look, what's that?

MARIA: It's a dinosaur!

RAJ: With those two huge horns and that bony frill, that's got to be a triceratops.

ACTRESS 2: Ro-o-oar!

KESTER: There's another one.

RAJ: I think that's a stegosaurus.

AIMEE: How can you tell?

RAJ: It's got those rows of bony plates all down its back.

GRACE: These guys are really big.

MARIA: Yeah. Aren't you glad they're plant eaters?

ACTOR 2: Ro-o-oar!

RAJ: Uh-oh. This is a different story.

KESTER: Walking on its hind legs—two little
front legs—

GRACE: A huge head with powerful jaws—

AIMEE: And lots of long—sharp—teeth!

MARIA: Even I can tell what kind this is!

ALL TOGETHER: Tyrannosaurus!

ACTOR 2: Ro-o-o-o-oar!!!

*They scream and run
back to the time machine.*

GRACE: Time for a quick getaway!

AIMEE: I'll drive now. Where do
you want to go?

GRACE: How about West Africa?

RAJ: That's not time travel.

GRACE: All right then, make it last year when Nana and I went to The Gambia.

AIMEE: Okay. I've set the dials for last year.

RAJ: Here we go again!

They make time-machine noises. ACTORS *and* ACTRESSES 1 *and 2 start walking about, their voices overlapping as they chant the goods they are selling.*

ACTOR 1: Mangos here! Papayas here!

ACTRESS 1: Fresh passion fruit! Fresh jack fruit!

ACTOR 2: Milk, milk, sweet fresh milk! Fresh from the goat!

ACTRESS 2: Smell my fresh bread! Fresh bread!

GRACE: It's the open-air market, right in the middle of town.

KESTER: And the women all walk around carrying baskets and trays and everything on their heads.

AIMEE: Look at this. The money has pictures of crocodiles!

MARIA: This is more exciting than shopping at home.

RAJ: Grace, you were so lucky to really visit here.

GRACE: And there was one special food we had. I've never tasted anything like it. It was—um—um—

NANA *(coming into the yard):* Benachin.

GRACE: Benachin, yes!

NANA: You ate enough of it!

KESTER: What's benachin, Nana?

NANA: Oh, there's all kinds. We had some with beef, cabbage, and eggplant all cooked together in one big pot.

GRACE: What are you doing out, Nana? Do you need something?

NANA: No. I was taking a nap. The dinosaurs woke me up.

AIMEE: Sorry!

NANA: It's all right, Aimee. Looks like fun.

MARIA: It is. Let's give Nana a turn!

RAJ: Yeah! Come on, Nana!

NANA: Well now, I haven't ridden in a time machine for a good long while. *(They help her sit in the machine.)*

KESTER: Choose a place. Here, here's the atlas.

NANA: No question. Trinidad, where I was born. Here it is, see?

KESTER: It's an island!

NANA: It's just a wee, bitty island in the West Indies. But there's nowhere else in the world quite like it.

MARIA: And when would you like it to be?

NANA: Oh, when I was a little girl about your age. Let's say sixty years ago.

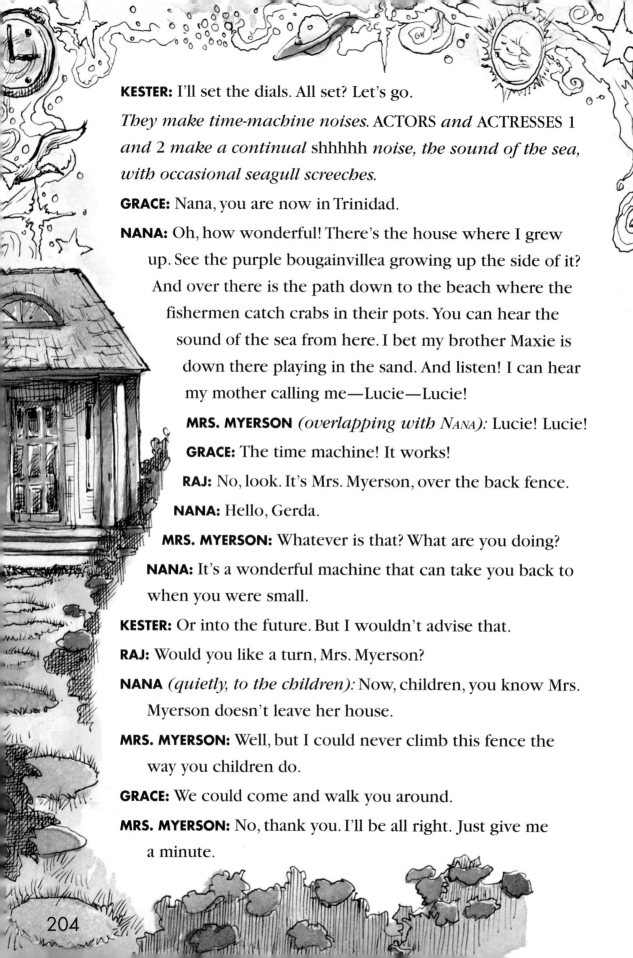

KESTER: I'll set the dials. All set? Let's go.

They make time-machine noises. ACTORS *and* ACTRESSES 1 *and* 2 *make a continual* shhhhh *noise, the sound of the sea, with occasional seagull screeches.*

GRACE: Nana, you are now in Trinidad.

NANA: Oh, how wonderful! There's the house where I grew up. See the purple bougainvillea growing up the side of it? And over there is the path down to the beach where the fishermen catch crabs in their pots. You can hear the sound of the sea from here. I bet my brother Maxie is down there playing in the sand. And listen! I can hear my mother calling me—Lucie—Lucie!

MRS. MYERSON *(overlapping with* NANA*):* Lucie! Lucie!

GRACE: The time machine! It works!

RAJ: No, look. It's Mrs. Myerson, over the back fence.

NANA: Hello, Gerda.

MRS. MYERSON: Whatever is that? What are you doing?

NANA: It's a wonderful machine that can take you back to when you were small.

KESTER: Or into the future. But I wouldn't advise that.

RAJ: Would you like a turn, Mrs. Myerson?

NANA *(quietly, to the children):* Now, children, you know Mrs. Myerson doesn't leave her house.

MRS. MYERSON: Well, but I could never climb this fence the way you children do.

GRACE: We could come and walk you around.

MRS. MYERSON: No, thank you. I'll be all right. Just give me a minute.

NANA *(getting out of the machine):* I must say I'm amazed. For as long as I've known her, Gerda Myerson has kept to herself.

MARIA: But what's wrong with her?

NANA: She had some very bad experiences during World War II. Her whole family was killed, and she was imprisoned for a long time. She survived, but usually she finds it hard to trust people. So she keeps her house all locked up. But you children seem to be bringing her back to life.

MRS. MYERSON: Well, here I am.

RAJ: Right this way, Mrs. Myerson.

KESTER: Please have a comfortable seat in our time machine. *(He helps her sit in the machine.)*

AIMEE: Now you must tell us where you would like to go.

MRS. MYERSON: Oh—Germany. My home in Heidelberg.

GRACE: And when?

MRS. MYERSON: Oh yes, before all that trouble. 1925.

MARIA *(dialing the timer):* I will be your captain for this voyage. Please remain in your seat while the vehicle is in motion. And we're off!

205

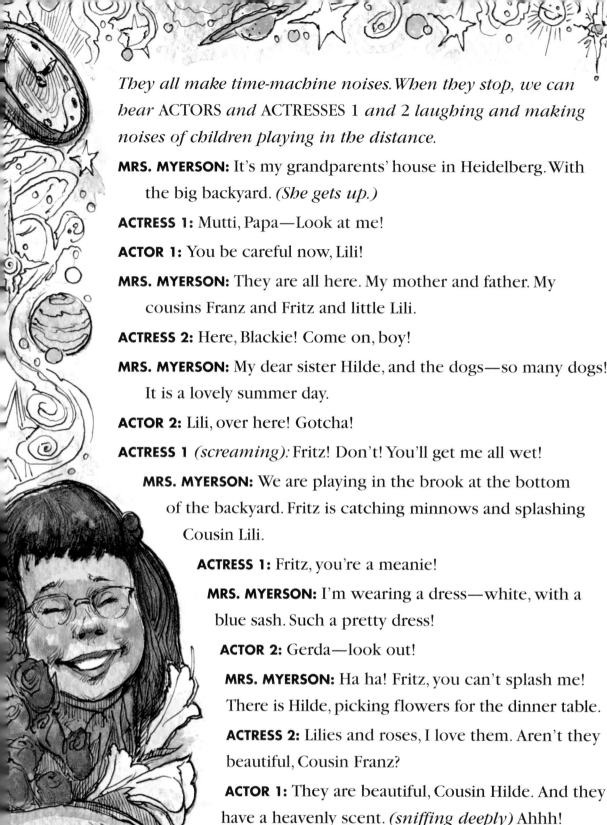

They all make time-machine noises. When they stop, we can hear ACTORS *and* ACTRESSES 1 *and* 2 *laughing and making noises of children playing in the distance.*

MRS. MYERSON: It's my grandparents' house in Heidelberg. With the big backyard. *(She gets up.)*

ACTRESS 1: Mutti, Papa—Look at me!

ACTOR 1: You be careful now, Lili!

MRS. MYERSON: They are all here. My mother and father. My cousins Franz and Fritz and little Lili.

ACTRESS 2: Here, Blackie! Come on, boy!

MRS. MYERSON: My dear sister Hilde, and the dogs—so many dogs! It is a lovely summer day.

ACTOR 2: Lili, over here! Gotcha!

ACTRESS 1 *(screaming):* Fritz! Don't! You'll get me all wet!

MRS. MYERSON: We are playing in the brook at the bottom of the backyard. Fritz is catching minnows and splashing Cousin Lili.

ACTRESS 1: Fritz, you're a meanie!

MRS. MYERSON: I'm wearing a dress—white, with a blue sash. Such a pretty dress!

ACTOR 2: Gerda—look out!

MRS. MYERSON: Ha ha! Fritz, you can't splash me! There is Hilde, picking flowers for the dinner table.

ACTRESS 2: Lilies and roses, I love them. Aren't they beautiful, Cousin Franz?

ACTOR 1: They are beautiful, Cousin Hilde. And they have a heavenly scent. *(sniffing deeply)* Ahhh!

MRS. MYERSON: I can smell them now. Ahhh—

AIMEE: Mrs. Myerson, are you all right?

RAJ: You're not crying, are you?

MRS. MYERSON: No, no. Well—yes.

KESTER: What's wrong?

MRS. MYERSON: Nothing. There is nothing wrong. Thank you, children. It is a wonderful machine.

NANA: I think maybe it's time to come back to the present and have a good strong cup of tea.

MRS. MYERSON: Oh, yes. That would be nice. But first—Maria, you have to bring me back. *(She reseats herself in the machine.)*

MARIA *(adjusting the dials)*: Right away. Here we go.

They all make time-machine noises. Ava enters and watches.

AVA: Grace, what's going on here? What is this contraption?

GRACE: Hi, Ma! It's a time machine, see?

NANA: It's a miracle. Not only did Gerda Myerson walk here from her house—she told us all about her childhood. She remembered how happy she was.

MRS. MYERSON *(getting up and joining them)*: I'm ready now, Lucie. Hello, Ava.

AVA: It's nice to see you, Gerda.

NANA: Yes. Let's go in then.

   (NANA and MRS. MYERSON go inside.)

GRACE: It was just as if she really did travel back in time, Ma.

AVA: Then your machine works, Grace. What a wonderful invention!

207

Reader Response

Open for Discussion In a way, a play is a time machine. It can take you to surprising times and places. Explain how that happens in this play.

1. What noises and movements are needed to make this play work on the stage?

2. Draw conclusions about Mrs. Myerson. Why does she keep to herself? Why is she excited to travel back in time?

3. What does the time machine allow Nana and Mrs. Myerson to do? Why is this nice for them?

4. When Grace's mother says that Nana is in *capable* hands, she means that Grace is able to take care of Nana. What else does Grace do to show that she is capable?

Look Back and Write Reread the ending of the play. Then write the reason that Ava says, "Then your machine works, Grace."

Mary Hoffman

Read other books by Mary Hoffman.

Mary Hoffman, who lives in England, has written more than eighty books on all sorts of topics. But she is best known for her books about Grace.

It all began in 1991, when she published *Amazing Grace.* This book told the story of Grace, an African American girl, who insisted she could play the role of Peter Pan, a white boy, even though everyone told her she couldn't. Ms. Hoffman has said, "Grace is really me— a little girl who loved stories." She remembers that as a child "I played all the leading parts—it didn't matter to me if they were for boys or girls." Readers loved Grace, and the book became very popular.

Ms. Hoffman has since written more books about Grace's dreams and adventures, including her trip to West Africa. Musical plays about Grace have been performed throughout the United States, and there are even Grace dolls. Ms. Hoffman says she receives fan mail from Grace-lovers everywhere.

Amazing Grace

Boundless Grace

What's There to Do?

adapted from *101 Outdoor Adventures* by Samantha Beres

Expository Nonfiction

Genre

- Expository nonfiction can introduce new ideas about people, places, and things.

- Though usually illustrated with photos, it is sometimes illustrated with art.

Text Features

- Subheads separate different parts of the text.

- The art gives ideas for the activity suggested.

Link to Social Studies

Work with a partner to come up with another activity idea. Include helpful hints about how to successfully complete the activity. The class might create a master list of new ideas.

Grace and her friends built a time machine. Here are some other activities you can do with friends on a summer day.

Help a Neighbor

Any time is a good time to give a gift. This gift can't be wrapped with paper and ribbon—it's a gift of time.

If you have a neighbor whom you know and who could use your help, organize a squad of friends to lend a helping hand. If your neighbor has a yard, you might cut the grass, pull weeds, or even help plant flowers or vegetables. If your neighbor doesn't have a yard, offer to clean windows, wash the car, help get groceries, run an errand, or paint something.

If your neighbor tries to pay you, don't accept. After all, you don't pay someone who gives you a birthday gift, do you?

210

Put On an Arts-and-Crafts Show

If you have some artistic friends and relatives, you can have your own arts-and-crafts show.

Decide where to have the show—outside on the sidewalk, in your front yard, or in a park. If you have a show in a public place, ask permission.

To prepare, ask friends and family if they would like to display their art in public. Make a list of things they would like to enter and ask them to have their items ready by the date of the show. Also ask them to label each piece with their name, a phone number, and a price, in case someone wants to buy it.

Before the show, figure out what you'll need to set up. You will need a table and maybe a clothing rack, if you have handmade clothes, quilts, or blankets to sell. A child's easel or a clothesline and clothespins are a good way to show off pictures.

Send out announcements (e-mail messages would work) or put up posters to advertise the show. Here's a list of arts and crafts you might try to include: drawings, paintings, photographs, sculptures, pottery, quilts, handmade jewelry, and knitted and crocheted items.

Reading Across Texts
Grace and her friends showed that they were creative. Which of the two activities in this selection do you think they would have enjoyed more?

Writing Across Texts
Write about why you think as you do.

Answer Questions Use prior knowledge to answer questions about this text.

211

Comprehension

Skill
Fact and Opinion

Strategy
Monitor and
Fix Up

 # Fact and Opinion

- A statement of fact can be proved true or false. You can look in a reference book, ask an expert, or use your own knowledge and experience.

- A statement of opinion cannot be proved true or false. It is a belief or judgment. It often contains a word of judgment, such as *best, should,* or *beautiful.* It may begin with the words *In my opinion* or *I believe.*

Statement	Fact? How Can It Be Checked?	Opinion? What Are Clue Words?

Strategy: Monitor and Fix Up

If you don't quite remember something you have read, you can skim the text to help you remember. You can use this same strategy to locate facts and opinions. To locate facts, scan for factual details, such as dates. To locate opinions, scan for opinion clue words.

 **Write**

1. Read "So You Want to Be a Lumberjack?" Find two statements of fact and two statements of opinion and record them in a graphic organizer.

2. Would you want to be a lumberjack? Make a graphic organizer. Then explain why or why not. Include at least two opinions and two facts.

So You Want to Be a Lumberjack?

At one time a vast forest covered much of the northern United States. This great north woods supplied lumber for homes and other buildings. Cutting down the forest trees for lumber was the job of lumberjacks.

Skill Look for a clue word in this paragraph that signals an opinion.

The life of a lumberjack, or jack, was one few people would want today. Lumberjacks didn't live at home. They lived in lumber camps in the forest. They had to get up at 5 o'clock in the morning and work outside 11 hours a day, 6 days a week, in all kinds of weather—rain, snow, cold, even steamy heat.

Strategy You could scan this paragraph to find evidence that facts have been given.

All the jacks slept in a bunkhouse, where bunks were nailed up the walls. In my opinion, those beds must have been very uncomfortable. There was just enough room to crawl into a bunk and turn over without bumping into the bunk above.

Strategy If you didn't catch the statement of opinion in this paragraph, you could scan now for clue words.

If you love food, however, you might have enjoyed being a lumberjack. Large, hearty meals were prepared by the camp cook and served in a big dining room.

Probably the best time of day for a lumberjack was the evening. Then lumberjacks would play card games and tell stories—many of them tall tales about Paul Bunyan, the biggest lumberjack of them all.

Skill There are several facts and one opinion in this last paragraph.

Words to Know

payroll

cord

immense

dismay

grizzly

Vocabulary Strategy
for Unfamiliar Words

Dictionary/Glossary When you are reading, you may come across a word you don't know. If you can't use the context, or words and sentences around the unknown word, to figure out its meaning, you can use a dictionary or glossary for help.

1. Look in the back of your book for a glossary. If there is no glossary, look up the word in a dictionary.

2. Find the entry for the word. The entries are in alphabetical order.

3. Read the pronunciation. Saying the word softly to yourself may help you recognize it.

4. Read all the meanings given for the word.

5. Choose the meaning that makes the best sense in the sentence.

As you read "Summer in the Woods," use a dictionary or glossary to find the meanings of the vocabulary words.

Summer in the Woods

My older brother spent a summer in the deep woods and mountains of Montana. No, he was not camping with the scouts. He was on the payroll of a fishing resort, though. It sounds easy, but believe me, he earned that money.

In letters home, he told about the cozy cabins with their neat stacks of firewood outside. Part of his job each day was to load a cord of wood into a wagon and resupply each cabin. All around the pines stretched as far as he could see. They rose so high, they blocked out the sky. Some were so immense, he said they must be hundreds of years old.

There was excitement too. One day, to his dismay, he found himself facing a fat grizzly bear over a stack of wood. He was so frightened, he froze and couldn't make a sound. Lucky for him, the bear wasn't hungry and strolled away.

Write

Write about an adventure you might have in the woods. Use some words from the Words to Know list.

Marven
of the Great North Woods

by Kathryn Lasky illustrated by Kevin Hawkes

Genre A **biography** is the story of a real person's life as told by someone else. As you read this biography, try to imagine yourself in Marven's place.

Is the great north woods a great place for Marven?

Ten-year-old Marven Lasky has left his parents and sisters and has traveled to the north woods to work there as a bookkeeper. Mr. Murray, who manages the lumber camp, shows Marven around the camp.

As they entered the camp, the longest shadows Marven had ever seen stretched across the snow, and he realized with a start that the shadows were the lumberjacks walking in the moonlight. He could smell hay and manure and saw the silhouettes of horses stomping in a snowy corral. From a nearby log building he heard the lively squeaks of a fiddle. It seemed for a moment as if the horses were keeping time to the music. Mr. Murray must have thought the same. "You want to watch the horses dance, or the jacks?" He laughed. "Come along, we'll take a look."

When they entered the building, the long shadows from the yard suddenly sprung to life. Marven stared. Immense men with long beards and wild hair were jumping around to the fiddler's tunes like a pack of frantic grizzly bears. They were the biggest and wildest men Marven had ever seen.

Marven could have watched the dancing all night, but Mr. Murray said, "Come on, Marven. We start early in the morning. I'll show you where you'll be living."

Mr. Murray took Marven to the small office where he would work and sleep. In Duluth, Marven had to share a bedroom with his two younger sisters and all of their dolls and toys, but this room was his—all his—and he liked it. A bed with a bearskin on it sat across from a woodstove; nearby, wood was stacked neatly. The big desk had cubbyholes for papers, envelopes, glue pots, and blotter strips. And on the desk there were blocks of paper and a big black ledger. There were pencils in a blue glass jar, as well as an inkwell.

Marven hoped that somewhere there was a very good pen—a fountain pen.

"In addition to keeping the payroll," Mr. Murray said, "you have another job. The first bell in the morning is at four o'clock; second bell at four-fifteen. Third bell is at four-twenty. By four-twenty-five, if any jack is still in the sack, he's *en retard,* 'late.' So you, son, are the fourth bell. Starting tomorrow, you go into the bunkhouse and wake *les en retards.*"

"How?"

"You tap them on the shoulder, give 'em a shake, scream in their ear if you have to."

Then Mr. Murray said good night, and Marven was alone again.

It seemed to Marven he had just crawled under the bearskin when he heard the first bell. The fire was out and the room was cold and dark. He lit the kerosene lamp and pulled on his double-thick long underwear, two pairs of socks, two pairs of knickers, and two sweaters. Then he put on his cut-down overcoat.

After the second bell, Marven heard the jacks heading toward the eating hall. It was nearly time for his first job.

He ran through the cold morning darkness to the bunkhouse, peeked in, and counted five huge lumps in the shadows. Five jacks in the sacks. Marven waited just inside the door.

At the third bell, Marven was relieved to see two jacks climb out of bed. He thought there must be a *broche,* a Hebrew blessing, for something like this. His father knew all sorts of *broches*—blessings for seeing the sunrise, blessings for the first blossom of spring. Was there a *broche* for a rising lumberjack? If he said a *broche,* maybe the other three would get up on their own.

One lump stirred, then another. They grunted, rolled, and climbed out from under the covers. Their huge shadows slid across the ceiling.

One jack was still in the sack. Marven took a deep breath, walked bravely over to the bed, reached out, and tapped the jack's shoulder. It was like poking a granite boulder. The jack's beard ran right into his long, shaggy hair; Marven couldn't even find an ear to shout into. He cupped his hands around his mouth and leaned forward.

"Up!"

The jack grunted and muttered something in French.

"Get up," Marven pleaded.

Another jack pulled on his boots, boomed, *"Lève-toi!* Jean Louis. *Lève-toi,"* and shuffled out the door.

"Lève-toi! Jean Louis. *Lève-toi,"* Marven repeated.

Jean Louis opened one eye. It glittered like a blue star beneath his thick black eyebrow. He squinted, as if trying to make out the shape in front of him, then blinked and sat up.

"Bonjour," Marven whispered.

"Qui es tu? Quel est ton nom?"

"I don't speak French—just *bonjour, derrière,* and *lève-toi."*

"That's all? No more?" The man opened his eyes wide now. "So what is your name?"

"Marven."

"Ah . . . Marven," Jean Louis repeated as if tasting the sound of his name.

"Will you get up?" Marven asked anxiously.

Jean Louis growled and fixed him in the hard blue squint of one eye.

"Please." Marven stood straight and tried not to tremble.

222

Jean Louis grunted and swung his feet from beneath the covers. They were as big as skillets, and one of his huge toenails was bruised black and blue. Marven tried not to stare.

Marven and Jean Louis were the last to arrive at the breakfast table. The only sounds were those of chewing and the clink of forks and knives against the plates. At each place were three stacks of flapjacks, one big steak, eight strips of bacon, and a bowl of oatmeal. In the middle of the table were bowls of potatoes and beans with molasses, platters with pies and cakes, and blue jugs filled with tea, coffee, and milk.

Marven stared at the food in dismay. *It's not kosher,* he thought. In Marven's house it was against ancient Jewish law to eat dairy products and meat together. And never, ever, did a Jew eat bacon. Marven came to a quick decision. One day he would eat the flapjacks and oatmeal with milk. The next day he would eat the steak and the oatmeal without milk. And never the bacon.

After breakfast, as they did every morning, the jacks went to the toolhouse to get their saws and axes. Then, wearing snowshoes and pulling huge sleds piled with equipment, they made their way into the great woods, where they would work all day.

Marven went directly to his office after breakfast. Mr. Murray was already there, setting out Marven's work. A fresh pot of ink was thawing in a bowl of hot water on the woodstove. There were two boxes on the desk filled with scraps of paper.

"Cord chits," Mr. Murray said. "The jacks are paid according to the numbers of cords they cut in a pay period—two weeks. You figure it out. I'm no good as a bookkeeper

and have enough other things to do around here. Each chit should have the jack's name—or, if he can't write, his symbol."

"His symbol?" Marven asked weakly.

"Yes. Jean Louis's is a thumbprint. Here's one!" He held up a small piece of paper with a thumbprint on it the size of a baby's fist. Marven blinked.

It was all very confusing. Sometimes two names were on one chit. These were called doublees; there were even some triplees. This meant more calculations. And sometimes chits were in the wrong pay-period box.

Marven sat staring at the scraps. "There is no system!" he muttered. Where to begin? His mother always made a list when she had many things to do. So first Marven listed the jacks' names alphabetically and noted the proper symbol for those who could not write. Then he listed the dates of a single pay period, coded each chit with the dates, and, with a ruler, made a chart. By the end of the morning, Marven had a system and knew the name or symbol for each man. There were many chits with the huge thumbprint of Jean Louis.

Every day Marven worked until midday, when he went into the cookhouse and ate baked beans and two kinds of pie with Mr. Murray and the cook. After lunch he returned to his office and worked until the jacks returned from the forest for supper.

By Friday of the second week, Marven had learned his job so well that he finished early. He had not been on his skis since he had arrived at camp. Every day the routine was simply meals and work, and Marven kept to his office and away from the lumberjacks as much as he could. But today he wanted to explore, so he put on his skis and followed the sled paths into the woods.

He glided forward, his skis making soft whisking sounds in the snow. This certainly was different from city skiing in Duluth, where he would dodge the ragman's cart or the milkman's wagon, where the sky was notched with chimney pots belching smoke, where the snow turned sooty as soon as it fell.

Here in the great north woods all was still and white.
Beads of ice glistened on bare branches like jewels. The
frosted needles of pine and spruce pricked the eggshell sky,
and a ghostly moon began to climb over the treetops.

Marven came upon a frozen lake covered with snow,
which lay in a circle of tall trees like a bowl of sugar. He
skimmed out across it on his skis, his cheeks stinging in the
cold air, and stopped in the middle to listen to the quietness.

And then Marven heard a deep, low growl. At the edge
of the lake a shower of snow fell from a pine. A grizzly bear?
Marven gripped his ski poles. A grizzly awake in the winter!
What would he do if a bear came after him? Where could he
hide? Could he out-ski a grizzly?

Marven began to tremble, but he knew that he must
remain still, very still. Maybe, Marven thought desperately,
the grizzly would think he was a small tree growing in the
middle of the lake. He tried very hard to look like a tree.
But concentrating on being a tree was difficult because
Marven kept thinking of the bundle on the train platform—
his mother, his father, his two big sisters, his two little sisters.
He belonged in Duluth with them, not in the middle of the

great north woods with a grizzly. The hot tears streaming down his cheeks turned cold, then froze.

When another tree showered snow, Marven, startled, shot out across the lake. As he reached the shore, a huge shadow slid from behind the trees. The breath froze in Marven's throat

In the thick purple shadows, he saw a blue twinkle.

"Aaah! Marven!" Jean Louis held a glistening ax in one hand. He looked taller than ever. "I mark the tree for cutting next season." He stepped closer to the trunk and swung the ax hard. Snow showered at Marven's feet.

"Ah, *mon petit,* you cry!" Jean Louis took off his glove and rubbed his huge thumb down Marven's cheek. "You miss your mama? Your papa?" Marven nodded silently.

"Jean Louis," he whispered. The huge lumberjack bent closer. "I thought you were a grizzly bear!"

"You what!" Jean Louis gasped. "You think I was a grizzly!" And Jean Louis began to laugh, and as he roared, more snow fell from the tree, for his laugh was as powerful as his ax.

As they made their way back to the sled paths, Marven heard a French song drifting through the woods. The other jacks came down the path, their saws and axes slung across their shoulders, and Marven and Jean Louis joined them. Evening shadows fell through the trees, and as Marven skied alongside the huge men, he hummed the tune they were singing.

A Note from the Author

Marven Lasky was born in 1907 in Duluth, Minnesota. He was the first child born in America to Ida and Joseph Lasky, who had emigrated from Tsarist Russia to escape the persecution of Jews. The story of their escape in 1900 was told in my novel *The Night Journey*.

Marven at age ten

In 1918, an influenza epidemic swept through the United States. The disease was the worst in the cities, among large populations. Old people and young children were the most vulnerable. Ida and Joseph believed that they might save at least one of their children if they could arrange for that child to go far from the city. Marven was not chosen because he was loved most; Joseph and Ida loved all of their children. Girls in that era, however, were never permitted to travel far from home by themselves— and the last place a girl would ever be sent was to a logging camp. Marven, therefore, was sent by himself on a train to a logging camp in the great north woods of Minnesota.

The last time Marven Lasky, my father, skied was at age eighty-three in Aspen, Colorado. He died at age ninety-one.

He always had a good head for figures.

Marven in his late sixties

Reader Response

Open for Discussion Put yourself in Marven's place. What could you do to enjoy living in the lumber camp? How could you keep from getting too homesick?

1. The author describes the lumberjacks as "biggest and wildest" (page 218). What else does she tell you about them to prove her point?

2. That statement on page 218 ("They were the biggest and wildest men Marven had ever seen") seems to be a statement of opinion. Why is it really a statement of fact?

3. Marven has a problem about what to eat at breakfast (page 224). What would you do to understand why he has this problem?

4. Put yourself in Marven's place. Write a postcard that he might have sent his parents from logging camp. Use words from the Words to Know list and the selection.

Test Practice

Look Back and Write When Marven feels scared and homesick, who helps him? How? Reread pages 228–231, and then write the answer in your own words.

Kathryn Lasky

Read more books by Kathryn Lasky.

The Man Who Made Time Travel

Born in the Breezes: The Seafaring Life of Joshua Slocum

Kathryn Lasky grew up in the suburbs of Indianapolis, Indiana. Her father went to law school and later started his own company. Her mother encouraged her to write. Ms. Lasky recalls, "She said, 'Kathy, you love words. And you have such a great imagination. You should be a writer.' My mom always thought I was the best, even when teachers didn't."

Ms. Lasky has written more than one hundred books. Like *Marven of the Great North Woods,* many of her books are based on real events. She suspects her success as a writer comes from being a good observer and from constantly reading. She is not concerned with her readers learning a lot of facts or getting a message from her writing. She says, "What I do hope is that they come away with a sense of joy—indeed, celebration—about something they have sensed of the world in which they live."

Meet the Illustrator
Kevin Hawkes

Read other books illustrated by Kevin Hawkes.

Kevin Hawkes never planned to be an artist, but always loved art classes in school. His first job out of college was producing cartoons for Saturday morning television. In his words, "I was horrible!" When he went to work in the children's section of a bookstore, he read picture books morning, noon, and night. This helped him get a feel for his own style, which he has used in more than thirty books for children.

Kevin Hawkes lives with his family and assorted pets (a beagle, a bunny, a large iguana, various fish, and a hamster named Crabby) on an island off the coast of Maine.

Dreamland
by Roni Schotter

The Librarian Who Measured the Earth
by Kathryn Lasky

E-Mail

Genre

- An *e-mail* is an electronic message sent over the Internet from one computer user to another. To e-mail someone is to send that person an electronic message.

- You can e-mail some Web sites for information to help with school projects.

Text Features

- The "To:" box shows to whom the message is going. The "From:" box shows from whom the message is coming.

- The message itself looks like the body of a letter.

Link to Writing

Tell a friend about *Marven of the Great North Woods.* Write an e-mail that you might send to him or her.

Logging Camps

After reading *Marven of the Great North Woods,* Kenji wants to know more about logging camps. He finds a Web site for a logging camp in northern Wisconsin.

236

Take It to the NET™
ONLINE
more activities sfsuccessnet.com

The site gives an e-mail address to contact for more information. Kenji decides to e-mail the Web site.

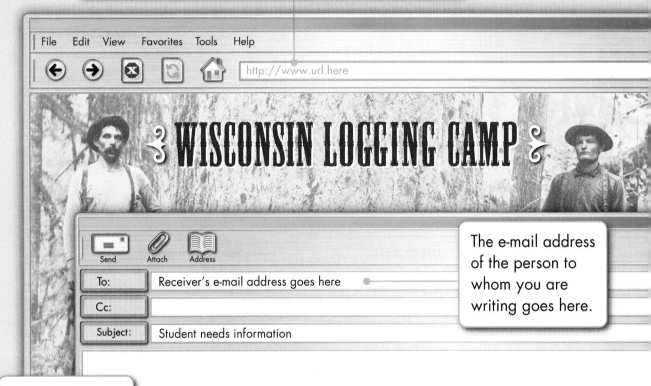

WISCONSIN LOGGING CAMP

Send   Attach   Address

To: Receiver's e-mail address goes here

Cc:

Subject: Student needs information

The e-mail address of the person to whom you are writing goes here.

If you do not know to whom to address your e-mail, use "Dear Sir or Madam."

Dear Sir or Madam:

I just read a story about a boy who goes to a logging camp in the north woods. Now I want to know more about logging camps. I have to give an oral report for class. Can you tell me where I might find more information about lumberjacks and how they lived? Thank you.

Kenji Shusizu

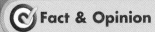 **Fact & Opinion**   Will the Web site Kenji has found provide facts *and* opinions?

The next day Kenji receives this reply.

From: Jensen, Kris
To: Shusizu, Kenji
Sent: Tuesday, November 1, 200_, 11:15 AM
cc:
Subject: Re: Student needs information

Hi Kenji,

Our Web site has several links that can help you learn about logging in this area. For information about how lumberjacks lived, follow the Cook Shanty & Bunkhouse link.

Thanks for visiting us. Let us know if we can be of further help.

Kris Jensen, Wisconsin Logging Camp

Kenji returns to the logging camp site and follows a series of links to the Cook Shanty & Bunkhouse link.

Home Visitor Center Cook Shanty &   Lumberjacks

COOK SHANTY & BUNKHOUSE   LUMBERJACKS

When Kenji clicks on the link, he finds this description of daily life in a camp.

File   Edit   View   Favorites   Tools   Help

http://www.url.here

Home   Visitor Center   Cook Shanty & Bunkhouse   Lumberjacks

COOK SHANTY & BUNKHOUSE

The cook shanty was where lumberjacks ate. The cooks were up before dawn to set the table and cook a breakfast of pancakes, salt pork, and coffee. The lumberjacks sat at long, oilcloth-covered tables. Talk was limited to requests for food.

The wanigan served as the camp store. Lumberjacks could buy clothing, shoes, blankets, tobacco, and some tools.

The bunkhouse was the crowded home for the lumberjacks during the logging season. Sleeping on bunk beds on mattresses of burlap, hay, straw, or branches, they found it difficult to keep the bedbugs or body lice away.

Reading Across Texts

What have you learned about life in a logging camp? Look at the information above and in *Marven* for details about how lumberjacks lived. List some of these details.

Writing Across Texts Use your list to write a description of life in a logging camp. Would you like to be a logger? Why or why not?

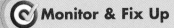 **Monitor & Fix Up**   How could you find out what *wanigan* means?

Comprehension

Skill
Main Idea and
Details

Strategy
Summarize

 # Main Idea
and Details

- The focus of a paragraph or an article—what it is all about—is the topic.

- The most important thing the author has to say about the topic is the main idea.

- Small pieces of information that tell more about the main idea are supporting details.

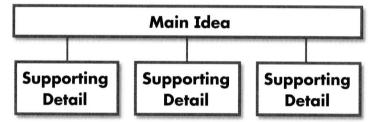

Main Idea		
Supporting Detail	**Supporting Detail**	**Supporting Detail**

Strategy: Summarize

Good readers summarize as they read. They decide which ideas are important and then put those ideas together into a short statement, or summary. Summarize as you read by pausing to think, "What are the most important ideas so far?"

Write

1. Read "A White House History." Make graphic organizers like the one above to help you find the main ideas of paragraphs two, three, and four.

2. Use your graphic organizers to write a summary of "A White House History."

A WHITE HOUSE HISTORY

The White House is where the U.S. President lives and works in Washington, D.C. However, our first President, George Washington, never even lived there! The building wasn't finished while he was in office. The White House was not begun until 1792.

Skill What is the main idea of the first paragraph?
(a) The White House is in Washington, D.C.
(b) The White House was begun in 1792.
(c) Unlike other Presidents, Washington didn't live in the White House because it wasn't finished.

Our second President, John Adams, moved into the White House in 1800. Even then, the building wasn't really finished. As a result, it was somewhat uncomfortable for daily life. The President's wife, Abigail, had nowhere to hang the family's laundry, so she used the East Room. Today that room is the biggest and grandest room in the house.

Strategy This is a good place to summarize. Tell the main ideas of the first two paragraphs.

In 1814, while our fourth President, James Madison, was in office, disaster hit the White House. The United States was again at war with England, and the British burned the White House. It had to be rebuilt.

Skill What is the main idea of the third paragraph?

Many people close to the President made their offices in the White House. By 1902, there were so many offices in the White House that our 26th President, Theodore Roosevelt, added more rooms—the West Wing. These rooms served as offices and freed up space in the White House for the President's six lively children and their pets.

Almost every President has made changes to the White House. The house doesn't belong to any one President, though. It belongs to the American people.

Strategy Summarize the article to help you remember its main ideas.

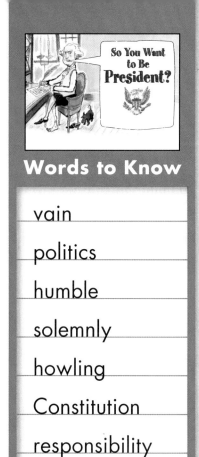

Words to Know

vain
politics
humble
solemnly
howling
Constitution
responsibility

Vocabulary Strategy
for Unfamiliar Words

Dictionary/Glossary When you are reading, you may come across a word you don't know. If you can't use the context, or words and sentences around the word, to figure out the word's meaning, you can use a dictionary or glossary to help you.

1. Check the back of your book for a glossary. If there is no glossary, look up the word in a dictionary.

2. Find the entry for the word. The entries are in alphabetical order.

3. Read the pronunciation to yourself. Saying the word may help you recognize it.

4. Read all the meanings given for the word.

5. Choose the meaning that makes sense in the sentence.

As you read "Class Election," use a dictionary or glossary to find the meanings of the vocabulary words.

Class Election

The students in Grade 4 are electing class officers. Four students are running for president.

Steven is vain about his looks. He puts just his name and his face on his signs. He says politics is dull, but winning is fun. Suzanne acts humble about how well she plays sports. Yet all her signs show her making the winning goal in last year's soccer championship. Omar solemnly promises that he will run a clean campaign. Then he makes fun of the other candidates. Still, his speeches are a howling success. Maya says that unlike the President of the United States, the president of Grade 4 does not have to "protect and defend the Constitution of the United States." However, she says the Grade 4 president does have a responsibility to all the students in Grade 4, not just the ones who voted for him or her. Maya was Grade 3 president and is captain of the softball team. If you were a student in Grade 4, whom would you vote for?

Suzanne
She is a winner!

Write

Answer the question at the end of the text. Give reasons for your choice. Use words from the Words to Know list.

Expository nonfiction gives information about real people and events. As you read, note new or surprising information about our country's Presidents.

So You Want to Be President?

by Judith St. George
illustrated by David Small

**What does it take to be
President of the United States?**

There are good things about being President, and there are bad things about being President. One of the good things is that the President lives in a big white house called the White House.

Another good thing about being President is that the President has a swimming pool, bowling alley, and movie theater.

The President never has to take out the garbage.

The President doesn't have to eat yucky vegetables. As a boy, George H. W. Bush had to eat broccoli. When George H. W. Bush grew up, he became President. That was the end of the broccoli!

One of the bad things about being President is that the President always has to be dressed up. William McKinley wore a frock coat, vest, pin-striped trousers, stiff white shirt, black satin tie, gloves, a top hat, and a red carnation in his buttonhole every day!

The President has to be polite to everyone. The President can't go anywhere alone. The President has lots of homework.

People get mad at the President. Someone once threw a cabbage at William Howard Taft. That didn't bother Taft. He quipped, "I see that one of my adversaries has lost his head."

Lots of people want to be President. If you want to be President, it might help if your name is James. Six Presidents were named James. (President Carter liked to be called Jimmy.) Four Johns, four Williams (President Clinton liked to be called Bill), three Georges, two Andrews, and two Franklins—all became President.

If you want to be President, your size doesn't matter. Presidents have come in all shapes and sizes. Abraham Lincoln was the tallest—six feet four inches. (His stovepipe hat made him look even taller.)

James Madison was the smallest—five feet four inches and only one hundred pounds. William Howard Taft was the biggest—more than three hundred pounds. He was so big that he had a special tub built for his White House bathroom. (Four men could fit in the tub!)

Though the Constitution says you'll have to wait until you're thirty-five, young, old, and in between have become President. Theodore (Teddy) Roosevelt at forty-two was the youngest. He had pillow fights with his children and played football on the White House lawn. "You must always remember that the President is about six," a friend said. Ronald Reagan was the oldest. When he first ran for President, he was sixty-nine. He joked that it was the thirtieth anniversary of his thirty-ninth birthday.

Do you have pesky brothers and sisters? Every one of our Presidents did. Benjamin Harrison takes the prize—he had eleven! (It's lucky he grew up on a six-hundred-acre farm.) James Polk and James Buchanan both had nine. George Washington, Thomas Jefferson, James Madison, and John Kennedy each had eight. (Two Presidents were orphans, Andrew Jackson and Herbert Hoover.)

A President in your family tree is a plus. John Quincy Adams was John Adams's son. George W. Bush was the son of George H. W. Bush. Theodore Roosevelt and Franklin Roosevelt were fifth cousins. Benjamin Harrison was William Harrison's grandson. James Madison and Zachary Taylor were second cousins.

Do you have a pet? All kinds of pets have lived in the White House, mostly dogs. Herbert Hoover had three dogs: Piney, Snowflake, and Tut. (Tut must have been a Democrat. He and his Republican master never got along.) Franklin Roosevelt's dog, Fala, was almost as famous as his owner.

George H. W. Bush's dog wrote MILLIE'S BOOK: ADVENTURES OF A WHITE HOUSE DOG (as reported to Mrs. Bush!). Ulysses Grant had horses, Benjamin Harrison's goat pulled his grandchildren around in a cart, the Coolidges had a pet raccoon, Jimmy Carter and Bill Clinton preferred cats.

Theodore Roosevelt's children didn't just have pets, they ran a zoo. They had dogs, cats, guinea pigs, mice, rats, badgers, raccoons, parrots, and a Shetland pony called Algonquin. To cheer up his sick brother, young Quentin once took Algonquin upstairs in the White House elevator!

Though most Presidents went to college, nine didn't: George Washington, Andrew Jackson, Martin Van Buren, Zachary Taylor, Millard Fillmore, Abraham Lincoln, Andrew Johnson, Grover Cleveland, and Harry Truman. (Andrew Johnson couldn't read until he was fourteen! He didn't learn to write until after he was married!)

Thomas Jefferson was top-notch in the brains department—he was an expert on agriculture, law, politics, music, geography, surveying, philosophy, and botany. In his spare time he designed his own house (a mansion), founded the University of Virginia, and whipped up the Declaration of Independence.

Almost any job can lead to the White House. Presidents have been lawyers, teachers, farmers, sailors, engineers, surveyors, mayors, governors, congressmen, senators, and ambassadors. (Harry Truman owned a men's shop. Andrew Johnson was a tailor. Ronald Reagan was a movie actor!)

There they are, a mixed bag of Presidents! What did they think of being head man? George Washington, who became our very first President in 1789, worried about his new line of work. "I greatly fear that my countrymen will expect too much from me," he wrote to a friend. (He was a howling success.) Some loved the job. "No President has ever enjoyed himself as much as I," Theodore Roosevelt said. Others hated it. "The four most miserable years of my life," John Quincy Adams complained.

Every President was different from every other and yet no woman has been President. No person of color has been President. No person who wasn't a Protestant or a Roman Catholic has been President. But if you care enough, anything is possible. Thirty-four Presidents came and went before a Roman Catholic—John Kennedy—was elected. Almost two hundred years passed before a woman—Geraldine Ferraro—ran for Vice President.

It's said that people who run for President have swelled heads. It's said that people who run for President are greedy. They want power. They want fame.

But being President can be wanting to serve your country— like George Washington, who left the Virginia plantation he loved three times to lead the country he loved even more.

It can be looking toward the future like Thomas Jefferson, who bought the Louisiana Territory and then sent Louis and Clark west to find a route to the Pacific. (They did!)

It can be wanting to turn lives around like Franklin Roosevelt, who provided soup and bread for the hungry, jobs for the jobless, and funds for the elderly to live on.

It can be wanting to make the world a better place like John Kennedy, who sent Peace Corps volunteers around the globe to teach and help others.

Every single President has taken this oath: "I do solemnly swear (or affirm) that I will faithfully execute the office of President of the United States, and will to the best of my ability, preserve, protect and defend the Constitution of the United States."

Only thirty-five words! But it's a big order when you're President of this country. Abraham Lincoln was tops at filling that order. "I know very well that many others might in this matter as in others, do better than I can," he said. "But . . . I am here. I must do the best I can, and bear the responsibility of taking the course which I feel I ought to take."

That's the bottom line. Tall, short, fat, thin, talkative, quiet, vain, humble, lawyer, teacher, or soldier—this is what most of our Presidents have tried to do, each in his own way. Some succeeded. Some failed. If you want to be President—a good President—pattern yourself after the best. Our best have asked more of themselves than they thought they could give. They have had the courage, spirit, and will to do what they knew was right. Most of all, their first priority has always been the people and the country they served.

Reader Response

Open for Discussion "What I enjoyed was. . . ." "What made me sad was. . . ." "What I learned was. . . ." Finish these sentences to give your reaction to *So You Want to Be President?*

1. An author's tone, or manner of writing, shows how the author feels about a topic. What is the author's tone in *So You Want to Be President?* Find parts of the selection that support your answer.

2. Reread page 250. What sentence states the main idea of this page? What supporting details can you find?

3. Suppose a friend announces plans to become President. What will you say to encourage him or her?

4. *Constitution* and *politics* are Words to Know that relate to government. Find other words in the selection that relate to government.

Look Back and Write On page 255 find three words that tell what the President is to do with the Constitution of the United States. Write them and tell what they mean.

256

Read more books by Judith St. George and David Small.

Judith St. George first discovered writing when she wrote a play in sixth grade. Since then she has gone on to write more than forty books. After publishing several books about American history, she decided to write about the presidency. She thought, "How about making my book on Presidents amusing and fun as well as informative?"

David Small, the illustrator, draws political cartoons for newspapers and illustrates children's books. *So You Want to Be President?* was a perfect opportunity for him to combine these two pursuits. "I hope readers will laugh first, and then begin to think a little more deeply," Mr. Small says. "Caricatures are not only funny pictures of people. The best ones make us see familiar faces in a new way. They exaggerate prominent aspects of a face to make us re-examine our heroes and other public figures in a different, more human light. The book concerns Presidents as the human beings they all are."

So You Want to Be an Inventor?

Imogene's Antlers

Expository Nonfiction

Genre

- **Expository nonfiction often presents facts and information in visual ways.**

- **Maps are important, with information being linked to them in some way.**

Text Features

- **With this brief article, a map of the United States shows the location of five national parks.**

- **Photos and facts provide details about the parks.**

Link to Social Studies

Look at a physical map of the United States. What natural landforms do you see? Choose a national park and make a list of the recreational activities people might enjoy there based on landforms that are part of the park.

OUR NATIONAL PARKS

by Susan Gavin

Did you know that the President of the United States has the power to set aside land for national parks? Ulysses S. Grant helped create the world's first national park, Yellowstone National Park, in 1872. In 1864, Abraham Lincoln set aside land that became Yosemite National Park in 1890.

Visit one of the 55 parks in the U.S. national park system. (A sampling is on page 259.) Walk through caves, climb mountains, and see wildlife, rain forests, and glaciers. As you enjoy these natural areas, remember that U.S. Presidents helped protect them.

Main Idea How would you state the main idea?

Sequoia
CALIFORNIA

Established: 1890
Size: 456,552 acres
Highlights: giant sequoia trees; Mt. Whitney (14,491 feet)

Mammoth Cave
KENTUCKY

Established: 1941
Size: 52,830 acres
Highlight: world's longest known network of caves

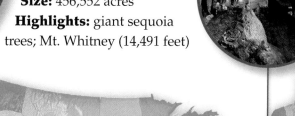

Everglades
FLORIDA

Established: 1947
Size: 1,399,078 acres
Highlight: largest subtropical wilderness in the United States

Death Valley
CALIFORNIA, NEVADA

Established: 1994
Size: 3,367,628 acres
Highlights: largest national park outside of Alaska; desert, dunes, gorges

Big Bend
TEXAS

Established: 1944
Size: 801,163 acres
Highlights: desert land; on the Rio Grande; dinosaur fossils

Reading Across Texts

"Our National Parks" tells that the President has the power to create national parks. What are some other good things Presidents have done that you read about in *So You Want to Be President?*

Writing Across Texts Make a list of three or four Presidents and tell something they each did that was good for the country.

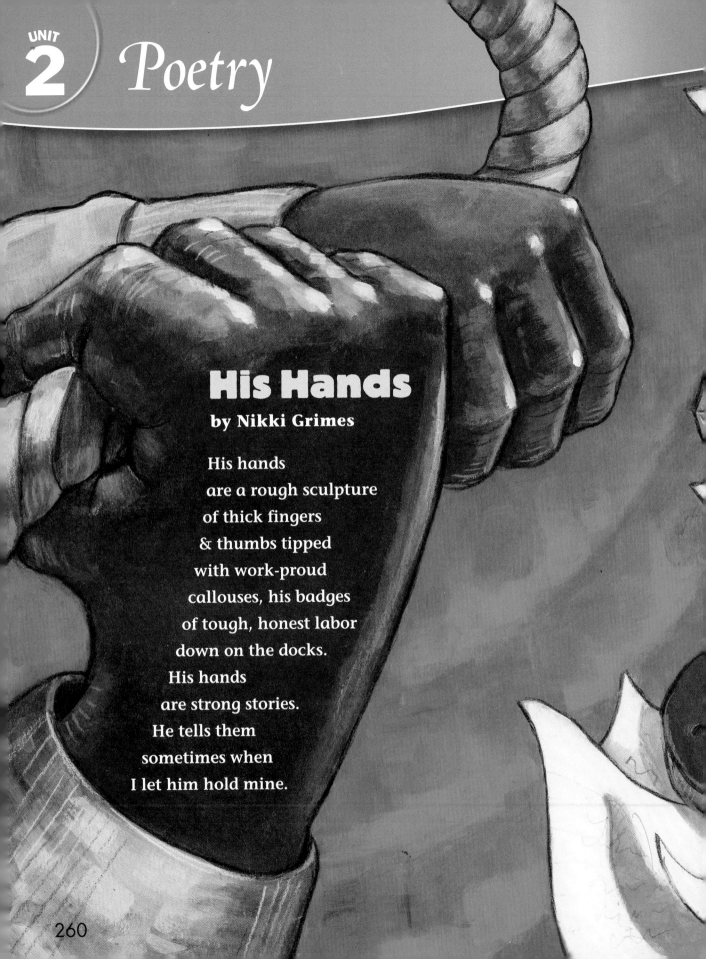

His Hands

by Nikki Grimes

His hands
are a rough sculpture
of thick fingers
& thumbs tipped
with work-proud
callouses, his badges
of tough, honest labor
down on the docks.
His hands
are strong stories.
He tells them
sometimes when
I let him hold mine.

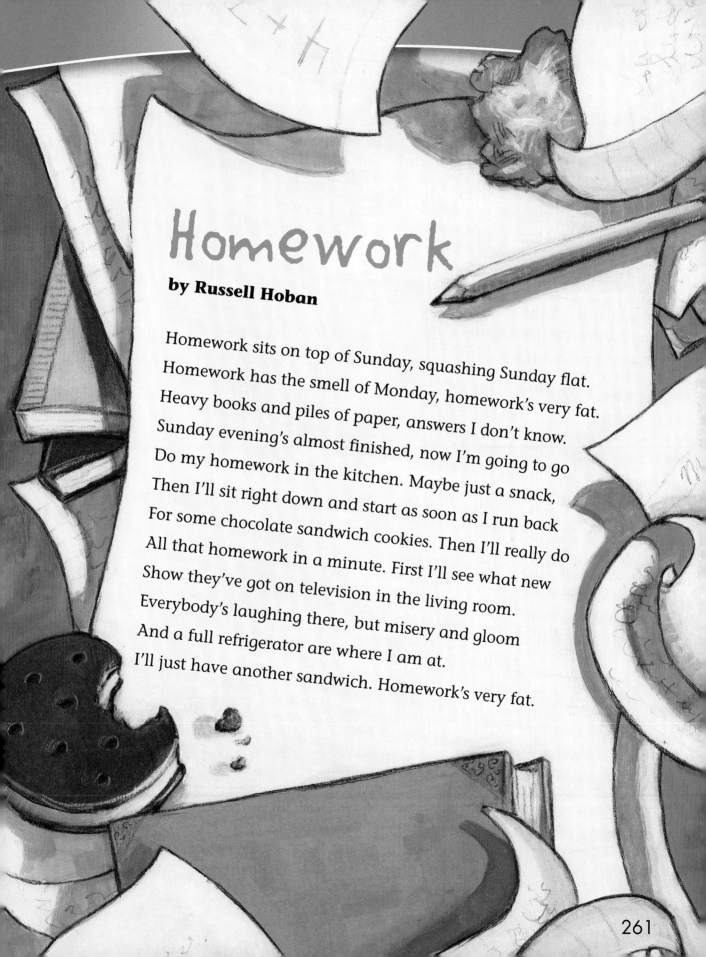

Homework

by Russell Hoban

Homework sits on top of Sunday, squashing Sunday flat.
Homework has the smell of Monday, homework's very fat.
Heavy books and piles of paper, answers I don't know.
Sunday evening's almost finished, now I'm going to go
Do my homework in the kitchen. Maybe just a snack,
Then I'll sit right down and start as soon as I run back
For some chocolate sandwich cookies. Then I'll really do
All that homework in a minute. First I'll see what new
Show they've got on television in the living room.
Everybody's laughing there, but misery and gloom
And a full refrigerator are where I am at.
I'll just have another sandwich. Homework's very fat.

Lem Lonnigan's Leaf Machine

by Andrea Perry

Lem Lonnigan's Leaf Machine cleans lawns with ease
by vacuuming all that falls down from the trees.
And as you might guess, he's quite busy in autumn.
Just look in a yard full of trees and you'll spot 'im!

He uses a special attachment to get
those few stubborn leaves that have not fallen yet,
extending its claws to reach sky-scraping heights
for snatching up stragglers and sometimes stray kites.

But if by mistake
his machine gets a nest
or a squirrel or bird
in its yard-cleaning zest,
then Lem hits the switch
to discharge it post haste
and carefully sees
that the tenant's replaced.

He's fast and efficient.
He's clean and he's neat
as he rides his machine
tree to tree down the street.
So don't waste time raking
and bagging this fall!
Lem's Leaf Machine's ready,
so give him a call!

Wrap-Up

New and Noteworthy

connect to **WRITING**

Think about something interesting that happened in school recently as you and your classmates worked or played together. Write a newspaper article telling about the event. Give your article a title. Be sure to include a main idea and details that tell *who, what, when, where, how,* and *why.* You might also add a photo or an illustration.

THE Class Chronicle

MAKING PEACE
ON THE PLAYGROUND

What is the value of work and play?

No More Child Labor

connect to
SOCIAL
STUDIES

Not too long ago many children worked instead of attending school. In some parts of the world today, children your age still work instead of attending school. Talk in a group about what kids your age and older could learn from working. Also, talk about what they would lose if they worked instead of going to school. Make a chart to summarize your ideas.

Children Who Work

What They Gain	What They Lose

Playtime Storyboard

connect to
ART

In *Grace and the Time Machine*, Grace and her friends come to a new understanding of another person by playing with a time machine. Make a storyboard with words and simple pictures to show something new you learned about yourself or another person by playing. Share your storyboard with a partner.

STORYBOARD

me →

Mom has my baseball.

She gives it to me.

1.
2.
3.

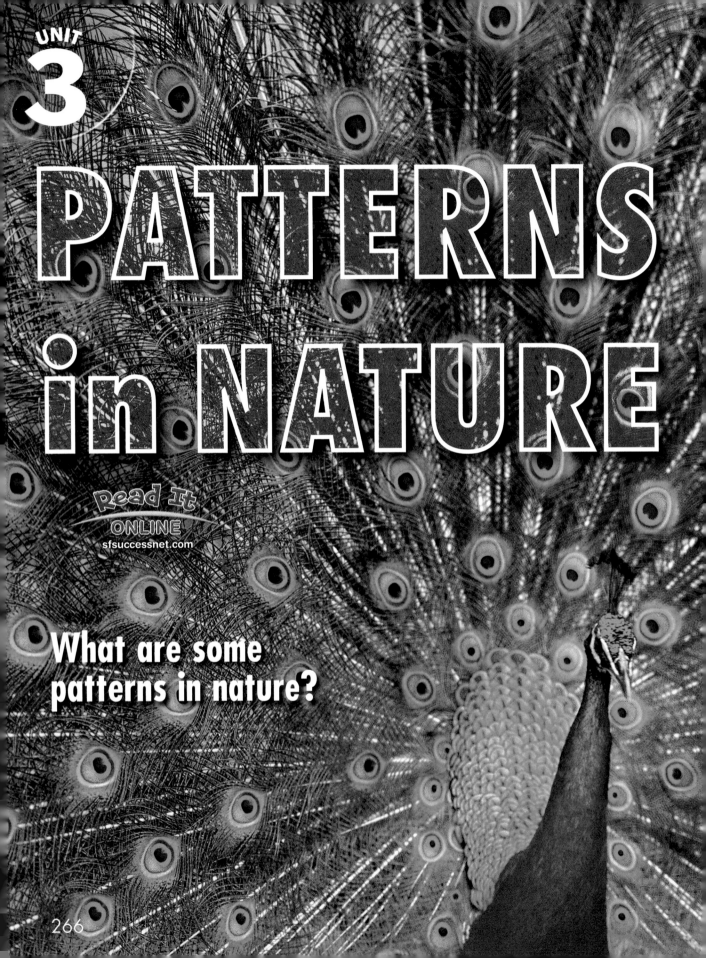

PATTERNS in NATURE

Read It
ONLINE
sfsuccessnet.com

What are some patterns in nature?

Comprehension

Skill
Cause and Effect

Strategy
Ask Questions

Cause and Effect

- Causes and effects are related. An effect is what happens. A cause is why it happens.

- Sometimes clue words, such as *because* and *so*, signal causes and effects. Other times you must figure out the causes and effects for yourself.

- Sometimes a cause has more than one effect.

Cause	→	Effect

Strategy: Ask Questions

Good readers ask themselves questions as they read. This helps them focus their reading because they are looking for answers. Asking questions is especially helpful when looking for causes and effects. You can ask yourself, "Why did this happen?" to find a cause. You can ask yourself, "What happened because of this?" to find an effect.

1. Read "Fall Harvest." Make a graphic organizer like the one above to help you find a cause and an effect.

2. Write two questions about the fall harvest, one beginning "Why?" and the other "What happens because of?" Then write the answers to your questions.

Fall Harvest

What do you think of when you hear the word *autumn*? Changing leaves and cooler weather? To a farmer, autumn means harvest time. After growing all summer, crops are ripe and ready to be harvested in the fall.

Skill Why is the fall a time of harvest? There is no clue word, so look for the information that tells *why*.

Grains like wheat are harvested with huge equipment called combines. A combine cuts plant stalks and separates the grain from the straw and other plant waste. It collects the grain and returns the straw to the ground.

Some farm equipment mows grasses like alfalfa and clover. Farmers let the mowed grasses lie in the fields. There they dry out and turn to hay. Then a machine called a hay baler gathers the hay and binds it into bales.

Strategy Ask yourself, "What happens to the grasses left in the field?" Then look for the answer.

Most apples are harvested in the fall. Because ripe apples are easily bruised, they must be carefully picked by hand. Apples can "keep" in cold storage for up to a year, so you can purchase apples all year long.

Skill Being able to buy apples year-round is the effect. What is the cause?

Pumpkins, too, are harvested by hand. They are cut from the vine with a sharp knife or shears. Below-freezing temperatures will kill a vine and damage the pumpkins. That's why farmers usually harvest their pumpkins in October, just in time for Halloween.

Strategy As you read this paragraph, ask yourself, "What are the effects of below-freezing temperatures?"

269

fascinated
timid
parlor
draft
etched
frost
terror

Remember

Try the strategy. Then, if you need more help, use your glossary or a dictionary.

Vocabulary Strategy
for Multiple-Meaning Words

Context Clues Sometimes when you are reading, you may see a word whose meaning you know, but that meaning doesn't make sense in the sentence. The word may have more than one meaning. You can look for clues to decide which meaning the author is using.

1. Try the meaning you know. Does it make sense in the sentence?

2. If it doesn't make sense, try to think of another meaning for the word. Does that meaning make sense?

3. If it doesn't make sense either, reread the words and sentences around the word. Use the context to predict a meaning for the unknown word.

4. Try that meaning in the sentence. Does it make sense?

As you read "The Old House on Dwyer Road," look for words that can have more than one meaning. Use the context to help you figure out which meaning is being used.

THE OLD HOUSE ON DWYER ROAD

Alec was fascinated by old houses. He heard that there was a really interesting old house on Dwyer Road. People said that strange things happened in the house at night—thumps, howls, groans. They said that it was not a place for the timid. Alec was intrigued. He got permission to stay overnight in the house.

The house had a parlor, dining room, kitchen, and storeroom on the first floor. Alec decided to stay in the parlor. He settled into a comfortable armchair and began to read his book. Suddenly Alec felt a cold draft, even though no door or window was open. Then he thought he heard footsteps in the hall. He got up and walked toward the parlor doors.

The doors had designs etched in the glass. It made them look as though they had frost on them. Shadowy forms seemed to flit past the doors. Alec reached for the door handles. Then terror seized him. He could not make himself open the doors.

Write

Write about a time when you were scared. What did it feel like? What did you do? Use some words from the Words to Know list.

The Stranger

text and art
by Chris Van Allsburg

272

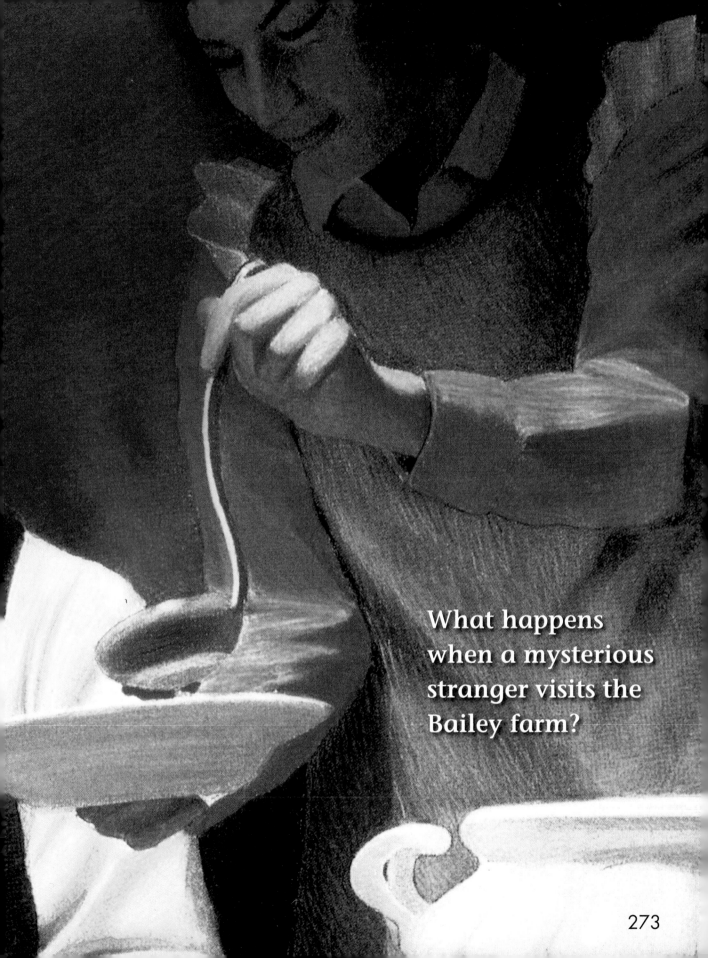

What happens when a mysterious stranger visits the Bailey farm?

It was the time of year Farmer Bailey liked best, when
summer turned to fall. He whistled as he drove along.
A cool breeze blew across his face through the truck's open
window. Then it happened. There was a loud "thump."
Mr. Bailey jammed on his brakes. "Oh no!" he thought. "I've
hit a deer."

But it wasn't a deer the farmer found lying in the road,
it was a man. Mr. Bailey knelt down beside the still figure,
fearing the worst. Then, suddenly, the man opened his eyes. He
looked up with terror and jumped to his feet. He tried to run
off, lost his balance, and fell down. He got up again, but this
time the farmer took his arm and helped him to the truck.

Mr. Bailey drove home. He helped the stranger inside, where Mrs. Bailey made him comfortable on the parlor sofa. Katy, their daughter, peeked into the room. The man on the sofa was dressed in odd rough leather clothing. She heard her father whisper ". . . must be some kind of hermit . . . sort of fellow who lives alone in the woods." The stranger didn't seem to understand the questions Mr. Bailey asked him. "I don't think," whispered Mrs. Bailey, "he knows how to talk."

Mr. Bailey called the doctor, who came and listened to the stranger's heart, felt his bones, looked in his eyes, and took his temperature. He decided the man had lost his memory. There was a bump on the back of his head. "In a few days," the doctor said, "he should remember who he is and where he's from." Mrs. Bailey stopped the doctor as he left the house. He'd forgotten his thermometer. "Oh, you can throw that out," he answered. "It's broken, the mercury is stuck at the bottom."

Mr. Bailey lent the stranger some clean clothes. The fellow seemed confused about buttonholes and buttons. In the evening he joined the Baileys for dinner. The steam that rose from the hot food fascinated him. He watched Katy take a spoonful of soup and blow gently across it. Then he did exactly the same. Mrs. Bailey shivered. "Brrr," she said. "There's a draft in here tonight."

The next morning Katy watched the stranger from her bedroom window. He walked across the yard, toward two rabbits. Instead of running into the woods, the rabbits took a hop in his direction. He picked one of them up and stroked its ears, then set it down. The rabbits hopped away, then stopped and looked back, as if they expected the stranger to follow.

When Katy's father went into the fields that day, the
stranger shyly tagged along. Mr. Bailey gave him a pitchfork
and, with a little practice, he learned to use it well. They
worked hard. Occasionally Mr. Bailey would have to stop
and rest. But the stranger never tired. He didn't even sweat.

That evening Katy sat with the stranger, watching the
setting sun. High above them a flock of geese, in perfect V
formation, flew south on the trip that they made every fall.
The stranger could not take his eyes off the birds. He stared
at them like a man who'd been hypnotized.

Two weeks passed and the stranger still could not remember who he was. But the Baileys didn't mind. They liked having the stranger around. He had become one of the family. Day by day he'd grown less timid. "He seems so happy to be around us," Mr. Bailey said to his wife. "It's hard to believe he's a hermit."

Another week passed. Farmer Bailey could not help
noticing how peculiar the weather had been. Not long ago
it seemed that autumn was just around the corner. But now
it still felt like summer, as if the seasons couldn't change. The
warm days made the pumpkins grow larger than ever.
The leaves on the trees were as green as they'd been three
weeks before.

One day the stranger climbed the highest hill on the Bailey farm. He looked to the north and saw a puzzling sight. The trees in the distance were bright red and orange. But the trees to the south, like those round the Baileys', were nothing but shades of green. They seemed so drab and ugly to the stranger. It would be much better, he thought, if all trees could be red and orange.

The stranger's feelings grew stronger the next day. He couldn't look at a tree's green leaves without sensing that something was terribly wrong. The more he thought about it, the more upset he became, until finally he could think of nothing else. He ran to a tree and pulled off a leaf. He held it in a trembling hand and, without thinking, blew on it with all his might.

At dinner that evening the stranger appeared dressed in his old leather clothes. By the tears in his eyes the Baileys could tell that their friend had decided to leave. He hugged them all once, then dashed out the door. The Baileys hurried outside to wave good-bye, but the stranger had disappeared. The air had turned cold, and the leaves on the trees were no longer green.

Every autumn since the stranger's visit, the same thing happens at the Bailey farm. The trees that surround it stay green for a week after the trees to the north have turned. Then overnight they change their color to the brightest of any tree around. And etched in frost on the farmhouse windows are words that say simply, "See you next fall."

Reader Response

Open for Discussion As you read this tale, what did you wonder? What questions did you ask yourself? Which did you answer?

1. The author gives clues about the stranger, such as the broken thermometer (page 276). What other clues does the author give?

2. Mr. Bailey brings the stranger home after he hits him with his truck. What happens at the farm while the stranger is there? What happens after he leaves?

3. What questions did you have about the setting of the story — where and when it takes place? How did you answer your questions?

4. How are the words *terror* and *timid* related? Which one describes a more extreme condition? What other words are related to them?

Test Practice

Look Back and Write What strange things happen at the Bailey farm every autumn? Look back at page 285 to help you remember. Then write your answer.

Chris Van Allsburg

Read other books by Chris Van Allsburg.

You have probably seen Chris Van Allsburg's illustrations in the award-winning books *The Polar Express* and *Jumanji*. But you might not know that he almost did not become an illustrator.

In fact, he started out as a sculptor, drawing only in the evenings for fun. Then, one day, an author and artist friend came over for dinner and saw Mr. Van Allsburg's drawings. He thought they were amazing and showed them to his editor. Before long, Mr. Van Allsburg published his first picture book, *The Garden of Abdul Gasazi*. The story begins with a picture of a fantastic garden with huge plants trimmed in the shape of animals.

"At first, I see pictures of a story in my mind," Mr. Van Allsburg says. "If I figure out what they mean, I can discover the story that's waiting."

The Garden of Abdul Gasazi

Zathura

Expository Nonfiction

Genre

- **Expository nonfiction gives information about the real world.**

- **It often explains ideas.**

Text Features

- **The author uses a question-and-answer format to explain changes in nature that take place in the fall.**

- **Graphic sources such as pictures and diagrams help explain the information.**

Link to Science

Think of another change in nature that takes place in the fall. Use reference sources to find out why this change takes place. Present your findings in the form of a question and an answer. Include a picture or diagram if needed.

TIME FOR A CHANGE

by Helen Strahinich

FROM FROSTY DAWNS TO FALLING LEAVES TO FLYING GEESE, AUTUMN IS A BUSY TIME OF YEAR.

WHY DO WE HAVE SEASONS?

The seasons are caused by the way the Earth moves around the sun. Imagine a line that runs from the top of the North Pole, through the center of the Earth, and out through the bottom of the South Pole. This line is called the Earth's axis. In some pictures of the Earth, its axis runs straight up and down. But as the Earth moves around the sun, its axis is really tilted.

For half of the year, the Earth's northern half, or Northern Hemisphere, is tilted toward the sun. This is when countries in the Northern Hemisphere, including most of the United States, have spring and summer. The days are long, sunny, and warm. But when the Northern Hemisphere is tilted away from the sun, these countries have autumn and winter.

The autumn equinox marks the first day of fall in the Northern Hemisphere, September 21, 22, or 23. On that day, the Earth gets 12 hours of daylight and 12 hours of darkness. From then on, the days grow shorter, and the weather gets cooler. Autumn ends on December 21 or 22. That day is known as the winter solstice. It is the start of winter and the shortest day of the year. Then it is time to brace for the snowstorms of winter.

THE REASON FOR SEASONS

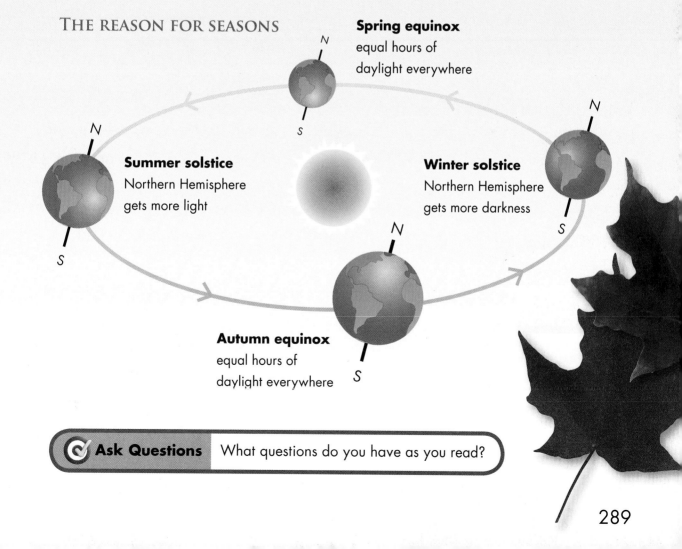

Spring equinox
equal hours of daylight everywhere

Summer solstice
Northern Hemisphere gets more light

Winter solstice
Northern Hemisphere gets more darkness

Autumn equinox
equal hours of daylight everywhere

Ask Questions What questions do you have as you read?

WHY DO LEAVES CHANGE COLOR IN THE FALL?

Leaves are like tiny factories. They make food that allows trees to grow. The energy that powers these tiny factories is sunlight.

Leaves contain a green substance called chlorophyll. This material gives leaves their green color during spring and summer. Leaves also have yellow- and orange-colored pigments, but in much smaller amounts. So you can't see them.

In the fall, the tree's food factories start to shut down for winter. As chlorophyll breaks down, the green color of the leaves fades. Now the yellow and orange colors burst through. In some trees, food trapped in the leaves turns the leaves red.

Seen from afar, these trees seem to put on a fireworks display each autumn. The best places to view these fireworks are in the eastern United States and southeastern Canada. These regions are thick with forests of leaf-bearing trees.

WHY DO CANADA GEESE MIGRATE SOUTH EACH AUTUMN?

Nobody knows for sure. It may be the cold or it may be instinct. Whatever the reason, these geese seem to have a kind of inner clock. It tells them to fly south before their ponds, lakes, and other nesting areas freeze over and snow covers their food.

Have you ever spotted Canada geese flying in their trademark V formation? It's a sight to see. The strongest geese take turns leading the flock. Each goose creates an airstream that makes it easier for those behind it to fly.

Most winters, Canada geese will move to regions like central Missouri, southern Illinois, and Tennessee.

In mild winters, many Canada geese will stay in places like Wisconsin. But harsh winters will drive Canada geese as far south as Mexico.

Don't worry, though. They always return home in the spring. Just like clockwork.

Reading Across Texts

Reread page 289 in "Time for a Change." Use the information given to determine which dates the stranger most likely visited the Baileys. Tell why you think so.

Writing Across Texts Write down the dates the stranger most likely visited the Baileys, and tell why you think this.

Cause & Effect   How does thinking about causes and effects help you?

Comprehension

Skill
Fact and Opinion

Strategy
Graphic
Organizers

Fact and Opinion

- A statement of fact can be correct or incorrect. You can check it by doing research.

- A statement of opinion should be supported. A valid opinion is supported by facts or good logic. A faulty opinion is not.

- Some sentences contain both statements of fact and statements of opinion.

Statement	Support	True or False/ Valid or Faulty
Statement of fact	Other facts	True
Statement of opinion	Logic or known facts	Valid
Statement of opinion	Weak opinion or incorrect facts	Faulty

Strategy: Graphic Organizers

Good readers organize their thoughts as they read. Jotting down lists or making charts can help you separate statements of fact from statements of opinion.

1. Read "Something Must Be Done." Make a graphic organizer like the one above to record statements of fact and opinion.

2. Write two statements of opinion from your chart. For each, tell how the author has supported it well or could have supported it better.

SOMETHING MUST BE DONE

What is the largest animal that ever lived? Is it an elephant? Not even close. This animal can be as big as four elephants. Is it a dinosaur? Guess again.

The largest animal in the world is the blue whale. This beautiful animal can grow as big as 100 feet long! You might think that an animal so enormous could survive anything. Not so.

In the 1800s and early 1900s, whaling was big business. People killed whales to make such things as oil and candles. Many whales were hunted almost to extinction. In time, other ways of lighting houses and workplaces were developed. People realized the harm the whaling business was doing to the whales. Now, most countries ban whaling, but even so, many species are still endangered.

Whales face other challenges too. They can get tangled in fishing nets and drown. (Remember, whales are mammals; they need to breathe air.) Also, they can get sick from pollution in the ocean. Sometimes, they collide with ships. Governments can make more laws to protect the whales and their habitats. For example, some shipping lanes were changed to make ships go around an area where mother whales bring their babies.

People should tell their governments that saving the whales is important. We can make a difference!

Skill Some sentences contain both a statement of fact and of opinion. The size of a blue whale can be proved. Yet, it is the author's opinion that the whale is a beautiful animal.

Strategy This is a statement of fact on your chart. Will the author prove it? Would you have to do research to prove it?

Skill How will the author support this statement of opinion?

Strategy This statement of opinion summarizes the article. Your graphic organizer should show how the author has supported it.

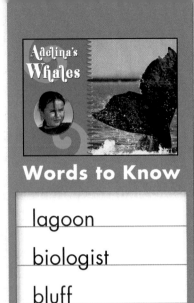

Words to Know

| lagoon |
| biologist |
| bluff |
| massive |
| rumbling |
| tropical |

Remember

Try the strategy. Then, if you need more help, use your glossary or a dictionary.

Vocabulary Strategy
for Homonyms

Context Clues Sometimes when you read, you may come to a word whose meaning you know, but that meaning doesn't make sense in the sentence. The word may be a homonym. Homonyms are words that are spelled the same but have different meanings because they have come into the English language from different languages. For example, *staff* can mean "a stick" or "a group of employees." You can use the context—the words and sentences around the word—to figure out which meaning is being used.

1. Reread the sentence in which the homonym appears. Look for clues to the homonym's meaning.

2. If that doesn't work, read the sentences around the sentence with the homonym. Look for clues to the homonym's meaning.

3. Try the meaning in the sentence. Does it make sense?

As you read "Paradise Island," look for homonyms. Use the context to figure out the meanings of the homonyms.

PARADISE ISLAND

Welcome to Paradise Island! Click on the following to find out more about what you can do on our island.

- Walk or run on the gorgeous white sand beaches that ring the whole island. They were voted the Best Beaches in the World last year by *Touring Magazine!*

- Swim in the beautiful blue-green waters of our lagoon. Protected from the ocean by a reef, the lagoon is also perfect for canoeing and kayaking.

- Take a walk with our staff biologist. You can learn about the many strange and colorful birds and other animals that call Paradise Island home.

- Climb the bluff for wonderful views of the island and the ocean. We offer climbs for beginners and experts.

- Take a day trip to the volcano. You can ride or hike to the top to look down into its massive crater. It has always been quiet (except for a rumbling noise every once in a while).

Paradise Island is a tropical paradise. Come see it for yourself and have the best vacation of your life!

Write

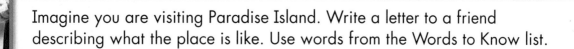

Imagine you are visiting Paradise Island. Write a letter to a friend describing what the place is like. Use words from the Words to Know list.

Adelina's Whales

text and photographs by Richard Sobol

Photo essays use words and pictures
to tell about someone or something. As you
read, notice how the words and images work
together to tell about Adelina and her whales.

What is so unusual about the
whales that visit Adelina?

La Laguna is the name of a quiet, dusty fishing village on the sandy shore of Laguna San Ignacio, in Baja California, Mexico. A few dozen homesites are scattered along the water's edge. These little houses are simple one- or two-room boxes patched together with plywood and sheet metal. Drinking water is stored outside in fifty-gallon plastic barrels, and electricity is turned on for only a few hours each day.

Adelina Mayoral has lived her whole life in La Laguna. She is a bright ten-year-old girl. She loves the ocean and the feeling of the ever-present wind that blows her long, dark hair into wild tangles. She knows what time of day it is by looking at the way the light reflects off the water. Adelina can tell what month it is by watching the kind of birds that nest in the mangroves behind her home. She can even recognize when it is low tide. Simply by taking a deep breath through her nose, she can smell the clams and seaweed that bake in the hot sun on the shoreline as the water level goes down.

In late January, every afternoon after school, Adelina walks to the beach to see if her friends—the gray whales—have returned. At this same time every year the whales come, traveling from as far away as Alaska and Russia. They slowly and steadily swim south, covering more than five thousand miles along the Pacific Coast during November, December, and January.

One night Adelina is awakened by a loud, low, rumbling noise. It is the sound of a forty-ton gray whale exhaling a room-size blast of hot wet air. As she has always known they would, the gray whales have come again to visit. Adelina smiles and returns to her sleep, comforted by the sounds of whales breathing and snoring outside her window. At daybreak she runs to the lagoon and sees two clouds of mist out over the water, the milky trails of breath left by a mother gray whale and her newborn calf.

The waters of the protected lagoon are warm and shallow. The scientists who have come to visit and study the whales have explained that Laguna San Ignacio is the perfect place for the mother whales to have their babies and then teach them how to swim. But Adelina knows why they really come—to visit her!

Adelina's family lives far away from big cities with highways and shopping malls. Her little village does not have any movie theaters or traffic lights, but she knows that her hometown is a special place. This is the only place on Earth where these giant gray whales—totally wild animals—choose to seek out the touch of a human hand. Only here in Laguna San Ignacio do whales ever stop swimming and say hello to their human neighbors. Raising their massive heads up out of the water, they come face-to-face with people. Some mother whales even lift their newborns up on their backs to help them get a better view of those who have come to see them. Or maybe they are just showing off, sharing their new baby the way any proud parent would.

The whales have been coming to this lagoon for hundreds of years, and Adelina is proud that her grandfather, Pachico, was the first person to tell of a "friendly" visit with one. She loves to hear him tell the story of that whale and that day. She listens closely as he talks about being frightened, since he didn't know then that the whale was only being friendly. He thought he was in big trouble.

Adelina looks first at the tight, leathery skin of her grandfather, browned from his many years of fishing in the bright tropical sun. From his face she glances down to the small plastic model of a gray whale that he keeps close by. As he begins to tell the story of his first friendly whale encounter, there is a twinkle in his eye and a large smile on his face. Adelina and her father, Runolfo, smile too, listening again to the story that they have heard so many times before.

In a whisper, her grandfather begins to draw them in. Adelina closes her eyes to imagine the calm and quiet on that first afternoon when his small boat was gently nudged by a huge gray whale. As the boat rocked, her grandfather's and his fishing partner's hearts pounded. They held tight and waited, preparing themselves to be thrown into the water by the giant animal. The whale dove below them and surfaced again on the opposite side of their boat, scraping her head along the smooth sides. Instead of being tossed from the boat, they were surprised to find themselves still upright and floating. For the next hour the whale glided alongside them, bumping and bobbing gently— as gently as possible for an animal that is as long as a school bus and as wide as a soccer goal. As the sun started to set behind them, the whale gave out a great blast of wet, snotty saltwater that soaked their clothes and stuck to their skin. The whale then rose up inches away from their boat and dove into the sea. Her first visit was over.

As her grandfather finishes the story, he looks to Adelina, who joins him in speaking the last line of the story: "Well, my friend, no fish today!" they say before breaking into laughter.

After this first friendly visit with the whales, word quickly spread of the unique encounter between a wild fifty-foot whale and a tiny fishing boat. Scientists and whale watchers started to come to Laguna San Ignacio to see the whales themselves. Perhaps word spread among the whales, too, because now dozens of whales began to approach the small boats. With brains as large as a car's engine, gray whales might even have their own language. They "talk" in low rumbles and loud clicks, making noises that sound like the tappings of a steel drum or the ticking that a playing card makes as it slaps against the spokes of a turning bicycle wheel. Maybe they told each other that it was safe to visit here.

Adelina's favorite time of the day is the late afternoon, when her father and grandfather return from their trips on the water, guiding visitors to see the whales. They sit together as the sun goes down behind them, and she listens to stories of the whales. She asks them lots and lots of questions.

Adelina has learned a lot about the gray whales. She knows that when a whale leaps out of the water and makes a giant splash falling back in, it's called breaching. When a whale pops its head straight up out of the water, as if it is looking around to see what is going on, it is called spyhopping. Adelina also learned how the whale's wide, flat tail is called a fluke, and when it raises its tail up in the air as it goes into a deep dive, that is called fluking.

Although her home is a simple shack on a sandy bluff hugging the edge of the Pacific Ocean, Adelina has many new friends who come to share her world. She has met people who come from beyond the end of the winding, bumpy road that rings the lagoon. Some are famous actors. Some are politicians. Some speak Spanish. Some speak English. Those that weigh forty tons speak to her in their own magical style. The whales have taught her that the world is a big place.

Adelina knows that she has many choices in her future. Sometimes she giggles with delight at the idea of being the first girl to captain a panga (a small open fishing boat) and teach people about the whales in the lagoon. Or sometimes she thinks she may become a biologist who studies the ocean and can one day help to unlock some of the mysteries of the whales in her own backyard. Or maybe she will take pictures like the photographer whom she watches juggling his three cameras as he stumbles aboard the whale-watching boat. But no matter what she chooses, the whales will always be a part of her life.

KUYIMA-5

For these three months Adelina knows how lucky she is to live in Laguna San Ignacio, the little corner of Mexico that the gray whales choose for their winter home. This is the place where two worlds join together. She wouldn't trade it for anything.

In the early spring the lagoon grows quiet. One by one the whales swim off, heading north for a summer of feeding.

On their heads and backs they carry the fingerprints of those they met, the memories of their encounters in Mexico. Maybe, as the whales sleep, they dream of the colorful sunsets of Laguna San Ignacio.

Every afternoon Adelina continues to gaze across the water. Sometimes now, when she closes her eyes, she can still see the whales swimming by. And if she listens *really* closely, she can even hear their breathing.

Reader Response

Open for Discussion What were your thoughts about gray whales as you read about them? What do you think your thoughts might be if you were to see real gray whales?

1. Why does the author tell you about gray whales the way Adelina sees and hears them?

2. A statement of fact can be proved true or false. Which two of the following are statements of fact?

    a. The whales go to Laguna San Ignacio to visit Adelina.

    b. Electricity is turned on for only a few hours each day in La Laguna.

    c. A whale's wide, flat tail is called a fluke.

3. Create a web to record what you learned about gray whales from the selection.

4. If Adelina wrote a description of Laguna San Ignacio, she might use the Words to Know *lagoon, tropical,* and *bluff.* What other words from the selection might she use?

Look Back and Write If you were to visit Laguna San Ignacio in January, what special sight would you see? Reread page 299 and then write your answer.

Richard Sobol

Read more books by Richard Sobol.

Richard Sobol says he "started photography in high school and never stopped." This passion led to a fast-paced career taking pictures of politicians and wildlife. Then he decided to write photo essays. He explains, "I was always insecure about my writing, but I was reluctant to leave the storytelling to someone else."

Mr. Sobol got the idea for *Adelina's Whales* while in Baja California, where Adelina's father was his whale guide. To take photographs for the book, he says, "I spent each morning and afternoon on a small boat waiting for the whales to approach. Most often, I was within twenty feet of the whales. Sometimes, though, they were right on the side of the boat!"

When asked what it was like to be so close to whales, Mr. Sobol answers, "I am still amazed that these totally wild animals chose to come so close to humans. I will never forget the slick rubbery sensation of rubbing the forehead of a huge gray whale that swam from one side of my boat to the other." He hopes his books inspire kids to value and protect the gray whale and other rare and endangered animals.

An Elephant in the Backyard

Seal Journey (with Jonah Sobol)

Expository Nonfiction

Genre

- Expository nonfiction gives facts and details about real people, places, animals, and things.

- Pictures and other graphic sources give information in a visual way, helping the reader better understand the text.

Text Features

- A paragraph introduces the article to the reader.

- Each section has a clever head that keeps the reader reading.

Link to Science

Research a sea or land animal that migrates. Make a poster with information about your animal, including its migration route.

Sea Animals on the Move

by Joanne Wachter

Some families take a trip to see relatives every Thanksgiving. Other families go to a cabin in the mountains every summer. Certain sea animals take trips to the same place year after year too. The trips these animals take are called *migration*.

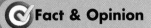 **Fact & Opinion**   Should there be many statements of opinion in this article?

Line Up!

One sea animal that migrates is the spiny lobster. Usually, the lobster stays close to its home, a crack in a rock deep in the ocean. When the first winter storm hits, however, something strange happens. The lobster starts a long trip. Groups of up to 60 lobsters line up, head to tail. Then they travel day and night, going 30 or more miles in a few days.

Other sea animals that migrate are sharks, eels, turtles, and whales. Some of these take very long trips. For example, sea turtles may travel more than 7,000 miles, one-third of the way around the Earth. Some fish have special ways to rest on their long trips. Lampreys use their sucking mouths to hold on to rocks for short breaks.

Trips with a Purpose

Why would an animal make such a trip? Some, such as spiny lobsters and sharks, move to warmer or cooler waters when the seasons change. Others, such as flashlight fish, migrate in search of food. The flashlight fish moves from deep to shallow water in order to feed. It uses a light that shines out of its body to find its way.

Many sea animals migrate to find safe places to lay eggs. Salmon live in the salty sea but travel to fresh water to have their young. The fish digs a hole in the river floor with its tail. Then it lays as many as 14,000 eggs. Sea turtles swim thousands of miles to have their babies on the same beaches where they hatched.

311

Traveling Without a Map

People would get lost very quickly if they tried to swim underwater from place to place. There are no signs or buildings to point the way in the ocean. Surprisingly, however, sea animals do not get lost.

Scientists think that sea animals use their senses to find their way. Some fish use their strong sense of smell. It helps them notice the familiar scents of rocks and plants along the way. Others use the sense of touch. They feel the movement of waves, tides, and currents. These clues help them map their journey.

Scientists have another interesting idea. They think that some sea animals have a sense that people do not. Something in the bodies of these animals may act like a compass. This sense may point them in the right direction.

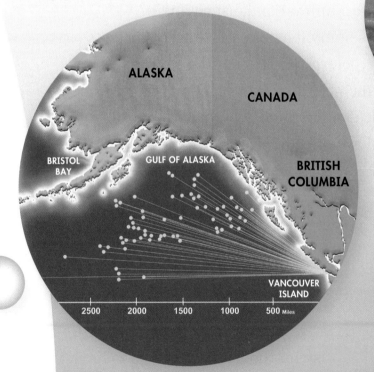

Scientists have tracked the distances traveled by some salmon. These salmon swam from the dots marked in the ocean to Fraser River in Canada.

Tag a Fish

Scientists are trying to learn more about migration. They have invented tools such as tagging to study how sea animals move. Researchers catch a sea animal, glue or strap a small tag to it, and then return the animal to the water. The tag gathers facts about the animal's journey and sends a report to satellites above the Earth. The satellites send the report back to computers on land. People use this information to learn about the patterns of the animals.

Reports about migration are useful. People from different countries are sharing what they learn so that we can all work together to protect sea animals. Dr. Barbara Block is one of these people. She believes, "The first step in protecting their [sea animals'] future on Earth is knowing where they go."

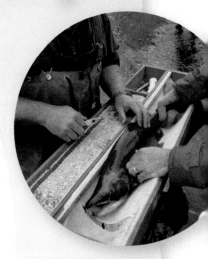

Researchers in Canada tag a sockeye salmon.

A tag on the fin of a loggerhead turtle relays information about the sea turtle's journey.

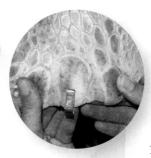

Reading Across Texts

How is Adelina's understanding of migration different from that of the scientists in this article?

Writing Across Texts Tell about the animal from these two selections whose migration you find the most interesting. Include the reasons for your choice.

Graphic Organizers How could a chart help you with this information?

Comprehension

Skill
Generalize

Strategy
Visualize

Skill

Generalize

- A generalization is a broad statement or rule that applies to many examples.

- A clue word such as *all, most, always, usually,* or *generally* signals that an author is making a generalization.

- Some generalizations are valid, which means that they are supported by facts or details. Some are faulty, which means that they are not supported.

Generalization	Clue Word?

Strategy

Strategy: Visualize

Good readers visualize as they read. They form mental pictures to help themselves understand ideas and information. Visualizing can help you understand generalizations. Trying to picture in your mind what the author is saying can help you decide whether or not the author's statement is valid.

1. Read "Call It a Day." Make a graphic organizer like the one above to note a generalization the author makes.

2. Does the amount of daylight in your hometown change more or less than it does at the equator? Write the author's generalization that helps you answer this question.

314

Call It a Day

When we say day, we often mean daytime, when it is light out—as opposed to nighttime, when it is dark. Daytime can vary. It depends on where you are and what time of year it is. Along the equator the length of day is always the same—about 12 hours.

North or south of the equator, hours of daylight change throughout the year. In general, the farther north or south you are, the greater the change. The longest "day" of the year in the Northern Hemisphere is usually June 21. On that day, New York has about 13 hours of daylight. The North Pole has 24!

Of course, 24 hours is another meaning of day. Daytime and nighttime together make up one day. We have day and night because of the Earth's spin, or rotation.

The Earth orbits around the sun. It also spins on its axis at a tilted angle. It takes about 24 hours for the Earth to spin around once. As it spins, the side of the Earth that is facing the sun has day. The side that is facing away from the sun has night. And for the half of the year that the Northern Hemisphere tilts toward the sun, daylight there is longer than darkness.

Skill Look for a generalization in this paragraph. The word *often* is a clue word.

Skill Look for two generalizations in this paragraph. Clue words signal them.

Strategy If you visualize traveling north and daylight changing more and more, you will better understand this generalization.

Strategy What could you visualize at this point to help you understand?

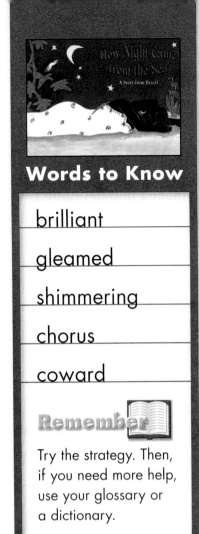

Words to Know

brilliant

gleamed

shimmering

chorus

coward

Remember

Try the strategy. Then, if you need more help, use your glossary or a dictionary.

Vocabulary Strategy
for Unfamiliar Words

Context Clues Sometimes when you are reading, you may come to a word you do not know. The context—the words and sentences around the unknown word—may give you clues to the word's meaning.

1. Read the words and sentences around the unknown word. The author may have included a definition, synonym, or other clue to the word's meaning.

2. If not, say what the sentence means in your own words.

3. Predict a meaning for the unknown word.

4. Try that meaning in the sentence. Does it make sense?

As you read "At the Edge of the Sea," look for context clues that can help you figure out the meanings of the vocabulary words.

At the Edge of the Sea

The two boys hesitated at the edge of the forest. They looked out at the sea. Waves caught the morning sun and sparkled in a thousand points like brilliant jewels. The white sand gleamed as though some servant of the wind had been polishing it all night. The boys knew it would soon be too hot to tread.

Still, they stood gazing out. The scene was like a painting. Its colors were bright and already shimmering with heat. Other than the waves and a few sea birds, nothing moved. It was all too radiant.

Perhaps it also did not seem real because a great journey lay ahead of them. They hoped for some omen of good luck.

At their backs, a chorus of birds began their songs. "May your travels be safe," they seemed to chant. "May your hearts be true and brave. May you never know the shame of the coward. Firm in your purpose, may you find what you seek."

The boys smiled then. They shifted the canoe on their shoulders and stepped forward onto the white sand.

Write

Imagine you are on the coast of a tropical sea. Write a letter home describing the sea and the coast. Use words from the Words to Know list.

Pourquoi tales are stories that explain how things in nature came to be. Think about how you would explain the cycle of day and night as you read this story.

How Night Came from the Sea

A Story from Brazil

retold by Mary-Joan Gerson
illustrated by Carla Golembe

Why do we have day—*and* night?

Long, long ago, at the very beginning of time, when the world had just been made, there was no night. It was always daytime.

No one had ever heard of sunrise or sunset, starlight or moonbeams. There were no night creatures such as owls and tigers, and no night flowers that secretly open their petals at dusk. There was no soft night air, heavy with perfume. Sunlight always filled the sky. The light jumped from the coconuts at the top of the palm trees, and it gleamed from the backs of the alligators wading at the edge of the sea. Everywhere there was only sunlight and brightness and heat.

In that time, the great African goddess Iemanjá dwelt in the depths of the sea. And Iemanjá had a daughter who decided to marry one of the sons of the earth people. With sorrow and with longing, the daughter left her home in the deep ocean and came to live with her husband in the land of daylight.

Iemanjá's daughter loved her husband, and she loved the magic of daylight that he showed her: the shimmering sand of the beach, the rows and rows of cocoa and sugarcane baking in sunlight, and the sparkling jewels and feathered costumes worn in harvest festivals.

But with time, the light became too bright and hard for
Iemanjá's daughter. The sight of the workers bent over in the
fields day after day hurt her eyes and her heart.

And finally even the brilliant colors worn by the dancers
at the festivals burned through her drooping lids.

"Oh, how I wish night would come," she cried. "Here
there is always daylight, but in my mother's kingdom there
are cool shadows and dark, quiet corners."

Her husband listened to her with great sorrow, for he
loved her. "What is this night?" he asked her. "Tell me about
it, and perhaps I can find a little of it for you."

"Night," she said, "is like the quiet after crying or the end of the storm. It is a dark, cool blanket that covers everything. If only we could have a little of the darkness of my mother's kingdom to rest our eyes some of the time."

Her husband called at once his three most faithful servants. "I am sending you on a very important journey," he told them. "You are to go to the kingdom of Iemanjá, who dwells in the depths of the seas. You must beg her to give you some of the darkness of night so that my wife will stop longing to return to her mother's kingdom and will be able to find happiness on land with me."

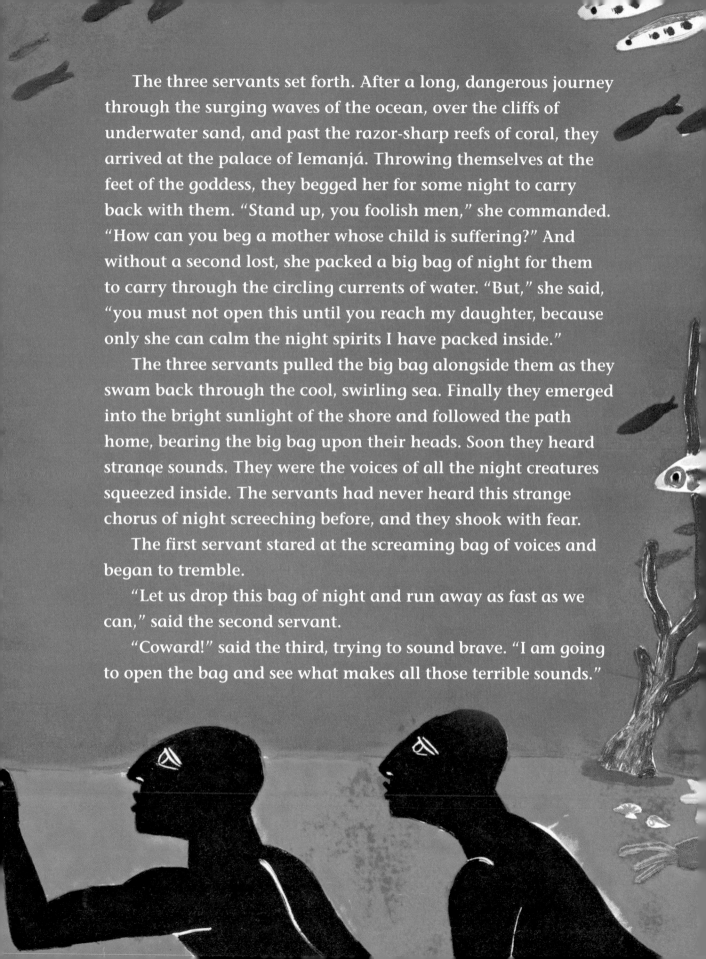

The three servants set forth. After a long, dangerous journey through the surging waves of the ocean, over the cliffs of underwater sand, and past the razor-sharp reefs of coral, they arrived at the palace of Iemanjá. Throwing themselves at the feet of the goddess, they begged her for some night to carry back with them. "Stand up, you foolish men," she commanded. "How can you beg a mother whose child is suffering?" And without a second lost, she packed a big bag of night for them to carry through the circling currents of water. "But," she said, "you must not open this until you reach my daughter, because only she can calm the night spirits I have packed inside."

The three servants pulled the big bag alongside them as they swam back through the cool, swirling sea. Finally they emerged into the bright sunlight of the shore and followed the path home, bearing the big bag upon their heads. Soon they heard strange sounds. They were the voices of all the night creatures squeezed inside. The servants had never heard this strange chorus of night screeching before, and they shook with fear.

The first servant stared at the screaming bag of voices and began to tremble.

"Let us drop this bag of night and run away as fast as we can," said the second servant.

"Coward!" said the third, trying to sound brave. "I am going to open the bag and see what makes all those terrible sounds."

He laid the bag on the ground and opened its sealing wax with his teeth. **Out rushed** the **night beasts,** the **night birds,** and all the **night insects. Out jumped** the **stars** and the **moon.** The servants ran terrified into the jungle.

But the servants were in luck, because Iemanjá's daughter
was standing at the shore, waiting and waiting for their return.
Ever since they had set out on their journey, she had stood in
one spot under a palm tree at the edge of the sea, shading her
eyes with her hand and praying for the darkness. And she was
still standing in that spot when the servants let night escape.

"Night has come. Night has come at last," she cried
as she saw the blue-black shadows gather on the horizon.
"I greet you, my kinship spirits." And when she spoke, the
night spirits were suddenly calmed, and there was hushed
darkness everywhere.

Then the gentle hum of the night creatures began, and moonbeams flickered across the sky. The creatures of the night appeared before her: the owl hunting by moonlight and the tiger finding its way through the forest by smelling the dark, damp earth. The soft air grew heavy with the smell of night perfume. To Iemanjá's daughter, this coming of night was indeed like the quiet after crying or the end of the storm. It was like a dark, cool blanket covering everything, and just as if a soft hand had soothed her tired eyes, Iemanjá's daughter fell fast asleep.

She awoke feeling as if she were about to sing. How rested she was after the coolness of her night dreams! Her eyes opened wide to the brightness of the glistening day, and in her heart she knew she would find peace in her husband's land. And so to celebrate the beauty of her new home, Iemanjá's daughter made three gifts.

To the last bright star still shining above the palm tree she said, "Glittering star, from now on you will be our sign that night is passing. You shall be called the morning star, and you will announce the birth of each day."

To the rooster standing by her, she said, "You shall be the watchman of the night. From this day on, your voice will warn us that the light is coming."

And to the birds all about her she called, "You singing birds, you shall sing your sweetest songs at this hour to announce the dawn of each day."

To this day, the gifts of Iemanjá's daughter help celebrate each new sunrise. In Brazil the early morning is called the madragada. As the madragada slides onto the horizon, the morning star reigns in the sky as queen of the dawn. The rooster announces the day's approach to the sleeping birds, and then they sing their most beautiful songs.

And it is also true that in Brazil night leaps out quickly like a bullfrog just as it leapt quickly out of the bag in the beginning of time. The night flowers suddenly open their petals at dusk. And as they do, the owl and tiger begin their hunt for food.

The beasts and birds and insects of the night begin to sing their gentle chorus. And when the dark, cool blanket of night covers everything, the people of the earth take their rest.

Reader Response

Open for Discussion As often happens, the three servants did not obey Iemanja's command. What resulted? Think of other stories in which a command is not obeyed. What happened?

1. A well-told story is like a play—it has action, dialogue, and setting. How is this telling of *How Night Came from the Sea* like a play?

2. What generalization could you make about the story or the characters in it? What examples lead to that generalization?

3. After the servants let night escape, they run "terrified into the jungle." What might the jungle at night be like? Describe what the servants might see, hear, smell, and feel.

4. Iemanja's daughter tells us what night means to her. Write your own "ode to night." Tell why it is important to you. Use words from the Words to Know list and the story.

Test Practice

Look Back and Write Page 330 of this story explains how three things came to be. Write what they are and why they are there at the end of the night.

Meet the Author and the Illustrator
Mary-Joan Gerson and Carla Golembe

Read more books by Mary-Joan Gerson and Carla Golembe.

Mary-Joan Gerson became interested in writing books for children when she and her husband were in Nigeria serving with the Peace Corps. After she returned to the United States, she wanted to write books so that American children could learn about Africa.

Ms. Gerson travels to learn about cultures. *How Night Came from the Sea* grew out of a trip she made to Brazil, where she went to experience the Yoruba culture. The tale shows the importance of women in Yoruba religion. In addition to her work as a writer, Ms. Gerson is a psychologist and on the faculty at New York University.

Carla Golembe is an artist, writer, and teacher. Her paintings have been displayed in art galleries. Of her art she says, "My paintings are the product of my dreams and experiences." Ms. Golembe loves to travel to warm places. When she paints jungles or oceans, she thinks of her experiences in Mexico, Belize, and Hawaii. She likes to use tropical colors in her illustrations.

People of Corn: A Mayan Story

Why the Sky Is Far Away: A Folktale from Nigeria

333

Pourquoi Tale

Genre

- Pourquoi tales explain how things in nature came to be.

- Often they are handed down from parents to children until they are finally written down.

Text Features

- This pourquoi tale is a legend told by Chief Lelooska.

- Look for italicized words in the story. These words are Kwakiutl, the language spoken by Chief Lelooska and the Kwakiutl Indians.

Link to Social Studies

Many Native American groups continue the tradition of storytelling. Do research in the library or on the Internet to find out more about Native American legends. Summarize one to share with your classmates.

THE ANT AND THE BEAR

from SPIRIT OF THE CEDAR PEOPLE

MORE STORIES AND PAINTINGS OF CHIEF LELOOSKA

 Visualize What senses will help you visualize?

Into the newly created world came Whone, the Changer. It was he who set the world right. Whone piled up earth and made the mountains. He planted trees on the hills and in the valleys. He planted all the edible roots that we now use for food. Then Whone took a stick and dug the rivers, and he called the salmon forth from the sea to feed the children of men.

After Whone had grown weary of all his good work, he called upon the animal people to help him make rules for the new world. One of the most important decisions was the proper length for the daylight and the dark. For in that time the daylight came and went as it pleased. A day might last a whole season or be as quick as a blink of the eye. Clearly something needed to be done, so Whone chose Ant and Bear for the task.

Bear was big and fat and lazy. He yawned, scratched himself, and looked down at the tiny Ant, the little Sky Yack, and said in a deep, gruff voice, "I am Chetwin! I am the Bear! I think half the year should be dark and half of it light. Then we bears could sleep for half the year and eat for the other half."

Ant was a scrawny little fellow, and he had a habit of tugging nervously at his belt when he talked. But Ant was also proud and stubborn. He was not about to let Bear decide anything for him. Ant pulled himself up as tall as he could and shouted up to the great Bear, "No, no! Never do! Never do! Never do! We must have *kai tacheelah, kai tacheelah, chowow, chaloose!* We must have daylight and dark, daylight and dark, every day!"

Bear, who was used to having his own way, leaned down and stared in Ant's face. "*Yo yoks! Sky ta che!*" he growled. "Half of the year dark and half of it light!"

And so the argument went on. Ant began to jump up and down in excitement, all the while yanking nervously at his belt and squeaking at the top of his voice, "Daylight and dark! Daylight and dark! Every day!"

Bear became very angry. He roared louder and louder, "Half the year dark and half of it light!"

On and on they shouted. How long they argued no one knows because there was no proper length for the daylight and the dark.

At last Bear grew weary. "All right, Ant, have it your way," he said. "Daylight and dark every day. But we bears will have it our way too! We will go into the mountains and sleep for half the year. Then we will wake up and eat."

Bear began to lumber away. Then he turned back to Ant. "And do you know what we will eat, Ant?" asked Bear with a big grin. "We will eat you! And all your relatives! We will tear open the old rotten logs and find you and eat you!"

"No, no, you will not," cried Ant. "We will grow wings and fly away!"

And so little Ant won the argument. There would be daylight and dark every day. Ant was pleased with himself, but then he looked down at his waist. In his excitement and all that yanking on his belt, Ant had cinched himself up so tight that he was almost cut in two. Ant had paid an awful price for his victory. He was left with the little skinny waist that all ants have to this very day.

We know this story must be true because ants do have tiny waists; they do grow wings and fly out of old rotten logs in the late summer; and bears do rumble off into the mountains and sleep for half the year. Most of all, we know it is true because we have daylight and dark every single day!

Reading Across Texts

Both *How Night Came from the Sea* and "The Ant and the Bear" are pourquoi tales that explain the cycle of day and night. Summarize each explanation.

Writing Across Texts

Which explanation of day and night do you like better? Write a paragraph that tells why you chose the one you did.

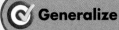 **Generalize**   Which characteristic of this one ant is generalized to all ants?

Comprehension

Skill
Graphic Sources

Strategy
Predict

Graphic Sources

- A graphic source shows or explains information in the text. Pictures, maps, charts, time lines, and diagrams are all examples of graphic sources.

- As you read, use graphic sources to help you understand information. Compare information in the text with information in the graphic sources.

Strategy: Predict

Good readers predict. They think about what will happen next. Before you read an article, try to predict what it will be about. (If there's a graphic source, be sure to look at it to help you predict.) As you read, think about what will come next. Patterns in the information in a graph or chart can help you predict too.

1. Read "Name That Hurricane." Explain in your own words how scientists in the year 2007 would use the list of names.

2. Create your own list of hurricane names. Use the same pattern as the list of names in the article.

NAME THAT HURRICANE

A hurricane is a huge storm with powerful winds that forms over the ocean and sometimes hits land. Weather scientists, or meteorologists, track these storms and warn people. To help communicate about hurricanes, meteorologists name them.

Hurricane names are taken from a list on a six-year cycle. In other words, every six years the same names are used. Not all the names are needed in any given year. It depends on the number of hurricanes that year.

Some hurricanes have been so destructive that their names have been "retired." For example, there will never be another Hurricane Andrew. This monster storm slammed into the Bahamas, Florida, and Louisiana in 1992, killing 54 people and causing billions of dollars in damage.

Strategy Look at the title and the graphic before you start reading. What do you predict this article will be about?

Skill Look at the title of the list. What is the next year after 2007 that the names on the list will be used?

Strategy Is it more likely that there will be a Hurricane Barry or a Hurricane Tanya? Explain your prediction.

Skill Look closely at this list. What can you tell about the order of the names in general and the order of the boy-girl names in particular?

Atlantic Ocean Hurricane Names for the Year 2007

1. Andrea
2. Barry
3. Chantal
4. Dean
5. Erin
6. Felix
7. Gabrielle
8. Humberto
9. Ingrid
10. Jerry
11. Karen
12. Lorenzo
13. Melissa
14. Noel
15. Olgar
16. Pablo
17. Rebekah
18. Sebastien
19. Tanya
20. Van
21. Wendy

Eye of the Storm

destruction

shatter

surge

inland

forecasts

expected

Remember

Try the strategy. Then, if you need more help, use your glossary or a dictionary.

Vocabulary Strategy
for Endings

Word Structure When you read, you may come across a word you don't know. Look at the end of the word. Does it have *-s* or *-ed*? You may be able to use the ending to help you figure out the meaning of the word. The ending *-s* is added to a noun to make it plural, or mean more than one. The ending *-ed* is added to a verb to make it past tense, or tell about past actions.

1. Put your finger over the *-s* or *-ed* ending.

2. Look at the base word. (That's the word without the ending.) Do you know what the base word means?

3. Try your meaning in the sentence. Does it make sense?

As you read "Hurricanes," look for words that have an *-s* or *-ed* ending. Use the ending to help you figure out the meanings of the words.

HURRICANES

A hurricane is a large storm with high winds and heavy rain. It needs heat and moisture to form, so the best hurricane-producing place is the warm tropical ocean. As warm, moist air rises, cooler air moves in. Then the air begins to spin. The winds spin around a calm center called the eye. The strongest winds are around the eye. They may be 200 miles per hour. A hurricane's winds may extend out 250 miles from the eye.

If a hurricane stays over water, it keeps pulling heat and moisture from the ocean. But it begins to lose its power as it reaches land, where the air is cooler and drier. Once it moves over land, it becomes weak very quickly.

The destruction from a hurricane comes from both wind and water. High winds shatter windows and uproot trees. Besides bringing heavy rain, a hurricane can cause a storm surge as winds push ocean water to areas far inland.

Meteorologists watch for and track hurricanes. They issue forecasts telling when a hurricane is expected to arrive so that people can prepare for the storm.

Write

Have you ever been in a hurricane, tornado, blizzard, flood, or other severe storm? Write about your experience. Use words from the Words to Know list.

Eye of the

by Stephen Kramer
photographs by Warren Faidley

Storm

Chasing Storms with Warren Faidley

Is the middle of a hurricane any place for a photographer?

343

Warren Faidley is a storm chaser. Beginning in April and continuing through November, he can be found on the trail of tornadoes, thunderstorms, and hurricanes, photographing their spectacular beauty and power. When he is not out chasing storms, Warren is at home in Tucson, Arizona, where he sells his photographs through his business, a stock photo agency.

Storm Seasons and Chasing

Storms are caused by certain kinds of weather patterns. The same patterns are found in the same areas year after year. For example, every spring, large areas of cool, dry air and warm, moist air collide over the central United States. If the winds are right, tornado-producing thunderstorms appear. That's why tornadoes in the south central United States are most likely to happen in spring. During July and August, shifting winds push moisture from the south up into the Arizona desert. When the cool, moist air is heated by the hot desert, storm clouds form. That's why Tucson has summer thunderstorms. In the late summer and early fall, when oceans in the northern Atlantic are warmest, tropical storms form off the west coast of Africa. A few of these turn into the hurricanes that sometimes batter the east and gulf coasts of North America.

April	May	June	July	August	September	October	November
Tornadoes		Thunderstorms			Hurricanes		

Because Warren is a storm chaser, his life also follows these weather patterns. Each spring, Warren goes on the road, traveling through parts of the United States likely to be hit by tornadoes. During the summer, he stays near Tucson so he can photograph the thunderstorms that develop over the desert. In the late summer and fall, he keeps an eye on weather activity in the Atlantic Ocean, ready to fly to the east coast if a hurricane appears.

Chasing Hurricanes

By the first or second week in September, Tucson's summer thunderstorms are ending. There won't be much lightning until the next summer. But that works out well for Warren, because August through November are months when hurricanes sometimes strike the east and gulf coasts of the United States.

Although Tucson is far from the areas where hurricanes hit, Warren begins his hurricane chases from home. He uses his computer to get information on tropical storms or hurricanes moving toward North America.

"I can't go out and look for a hurricane, or watch one develop, like I can with tornadoes and lightning," says Warren. "When a hurricane is forming, I look at satellite pictures, I listen to weather forecasters talk about it, and I pay attention to what scientists and meteorologists think the hurricane is going to do. Hurricane paths are very hard to predict. Often a hurricane will roar right up to the coast and then stop and go away. So I want to be sure that I'm going to have a storm to photograph before I travel all the way to the east coast!"

When weather forecasters predict that a hurricane will strike the eastern United States, Warren flies to a city near the place the storm is expected to arrive. Flying is faster than driving Shadow Chaser* all the way from Tucson. Besides, a vehicle would not be safe during a hurricane. Branches, boards, and other loose materials carried by hurricane winds quickly shatter windows and damage any cars left outside.

*Shadow Chaser is Warren's specially equipped four-wheel-drive vehicle.

"Hurricanes are the only type of storm where I'm shooting destruction in progress. With tornadoes, you're not usually close enough to shoot the destruction—if you are, you're in a very dangerous place! With hurricanes I'm shooting palm trees bending until they're ready to break and floodwaters splashing over the bank. Those kinds of shots really separate hurricane photos from the others. Most of my hurricane photos are wind shots with heavy rains.

"Finding a place to stay safe while I take hurricane photos is also a challenge. I like to find a solid garage. A good concrete garage is going to be able to withstand the high winds. Another danger with hurricanes is that the powerful winds can lift the seawater and carry it a long ways inland. This is called a storm surge, and it's like a flood from the ocean. When you're picking a spot to stay during the hurricane, you need to have some idea of how high the storm surge might be and how far inland it will go."

Hurricane Andrew

On Saturday, August 22, 1992, after a seven-hour flight from Tucson, Warren arrived in Miami, Florida. He had arranged to meet Mike Laca and Steve Wachholder, two other experienced hurricane chasers. Hurricane Andrew was expected to hit the Florida coast in two days, so Mike, Steve, and Warren had agreed to work together to predict where the storm was going to hit, scout out a safe place to stay, and photograph the storm.

When Warren arrived, the three compared notes. They knew, from weather reports and bulletins from the National Hurricane Center, that Andrew had the potential to become a very dangerous storm. The hurricane was about 520 miles from Miami. It was heading in their direction at about 14 miles per hour. The storm had sustained wind speeds of 110 miles per hour, and they were expected to increase. Warren, Mike, and Steve agreed to get a good night's sleep and meet at noon the next day to go over the latest forecasts. When they had a better idea of where the storm would hit, they could start looking for a safe place to stay.

Mike and Warren found a sturdy, seven-story parking garage in an area called Coconut Grove. It was built with thick concrete walls and looked like a fortress, but the outside walls also had large square openings that could be used for taking pictures. Fort Andrew, as Warren began calling the building, was located on a slight hill, which would help protect it from the storm surge.

Warren, Mike, and Steve find shelter in a seven-story parking garage.

Steve, Mike, and Warren set up a "command center" on the fifth floor of the garage. They stockpiled food, water, rope, and waterproof bags as well as their photography equipment. The three took turns monitoring the latest updates on TV and radios.

As the sun set, Warren and his friends waited anxiously. By 11:00 P.M., there was still no sign of the storm. They began to wonder whether the hurricane had changed direction. But reports on the TV and radio kept saying that Andrew was still headed straight for land—and its strongest winds were expected to hit the area where Warren, Steve, and Mike were staying.

About 2:30 A.M., Hurricane Andrew finally arrived. Warren was watching when bright flashes began appearing in the northeast. The lights looked like fireworks. Actually, they were sparks and explosions as the approaching winds knocked down power lines and transformers. Warren will never forget the sounds of that night:

"At first, there was just the noise of sparking electrical lines and trash cans rolling down the street. But as time passed, the wind just kept getting louder and louder and scarier and scarier."

During the next hour, Steve and Warren tried several times to measure the wind speeds with an instrument called an anemometer. Steve held the instrument out an opening in the wall and Warren used his flashlight to read the dial. When the wind reached 65 miles per hour they gave up.

"I can't hold on anymore," Steve called above the howling winds. "It's too dangerous! I can't hold on!" The winds were carrying raindrops sideways through the air.

"Around 3:45 A.M., we began to hear bursts of breaking glass, as the winds became strong enough to blow in windows. Sometimes the crack of breaking glass was followed by a tinkling sound, like wind chimes, as the wind blew the broken glass along the streets. Inside the garage, car alarm sirens wailed as cars were hit by blasts of wind. Later, even the sound of alarms and the crack of breaking glass disappeared in the roar of the hurricane winds."

As the wind wailed in the darkness, Warren wondered how he was ever going to get any pictures. He worried that by the time it became light, the hurricane winds would die down. He worried about missing the chance to see what was going on outside.

About 5:15 A.M., the hurricane winds reached their peak. The parking garage began to shake. Wind slammed into the concrete walls with the force of bombs. Large sprinkler pipes fastened to the ceilings in the garage began to work their way loose. Several pipes collapsed and fell to the floor.

Now the winds were blowing so hard inside the garage that it was impossible to walk even a few feet in areas that weren't blocked by walls. The roar of the wind turned into a sound like the constant blast of jet engines.

Finally, around 6:00 A.M., with the winds still howling, Warren saw the first faint light of the new day. As the sky gradually turned a strange blue color, Steve, Mike, and Warren looked out on a scene of terrible destruction. Broken boats, and parts of boats, had been carried by the storm surge from the marina almost to the garage. A tree that had been torn from the ground during the night had smashed into the side of a parked truck. Although most of the buildings around the garage were still standing, many had been heavily damaged.

When there was finally enough light for his camera, Warren headed outside. Leaning into the strong winds, he carefully made his way toward the marina. At times, gusts of wind knocked him to the ground. Wreckage from boats and buildings was still flying through the air. Warren took pictures of the wind bending the trees near the marina and the broken boats on the shore.

Warren continued walking along the beach, shooting more pictures as the sky turned light. After about an hour, the wind began to quiet and the rain became more gentle. Now Warren began to wade carefully toward the marina, taking more pictures of the wreckage ahead of him. Other people were arriving to look at the damage and to see if their boats had survived.

After a tour of the marina, Warren went back to the beach. It was littered with boat parts, clothing, and dead fish. There was even a photo album opened to a wet page. More and more people arrived to see what remained of their homes or boats.

Warren finally returned to his motel, where he slept for ten hours. The next day, when he drove back to the Miami airport, his camera bags were filled with rolls of exposed film. His arm ached where the wind had slammed him into a railing after he left the parking garage. Still, as the airplane took off from Miami, it was hard for Warren to imagine that two nights earlier he had been watching, listening to, and photographing the destructive winds of Hurricane Andrew.

Reader Response

Open for Discussion When is it wise to chase a storm? When is it foolish? If you went storm chasing with Warren Faidley, would you be wise or foolish? Explain.

1. Were you surprised that the hurricane got inside a thick concrete building? How did the author use details to show you the force of that invasion?

2. The selection's photos, captions, and diagram are graphic sources. What kind of information do they provide that the text cannot? How do these features add to your understanding of the selection?

3. Do you think Warren Faidley will continue to chase storms? Why do you think this?

4. Make a chart labeled "Sights and Sounds of Hurricane Andrew." Write words and phrases from the Words to Know list and the selection that fit into each category.

Look Back and Write To photograph a hurricane, Warren Faidley needs a safe place to stay. What does he look for in a shelter? Look back at page 347 for information to write your answer.

Hurricanes

Read more books by Stephen Kramer.

When Stephen Kramer interviewed Warren Faidley for this book, he was impressed by Warren's enthusiasm. "Warren loves the excitement of trying to be in the right place at the right time to capture the perfect photo of a storm. I also learned about Warren's respect for the danger of lightning, tornadoes, and hurricanes. Warren knows how to stay safe in dangerous weather."

About himself, Mr. Kramer says, "I've been picking up leaves, looking at flowers, and learning about animals for as long as I can remember." Mr. Kramer studied biology in college. While attending graduate school in Arizona, he did research on the songs of a bird called the Townsend's Solitaire. Now he teaches fourth grade near Vancouver, Washington. "I write science books because I love science and want to share my excitement with young readers," he says. "Science helps us uncover the beauty and wonder of nature. I also hope that my books might inspire some of my readers to become scientists!"

Caves

Hidden Worlds: Looking Through a Scientist's Microscope

Reading Online

Severe Weather Safety

Web Site

Genre

- Web pages are found on Internet Web sites.

- A Web site is created and maintained by a person called a Web master.

Text Features

- Every Web site has a home page. The home page is like the table of contents in a book. You can move around a Web site by clicking on links on the home page.

- Links are buttons or words that are printed in a different color or underlined. When you click on one, your computer opens a new Web page that contains the information indicated by the link.

Link to Science

Research a topic related to severe weather. Share your results with the class.

After reading *Eye of the Storm*, Natalia wants to know more about storm safety. Where she lives, in northern Illinois, thunderstorms are frequent during the spring and summer. What should she do if she is caught outside during a thunderstorm, she wonders. And if she is inside during a storm, are there any things she shouldn't do?

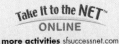

Take It to the NET
ONLINE
more activities sfsuccessnet.com

Natalia decides to search for information on the Internet. Her search takes her to the Web site of a regional weather service office.

File   Edit   View   Favorites   Tools   Help

http://www.url.here

Regional Weather Service Office

Staying Safe in Severe Weather

Contents

Tornado Safety

Flash Flood Safety

Lightning Safety

Winter Storm/Blizzard Preparedness and Safety

Hurricane Safety

Other Severe Weather Safety Links

Natalia clicks on a series of links that takes her to a Web page about severe weather safety. After skimming the contents of the page, she decides to click on the Lightning Safety link.

In the United States, lightning causes about 100 deaths each year. This is more than tornadoes and hurricanes combined.

 **Graphic Sources**   How can you tell that Flash Flood Safety is a link?

Clicking on the <u>Lightning Safety</u> link opens a new Web page on Natalia's computer screen. As the link indicates, the Web page contains information about lightning safety.

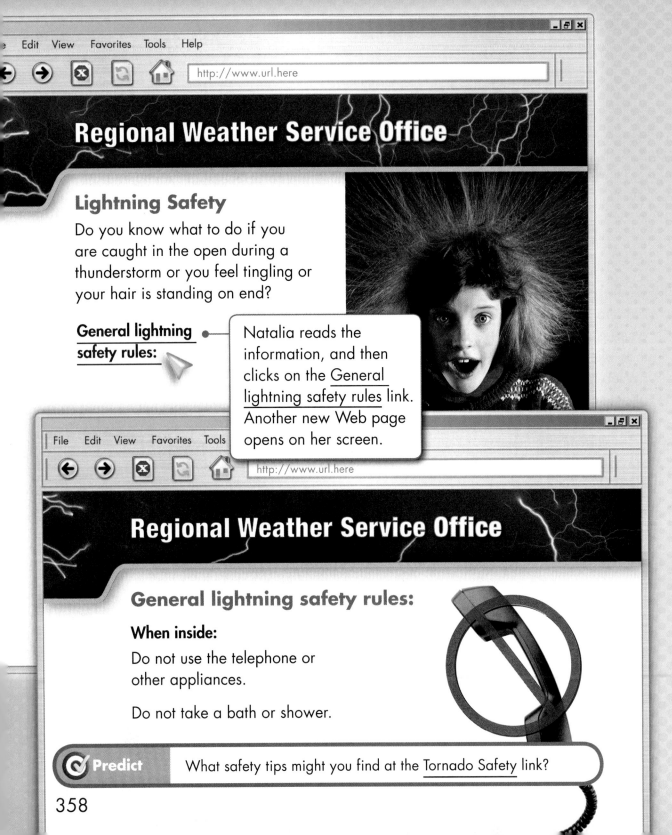

Regional Weather Service Office

Lightning Safety

Do you know what to do if you are caught in the open during a thunderstorm or you feel tingling or your hair is standing on end?

<u>General lightning safety rules:</u>

Natalia reads the information, and then clicks on the <u>General lightning safety rules</u> link. Another new Web page opens on her screen.

Regional Weather Service Office

General lightning safety rules:

When inside:

Do not use the telephone or other appliances.

Do not take a bath or shower.

Predict What safety tips might you find at the <u>Tornado Safety</u> link?

358

Regional Weather Service Office

When outside:

Go to a safe place right away, such as inside a strong building. A hard-top automobile with the windows up can also offer fair protection.

If you are boating or swimming, get out of the water right away and move to a safe place away from the water!

If you are in a wooded area, take cover under a thick growth of relatively small trees.

If you feel your hair standing on end, squat with your head between your knees. **Do not lie flat!**

Stay away from: isolated trees or other tall objects, bodies of water, sheds, fences, convertible automobiles, tractors, and motorcycles.

If you are outside and your hair stands on end, squat with your head between your knees.

Reading Across Texts

Both hurricanes and tornadoes produce lightning. Compare the lightning safety tips with how Warren, Steve, and Mike faced lightning in *Eye of the Storm.*

Writing Across Texts Use both selections to prepare a "Lightning Dos and Don'ts List."

Comprehension

Skill
Generalize

Strategy
Story Structure

Skill

Generalize

- A generalization is a broad statement based on several examples.

- A generalization can be valid (logical) or faulty (wrong) depending on the number of examples on which it is based and on how logical and careful the thinking is.

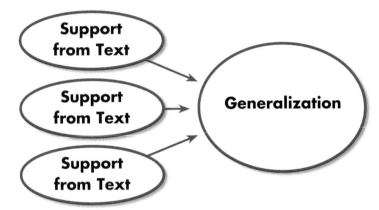

Support from Text → Generalization

Support from Text → Generalization

Support from Text → Generalization

Strategy

Strategy: Story Structure

Good readers pay attention to story structure—how a fictional story is put together. As you read, notice how the story begins (the problem), how it builds through the middle (rising action and climax), and how it ends (resolution). You can generalize about characters to help you make predictions.

Write

1. Read "The Biggest Snake in the World." Make a graphic organizer to show how a character generalized.

2. Is the generalization by the character you chose valid or faulty? Write your explanation.

The Biggest Snake in the World

Max the python was big for his age, and he never stopped bragging about it. "Look at all my short friends! I'm the biggest snake in the meadow! I'm the biggest snake in the *world!*"

So one day his grandfather sent him on an educational trip to South America.

In the rain forest, Max saw a GIANT log about 30 feet long floating down a stream near the Amazon River. Only—it wasn't a log. It was a snake!

"I'm an anaconda," the snake explained. "I'm the biggest snake in the world. I've heard there's some guy crawling around claiming that he's the biggest. Makes me mad, I tell you."

"Do you, um, know who this guy is?" gulped Max.

"Oh, just some python from Southeast Asia," said the anaconda. "Thinks because he's thirty feet long that he's the biggest. But I'm heavier, so it's clear that I'm the biggest. Who does he think he is? Honestly, if there's one thing I CAN'T STAND, it's bragging!"

"Um, right!" said Max. "See ya!"

When Max got home safe and sound, his grandfather said, "Well, my boy. Do you still think you're the biggest snake in the world?"

"No," said Max. "But I just might be the fastest!"

Skill What is Max's generalization? How does he reach it? Is Max's meadow the same as the world?

Strategy Based on the structure of stories, the rising action will bring about several events. What do you predict for Max?

Skill How could this statement be stated as a generalization—a statement that applies to many examples?

Strategy Usually a problem is solved at the end of a story. This is called the resolution. What is the resolution of this story?

361

Words to Know

canopy

dangle

dappled

fragrant

pollen

pollinate

slithered

wondrous

Remember

Try the strategy. Then, if you need more help, use your glossary or a dictionary.

Vocabulary Strategy
for Suffixes

Word Structure Suppose you are reading and you come to a word you don't know. Does the word have *-ous* or *-ate* at the end? You can often use a suffix to help you figure out a word's meaning. The suffix *-ous* can make a word mean "full of ___," as in *joyous*, or "full of joy." The suffix *-ate* can make a word mean "supply or treat with ___," as in *hydrate*, or "supply or treat with water."

1. Look at the unknown word to see if it has a base word you know.

2. Check to see if the suffix *-ous* or *-ate* has been added to the base word.

3. Ask yourself how the suffix changes the meaning of the base word.

4. Try that meaning in the sentence. Does it make sense?

As you read "The Busy Rain Forest," look for words that end with *-ous* or *-ate*. Use the suffixes to help you figure out the meanings of the words.

THE BUSY RAIN FOREST

The rain forest is a world filled with life. From the ground all the way up to the canopy, every square foot is packed with organisms. There are huge trees that tower over everything else, taking in the hot sun. From their branches dangle fat vines. Monkeys and sloths are right at home on these.

In the dappled shade, thousands of kinds of insects buzz. Some are drawn to big, fragrant blossoms. They will tramp in the flowers' pollen as they find their meal. Then they carry it on legs or wings to the next flower.

In this way, insects pollinate the rain forest plants. Both plants and animals win.

Brilliant birds and frogs flash their bright red, blue, yellow, and green colors. They seem to advertise with each flight or leap: Here I am! Other animals are not so easy to see. A dark poisonous snake has slithered across the damp ground. It may be invisible until you are right upon it. A big cat makes its way through the forest in silence. These are just a few of the living things that make their home in the wondrous rain forest.

Write

Write a description of a plant you can observe or look up in a book. Include details about some of the life that goes on around the plant. Use words from the Words to Know list.

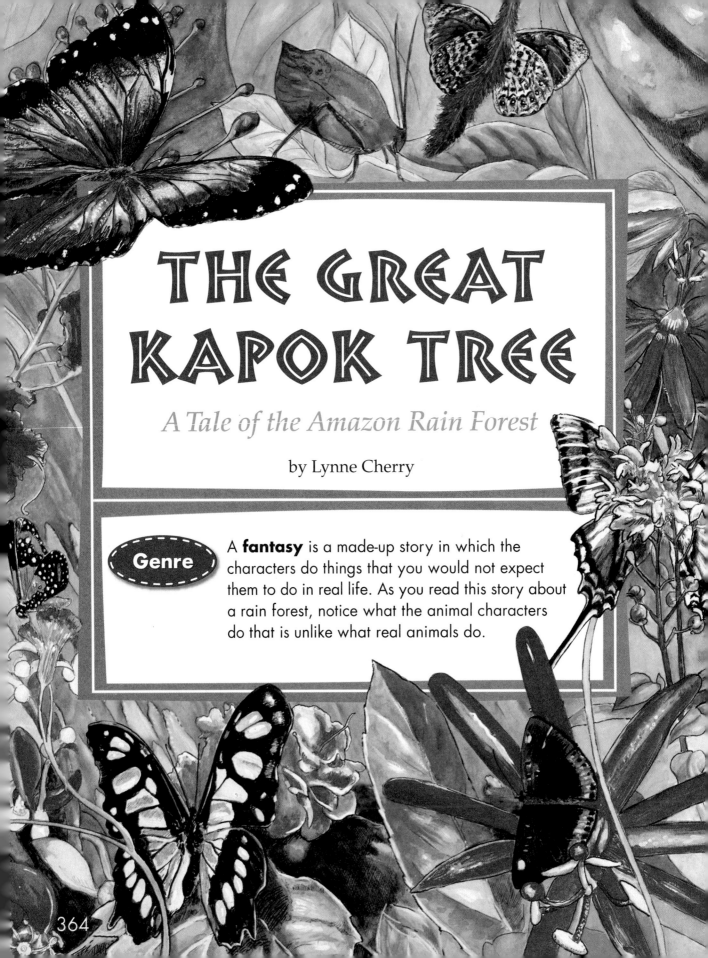

THE GREAT KAPOK TREE

A Tale of the Amazon Rain Forest

by Lynne Cherry

How can one
tree in the
rain forest
be so
important?

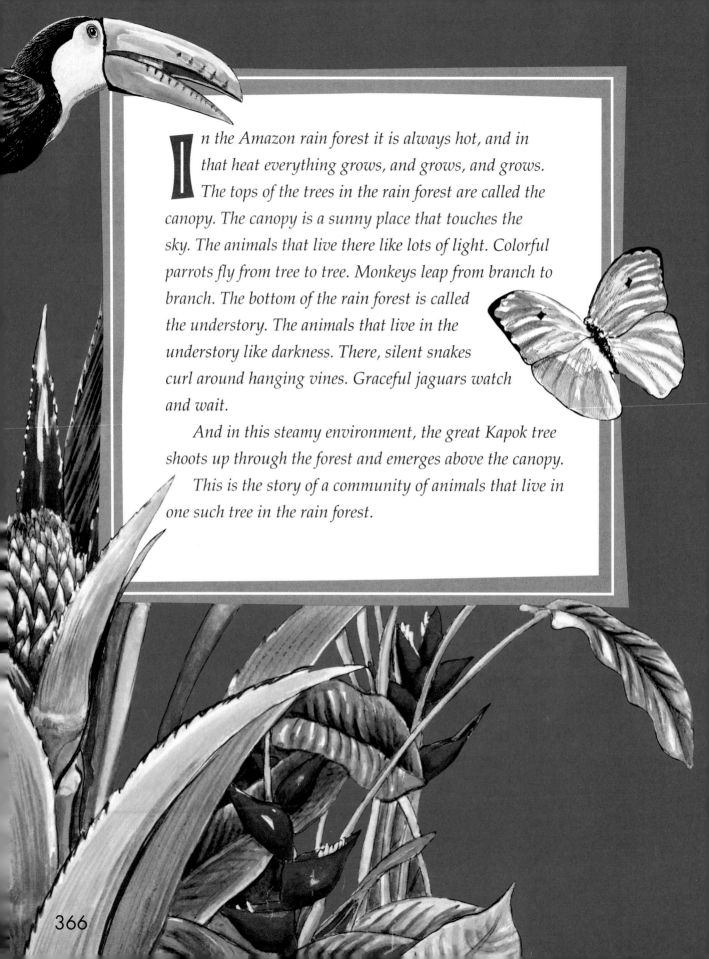

In the Amazon rain forest it is always hot, and in that heat everything grows, and grows, and grows. The tops of the trees in the rain forest are called the canopy. The canopy is a sunny place that touches the sky. The animals that live there like lots of light. Colorful parrots fly from tree to tree. Monkeys leap from branch to branch. The bottom of the rain forest is called the understory. The animals that live in the understory like darkness. There, silent snakes curl around hanging vines. Graceful jaguars watch and wait.

And in this steamy environment, the great Kapok tree shoots up through the forest and emerges above the canopy.

This is the story of a community of animals that live in one such tree in the rain forest.

Two men walked into the rain forest. Moments before, the forest had been alive with the sounds of squawking birds and howling monkeys. Now all was quiet as the creatures watched the two men and wondered why they had come.

The larger man stopped and pointed to a great Kapok tree. Then he left.

The smaller man took the ax he carried and struck the trunk of the tree. Whack! Whack! Whack! The sounds of the blows rang through the forest. The wood of the tree was very hard. Chop! Chop! Chop! The man wiped off the sweat that ran down his face and neck. Whack! Chop! Whack! Chop!

Soon the man grew tired. He sat down to rest at the foot of the great Kapok tree. Before he knew it, the heat and hum of the forest had lulled him to sleep.

A boa constrictor lived in the Kapok tree. He slithered down its trunk to where the man was sleeping. He looked at the gash the ax had made in the tree. Then the huge snake slid very close to the man and hissed in his ear: "Senhor, this tree is a tree of miracles. It is my home, where generations of my ancestors have lived. Do not chop it down."

A bee buzzed in the sleeping man's ear: "Senhor, my hive is in this Kapok tree, and I fly from tree to tree and flower to flower collecting pollen. In this way I pollinate the trees and flowers throughout the rain forest. You see, all living things depend on one another."

A troupe of monkeys scampered down from the canopy of the Kapok tree. They chattered to the sleeping man: "Senhor, we have seen the ways of man. You chop down one tree, then come back for another and another. The roots of these great trees will wither and die, and there will be nothing left to hold the earth in place. When the heavy rains come, the soil will be washed away and the forest will become a desert."

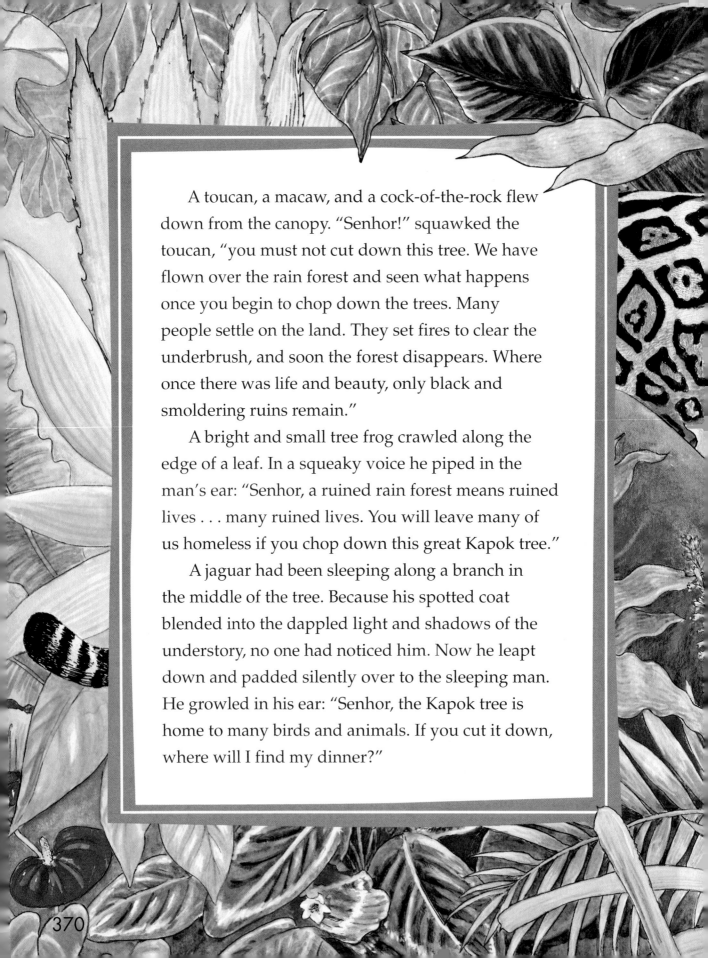

A toucan, a macaw, and a cock-of-the-rock flew down from the canopy. "Senhor!" squawked the toucan, "you must not cut down this tree. We have flown over the rain forest and seen what happens once you begin to chop down the trees. Many people settle on the land. They set fires to clear the underbrush, and soon the forest disappears. Where once there was life and beauty, only black and smoldering ruins remain."

A bright and small tree frog crawled along the edge of a leaf. In a squeaky voice he piped in the man's ear: "Senhor, a ruined rain forest means ruined lives . . . many ruined lives. You will leave many of us homeless if you chop down this great Kapok tree."

A jaguar had been sleeping along a branch in the middle of the tree. Because his spotted coat blended into the dappled light and shadows of the understory, no one had noticed him. Now he leapt down and padded silently over to the sleeping man. He growled in his ear: "Senhor, the Kapok tree is home to many birds and animals. If you cut it down, where will I find my dinner?"

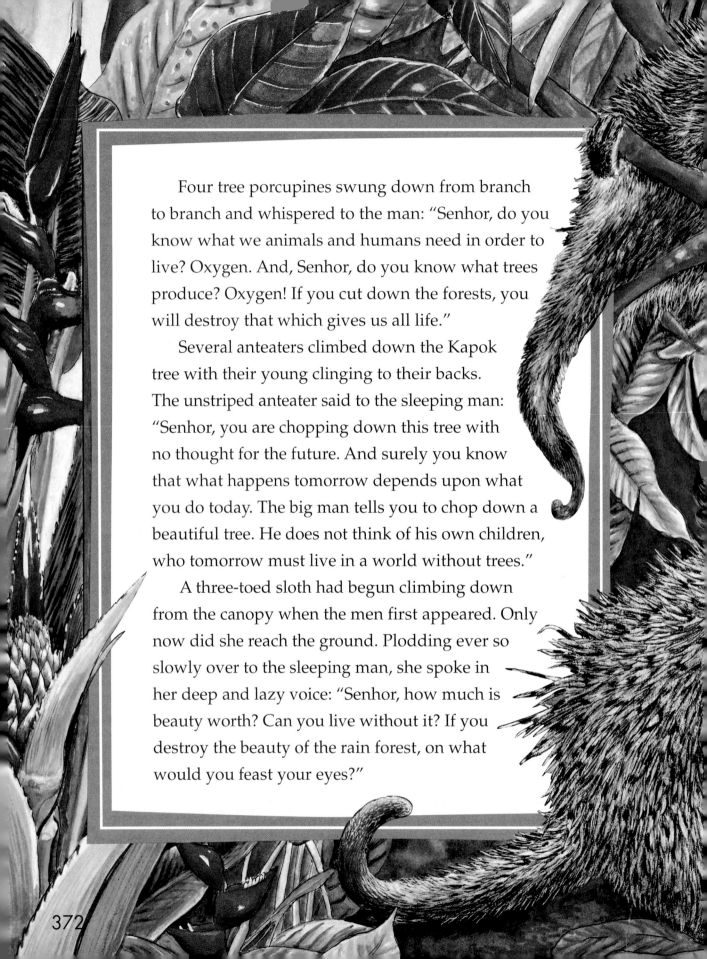

Four tree porcupines swung down from branch to branch and whispered to the man: "Senhor, do you know what we animals and humans need in order to live? Oxygen. And, Senhor, do you know what trees produce? Oxygen! If you cut down the forests, you will destroy that which gives us all life."

Several anteaters climbed down the Kapok tree with their young clinging to their backs. The unstriped anteater said to the sleeping man: "Senhor, you are chopping down this tree with no thought for the future. And surely you know that what happens tomorrow depends upon what you do today. The big man tells you to chop down a beautiful tree. He does not think of his own children, who tomorrow must live in a world without trees."

A three-toed sloth had begun climbing down from the canopy when the men first appeared. Only now did she reach the ground. Plodding ever so slowly over to the sleeping man, she spoke in her deep and lazy voice: "Senhor, how much is beauty worth? Can you live without it? If you destroy the beauty of the rain forest, on what would you feast your eyes?"

372

A child from the Yanomamo tribe who lived in the rain forest knelt over the sleeping man. He murmured in his ear: "Senhor, when you awake, please look upon us all with new eyes."

The man awoke with a start. Before him stood the rain forest child, and all around him, staring, were the creatures who depended upon the great Kapok tree. What wondrous and rare animals they were!

The man looked about and saw the sun streaming through the canopy. Spots of bright light glowed like jewels amidst the dark green forest. Strange and beautiful plants seemed to dangle in the air, suspended from the great Kapok tree.

The man smelled the fragrant perfume of their flowers. He felt the steamy mist rising from the forest floor. But he heard no sound, for the creatures were strangely silent.

The man stood and picked up his ax. He swung back his arm as though to strike the tree. Suddenly he stopped. He turned and looked at the animals and the child.

He hesitated. Then he dropped the ax and walked out of the rain forest.

emerald
tree boa

scarlet
macaw

toucan

Brazilian
tree frog

coati

golden
tanager

tree
frog

three-toed sloth

urania
butterfly

cock-of-
the-rock

tree
porcupine

ARCTIC OCEAN

GREENLAND

NORTH
AMERICA

EUROPE

AFRICA

ATLANTIC
OCEAN

Central
America

CARIBBEAN
SEA

THE
AMAZON RAIN FOREST
Rio Negro   Manaus
AMAZON RIVER

Brazil

Equator

Madagascar

SOUTH
AMERICA

PACIFIC
OCEAN

☐ today's rain forests
☐ original extent of rain forests

Tropical Rain Forests of the World

mother & baby
giant anteater

Vindula
arsinoë
butterfly

baby
hoatzin

poison
arrow
frog

Anteos
menippe
butterfly

376

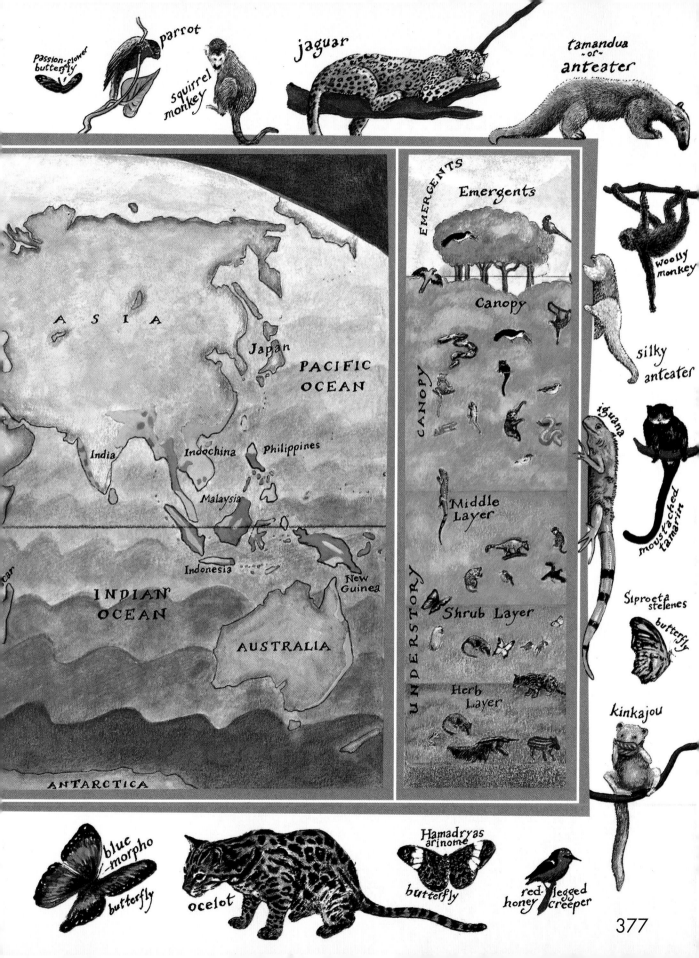

passion-flower butterfly

parrot

squirrel monkey

jaguar

tamandua ~or~ anteater

ASIA

Japan

PACIFIC OCEAN

India

Indochina

Philippines

Malaysia

Indonesia

New Guinea

INDIAN OCEAN

AUSTRALIA

ANTARCTICA

EMERGENTS

Emergents

Canopy

CANOPY

Middle Layer

UNDERSTORY

Shrub Layer

Herb Layer

woolly monkey

silky anteater

iguana

moustached tamarin

Siproeta stelenes butterfly

kinkajou

blue ~morpho~ butterfly

ocelot

Hamadryas arinome butterfly

red-legged honey creeper

377

Reader Response

Open for Discussion If animals can talk in a story, perhaps a tree can talk too. What would the Kapok tree say to the animals, the man, and the child?

1. Authors have a purpose—to make you laugh, to scare you, to surprise you, and so on. What do you think the author's purpose is in *The Great Kapok Tree*? Why do you think this?

2. Look back at the illustrations. Make a generalization about what a rain forest is like.

3. The author introduces a problem in the beginning of the story. What is this problem and how does it affect the events that follow?

4. Think about the messages the animals and the child whisper in the ear of the sleeping man. Write a message of your own to tell the man about saving the rain forest. Use words from the Words to Know list and the story.

Test Practice

Look Back and Write The bee says something important—a lesson or theme for the whole story. Write that part of what the bee says and tell why it is important.

Meet the Author and Illustrator

LYNNE CHERRY

Read more books by Lynne Cherry.

A River Ran Wild

The Armadillo from Amarillo

Lynne Cherry says, "I wrote *The Great Kapok Tree* so that children would know about the threat to the world's rain forests and, hopefully, try to save them." She wrote the draft for the book on a train from Connecticut to Washington, D.C. But she traveled to the Amazon rain forest in Brazil to research the illustrations.

"All my life I've been a nature lover," Ms. Cherry writes in a letter to readers. "When I was a little girl I spent most of my waking hours in the warmer months out in the woods. I brought books to read there. There was peace and quiet, beauty, and the wonderful smells of earth and green, growing things. Natural settings have always provided me with places for my thoughts to wander and my imagination to fly."

Ms. Cherry believes that children can make a difference in a democratic society. She encourages everyone to work for preserving natural resources.

379

Expository Nonfiction

Genre

- Expository nonfiction informs about things that are real.

- Both pictures and words provide information on a particular topic.

Text Features

- Introductory paragraphs name the animals to be described and give a basic definition.

- Subtitles and subheads summarize each section to be read.

- Colorful photographs show the animals described in the text.

- "Did You Know?" boxes provide other interesting facts.

Link to Science

Research other animals that use camouflage to get food or escape danger. Write a paragraph about one of them.

Living in a World of GREEN

Where Survival Means Blending In

by Tanya Lee Stone

What do tree frogs, butterflies, sloths, and emerald tree boas have in common? They all live in a world of green. They make their homes in forests and jungles.

These animals are perfectly suited to their environment. And each relies on camouflage to survive. When something is camouflaged, it blends into its surroundings and is difficult to see. Camouflage helps these animals get food and escape danger. How do they do it?

Tree Frogs
Shades of Green

The green tree frog is an amphibian (an animal that lives both on land and in the water). This tree frog loves forested areas near ponds, lakes, rivers, or marshes. Its beautiful color helps it blend in well in its damp, green environment. The green tree frog can also change color when it needs to. If it is a bright sunny day, the frog's color fades a bit. This helps it absorb less heat and stay cooler. If it is a cloudy day, the frog can darken to soak up more light and heat. It can even fade to a grayish color during the winter to blend in with the duller colors of that season.

Did You Know?

- The green tree frog has large, sticky toe pads that help it cling to plants. It also has long legs for jumping—it can leap up to 10 feet (3 meters)!

- The famous Muppet, Kermit the Frog, is a green tree frog.

Butterflies
Flight and Fright

Butterflies are easy prey for birds, wasps, lizards, and spiders. One of the best ways they avoid danger is to fly away. But some butterflies can't fly very fast. And none can outfly a bird. Butterflies use some of the same camouflage defenses as caterpillars. Some have eyespots that frighten predators away. Others have markings that mimic poisonous or bitter-tasting butterflies. This camouflage helps keep the non-poisonous butterflies safe. And lots of butterflies have coloring that blends into the surroundings. They can be drably colored and hard to tell apart from tree branches or bark.

Did You Know?

The female Queen Alexandra's birdwing butterfly is the largest butterfly in the world. Its wings stretch out more than 12 inches (31 centimeters).

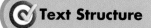 **Text Structure** How does the author's way of organizing the text help you?

Sloths

Hangin' Around

What spends its whole life hanging upside down in a tree? A sloth. Sloths live in rain forests. They hardly move at all. To eat, they slowly reach out and grab nearby leaves and buds. A sloth has sharp claws and will fight an enemy if attacked. But an animal that moves so slowly can't run away from predators, such as jaguars, snakes, and large birds. It needs a different way to stay out of danger. A sloth's natural gray-brown color blends in well with the forest. This camouflage gets an extra boost from greenish algae that grow in a sloth's fur. A sloth sleeps during the day with its head curled up between its front legs. Together, a sloth's coloring, its sleeping position, and the fact that it barely moves, make a sloth look like a stumpy tree branch or a bird nest to predators.

Did You Know?

A sloth only climbs down from its tree once a week. It can take up to an hour for the sloth to reach the ground!

Emerald Tree Boas

Sneaky Snakes

The emerald tree boa is a top-notch hunter. But it doesn't usually go searching for prey. Instead, it curls around a tree branch and waits. Camouflage helps this snake stay hidden so it can make a surprise attack when a lizard, bird, or small mammal is nearby. The beautiful green color of the emerald boa blends in well with the rich green colors of the rain forest. It also has white markings to help camouflage it. These markings break up the snake's body shape, making it even harder to see. The white can also look like sunlight streaming through the forest.

Did You Know?

This large, heavy snake can race through the trees when it wants to go hunting.

Reading Across Texts

Both *The Great Kapok Tree* and this selection are about survival among predators. What kind of predator does each deal with?

Writing Across Texts Tell which predator you think presents the greater danger and why.

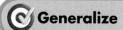 **Generalize** Why can't you generalize that all camouflage is green?

Autumn

by Charlotte Zolotow

Now the summer is grown old
the light long summer
                    is grown old.
Leaves change
and the garden is gold
with marigolds and zinnias
tangled and bold
blazing blazing
orange and gold.
            The light long summer
            is grown old.

Falling Snow

author unknown

See the pretty snowflakes
　　Falling from the sky;
On the walk and housetop
　　Soft and thick they lie.

On the window-ledges
　　On the branches bare;
Now how fast they gather,
　　Filling all the air.

Look into the garden
　　Where the grass was green;
Covered by the snowflakes,
　　Not a blade is seen.

Now the bare black bushes
　　All look soft and white,
Every twig is laden—
　　What a pretty sight!

EARLY SPRING

by Shonto Begay

In the early spring, the snowfall is light
upon the mesa.
It does not stick to the ground very long.
I walk through this patchwork of snow and earth,
watching the ground for early signs.
Signs of growth. Signs of rebirth.

Larkspur and wild onions are still
within the warmth of the earth.
I hear cries of crows off in the distance.
A rabbit bounds off into the sagebrush flat.
A shadow of a hawk disturbs the landscape momentarily.
It sees food and life abundant below that I cannot see.
The cycle of life continues.

Even as I stand here shivering in the afternoon chill,
just below me, young seedlings start
their upward journey.
Insects begin to stir.
Rodents and snakes are comfortable in their burrows.
Maybe to them we also disappear with the cold.
Not to be seen until spring.

For this generation, and many more to come,
this land is beautiful and filled with mysteries.
They reveal themselves and their stories—
if you look carefully, and listen. . . .

Again and Again

connect to
WRITING

Patterns are all around you in nature—in the seasons and in the rhythms of your daily life. Think about how some patterns in nature affect you. Write at least three journal entries as you think about this.

December 5th

Today I saw the first snowflake of the season.

What are some patterns in nature?

Visual Patterns

connect to
ART

Look at the natural environment around you. Where do you see patterns? Let these patterns inspire you as you make a colorful drawing or painting. Share your artwork with others. Tell them about the patterns that inspired you.

The Science Behind the Scenes

connect to
SCIENCE

Think about the repeating events in nature that you read about in this unit, such as the whales that return to Laguna San Ignacio each year. What scientific event is the basis for each selection in this unit? Identify the key event and give a brief scientific explanation of it. Record your ideas in a chart like the one below. Then list several reference sources that could provide more facts about each topic.

	Scientific Event	Explanation	Where to Find More Facts
The Stranger			
Adelina's Whales			
How Night Came			

389

UNIT 4

PUZZLES AND MYSTERIES

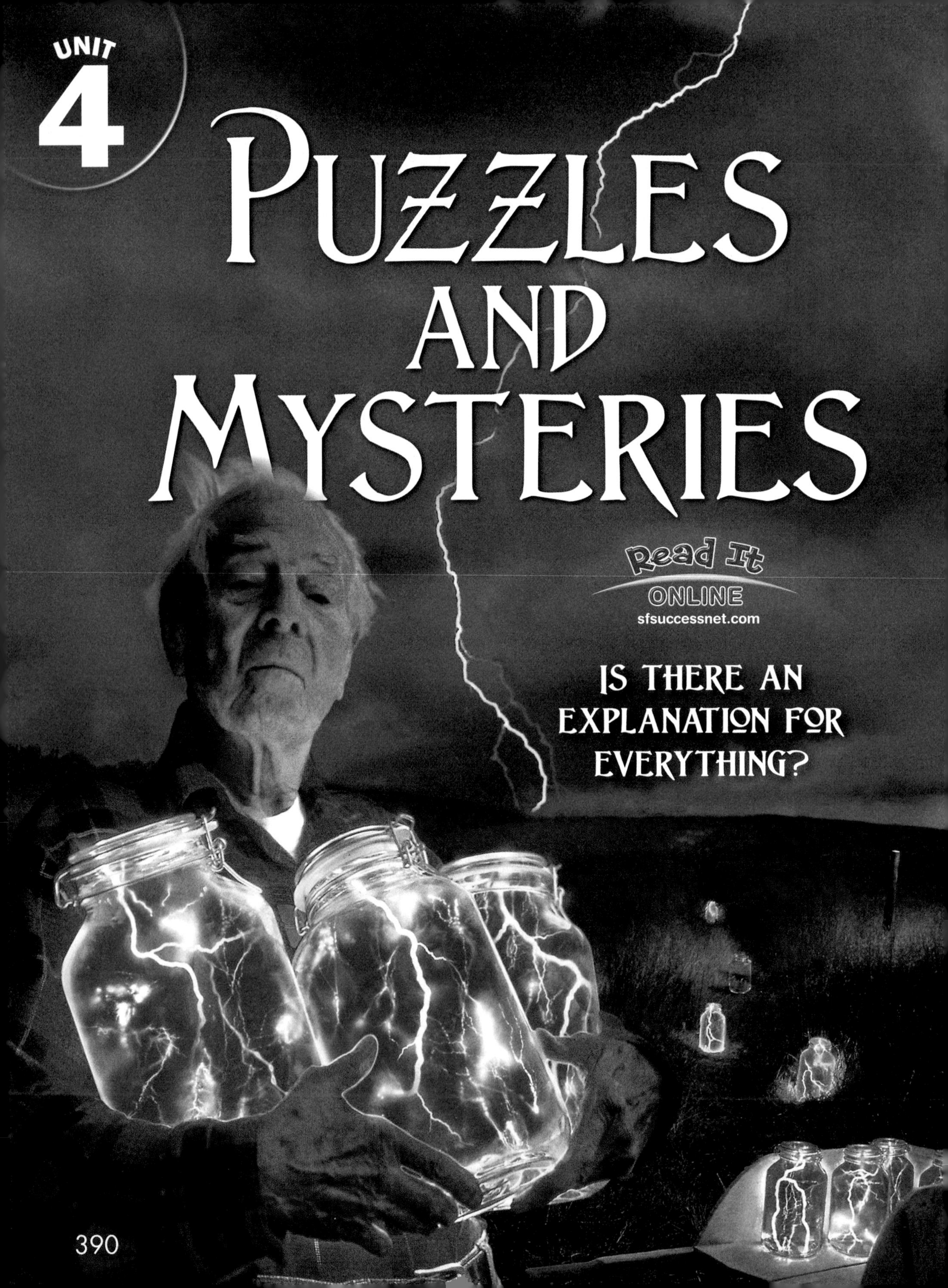

Read It ONLINE
sfsuccessnet.com

IS THERE AN EXPLANATION FOR EVERYTHING?

Comprehension

Skill
Compare and Contrast

Strategy
Predict

Compare and Contrast

- When you compare and contrast, you tell how two or more things are alike and different.

- A chart can help you compare and contrast. You can compare and contrast two things you read about or something you read about with something you already know.

	Alike	Different
Two things in the text		
One thing in the text with something I already know		

Strategy: Predict

Active readers predict. They use what they know as well as what the author tells them to form ideas about what might happen next. When you read, you can also predict how something will be like or unlike something you know about from your own life.

Write

1. Read "How Did He Do That?" Make a chart like the one above to compare and contrast Harry Houdini with the magicians mentioned in the text. If there is a magician you already know about, compare and contrast Houdini with that person.

2. Use your chart to sum up what made Houdini like and unlike other magicians.

How Did He Do That?

One day a boy named Erich read a book about a great magician, Robert Houdin. Erich dreamed of becoming a magician himself. He decided to change his name to Harry Houdini. Harry went on to become the greatest magician of his day.

In Houdini's day, magicians sawed ladies in half. They walked through walls. They made people float in the air. In other words, they were masters of illusion. They made things appear to be real that were not.

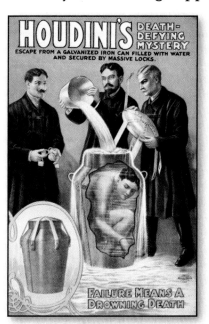

HOUDINI'S DEATH-DEFYING MYSTERY
ESCAPE FROM A GALVANIZED IRON CAN FILLED WITH WATER AND SECURED BY MASSIVE LOCKS.

FAILURE MEANS A DROWNING DEATH

Yet Houdini did do something real, and he did it better than anyone else could. Houdini ESCAPED! He could get free of ropes and handcuffs and straitjackets and locked boxes—you name it!

Thousands came to see Houdini perform. The suspense would be almost too much to bear. Would Houdini get out alive? He always did. How?

Houdini's secret was this. He exercised to become very strong, he became an expert at locks, and he trained himself to keep calm in dangerous situations. How dangerous? Imagine being chained upside-down in a locked tank filled with water!

Strategy Make a prediction. Will this article be about Erich's dream of becoming a magician? What are the clues?

Skill This paragraph describes other magicians of Houdini's day. How are they similar to or different from magicians you know of?

Strategy Do you predict that Houdini performed the same kind of magic as other magicians? Why or why not?

Skill What was different about Houdini's act? Did he do anything like other magicians? Think of magicians you may know about, and complete your graphic organizer.

393

Words to Know

magician
vanished
crumbled
bustling
escape
appeared
monument

Remember

Try the strategy. Then, if you need more help, use your glossary or a dictionary.

Vocabulary Strategy
for Synonyms and Antonyms

Context Clues When you read, you may come across a word you don't know. Sometimes the author will use a synonym or an antonym as a clue to the word's meaning. Synonyms are words that mean almost the same thing. Antonyms are words with opposite meanings.

1. Reread the sentence with the unknown word. Look for a synonym or an antonym of the word. If you find one, try it in the sentence. Does the synonym make sense in the sentence? Does the antonym give the sentence an opposite meaning?

2. If there is not a synonym or an antonym in the same sentence as the unknown word, check the sentences around it. The author may use a synonym or an antonym there. If you find one, try it in the sentence.

3. If you cannot find a synonym or an antonym of the unknown word, think about the context—the meaning of all the sentences together. Decide on a meaning of the word that makes sense in the context.

As you read "A Little Magic," look for synonyms and antonyms to help you understand the meanings of vocabulary words.

A Little Magic

A historian is someone who writes about the past. In some ways, he or she is like a magician. With a wave of the hand, a magician brings back things that have disappeared. In much the same way, the person who writes history calls up people, places, and events that vanished long ago.

A building has crumbled. All that is left are a few columns standing on a hill. The writer of history brings it to life. We can see it as a bustling center of government in Greece thousands of years ago. It is where men meet to discuss and vote on leaders and wars.

A magician may escape from a trunk that has been locked and chained shut. In just a few seconds, he or she is free of the box and has appeared on stage. How is this possible?

A historian may draw us to the monument, or tombstone, of a great leader. In just a few pages, he or she has brought that person to life with words. We understand what made that person unforgettable.

Write

Imagine that your school put on a talent show that featured a magic act. Describe the act. Use as many of the Words to Know as you can.

THE HOUDINI BOX

Genre

Historical fiction has characters and events based on real people and events in history. As you read, look for historical details.

*Will Victor learn
the secrets of Harry
Houdini's tricks?*

BRIAN SELZNICK

 **OUDINI** was a magician. He could pull rabbits from hats, make elephants disappear, and do a thousand card tricks. Locks would fall open at his fingertips, and he could escape from ropes and chains and cabinets and coffins. Police from around the world couldn't keep him in their jails, and the oceans couldn't drown him. Bolt Houdini into a metal box and throw him in the water; he will escape. Lock him up in a jail, handcuffed and helpless, in any city in the world—Moscow, New York, Vienna, Paris, or Providence; Houdini will escape.

Everyone was wonderstruck by Houdini, but children were especially delighted. Children want to be able to escape from their rooms when they are sent there for being bad. They want to make their dinners disappear and their parents vanish. They want to pull candy from their pockets without putting any in, turn their sisters into puppies and their brothers into frogs (although some children want to turn their puppies and frogs into sisters and brothers). Children liked Houdini because he could do the unexplainable things that they wanted to do. Houdini was a magician. Magicians can do anything.

Victor was ten. He wanted to be a magician too.

When Victor was eight, he read in the newspaper that Houdini had escaped from an iron milk can in under twenty seconds.

Victor found his grandmother's trunk and closed himself inside. The locks snapped shut behind him. He tried and tried, but he could not escape in under twenty seconds. In fact, he could not escape at all.

So Victor cried and yelled until his mother came home and undid the locks. She was very upset that her son had shut himself up in Grandmother's trunk. Victor was very upset that he couldn't get out.

When Victor was nine, he found out that Houdini could hold his breath for over five thousand seconds while escaping from a crate dropped into the ocean. If Houdini could hold his breath for five thousand seconds in his crate in the ocean, then Victor could certainly hold his breath for five thousand seconds in his tub in the bathroom. So during bath time, he put his head underwater and counted as fast as he could. But he never got to five thousand. His mother kept making him get out of the tub and breathe.

Victor got this idea when he read that Houdini could walk through brick walls. Victor was sure he could do that. First he tried walking slowly into a living-room wall and pushing his way through. Nothing happened. Next he tried backing up across the room and running through the wall. He almost broke the lamp, the table, a few pictures, and his nose—but he didn't make it to the other side. Later that evening, after many unsuccessful hours, Victor finally got through the wall. He used the door.

Victor's mother was going crazy unlocking her son from trunks, reminding him to breathe when he took a bath, and telling him not to walk into walls. She decided she would take him to visit Aunt Harriet. Maybe a weekend in the country would calm him down.

It was while they were traveling there that the most incredible thing happened.

Victor was looking around the huge, bustling train station when he saw, way across the crowds, Harry Houdini himself, buying tickets with his wife.

Victor broke free from his mother's hand and ran straight to Houdini. He was filled with questions, millions and billions of questions, but which should he ask first? He took a deep breath, and this is what he said:

"How can I escape from my grandmother's trunk in under twenty seconds? How do I hold my breath in the tub without running out of air? Why can't I walk through a wall, like you can? How do you escape from jails and handcuffs and ropes and make elephants disappear? How—"

"Congratulations, my young man," interrupted the smiling magician. "No one has ever asked me so many questions in such a short amount of time. Are you a magician?"

"I want to be one," said Victor.

Houdini remained silent for several moments. After looking at Victor, and then at his wife, he finally said, "Then listen. Give me the tag from your suitcase."

"Why?"

"Your name and address are on it. When I write you a letter, I'll need to know where to send it, won't I?"

Victor immediately undid the little buckle and handed the tag to Houdini.

After reading it, the magician bent down so he was face to face with the boy. He whispered, "You want me to tell you things I can't talk about in the middle of a busy train station, son. And if I'm not mistaken, I see your mother heading this way. If it looks like you're going to get in trouble, you can blame everything on me." Then, grinning ever so slightly, he added, "Tell her Houdini tied you up for a moment. I'll write you a letter. Wait. Just you wait."

Houdini slipped the nametag into his pocket and disappeared into the crowd with his wife.

The weekend in the country was not as restful as Victor's mother had hoped. Her son was so excited about having seen Houdini that he locked himself in Aunt Harriet's dresser and in the cabinet of her clock. He walked very fast into her walls and almost broke all of her old framed photographs. Aunt Harriet was not sad when they left.

Back at home, Victor locked himself in the closet under the staircase, the cupboard in the kitchen, and his grandmother's trunk. How he hoped Houdini would write him quickly!

Victor thought and dreamt about the magician's letter. When you are a boy expecting the secrets of the world to arrive in the mail, it is almost impossible to be patient. If only Victor were already a magician! A magician could make the letter appear out of thin air. But Victor was still just a boy, and patiently or not, he had to wait. And so he did, until one day when he was locked up tight inside an old suitcase, he finally heard his mother say, "Victor, there's a letter here for you."

She unlocked the suitcase and handed him the letter. The handwriting was thick and round and perfect:

A thousand secrets await you. Come to my house...

Then Houdini gave the time and date for the meeting.

But it seemed so far away! Victor knew he couldn't wait so he went to the magician's house that evening.

His hands were shaking as he knocked on the door. With a heavy sigh it opened, and there before him was Harry Houdini's wife. Victor was suddenly too nervous to speak. He stood silently, staring at the sad woman in the light of the doorway.

She handed him some candy and softly asked, "What are you supposed to be?"

Victor didn't understand what she meant until he saw a ghost, a cowboy, and two little goblins running down the street. In all of his excitement, he had forgotten that tonight was Halloween!

And now he knew what he was supposed to be. "I'm a magician!" he said, and handed Mrs. Houdini the letter.

Mrs. Houdini read it and began to cry. She asked him to please wait inside, and vanished up the staircase into the magician's library, a dark place alive with books and dust and magical things. He held his breath, waiting for Houdini to greet him with outstretched arms and lead him back into that mysterious room.

When someone finally appeared in the hallway, though, it was only Mrs. Houdini again, alone. She came to Victor and handed him a small locked box. Then she opened the front door, and as she showed him out, he heard her whisper, "Houdini died today."

The magician's wife closed the door and left Victor alone with the box. "Bye," he said to the door, and went out, into the streets, toward home.

That night, while he was trying to open the lock on the box with pins and pens and all the small keys from the suitcases and clocks around the house, Victor found the owner's initials engraved on the bottom:

E. W.

This wasn't Houdini's box at all! The owner was E. W. There could be no secrets in here.

Imagine, as you read this, how it would feel if you had one dream, one hope, one mysterious wish, and then saw it disappear into thin air. That's how Victor felt, and that's why he did what he did next. He took the box that belonged to E. W. and buried it forever at the bottom of his closet. As he closed the door, he made this promise: "Houdini is gone. I will never think about him again or try to do any of his tricks. Cross my heart and hope to die."

So Victor grew up and got married. He and his wife had a child, and they named him Harry (in honor of Aunt Harriet, who had passed away one October long ago; he was not named in honor of a certain magician, because Victor said he never, not even once, thought about Houdini).

One chilly day, several years later, Victor and Harry were playing ball in a large field near a graveyard behind their house. Victor was pitching and Harry was swinging his bat, but he could never quite hit the ball. It was nearing dark, and there was time for just one more try. Victor gave Harry a few last-minute batting tips, and then, with all the gentle power that he had, threw the day's final pitch to his son.

Harry closed his eyes, and at exactly the right moment, he swung his bat. He heard a loud crash, opened his eyes, and was amazed to see the ball fly through the sky and land somewhere in the middle of the graveyard.

Victor congratulated his son, and together they climbed over the iron fence to look for the winning baseball. At last they found it, lying in the corner of a dark monument. Whether it had landed there by chance, or by some strange, powerful magic, no one will ever know. But the ball that Victor's son had hit so perfectly had come to rest right on the grave of Houdini!

Victor read the monument. Two smaller words appeared directly below "Houdini," and Victor said them over and over again because they seemed so familiar. It wasn't until he traced the first letters with his fingers that he understood what he was reading. This was Houdini's real name.

Before he became Houdini, the magician had been a boy named Ehrich Weiss. E. W.!

Victor's head spun, and he laughed out loud. Carrying his son, he ran out of the graveyard, through the baseball field, and into his house.

He was out of breath and crazy with excitement, but he couldn't tell his wife or son what was going on. He waited until they were fast asleep, and then he snuck upstairs into the attic.

Victor found the forgotten box in a moonlit corner under a steady leak in the roof. He carefully picked it up and dried it off. His hand brushed across the lock, and it suddenly crumbled. The water had rusted through the tiny thing completely. How easy it would be to open the box now!

And that night, while his wife and son slept downstairs and the attic shadows vanished in the pale, blue fall of moonlight, Victor locked himself inside his grandmother's trunk and escaped in under twenty seconds.

Reader Response

Open for Discussion Houdini was a great magician who performed amazing tricks. What did you wonder about Houdini as you read *The Houdini Box?*

1. Brian Selznick, the author of *The Houdini Box,* drew his own pictures for the story to help communicate certain feelings. What do you think the picture of Victor on page 401 communicates to the reader?

2. How does Victor feel before and after he visits Houdini's house? Why do you think his feelings change?

3. Do you think Victor's life will change now that he has opened Houdini's box? Why or why not?

4. A new movie is coming out about Houdini. Write copy to use on a poster advertising the movie. Use words from the Words to Know list and the story.

Look Back and Write Did Victor learn the secrets of Houdini's tricks? Why do you think as you do? Support your answer with details from the story.

Meet the Author and Illustrator
BRIAN SELZNICK

You can find more of Brian Selznick's art in these books:

The Houdini Box was Brian Selznick's first book. He chose magician Harry Houdini as the subject because he had been fascinated by Houdini as a child and had recently created a college art project about Houdini. Writing and illustrating his first book was not easy. Mr. Selznick considers himself more an artist than a writer, and it took a year and a half of rewrites before *The Houdini Box* was finished. He has received many awards for it.

Mr. Selznick says about the story, "Houdini really did die on Halloween, but in Detroit while on tour, not in New York, as in my story. I sent Houdini and his wife home so Victor could find them there that day. As for the Houdini box, I made it up—or at least I thought I did. Shortly after I wrote this story I found a newspaper article dated 1974, with the headline 'Magician's Box Still Being Sought.' Supposedly, on the 100th anniversary of Houdini's birth, 'a box containing his cherished secrets would be made public. . . . ' The article also said that the box had not yet been found."

Doll People by Ann M. Martin

Riding Freedom by Pam Muñoz Ryan

411

So You Want to Be an Illusionist

by Tui T. Sutherland

Expository Nonfiction

Genre

- Expository nonfiction gives factual information or explanations about a topic.

- Frequently, photos or artwork help explain the information.

Text Features

- The author uses headings to organize the text into meaningful parts.

- Captioned diagrams help you "see" and understand information in the text.

- Preview the title, headings, diagrams, and captions. This will prepare you to better understand what you read.

Link to Science

Do research in the library or on the Internet to find out more about optical illusions. Re-create one simple optical illusion you find and share it with your class.

Most magicians start their careers with illusions. A classic example is pulling a rabbit out of a hat. Harry Houdini wanted to take illusions to a whole new level. And he did.

A lot of magicians make things "disappear"—a rabbit, a coin, even a person. But Harry wanted to perform the biggest disappearing act in the world. That's how he came up with his trick: The Vanishing Elephant.

Harry performed this illusion only in the biggest theaters where there was room on stage for an elephant.

Predict   What will this article be about?

Vanishing Elephant

He would start out by introducing his elephant, who was named Jenny. Then Harry's assistants would roll in a very large box on wheels, large enough to hold Jenny. Harry would walk around the box, opening the doors on all sides, so the audience could see that there were no hidden sections at the back. Harry would lead Jenny inside and close all the doors.

A few seconds later, Harry would sweep open the doors again. Jenny was gone. Once again, he'd walk around the box and open all the doors. She had vanished!

Audiences were amazed. How did he do it? The trick was in the construction of the box. But as far as the audience could tell, Harry had made the elephant disappear.

1 Harry leads Jenny the elephant to a large cabinet on the stage. Jenny enters the cabinet through the curtains and is out of the audience's view.

2 The cabinet is folded open to reveal that Jenny has vanished.

3 The Trick

3 Through spring doors at the rear of the cabinet, Jenny enters a hidden cage on wheels, where Jenny is trained to find her favorite foods.

4 With the cabinet open, the audience does not see the assistants removing the secret cage.

Brick Wall Trick

Another one of his illusions used screens and an actual brick wall. Harry would have a team of bricklayers build a wall down the center of the stage, right in front of the audience. The stage floor was covered with a large sheet, pinned underneath the wall, and Harry would ask volunteers to come up and stand around the edges of the sheet. Then he would stand on one side of the wall, and his assistants would put a screen around him. They would put another screen on the other side of the wall. Then everyone would stand back and wait.

Harry, waving his hand over the top of the screen, would call, "You see, I am over here!" Then the hand would disappear, his assistants would take away the screen, and—no Harry. A moment later, Harry would walk out from behind the screen—on the other side of the wall.

How did he do it? The people onstage would see that he didn't walk around the back. The audience had seen the wall being built, so they knew there wasn't a secret door or way through it. And surely the sheet on the stage floor guaranteed that he hadn't somehow gone under the wall.

Well, not exactly. In actual fact, that's just what he did. There was a trapdoor in the stage just under the wall. Once everything was in place, one of his assistants would hide under the stage and open the trapdoor. There was just enough room for Harry to squeeze between the bottom of the wall and the sheet. Everyone standing on the sheet kept it from moving while Harry squeezed through. They thought they were preventing Houdini from tricking them. Instead, they were actually helping him.

1 A sheet is laid on the stage floor and a brick wall is built on a wheeled frame.

2 Audience volunteers inspect the wall as assistants place screens on both sides of the wall.

3 Houdini moves behind the screen on one side of the wall and then emerges from the other side.

4 The Trick

stage

trapdoor

An assistant releases a trapdoor below the stage, allowing the sheet to sag just enough for Houdini to crawl beneath the wall.

Reading Across Texts

You read about magic tricks in both *The Houdini Box* and "So You Want to Be an Illusionist." Which trick impressed you the most?

Writing Across Texts Write about why you chose the trick you did.

Compare & Contrast How useful is the art compared to the text?

Comprehension

Skill
Compare and
Contrast

Strategy
Visualize

Skill

Compare and Contrast

- To compare is to tell how two or more things are alike. To contrast is to tell how two or more things are different.

- Clue words such as *like* and *as* show a comparison. Clue words such as *but, instead,* and *unlike* show a contrast. Often, however, there are no clue words.

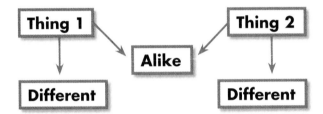

Strategy

Strategy: Visualize

Good readers visualize as they read. This means they create pictures in their minds. Sensory words such as *sticky* and *crackle* can help you experience what you are reading. You can use visualizing to help you compare and contrast as you read. It will help you "see" how things are alike and different.

1. Read "It's a Jungle Out There!" Make a graphic organizer like the one above to compare and contrast the rain forest and jungle.

2. Suppose you take a trip through the rain forest and then the jungle. Write a letter home about what you see and do in each.

IT'S A JUNGLE OUT THERE!

Well, actually, it's a tropical rain forest out there. It's easy to confuse the terms *rain forest* and *jungle,* but they don't mean exactly the same thing. A jungle is a particular part of the rain forest.

In the rain forest, thousands and thousands of huge trees grow so close together that their tops overlap to form a kind of roof high above the forest floor. This leafy roof is called the canopy.

> **Strategy** Visualize a rain forest tree. See its height, its colors, its trunk, and its leaves. Now picture thousands of such trees together.

You can walk around fairly well on the forest floor under the canopy. That's because the tops of the tall trees grow so thickly together that they shut out most of the sunlight. Plants need sunlight to grow, but there's not enough light for them to grow under the canopy.

> **Skill** The topic is shifting to the jungle. Pay attention to how it is both like and unlike the rain forest.

The jungle is another matter. In the rain forest there are clearings (for example, on the banks of rivers) where there are not as many gigantic trees. Here the sunlight can reach the ground, so smaller trees and plants can grow. And do they ever! This wild, thick tangle of plants is the jungle. You would need a big, sharp knife called a machete to hack your way through it. Good luck!

> **Skill** Ask yourself how this is different from the rain forest.

> **Strategy** Picture yourself trying to go through the jungle.

Words to Know

dolphins

surface

pulses

aquarium

flexible

enchanted

glimpses

Remember

Try the strategy. Then, if you need more help, use your glossary or a dictionary.

Vocabulary Strategy
for Multiple-Meaning Words

Context Clues When you read, you may find that the meaning of a word you know does not make sense in a sentence. This may be because the word is a multiple-meaning word, or a word with more than one meaning. For example, *story* can mean "an account of what happened." It can also mean "a lie, or falsehood."

1. Try the meaning you know. Does it make sense in the sentence?

2. If it does not make sense, think of another meaning for the word. Try that meaning in the sentence. Does it make sense?

3. If necessary, consider other meanings for the word. Decide on the best meaning and read on.

As you read "Dolphins," look for words that can have more than one meaning. Try each meaning to see which one makes sense in the sentence.

Dolphins

Dolphins are animals that live in the sea. Unlike many sea animals, they are mammals, not fish.

Dolphins have long, smooth bodies, and flippers, not fins. When they swim, they move their tails up and down, not side to side like fish do. Dolphins have to go to the surface of the water to breathe. They breathe through a hole on top of their head.

Dolphins use sounds to find things. They send out pulses of sound. The sounds bounce off an object and back to the dolphins. They use the sounds to tell where the object is.

If you take an expedition to an aquarium or a zoo, you will most likely see bottle-nosed dolphins. They are the ones that look like they are smiling. They are also friendly and smart. They can be trained to jump through hoops, throw balls through nets, and "walk" backwards on the water using their flexible tails.

People have long been enchanted by dolphins. The ancient Greeks drew pictures of them on pottery and walls. For centuries sailors have believed that catching glimpses of dolphins following their ships would bring them good luck.

Write

Imagine that you have a small aquarium in your home. What plants, animals, and other objects, such as rocks or shells, would you place in it? Describe your aquarium. Use words from the Words to Know list.

ENCANTADO:

by Sy Montgomery

Pink Dolphin of the Amazon

In what ways are
PINK DOLPHINS
mysterious?

421

ENCOUNTERS with ENCANTADOS

You're traveling to a world that is full of water.

In the Amazon, the wet season lasts half the year. During the rainiest part of the wet season, from March through May, it rains every day. Not all day but every day. Sometimes the rain lasts less than an hour, and then the bright, hot sun comes out to burn your skin. But every day there is some kind of downpour.

The wet season is the best time of year to explore the Amazon. You'll soon see why. So bring a poncho. On your expedition, you will watch the rain remake this jungle world. Swollen with rainwater, the Amazon River and its many branches—smaller rivers called tributaries—overflow their dry-season banks. The rivers flood people's gardens. Water covers the village soccer fields. The school playgrounds are underwater. Instead of taking a school bus to class, the kids take a canoe.

The village school is like a treehouse, perched high on stilts. Many of the village houses are built on stilts, too. Others float on the river, like rafts. People have to tie their floating houses to big trees so they don't drift away.

On your expedition, you'll sleep in a jungle lodge on stilts. You'll visit Amazon villages where the little girls play with real baby caimans (a kind of crocodile) the way girls at home play with dolls—and where the people will tell you stories about amazing creatures they call "encantados."

Encantado means the same thing in Portuguese (the language most people speak in Brazil) and in Spanish (which people speak in Peru and many other South American countries). It means "enchanted." And once you meet an encantado on the river, you'll know why.

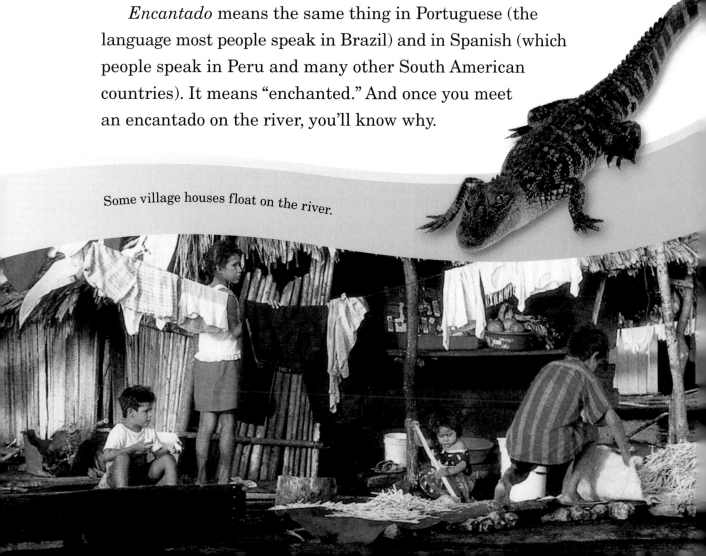

Some village houses float on the river.

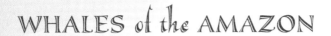

WHALES of the AMAZON

Everything about them sounds impossible: pink dolphins! Dolphins who live in rivers, not in the ocean. And not just any rivers: these are rain-forest dolphins, who swim in a submerged jungle.

And look how they do it. Unlike the athletic dolphins who jump through hoops for aquarium shows, pink dolphins don't leap out of the water. Watch: they swim slowly, low in the water. They don't look like "regular" dolphins, either: Unlike the ones who swim in the sea, the pink dolphin doesn't have a tall, pointed fin on the back, sticking out of the water like a shark's. Pink dolphins just have a low ridge, which makes them difficult to spot.

Besides making sounds from their mouths, dolphins (as well as many whales) can also send out pulses of sound, like an invisible beam of light, from inside their foreheads. The sound beams are too high-pitched for our ears. Listening with the help of special underwater microphones and recording devices, scientists have learned that these sounds are a series of pulsed clicks. The clicks travel through the water. When they hit an object—a tree branch, a tasty fish, or even a swimming person—the sounds come bouncing back to the dolphin. That's right—it's an echo. Dolphins can locate objects by their echoes. That's why this sense is called echolocation. It's also sometimes called sonar, which ships and submarines use to probe the water, too.

In fact, the echoes form a three-dimensional image in the dolphin's brain, allowing the animal to "see" not only the object's shape and size but also its insides.

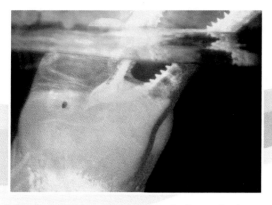
Pink dolphins make sounds from their mouths. They also send out pulses of sound from inside their foreheads.

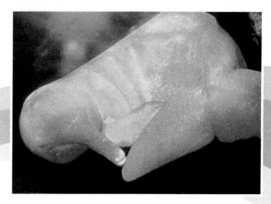
Dolphin doughnut: a pink dolphin touches its tail to its nose.

In addition to this super-sonar, pink dolphins have another special talent. Ocean dolphins' bodies don't bend very well. They'd never be able to get around all the branches in the Amazon. Pink dolphins can bend their bodies to twist gracefully through the underwater treetops. They are so flexible they can even touch their tail to their nose—like a dolphin doughnut.

Because of their unique flexibility, pink dolphins can also swim in shallow waters that ocean dolphins can't manage. Sometimes they get stuck—but not for long. You probably have already noticed that pink dolphins have really big front flippers—almost like wings. At moments like these, those flippers come in handy. Pink dolphins can use their front flippers not just to swim but also to crawl—both out of and back into the water!

Sometimes pink dolphins' behavior seems downright weird. Here's another example: sometimes they sleep upside down. Imagine finding a 300-pound dolphin floating upside down like a dead goldfish! Why do they do this? Why don't other dolphins?

No one knows. And that's just one of the mysteries about them.

Moises Chavez at the helm of the canoe.

NIGHTMARE DREAM WORLD

Canoeing through the flooded forest feels like a dream.

Strange lives cling to every tree. Fist-sized, hairy megalomorph spiders, who look like tarantulas, hunt for bugs in tree holes. The purselike nests of little birds called oropendulas hang from the tips of branches. Centipedes curl in the cracks of bark. Snails cling to the undersides of leaves.

"Duck!" Moises Chavez (MOY-sess SHAH-vez), your Peruvian guide, calls out from the front of the boat.

A duck? Where? But no—he motions you to get your head down, fast. You don't want to smack your head on a low branch as the canoe glides beneath it. Particularly this branch—because hanging down from it is a wasp nest the size of a pumpkin.

426

Fortunately, Moises knows these waterways well. He can warn you of the dangers. He grew up in the Amazon rain forest. His father was a teacher working in Amazonian Indian villages. Moises speaks some of the Indian languages, as well as Spanish and English. He has learned many of the jungle's secrets, including where to find the pink dolphins.

Today he's taking you to his favorite lake, where he knows you'll see pink dolphins. But to get there, you have to thread through twisting waterways, the heart of the Amazon rain forest.

Trees poke out of the water on all sides. Moises explains that it's important to keep your hands away from the sides of the boat. It's easy to see why. Some of the trees have spines growing out of their trunks. "They're sharp as needles," he says. "Don't touch the trees! See this guy"—he points to a tree with smooth bark—"this guy has sap that can burn your skin. And this guy," he says, pointing to a short tree with yellow flowers, "from its leaves you can make a tea to cure yellow fever. And this guy—"

Electric eels live in the Amazon River.

A centipede.

Hairy megalomorph spiders defend themselves with the hairs on their legs.

BANG!

Your canoe has come to an abrupt halt. The bottom is hung up on an underwater tree limb.

Your canoe is stuck in the treetops!

But Moises quickly gets the situation under control by pushing against a tree to free the canoe.

You're over the log, but you're not out of trouble.

"Watch out!" calls Moises. "Tangarana tree!"

Moises recognizes the tree's long, oval leaves right away. And he also knows that its hollow stems teem with thousands of stinging black tangarana ants. Each ant is more than an inch long. When something bumps against the tree, the ants think it's an attack on their home. Bravely, they'll rush to defend it. They'll even jump off branches into your canoe to sting you if they think their tree is threatened.

At the last minute, with some skilled paddling, Moises veers the canoe away from its dangerous path. You miss the ant tree by inches.

And then, pushing aside some branches like a curtain on a stage, Moises reveals your destination: the dolphin lake. You've made it.

During the dry season, the lake is little more than a puddle. But now, full of rainwater, it covers an area larger than a thousand football fields. It's shaped like a figure eight, with the crown of a mimosa tree poking up the middle.

Across the lake you can hear a dolphin blowing: "CHHHAAA!"

Some trees protect themselves with sharp spines.

428

The tangarana tree is home to thousands of stinging black tangarana ants.

REFLECTIONS on the WATER

You're surrounded.

At first, it seemed that you would see the dolphins only far away—just a pink shimmer on the water's surface. At first glance, you weren't sure whether you really saw one or just imagined it.

But Moises had a great idea. "Let's call them," he suggested. He leaned over the side of the canoe and, reaching underwater, banged on the side of the boat with his knuckles. The dolphins responded. And now they are all around you.

Right behind your canoe, you hear one blow. You twirl around, but all you see is the dolphin's wake, the wave it made when it dived just a split second ago. Then—"CHAAHHH!" A dolphin surfaces in front. "Look!" cries Moises—but you see only a trail of bubbles.

A diving dolphin leaves a wake and a trail of bubbles.

430

This pink dolphin looks almost like a reflection on the water.

SPLASH! Off to your left, a big pink form has surfaced. But by the time you turn, you see only a tail.

If the water were clear, as in an aquarium tank, you could see them swimming beneath the surface. But the water in the lake is as dark as night. It's not polluted; it's stained with natural chemicals from decaying rain-forest leaves.

Because of the dark water, it's impossible to count the dolphins. It certainly seems there are several. After all, one surfaced in back of the boat, then one in front of the boat. Another rose to the side. Does that mean there were three dolphins?

Maybe not. Remember that pink dolphins, with their bendy bodies, don't have to swim in a straight line. You can't predict where they might surface next. They can turn and twist beneath the water, even whirl around like a Ferris wheel. Maybe the three glimpses you had were all of the same dolphin.

How would you tell? Most animals, including dolphins, look as different from one another as people do. You just have to learn to see the differences. Some are bigger than the others, some are darker. One might have a notch or a scar on the back or head. One might have a bent snout.

But here's the problem: because pink dolphins don't leap out of the water, and because the lake water is so dark, you never see much of any individual dolphin at one time. You get only little glimpses: the glistening pink top of a head here, a tail there, a quick look at the low fin on the back here. And you can't identify them by color, because these dolphins grow pinker with exercise, just as people do.

For half an hour, the dolphins, whether one or several, continue to visit near your canoe. Could they be as curious about you as you are about them?

As you and Moises paddle back to the lodge for dinner, you're full of questions about the dolphins. How many of them visit the lake? Do they stay there all year, or do they move to other lakes and rivers? Are there mothers with babies among them? What kinds of fish do they like to eat?

Moises knows a lot about the wildlife in the Amazon. But even he doesn't know the answers to your questions. "The bufeo*, they are very mysterious," he says.

*__Bufeo colorado__ (Boo-FEY-oh co-low-RAH-doe) is another name for the pink dolphin. *Bufeo* is the local word for *dolphin*. *Colorado* is a Spanish word that means "ruddy or reddish."

Because they are difficult to study in the wild, pink dolphins remain a mystery to scientists.

The water is so dark you can't tell who might be swimming in there with you! This nose (above) belongs to a huge Amazonian manatee.

433

Reader Response

Open for Discussion A person who reads about travel is an armchair traveler. So you are an armchair traveler. Which sights and sounds impressed you as you traveled in the Amazon rain forest?

1. How does the author involve you in her journey to the Amazon? Find sample sentences that show how she brings the reader along to the rain forest.

2. Describe the special body structure of the pink dolphin. What is it able to do because of this body structure?

3. Use details from the selection to create a mental image of daily life in the Amazon during the rainy season. What is it like? How does it compare to your own daily life?

4. Write an article for the school newspaper about a class trip to a dolphin show. Make it exciting for your classmates. Use words from the Words to Know list and the selection.

Test Practice

Look Back and Write Why are pink dolphins called *encantado,* or "enchanted"? Support your answer with details from the selection.

Meet the Author

Sy Montgomery

Read more books by Sy Montgomery:

Sy Montgomery really gets to know the animals she writes about. For *Encantado,* she traveled to Peru and Brazil to study and even swim with dolphins. She remembers, "They would sometimes swim underneath me and blow bubbles up at me. The bubbles sizzled on my skin. Researchers believe they blow bubbles to give each other a tickly, calming feeling—like a whirlpool bath or massage."

Ms. Montgomery has written many books about nature for both adults and children. She especially loves writing for children. "When we are young, we find in books hopes and dreams and futures we never would have found otherwise. It is my hope in writing for kids that my readers find we share the same dream: a world in which people, animals, land, plants, and water all are seen as precious and worthy of protection."

The Snake Scientist

The Man-Eating Tigers of Sundarbans

Expository Nonfiction

Genre

- An expository article gives facts and information.

- The author often includes photographs and diagrams to support the text.

Text Features

- Headings in an interesting typeface capture the reader's attention and organize the text into parts. Sidebar diagrams add information that is not in the text.

- Preview the article. Looking at the title, headings, and other text features will help prepare you to read.

Link to Science

Choose one of the animals in "Mysterious Animals" and use reference materials to learn more about it. Make a poster with a picture of the animal and the facts you find.

Mysterious Animals

Some animals puzzle us. They look strange and they behave in strange ways. Now you can get to know four of these mysterious animals.

Wrinkle-Faced Bat

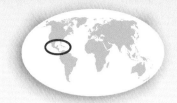

The wrinkle-faced bat sleeps during the day and goes out to look for food at night (like other bats). It does not look like other bats, however. Its face is covered with folds of skin. Why it has all that extra skin is still a mystery.

Where it lives: Mexico, Central America, and the West Indies

Favorite food: fruit

Weight: 1 ounce or less

Size: 2–3 inches

3 inches

3 inches

Raccoon Dog

Where it lives: Northern Asia and parts of Europe

Favorite foods: plants, fruits, insects, fish, and small animals

Weight: 8–22 pounds

Size: head and body: 1.5–2 feet long; tail: 5–10 inches long

3 feet

This strange dog looks like a raccoon. It sleeps through the winter like a bear. Oddly, this dog does not bark. Hunters prize this animal for its fur.

 Visualize | Which words help you "see" the bat's face?

Grasshopper Mouse

This small mouse is not timid or quiet. It has sharp teeth and big jaw muscles for killing and eating its prey. Unlike some other mice, it does not squeak softly. Instead, it stands on its back legs and roars! Its cry can be heard more than 100 yards away.

Where it lives: North America

Favorite foods: insects and small animals

Weight: 1–2 ounces

Size: 2 inches tall with a head-body length of 3–5 inches

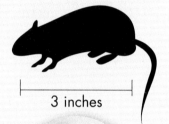

3 inches

Compare & Contrast Think beyond the obvious when you compare.

438

Bush Dog

These dogs are equally at home on land and in the water. With their webbed feet, they can swim and dive underwater. Though they may swim like fish, these strange dogs sound like birds. Their "bark" resembles a whistle or chirp.

Where it lives: parts of Central and South America

Favorite foods: birds and rodents

Weight: 11–15 pounds

Size: head and body: 1.75–2.5 feet; tail: 4–6 inches

3 feet

Reading Across Texts

Encantado takes place in Brazil, a country in South America. Which of the animals in "Mysterious Animals" also makes its home in South America?

Writing Across Texts Tell two ways in which pink dolphins and one of these animals are alike and two ways in which they are different.

Skill
Character
and Setting

Strategy
Monitor and
Fix Up

 Skill

Character and Setting

- Characters are the people in a story. You can learn about characters by noticing what they say and do and by noticing how they interact with other characters.

- The setting is the time and place of a story.

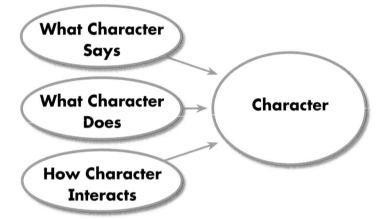

What Character Says

What Character Does

How Character Interacts

Character

 Strategy

Strategy: Monitor and Fix Up

Good readers make sure they understand what they read. If they don't, they may use text features to fix up the problem. A play's text features can help you. For example, directions in parentheses tell you how a character should speak and act.

1. Read "Frog Prince: The Sequel." Make a graphic organizer like the one above for the character of the Bad Fairy.

2. Use your graphic organizer to write a paragraph describing the Bad Fairy.

Frog Prince: The Sequel

CHARACTERS: BAD FAIRY, PRINCESS

A telephone conversation in fairy tale land.

BAD FAIRY: Nasty Spells Complaint Department. What do you want?

PRINCESS: Hello, this is the princess up at the castle.

BAD FAIRY: Just a minute, Sweetie. Let me pull up your file. Oh, right, right. You kissed the frog and turned him back into a prince. How's that working out?

PRINCESS: It's totally not!

BAD FAIRY: What's the problem? He's not *handsome* enough for you?

PRINCESS: No, no, it's not that. I mean, he's a really cute guy and everything, but . . .

BAD FAIRY: But what?

PRINCESS: He jumps out at people. And he makes these disgusting rib-bet noises. And—and he eats flies!

BAD FAIRY: Boys will be boys. *(She chuckles.)*

PRINCESS: But he's not acting like a boy. He's acting like a *frog!*

BAD FAIRY: *(in a no-nonsense way)* Sorry, Sweetie. We have a strict no-returns policy on frogs turned human.

PRINCESS: Then what am I going to do?

BAD FAIRY: Live hoppily ever after?

Skill Where does the Bad Fairy work? What does she say? What do these things tell you about her?

Strategy The word *handsome* is in italics. That's a signal that the Bad Fairy should emphasize it. How should she say this line?
(a) in a sweet way
(b) in a mocking way
(c) in a sad way

Strategy If you are not sure about how the Bad Fairy should say these lines, reread the stage direction.

Skill How would you describe the Bad Fairy after reading this line?

The King in the Kitchen

Words to Know

- majesty
- genius
- peasant
- noble
- duke
- furiously
- dungeon
- porridge

Vocabulary Strategy
for Unfamiliar Words

Dictionary/Glossary You can use a glossary or a dictionary to find out the meaning of an unfamiliar word. A glossary is part of a book. It lists important words and their meanings. A dictionary is its own book. It gives the meanings of most of the words in a language. The words in a glossary or dictionary are listed in alphabetical order.

1. Look at the first letter in the unfamiliar word.

2. Open the glossary or dictionary to the section for that letter.

3. Find the word.

4. Read the entry for the word. If the word has more than one meaning, decide which meaning fits in the sentence.

5. Try that meaning in the sentence to see if it makes sense.

As you read "Keeping a Secret," use a glossary or dictionary to find the meanings of unfamiliar vocabulary words.

Keeping a Secret

Once upon a time, there was a king who had really big ears. The only person who knew this was the king's barber. The king told the barber, "Never tell anyone what you have seen." The barber nodded vigorously and replied, "Oh, yes, of course, your majesty."

The barber was a genius at snipping hair but not at keeping secrets. He went into a field and dug a hole. He whispered into the hole, "The king has really big ears." Then he filled the hole and went home.

Oats grew in the field and when the wind blew, the oats whispered, "The king has really big ears." A peasant heard the oats. He told his wife, who told the neighbors, who told the noble lord, who told the duke, who told everyone else.

The king soon realized that everyone knew his secret. He confronted the barber and shouted furiously, "Guards, take this man to the dungeon!"

Alone in the dark dungeon, the poor barber puzzled over how the secret had gotten out. A guard brought him a bowl of porridge (which is made from oats). As the barber lifted the bowl, he heard a faint whisper, "The king has really big ears."

Write

Why do you think the barber couldn't keep a secret? What would you have told him to do? Write your advice to the barber. Use words from the Words to Know list.

Genre

Plays are stories written to be performed. As you read, try to imagine actors performing this story on a stage.

The King
in the
Kitchen

by Margaret E. Slattery
illustrated by Matthew Trueman

What could a king
be doing in the kitchen?

Characters

COOK

1ST KITCHEN MAID

2ND KITCHEN MAID

PEASANT

KING

PRINCESS

GUARD

DUKE

SETTING: *The palace kitchen. Large table with pots and pans is upstage center. Several stools are placed around stage.*

AT RISE: COOK *is standing behind table, fussing with the pots and pans.* 1ST KITCHEN MAID *sits on a stool, peeling potatoes.* GUARD *enters, leading* PEASANT *by the arm. They start to walk across the stage.*

COOK *(Looking up):* Ho, there! You! Guard!

GUARD *(Stopping):* What is it, Cook?

COOK: Where are you taking that man?

GUARD: To the dungeon.

1ST KITCHEN MAID: Oh, my!

COOK: To the dungeon! Why, what's he done, poor fellow?

PEASANT: It was nothing, really. All I did was to ask the King for the Princess's hand in marriage.

GUARD: And him a peasant!

COOK: A peasant! Why, a peasant can't marry the Princess.

PEASANT: I don't see why not. I'm handsome and clever, and I'm awfully fond of the Princess. She's awfully fond of me too.

1ST KITCHEN MAID (*Staring*): She is?

PEASANT: Oh, my, yes. I come to the palace every day to deliver vegetables. The Princess thinks I'm wonderful, and I think she's wonderful.

COOK: The Princess can't marry a peasant, I tell you. She has to marry someone rich and famous and noble and—

1ST KITCHEN MAID: Like the Duke.

PEASANT: The Duke is fifty years old, and dull too. The Princess will never marry him.

COOK: The Princess will marry whomever her father tells her to marry. I'm sure he'll want a wealthy son–in–law because they say the Royal Treasury is almost empty.

GUARD: Besides, I told you not to ask the King today. If you'd asked him some other time, he might only have exiled you. But he's awfully upset today.

COOK: Why?

GUARD: It was the soup you sent up. He said it was horrible and threw it on the floor.

1ST KITCHEN MAID: Oh, my!

GUARD: Well, come on, peasant. *(Takes PEASANT's arm and starts toward door.)*

PEASANT *(Sings to tune of "London Bridge"):* To the dungeon we must go, we must go, we must go. To the dungeon— *(Exits with GUARD)*

COOK *(Tearfully):* Oh, dear, the King didn't like the soup and I took such trouble with it.

2ND KITCHEN MAID *(Rushing in breathlessly):* Cook, Cook! Something terrible!

COOK: What's the matter?

2ND KITCHEN MAID: It's the King. He's coming here!

COOK *(Flustered):* What?

1ST KITCHEN MAID: The King! But he's never been in the kitchen before.

COOK: This is terrible. Here now, both of you start working. We'll have to straighten this kitchen up. *(ALL rush around, trying to straighten up, bumping into each other and dropping pots and pans.)*

KING *(Striding in):* Well, so this is the kitchen. *(Looks around.)* Hmm. At least you're working. Now, who made that awful soup?

COOK *(Curtseys):* I—I did, your Majesty.

KING: It was horrible! Horrible, do you hear me?

COOK: But, your Majesty, it's really not my fault. The ingredients we've been getting lately have been very inferior.

KING: Stuff and nonsense! I could make a better soup than that with my eyes shut. In fact, I'll do it!

2ND KITCHEN MAID *(Shocked):* Your Majesty!

KING: Yes, that's exactly what I'll do. And with my eyes shut. Now, out of my way, everybody. *(Marches behind table, looking at things on it. Picks up mixing spoon.)* What's this?

COOK: A mixing spoon, your Majesty.

KING: Well, I guess I'll need it. Now let me see, what do I want?

2ND KITCHEN MAID: Maybe a bowl, your Majesty? *(Hands him a bowl.)*

KING: Of course. The very thing. You're a smart girl. *(Puts bowl on table.)* All right, I'm ready. Now, Cook, give me your apron.

COOK: But your Majesty—

KING: Hurry up! *(Takes apron from COOK and puts it on.)* Now, I'll show you I can do this with my eyes shut. Tie something around my eyes, Cook.

COOK: Your Majesty, I don't really think—

KING: Be quick about it. (COOK *ties dish towel around* KING's *eyes.*) There! I'm ready to begin.

1ST KITCHEN MAID: What will you do first, your Majesty?

KING: Ah, let me see. Have we any water?

COOK: Oh, a nice kettle full, your Majesty.

KING: Well, pour some in the bowl. (COOK *pours some in.*) Now, I think I'd like a little flour. (COOK *dumps some in a bowl.* KING *feels about table and picks up a bottle.*) What's this?

COOK: That's sauce, your Majesty. You don't want that for soup.

KING: Silence! That's exactly what I do want.

COOK: But, your Majesty—

KING: Who's making this, you or I?

COOK: You are, your Majesty.

KING: Very well then. *(Pours some sauce in bowl.)* Now, what next?

1ST KITCHEN MAID: Maybe a little salt.

KING: That's just what I was about to say myself. Put some in. (KITCHEN MAID *pours a little salt in a teaspoon and dumps it in.)* How much did you put in?

1ST KITCHEN MAID: Oh, just a dash, as the good cookbooks say.

KING *(Screaming):* Cookbooks! Cookbooks! What do I care about cookbooks? You, Cook! Do you use cookbooks?

COOK: Oh, yes, your Majesty.

KING: Then that's what's the matter with your cooking. No imagination. Who ever heard of a dash of salt? We want this to have flavor, don't we? Here, where's that salt shaker? *(Pulls towel off eyes and grabs up shaker.)* This is the way to do it. *(Holds salt shaker in both hands upside-down over bowl. Shakes it furiously.)* There, that's better. *(Stirs it vigorously with mixing spoon. Enter PRINCESS.)*

PRINCESS: Oh, here you are, Father. I've been looking everywhere for you.

KING: Now, now, my dear, don't bother me. I'm very busy.

PRINCESS: Father, I must talk to you. Have you seen my peasant anywhere? He's usually here by eleven o'clock with the vegetables.

KING: Oh, him. Yes, I saw him and threw him in the dungeon.

PRINCESS *(Shrieking):* What!

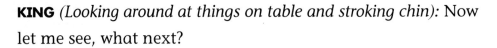

KING (*Looking around at things on table and stroking chin*)**:** Now let me see, what next?

PRINCESS: But, Father, why?

KING: Are you still here? Go away.

PRINCESS: Father, why did you throw him in the dungeon?

KING: Who?

PRINCESS (*Stamping foot*)**:** Father, stop it. You know who I mean.

KING: Oh, that peasant. Yes, I had to throw him in the dungeon. He had the colossal nerve to ask for your hand in marriage.

PRINCESS (*Clapping hands*)**:** He did? You have to let him out of the dungeon. I want to marry him.

KING: Nonsense, you can't marry a peasant and you know it. What this family needs is a relative with some money. Now find someone with royal blood and lots of money and you can marry him.

PRINCESS (*Sitting down on chair and crying*)**:** I want to marry my peasant.

KING: There, don't cry. Look at this nice thing Daddy made for you here. See? (*Holds bowl out to her.*)

PRINCESS (*Sniffing*)**:** What is it?

KING: I don't know. Why don't you taste it?

PRINCESS (*Peering at it*)**:** It looks awful. What do you suppose it is, Cook?

COOK (*Coming over and taking bowl*)**:** I'm sure I don't know, your Highness. (*Stirs it around a little.*) It's not porridge.

KING: Of course it's not porridge. It's—it's—well, don't all of you stand there. What is it?

1ST KITCHEN MAID: I really don't think it's soup.

2ND KITCHEN MAID: Nor stew.

KING *(Stroking chin):* Hmm. This is a problem. *(Paces floor.)* I have it! One of my wonderful ideas!

COOK: Oh, dear! (KITCHEN MAIDS *groan.*)

PRINCESS: Oh, Father, what is it this time?

KING: We'll have a contest. Whoever can guess what this is, wins a reward.

COOK: And what will the reward be, your Majesty?

KING: Why, the hand of the Princess in marriage, of course.

PRINCESS *(Jumping up):* Father!

KING: Certainly. You want to have a lovely wedding and get lots of presents, don't you?

PRINCESS: Yes, but—

KING: Now, let me see. Whom shall we have enter the contest?

1ST KITCHEN MAID: What about the Duke, your Majesty?

KING: Of course. Now, Kitchen Maid, run quickly and tell the Guard to tell the Footman to send the Duke here immediately. (*Exit* 1ST KITCHEN MAID.)

PRINCESS: But I don't want to marry the Duke. He's the dullest man in the palace.

KING: Well he can't be so dull he won't be able to tell what this is.

PRINCESS: How will you know if he's right anyway? You don't know what it is yourself.

KING: Nonsense! Why, it's—it's—*(Noise outside.)* Ah, here comes the Duke now. *(Enter* GUARD *and* DUKE.)

DUKE: Ah, your Majesty, good afternoon. Making a little tour of the kitchens, I see? We in this country are so fortunate to have a king who takes an interest in these simple matters. I have always said—

KING: Save that for an after-dinner speech.

DUKE: Ahem, yes. And, your Highness. *(Bows to* PRINCESS.) How beautiful you look today!

KING: All right, all right, let's get on with it. Now, Duke, can you tell me what I've made here in this bowl? *(Points to bowl* COOK *is holding.)*

DUKE: Er—what *you've* made, your Majesty?

KING: Yes, of course I made it. And if you can tell me what it is, you win the hand of the Princess in marriage.

DUKE: Well, that would indeed be an honor. *(Takes bowl.)* Now let me see. *(Stirs it around.)* Ah–er—could it be—pudding?

KING: Pudding! Of course not, you nincompoop! Why would I make a pudding? You must really be dull.

DUKE: Oh, no I'm not—not at all, your Majesty. Maybe if I could just taste it—*(Takes some up on mixing spoon.)* I'm sure it will be delicious. *(Puts spoon to mouth.)*

KING: Well?

DUKE *(Choking and coughing):* Ah—ugh—er *(Claps hand over mouth.)*

KING: What? Speak up, man!

DUKE *(Muttering through hand over mouth):* Ug—mmph— mm—er—

KING: What is he trying to say?

455

PRINCESS: I don't know. I told you he was dull.

DUKE *(Sitting down on stool in corner):* Mmph—er—*(Covers face with hands.)*

PRINCESS: Well, there you are, Father. He doesn't know what you've made so I don't have to marry him.

COOK: Congratulations, your Highness.

KING: Well, just because he's dull doesn't mean everyone is. Let's see, whom shall we ask next. *(Looks about room.)* Ah, what about you, Guard?

PRINCESS: Father!

GUARD: Oh, I'm afraid it wouldn't be fair for me to enter the contest, your Majesty. I'm already married.

KING: Well, don't stand there gaping. Go and find someone. *(Exit GUARD.)*

PRINCESS: Father, this is so silly.

KING: Not at all. By now I'm curious myself to find out what I've made. It's too thick for soup.

COOK: And too thin for porridge. *(Enter GUARD.)*

GUARD: Your Majesty, I have someone for the contest.

KING: Well, send him in, send him in.

GUARD *(Calling offstage):* All right, you. Come on in. *(Enter PEASANT.)*

PRINCESS: My peasant! My very own dear peasant!

PEASANT *(Going down on one knee before PRINCESS):* My Princess! My very own dear Princess!

KING: What is all this?

PEASANT *(Rising):* Your Majesty, this is an unexpected pleasure. But you really didn't have to come all the way down to the kitchen to see me. I would have been glad to come upstairs to the throne room.

KING: Who let you out of the dungeon?

GUARD: I did, your Majesty. You said you wanted someone to enter the contest.

KING: Guard! I didn't tell you to empty out the dungeon. Can't you find anyone in this palace with royal blood?

PRINCESS: Oh, this is wonderful! Father, please let him try. He's so clever! You will win the contest so you can marry me, won't you, dear peasant?

PEASANT: Of course. What is the contest?

KING: I've made a perfectly wonderful dish of something or other, and whoever can tell me what it is, receives the hand of the Princess in marriage.

PRINCESS: Go ahead, dear. Guess what Father's made.

PEASANT *(Goes over to bowl. Sniffs. Stirs it a little. Sniffs again):* Ah!

KING: Delicious, isn't it?

PEASANT: Indeed, yes. *(Peers at it.)* Let me see. Ah, of course! I have it. *(Sits down on chair.)*

PRINCESS *(Excitedly):* What is it? What is it?

PEASANT: Now just a minute—*(Takes off shoe, picks up a little of the liquid on a spoon and drops it on edge of sole. Makes motions of pressing sole tight against shoe.)* There!

KING: What are you doing?

457

PEASANT *(Putting shoe back on):* Now we'll see. *(Gets up and walks around a little. Then bends down and looks at shoe.)* Ah–ha, just as I thought! Congratulations, your Majesty.

KING: What for?

PEASANT: You have just made a bowl of the most wonderful glue I've ever seen.

KING *(Bellowing):* What!

PRINCESS: Glue!

COOK: Glue!

KITCHEN MAIDS *(Together):* Glue!

PEASANT: You are a genius! An absolute genius. Why, this glue is strong as iron. See? *(Lifts up foot.)* The sole of my shoe was almost falling off. Now it's on tight as new.

KING: So you think I'm a genius, do you?

PEASANT: Certainly. You'll be famous. Rich, too. We'll put this in bottles and sell it everywhere. Let's see. We could call it King's Glue. *(Sings)*

> Go out today and buy King's Glue.
> Through thick and thin, it sticks with you.

PRINCESS: I knew you were clever. We gave some to the Duke and he didn't know what it was.

PEASANT: The Duke ate some? *(Rushes over to DUKE. Peers at him.)* Just as I thought. His teeth are stuck together.

KITCHEN MAIDS *(Together):* Oh my! *(Hurry over and look at DUKE.)*

KING: It serves him right. The fellow ought to have known better than to eat glue. Here, Guard, take him off to the Royal Dentist.

DUKE *(Getting up):* Mmph! (GUARD *takes him by arm and leads him off.*)

KING *(Stirring spoon in bowl):* It does look a little like glue. How clever I am.

PRINCESS *(To* PEASANT*):* You've won the contest! Now we can be married.

KING: This is terrible. What will my Prime Minister say when he hears I am to have a peasant for a son–in–law?

PEASANT: Never you mind. When we tell him how much money will go into the Royal Treasury from your glue, he won't care about anything. Of course, it will mean you will have to spend most of your time in the kitchen.

KING: It's not so bad down here. And I'll always have something to eat. As for you, Cook—

COOK: Y–y–yes, your Majesty?

KING: Off to cooking school you go, and don't come back till you have a diploma. Take the Kitchen Maids with you. (*Exit* COOK *and* KITCHEN MAIDS.)

KING: Now you two run along. I want to start working.

PEASANT: All right, your Majesty. See you at the wedding. (*Exit* PRINCESS *and* PEASANT.)

KING *(Fussing about with pots and pans):* Now let me see. What did I do first? *(Places pan in front of him and pours some water in.)* Did I put one cup of flour in? Or was it two? And how much salt? *(Picks up shaker and shakes some in.)* Oh, well—*(Stirs it up singing.)*

Go out today and buy King's Glue.
Through thick and thin, it—sticks—with—you!

The End

Reader Response

Open for Discussion Suppose your class is putting on a performance of *The King in the Kitchen.* Which character would you like to play? What are three adjectives that describe that character?

1. Suppose someone says to you, "This play isn't real. It could never happen!" What do you think the author would say?

2. The setting is the time and place in which a story occurs. What is the setting of *The King in the Kitchen?* What details in the text and the illustrations help you determine this?

3. The Princess loves the Peasant because he's clever. Think about what you know about being clever. How was the Peasant clever in his encounter with the King?

4. Some of the characers in the play are royals. Some are servants. Make a chart. List the characters in each category. Add other words you know that fit into each category.

Look Back and Write The King went to the kitchen to find out who made his soup. What else did he accomplish while he was there? Support your answer with details from the play.

Meet the Illustrator

Matthew Trueman

Read other books with plays you can perform.

Matthew Trueman's family moved from the United States to Italy when he was four. He remembers, "I didn't know Italian at first, so I spent a lot of time drawing by myself. I didn't have very many toys, but if I had paper and something to draw with, I could play with castles, robots, mountains, airplanes, soldiers, horses, swords . . . anything I could think of." He now lives in the United States, where he creates illustrations for children's books, magazines, newspapers, and advertisements.

Before he illustrates a story, Mr. Trueman tries to form a picture of the characters. He says, "The first and most important part for me is finding the characters—the way a director might experiment with different actors for a film. If I get the characters right, they become almost like real people to me, and they act out the story." Of the characters in *The King in the Kitchen,* he says, "I like the way the King and his daughter seem a little crazy!"

12 Fabulously Funny Fairy Tale Plays by Justin McCory Martin

Theatre for Young Audiences edited by Coleman A. Jennings

463

Poetry

Genre

- Poetry is imaginative and can show us new ways of looking at things.

- Many poems have lines that end with words that rhyme.

- Many poems have lines that have a certain rhythm—a regular pattern of unstressed and stressed syllables, or beats, that is noticeable when the poem is read aloud.

- Two of these poems are limericks. Limericks have five lines. Lines 1, 2, and 5 have the same number of beats and end with rhyming words. Lines 3 and 4 have fewer beats, but also end with rhyming words.

Link to Writing

As you read the two limericks, count the beats. Then write your own limerick with words that rhyme.

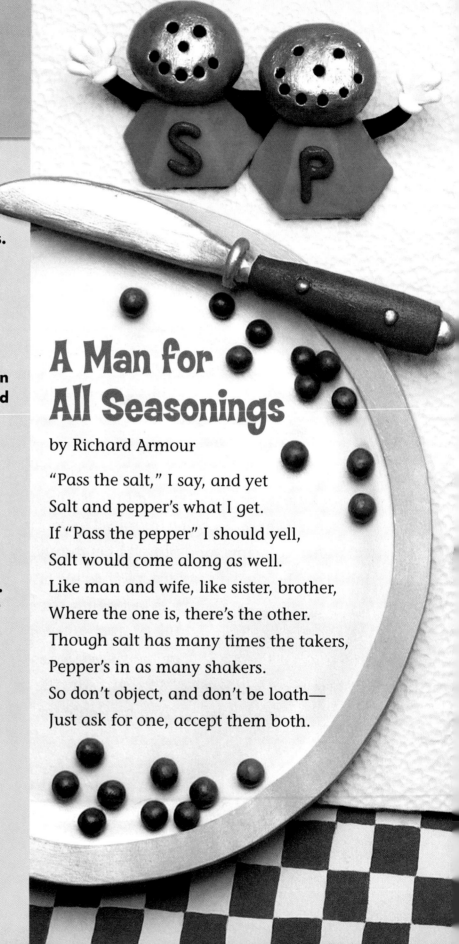

A Man for All Seasonings

by Richard Armour

"Pass the salt," I say, and yet
Salt and pepper's what I get.
If "Pass the pepper" I should yell,
Salt would come along as well.
Like man and wife, like sister, brother,
Where the one is, there's the other.
Though salt has many times the takers,
Pepper's in as many shakers.
So don't object, and don't be loath—
Just ask for one, accept them both.

464

A Confectioner

by Myra Cohn Livingston

A confectioner living in Skittle
Once confessed, "I'm so skinny and little
    That unless I put glue
    On the sole of my shoe
I'd fall into my own peanut brittle."

Expert

Author Unknown

A prominent lady in Brooking
Was a recognized genius at cooking.
    She could bake thirty pies
    All quite the same size
And tell which was which without looking.

Reading Across Texts

Find words in these poems that link them to
The King in the Kitchen.

Writing Across Texts Write a limerick of
your own about the king. The first line might
be: "There once was a king from Chinook . . . ."

Monitor & Fix Up   What might you misunderstand in poetry?

465

Comprehension

Skill
Graphic Sources

Strategy
Ask Questions

Graphic Sources

- A graphic source, such as a picture, a map, or a chart, organizes information and makes it easy to see.

- You can use a graphic source to help you understand what you read.

Strategy: Ask Questions

Active readers ask themselves questions before they read, while they read, and after they read. Look at a graphic source before you read. Ask yourself, "What does this show? What do I think the article will be about?" As you read, ask, "How does this graphic source compare with the text?" After you read, ask, "Do I understand this graphic source now? Do I have any questions about it?"

1. Read "Picture This." Draw a shape like an Egyptian cartouche (see below). Write your name in the cartouche in hieroglyphics.

2. Write a sentence using hieroglyphics. Exchange your sentence with a partner. Write each other's sentences in English.

Picture This

In ancient Egypt, people used a form of picture writing known as **hieroglyphics.** This word means "sacred writing." Hieroglyphics were carved on the walls of temples and tombs, but they were used on other things as well. For example, a cartouche was an oval figure that contained the name of a ruler in hieroglyphics.

English writing is made up of letters. The letters represent the sounds of the language. Hieroglyphics were just pictures—no letters at all! Sometimes a picture stood for the thing it showed. For example, sometimes ∧∧∧∧ meant "water." Other times ∧∧∧∧ stood for the sound /nnn/ from the Egyptian word for *water.* This chart shows hieroglyphics that can be used for English letters.

Strategy Look at the chart below. Ask, "What does this chart show? What will this article be about?"

Skill Look below to see how this information relates to the chart.

Skill Which hieroglyphic can be used for *d*? Which letters have the same hieroglyphic?

Strategy What questions do you have about this chart?

A	D	H	L	O/U/W	S/Z	U/W/O
Eagle (1)	Hand (5)	House (9)	Lion (13)	Lasso (18)	Cloth (22)	Chick (26)
A	E/I/Y	H	M	P	SH/CH	X
Arm (2)	Two Strokes (6)	Flax (10)	Owl (14)	Door (19)	Pool (23)	Basketcloth (27)
B	F/V	I/Y/E	M	Q	T	Y/E/I
Foot (3)	Viper (7)	Reed (11)	Bar (15)	Slope (20)	Loaf (24)	Double Reed (28)
C/K	G	J	N	R	TH	Z/S
Basket (4)	Jar (8)	Cobra (12)	Water (16)	Mouth (21)	Rope (25)	Bolt (29)
			N			
			Crown (17)			

Words to Know

ancient
temple
scholars
seeker
translate
link
triumph
uncover

Remember

Try the strategy. Then, if you need more help, use your glossary or a dictionary.

Vocabulary Strategy
for Greek and Latin Roots

Word Structure Many words in English come from the Greek and Latin languages. You may be able to use what you already know about Greek and Latin words to help you figure out the meaning of an unknown word.

1. Check the word for any Greek or Latin word parts whose meanings you already know. For example, you might know that the *trans-* in *translate* means "across, through, or beyond."

2. Use the meaning of the word part to help you figure out the meaning of the unknown word.

3. Check the word to see if it looks like another word you know. For example, the *schol-* in *scholars* may remind you of the word *school.*

4. Use the meaning of the similar word to help you figure out the meaning of the unknown word.

As you read "The Rosetta Stone," use what you know about Greek and Latin words to help you figure out the meanings of unknown vocabulary words.

The Rosetta Stone

In 1799, a French army officer found a stone slab near the city of Rosetta in Egypt. On the stone was the same announcement in three different languages. At the top was hieroglyphics, a writing that uses pictures or symbols to stand for ideas and sounds. This writing was used in ancient Egypt. In the middle was an Egyptian language called demotic. At the bottom was the Greek language.

For more than 3,000 years, the ancient Egyptians used hieroglyphics on their temple walls and monuments. But over time the language was forgotten.

For hundreds of years, scholars were unable to figure out how to read hieroglyphics.

Jean-François Champollion was a French scholar who wanted to be the first to read hieroglyphics. He studied the language his whole life. He was a true seeker of knowledge. He used the Greek part of the Rosetta Stone to translate the Egyptian part. The Rosetta Stone gave him a link between the known and the unknown.

Champollion's work was a triumph. It allowed other scholars to uncover the history of ancient Egypt.

Write

Imagine that you have made an important discovery. Write about your discovery. Use words from the Words to Know list.

SEEKER OF KNOWLEDGE

THE MAN WHO DECIPHERED EGYPTIAN HIEROGLYPHS

text and illustrations
by James Rumford

Genre

A **biography** is the story of a real person's life as told by another person. As you read this biography, notice how the author uses words and images to tell his story.

WHO WILL
DISCOVER
THE KEY TO
EGYPTIAN
HIEROGLYPHS?

There is a jumping, free-spirited kid goat in the Egyptian word "imagine."

There is a sharp-eyed ibis bird in the word "discover."

There is a long-necked, far-seeing giraffe in "predict."

In 1790, a French boy named Jean-François Champollion was born.

When he was seven, his older brother told him about General Napoleon, the great leader of France, who was in Egypt uncovering the past.

"Someday I'll go to Egypt, too!" Jean-François told his brother as he sat spellbound, imagining himself with Napoleon, making his own discoveries.

When Jean-François was eleven, he went to school in the city of Grenoble. There, his brother took him to meet a famous scientist who had been in Egypt with Napoleon.

The scientist's house was filled with Egyptian treasures. Each one captured the boy's imagination.

"Can anyone read their writing?" asked Jean-François.

"No. No one," the scientist replied.

"Then I will one day," said Jean-François, and he left the house full of enthusiasm, sure that he would be the first to discover the key to Egyptian hieroglyphs.

Back home, his brother helped him get down all the books they had on Egypt. On moonlit nights, Jean-François stayed up reading long after he should have been asleep.

His brother nicknamed him "the Egyptian" and bought him notebooks. Jean-François filled them with hieroglyphs. There were prowling lions 🐅, angry monkeys 🐒, trumpeting elephants 🐘, and sharp-eyed ibis birds 🐦 with their long, curved bills. He could not read the Egyptian words, but he dreamed that one day he would, as he sailed up ⛵ the Nile.

Jean-François had a favorite animal. It was the lion because there was one in his name: JEAN-FRANÇOIS CHAMPOL**LION**.

There are strongly woven sandals firmly planted on the ground in "never give up."

When Jean-François finished school at sixteen, his brother took him to Paris to meet  the scholars who were studying a black stone from Rosetta, Egypt. The stone was covered with Egyptian and Greek words and told of a king of Egypt named Ptolemy. By reading the Greek, the scholars hoped to decipher the Egyptian. But the work was difficult—certainly too difficult for a boy— and the scholars turned Jean-François away .

They did not see the fire burning bright in his eyes. They did not recognize the genius who had already learned all the known ancient languages. They did not know that he was a seeker of knowledge, one who would not rest until he had found the answer.

Jean-François gathered his notebooks and returned to Grenoble. There he taught school. His students often came to hear him talk about Egypt—her pharaohs and gods and the mysterious writing.

Once, even Napoleon came to Grenoble and sat up all night, listening spellbound as Jean-François told the great man of his dreams.

Napoleon promised to send Jean-François to Egypt when he conquered the world. Napoleon dreamed of glory. Jean-François dreamed of discovery .

There are two regal, heads-up-high leopards in the word "glory."

Thoth, one of the ancient gods

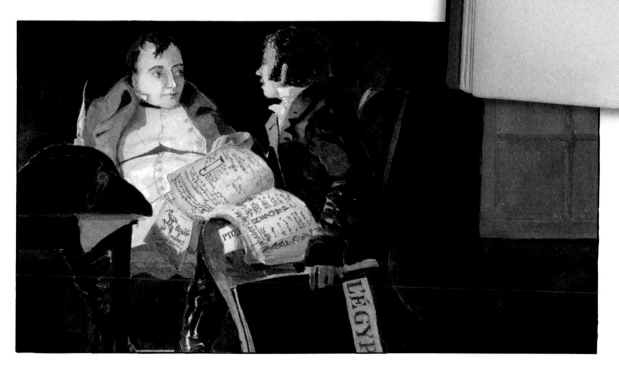

There is a roaming, black-as-night jackal in the word "mystery."

There is an unblinking crocodile lurking in the word "trouble."

But a few months later, Napoleon was defeated at the Battle of Waterloo. France was now defenseless. Her enemies poured in. They surrounded Grenoble and in the early morning bombarded the city. Jean-François ran 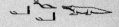 to save his notebooks from the flames.

The people were angry with Napoleon and anyone who knew him. They pointed fingers at Jean-François and called him a traitor. He fled into the woods, leaving his notebooks behind. There he lived like a hunted dog . It was weeks before it was safe to come out and months before he saw his notebooks again.

During these troubled times, scholars everywhere were racing to solve the mystery of Egyptian writing. Unbelievable things were said. Ridiculous books were written. No one had the answer. Then an Englishman discovered that a few of the hieroglyphs on the Rosetta Stone were letters, and he deciphered King Ptolemy's name. Everyone said that the Englishman would be the first to unlock the door to Egypt's past—everyone except Jean-François .

When Jean-François was thirty, he gathered up his notebooks and left Grenoble. He made his way back to Paris—to his brother.

The letter **P** *in Ptolemy's name*

The letter **T** *in Ptolemy's name*

To Jean-François, this was the letter **A.**

The letter **W**

In Paris, Jean-François studied the Rosetta Stone and other inscriptions. He compared the Greek letters with the Egyptian hieroglyphs and herded together his own alphabet of eagles and lions and dark-eyed chicks . But this wonderful list of letters was no help in reading the language. There were too many pictures he did not understand. What to make of a fish with legs , a jackal with wings , or an ibis god with a long, curved bill ? There had to be a link between the pictures and the Egyptian letters. But what was it? Jean-François slept little. He ate almost nothing.

Then, on a September morning in 1822, Jean-François found a small package on his doorstep—from a friend in Egypt! In it were the names of pharaohs copied

from a temple wall. Each name was a jigsaw puzzle of letters and pictures. Jean-François studied the names and saw the link! The pictures were sounds, too. Not single letters, but syllables, even whole words!

One of the names drew him. It began with the hieroglyph of an old, silent friend perched on a sacred staff . This was a picture of the god of writing, Thoth, followed by the letters *m* and *s*.

"Thothmes!" Jean-François suddenly exclaimed, and the rushing sound of the pharaoh's name, as if carried on wings across the centuries, filled the room.

The royal cartouche, *or ring of rope, encircling* Thothmes's name

Thothmes (*also written* Thutmose *or* Thutmosis), *one of the ancient pharoahs*

There is a blue lotus, its center as bright as the yellow sun, in the word "joy."

There are rippling river waves in the word "Nile."

Jean-François raced  down the street to his brother's office. He burst through the door, exclaiming, "I have the key!"

Then he collapsed . He had not eaten. He had not slept. For five days, he lay near death.

On the fifth day, he awoke. "Pen and paper," he whispered, and he wrote of his discovery to the world.

People all over France celebrated his triumph as Jean-François became the first to translate the ancient writing and open the door to Egypt's past.

A few years later, the people of France sent Jean-François to Egypt on an expedition to uncover  more secrets. He knew Egypt so well in his mind that he felt he was going home. As Jean-François had imagined a thousand times in his dreams, he sailed up the Nile.

Once ashore, he entered the ruins of a temple. A magnificent flock of ibis suddenly rose up from the reeds and took flight.

Below, the ibis saw the seeker of knowledge touch the stone walls.

His fingers dipped into the carved pictures. He pressed his ear to the stone and listened to the ancient voices.

Reader Response

Open for Discussion Imagine that you are Jean-François Champollion. How would you answer this question: What made you so determined to decipher hieroglyphs?

1. The author of this biography placed small pictures among his sentences. Find one and explain why you think the author included it.

2. On many pages of the selection, part of a notebook appears next to the text. What is the purpose of this graphic element?

3. What questions did you have about Jean-François as you read about him? How were your questions answered?

4. Create a hieroglyph for some of the words on the Words to Know list or in the selection.

Look Back and Write Jean-François was the first to uncover the secrets of Egyptian hieroglyphs, but he had help along the way. Who were the people who helped him? Use details from the biography to support your answer.

JAMES RUMFORD

Here are two more books by James Rumford.

James Rumford began writing books in his forties. Before that, he worked for the Peace Corps and taught English all over the world, including in Africa, the Middle East, and Asia. He currently lives in Hawaii, where he runs a small publishing company. He handles every step of the book-making process, from making his own paper to setting type to printing pages on a hand press. He even binds his books—one at a time. The books he prints contain both Hawaiian and English.

Mr. Rumford can speak or translate many languages. For *Seeker of Knowledge,* he taught himself hieroglyphics.

"I think all kids are like Jean-François Champollion," says Mr. Rumford. "When they're 10, 11, 12 years old, most of them have a clear picture of what they want to do." Mr. Rumford wants kids to know that dreams can come true with hard work.

Traveling Man: The Journey of Ibn Battuta, 1325–1354

The Island-below-the-Star

James Rumford with young readers of his book *Calabash Cat* in Hawaii ▶

483

Search Engines

Genre

- A tool called a search engine can help you find Web sites on the Internet.

- You can focus your search by brainstorming a list of important words, or keywords.

Text Features

- Every search engine has a window in which you type keywords.

- Clicking on the SEARCH button starts the search.

- Search results are displayed in a list below the search window. Each item is a link to a Web site that contains the keywords.

Link to Social Studies

How do hearing-impaired people communicate? Search the Internet for information on ASL, American Sign Language.

Word Puzzles

To Jean-François Champollion, the Rosetta Stone was a giant word puzzle. If you wanted to know more about word puzzles, you could type "word puzzles" into a search engine window and click the SEARCH button.

484

Take It to the NET
ONLINE
more activities sfsuccessnet.com

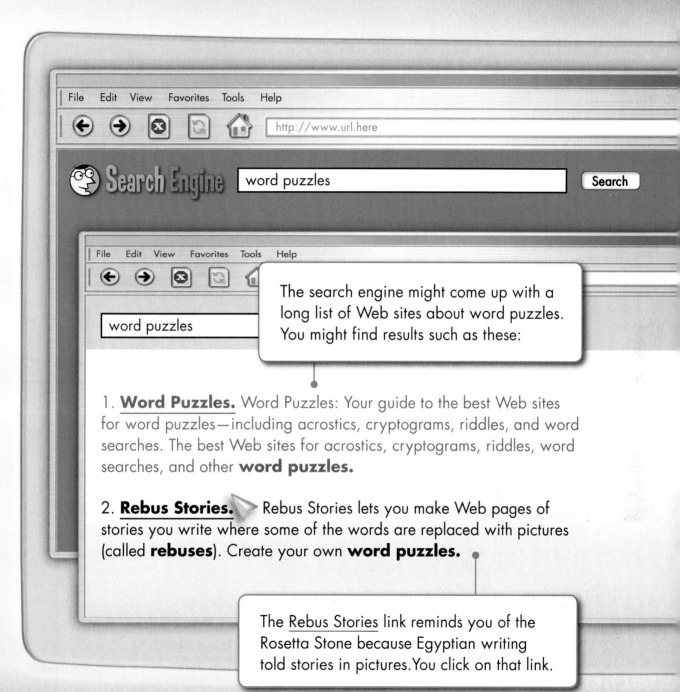

File   Edit   View   Favorites   Tools   Help

← → ⊠ ⟳ ⌂   http://www.url.here

Search Engine | word puzzles | | Search |

File   Edit   View   Favorites   Tools   Help

← → ⊠ ⟳ ⌂

| word puzzles |

The search engine might come up with a long list of Web sites about word puzzles. You might find results such as these:

1. **Word Puzzles.** Word Puzzles: Your guide to the best Web sites for word puzzles—including acrostics, cryptograms, riddles, and word searches. The best Web sites for acrostics, cryptograms, riddles, word searches, and other **word puzzles.**

2. **Rebus Stories.** ▷ Rebus Stories lets you make Web pages of stories you write where some of the words are replaced with pictures (called **rebuses**). Create your own **word puzzles.**

The Rebus Stories link reminds you of the Rosetta Stone because Egyptian writing told stories in pictures. You click on that link.

Ⓠ Ask Questions   What questions do you have about search engines?

The link takes you to the Rebus Stories Web site. This is what you see:

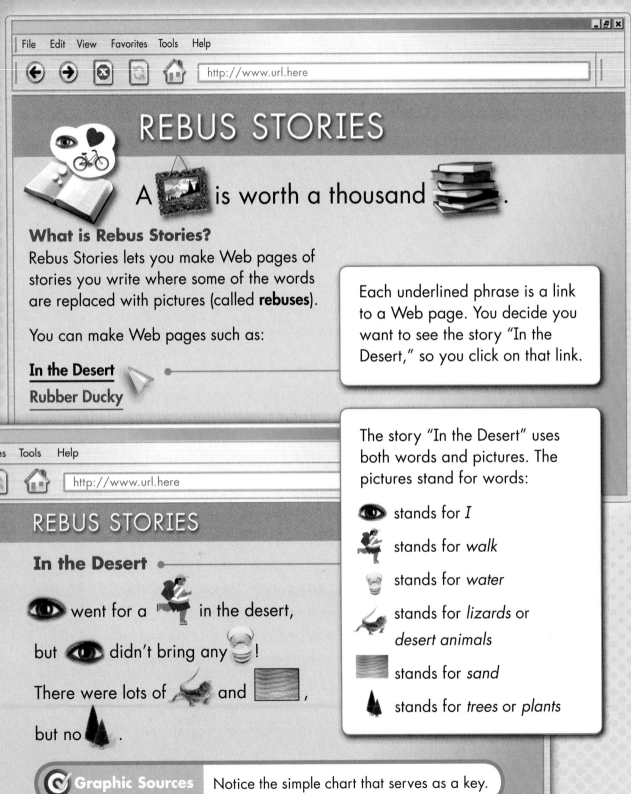

REBUS STORIES

A [picture] is worth a thousand [books].

What is Rebus Stories?
Rebus Stories lets you make Web pages of stories you write where some of the words are replaced with pictures (called **rebuses**).

You can make Web pages such as:

In the Desert
Rubber Ducky

Each underlined phrase is a link to a Web page. You decide you want to see the story "In the Desert," so you click on that link.

REBUS STORIES

In the Desert

[eye] went for a [walk] in the desert, but [eye] didn't bring any [water]!

There were lots of [lizard] and [sand], but no [tree].

The story "In the Desert" uses both words and pictures. The pictures stand for words:

[eye] stands for *I*

[walk] stands for *walk*

[water] stands for *water*

[lizard] stands for *lizards* or *desert animals*

[sand] stands for *sand*

[tree] stands for *trees* or *plants*

Graphic Sources   Notice the simple chart that serves as a key.

REBUS STORIES

Other Rebuses
Can you figure out what each of these rebus sentences says?

2 ride my 2 every day.

Did **U C** that dunk that ?

went **2** her **2** get her poor

a .

Reading Across Texts

Both selections tell about how using symbols can be a way to communicate. How are Egyptian hieroglyphics and rebuses alike and different?

Writing Across Texts Write a rebus story that tells something about Jean-François Champollion.

Comprehension

Skill
Plot

Strategy
Prior Knowledge

Plot

- A plot, or underlying story structure, is found only in fiction.

- A plot begins when a character has a problem or conflict.

- The problem builds up during the rising action, is met directly at the climax, and comes to an end, with the action winding down, during the resolution.

Problem → Rising Action → Climax → Resolution

Strategy: Prior Knowledge

Good readers use their prior knowledge as they read. They ask themselves, "What do I already know about what is happening in this story?" You can use things you already know to help you understand the events in the rising action and the climax.

1. Read "Oh, NO!" Make a graphic organizer like the one above to outline the parts of the story's plot.

2. Use your graphic organizer to write a summary of the plot.

Catherine was very excited when she learned that both she and her friend Shelley had gotten parts in the class play. She had always wanted to try acting. Mr. Kiley, the director, explained that it was important for everyone to attend each rehearsal. ●

On the fourth day of rehearsals, Catherine felt feverish. That night her fever became worse, and the next morning she had to remain in bed. ●

The doctor told Catherine that she would probably miss a week of school. "Oh, *no!* I can't miss that much!" she cried. "I'll be replaced in the class play."

That evening Catherine heard the telephone ring. Several minutes later her mother came into her bedroom.

"That was Mr. Kiley, your director, on the telephone," she told Catherine.

"He called to tell me I've been replaced, no doubt," Catherine moaned, suddenly feeling worse. ●

"No," said her mother. "He asked if Shelley could visit you after each rehearsal to keep you informed about the play. Then you'll be able to catch up when you get back next week."

"Oh, *yes!*" Catherine screamed excitedly and jumped out of bed. ●

"Hey!" laughed her mother. "Do you want your fever to *ever* go down?"

Skill What does Catherine want to do? Could something prevent that from happening? This is the problem.

Strategy Use your knowledge of being very sick. How did you feel? Did you miss school? What will happen to Catherine?

Skill You might conclude that this is where the problem will be met directly. What do you predict will happen?

Strategy How have you felt when you expected bad news and received good news? Can you understand Catherine's reaction?

lizards

salamanders

reptiles

amphibians

stumped

reference

exhibit

crime

Try the strategy. Then, if you need more help, use your glossary or a dictionary.

Vocabulary Strategy
for Synonyms and Antonyms

Context Clues When you read, you may come across a word you don't know. Sometimes the author will use a synonym or an antonym as a clue to the word's meaning. Synonyms are words that mean almost the same thing. Antonyms are words with opposite meanings.

1. Reread the sentence with the unknown word. Look for a synonym or an antonym of the word. If you find one, try it in the sentence. Does the synonym make sense in the sentence? Does the antonym give the sentence an opposite meaning?

2. If there is not a synonym or an antonym in the same sentence as the unknown word, check the sentences around it. You may find a synonym or an antonym there. If you do, try it in the sentence.

As you read "It Is Not All in the Family," look for synonyms and antonyms to help you understand the meanings of vocabulary words.

IT IS NOT ALL IN THE FAMILY

Are you interested in the world of snakes, frogs, turtles, lizards, toads, and salamanders? You probably think of all of these animals as one big creepy family. In fact, they are not. Snakes, turtles, and lizards are all reptiles. Frogs, toads, and salamanders are all amphibians. Look at pictures of these animals. Can you tell how they are different? If you are stumped, read on.

Amphibians have skin that must be kept wet. If you touch the skin, it feels slimy. This is because amphibians live near water. They lay their eggs in water because the eggs have no shell. Reptiles, on the other hand, have dry skin that is covered with scales. Their eggs have a tough covering. These eggs can be laid on land.

If you are still baffled or confused about these animals, read about them in a reference book, such as an encyclopedia. The next time you are at a zoo, look them up. A zoo exhibit has live animals that you can see up close. The display gives facts about the animals. And remember, it is not a crime to ask questions! Zoo workers like to share what they know.

Write

Be a reporter. Write a news story about a group of young people who are helping the environment. Use as many Words to Know as you can.

ENCYCLOPEDIA

written by DONALD J. SOBOL

Genre

Realistic fiction tells about events that could really happen. As you read, think about how the events in this story are similar to events in real life.

BROWN and the Case of the Slippery Salamander

illustrated by **BRETT HELQUIST**

Can a boy detective solve the mystery of a missing salamander?

To a visitor, Idaville looked like an ordinary seaside town.

It had churches, two car washes, and three movie theaters. It had bike paths, sparkling white beaches, a synagogue, and plenty of good fishing spots.

But there was something out of the ordinary about Idaville: For more than a year, no child or grown-up had gotten away with breaking a law.

People wanted to know: How did Idaville do it?

The secret resided in a red brick house at 13 Rover Avenue. That was where Idaville's police chief lived with his wife and son.

Chief Brown was a smart, kind, and brave man. But he wasn't the one who kept crooks from getting away with their crimes. No, the brains behind it all was his ten-year-old son, Encyclopedia.

Encyclopedia's real name was Leroy. But only his parents and teachers called him that. Everyone else called him "Encyclopedia" because his brain was filled with more facts than a reference book.

Sometimes the Brown family was tempted to tell the world about Encyclopedia's amazing talent as a crime-solver. But so far they hadn't leaked a word. For one thing, the Browns didn't like to boast. For another, who would believe that Idaville's top detective was a fifth-grader?

13 Rover Avenue, Idaville

One Monday night Chief Brown sat at the dinner table, staring at his plate of spaghetti. So far he hadn't slurped up a single strand. Encyclopedia and his mother knew the reason.

The chief wasn't eating because he had come up against a crime that he couldn't solve.

Encyclopedia waited for his dad to tell him about the case. Whenever Chief Brown was stumped, Encyclopedia cracked the case for him, usually by asking just one question.

At last Chief Brown looked up. "There was a theft at the aquarium today," he said, rubbing his forehead.

Last summer an aquarium had opened near the beach. The most popular attractions were the giant shark tanks, the dolphin shows, and the Den of Darkness.

The Den of Darkness was a huge indoor exhibit of reptiles and amphibians. Encyclopedia especially liked visiting the frogs and salamanders in the amphibian section.

Fred

"I hope the great white sharks weren't stolen," Mrs. Brown said with a smile. "That would certainly take a bite out of business!"

Chief Brown shook his head. "It wasn't the sharks."

Encyclopedia put down his fork and listened carefully as his father explained that Fred, a tiger salamander, had been stolen.

"Fred was shipped to the aquarium only two days ago," Chief Brown said. "He was being kept apart from the other animals until the officials were sure he was healthy. If he got a clean bill of health, he was to go on display next month."

"Do you have any clues, dear?" Mrs. Brown asked.

The chief frowned. "Not many. All we know is that the salamander disappeared this morning, sometime between ten-thirty and eleven forty-five."

"Why would someone steal a salamander?" Mrs. Brown wondered.

"Fred is the aquarium's only tiger salamander," her husband explained. "From what the director of the aquarium told me, someone could sell him for a lot of money."

"Really?" Mrs. Brown's eyes widened. "Do you think a visitor might have stolen him?"

496

Mrs. King
Sam Maine
Dr. O'Donnell

"It's very unlikely," Chief Brown replied. "Employees and volunteers are the only ones who have access to the back room in the Den of Darkness where Fred was being kept."

Chief Brown told Encyclopedia and Mrs. Brown that three people had been working at the exhibit that morning: Mrs. King, who volunteered at the aquarium every Monday; Sam Maine, the man in charge of cleaning and maintaining the exhibits; and Dr. O'Donnell, an expert on reptiles and amphibians.

"Did you question the three of them?" Mrs. Brown asked.

The chief nodded. "Dr. O'Donnell spent the morning examining a new crocodile from Australia. Sam Maine told me he was busy cleaning out exhibits and feeding some of the lizards. Several people saw him working," Chief Brown added, "so it looks like he's telling the truth."

"What about Mrs. King?" his wife prodded.

497

Chief Brown frowned. "Actually, Sam Maine seems very suspicious of Mrs. King," he confided. "And after talking with her I can see why. Mrs. King is fascinated with salamanders."

"Fascinated with salamanders?" Mrs. Brown echoed.

The chief nodded again. "She told me she has dozens of them at home as pets, and that Fred is the first tiger salamander she's ever seen." He shook his head. "Mrs. King does seem odd—she thinks salamanders are sacred creatures with magical powers."

Encyclopedia spoke up. "In ancient times, people used salamanders for medicine. They also believed that salamanders could eat fire and live in flames."

"Maybe Fred wasn't stolen for money," Mrs. Brown said thoughtfully. "Maybe Mrs. King took Fred just because she thinks he's a special specimen!"

"That's exactly what I've been thinking," Chief Brown admitted. "But there's no proof that Mrs. King had the opportunity to steal Fred. She was with a group of school children from ten-thirty to eleven-fifteen. After that she went over to the cafeteria for a coffee break. One of the cashiers said he saw her there."

Chief Brown sighed with frustration. "I hate to admit it, but this case has me baffled!"

Encyclopedia closed his eyes. His parents watched him hopefully. They knew that when Encyclopedia closed his eyes, it meant he was doing his deepest thinking.

A moment later Encyclopedia was ready. He opened his eyes and asked his one question:

"Has Sam Maine been working at the aquarium long, Dad?"

"Actually, he was hired only two weeks ago," Chief Brown answered. "But he has a lot of experience. Sam told me he's been taking care of salamanders and other lizards for more than nineteen years."

That was all Encyclopedia needed to hear.

"Oh no, he hasn't!" Encyclopedia declared with a satisfied smile. "If he's a lizard expert, then I'm the Queen of England! Sam Maine is lying, and I can prove it!"

How does Encyclopedia know?

SOLUTION to the Case of the Slippery Salamander

Encyclopedia knew that Sam Maine was lying because he told Chief Brown he'd been taking care of "salamanders and other lizards for more than nineteen years." Anyone who'd been taking care of salamanders for that long would know that salamanders are not lizards. They are classified as amphibians. Lizards are classified as reptiles.

Sam Maine admitted stealing the valuable new tiger salamander that morning. After he returned Fred to the aquarium, he was fired from his job as caretaker.

Reader Response

Open for Discussion Does Encyclopedia Brown remind you of anyone you know? Does he remind you of someone you would like to know? Explain your thoughts.

1. Idaville isn't real, but the author includes details to make it seem like a real town. Find at least three details that make Idaville seem real.

2. A plot has a conflict, but the conflict isn't always between two characters. What is the conflict in this story? How is the conflict solved?

3. Think about what you know about how crimes are solved. What does Chief Brown do that most detectives would do? What does he do that's different?

4. As a detective on the case, what notes might Encyclopedia Brown have jotted in his notebook? Write some of them, using words from the Words to Know list and the story.

Look Back and Write Whom do you think Chief Brown suspects of stealing the salamander before Encyclopedia solves the crime? Use details from the story to support your answer.

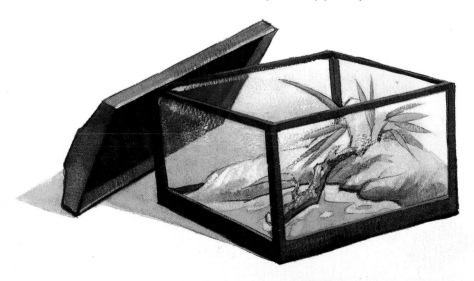

Read other books by Donald J. Sobol.

Encyclopedia Brown Sets the Pace

Encyclopedia Brown and the Case of the Jumping Frogs

Donald J. Sobol was born in New York City in 1924. *Encyclopedia Brown: Boy Detective,* his first story about this famous character, was published in 1963. Since then, he has written over twenty books about Encyclopedia Brown. In most of these books, there are ten mysteries, with the solutions to the mysteries at the back of the book. Leroy "Encyclopedia" Brown is the ten-year-old sleuth who solves the mysteries— even though his father is the town's police chief!

Mr. Sobol once said, "Readers constantly ask me if Encyclopedia Brown is a real boy. The answer is no. He is, perhaps, the boy I wanted to be—doing the things I wanted to read about but could not find in any book when I was ten." Now in his eighties, Mr. Sobol lives in Florida, where he continues to write Encyclopedia Brown stories for a new generation of fans.

Donald J. Sobol

Read other books illustrated by Brett Helquist.

Brett Helquist is best known as the illustrator of the Lemony Snicket books, *A Series of Unfortunate Events*. While illustrating those books might seem like enough danger for one man, Mr. Helquist has also illustrated many other children's books.

Mr. Helquist was born in Ganado, Arizona, and grew up in Orem, Utah. He studied art at Brigham Young University in Provo, Utah. Soon after graduating from college, he moved to New York City. He and his wife live in Brooklyn. Mr. Helquist has done illustrations for many newspapers and magazines, including *The New York Times*, *Time for Kids*, and *Cricket*.

It Came from Beneath the Bed! by James Howe

Bud Barkin, Private Eye by James Howe

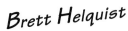

Brett Helquist

Newspaper Article

Genre

- Newspaper articles provide information about current events and topics of human interest.

- News stories are usually short and to-the-point. They tell *who, what, when, where,* and *why.* Human-interest stories are generally longer and more descriptive.

Text Features

- A catchy title, or headline, grabs the reader's attention.

- The first paragraph summarizes the article and prepares readers for what comes next.

- The use of direct quotations makes the article personal and interesting.

Link to Science

Make a set of fingerprints. Then compare and contrast your fingerprints with those of a classmate.

The D

Crime scene investigation: Students use tools such as a microscope to evaluate evidence at the scene of a "crime."

Daily Journal

Monday

Young Detectives
of Potterville Middle School

by Bonnie Kepplinger

Sixth-graders in a Michigan middle school solve crimes during one class period each day. Their classroom has become a crime lab. Their tools are microscopes, rubber gloves, goggles, and fingerprinting brushes and powder. These students work together to evaluate evidence at a "crime" scene. Hair and fiber analysis can answer questions that identify criminals. Does this hair belong to a dog, a cat, or a human? What kinds of fibers were found on the victim's clothes? What do clues tell us about anyone else present at the scene of the crime?

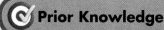 **Prior Knowledge** Think about what you know about what detectives do.

A young detective analyzes "blood" samples.

"We rush to this class," said one student. "No one's ever really tardy because we like to come."

"I don't want to leave this class," added another student. "We get to solve crimes. It's fun because we get to find out by ourselves instead of having someone else tell us or show us."

Several high schools in mid-Michigan offer forensic science classes. (*Forensic* refers to science that can be used in legal courts.) However, Potterville Middle School is believed to be the first in the area to bring such classes to younger students. These classes teach students how to think, question, and solve problems. Young Potterville detectives enjoy improving their science skills through investigation.

During the nine weeks of classes, students have several projects. One week they were given a burglary scene with four possible suspects. Their job was to analyze fake blood samples. Then they matched one suspect's blood type with the sample found at the crime scene.

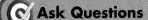

Ask Questions What questions do you have that the author answers?

506

Teachers say that this is a way to get students interested in and excited about science. "We have never seen kids this excited about science as we have this year," said sixth-grade teacher Maureen Dykstra. "They have become close observers and careful recorders of data." Like all good detectives, students learn how to collect and weigh information. They even draw pictures of the crime scene. Students also have a place to stage the crimes. This is a portable unit outside the school that used to be a music room.

Guest speakers visit the class to talk about careers. Visitors have included a forensic scientist, a police officer, and a detective. Jeff Hudak is a crime investigator for the local police department. He knows that working with young students encourages them to think about future jobs. "It lets them know what they have to do to get involved in crime scene investigation," he said. "It's never too early to get them interested."

Reading Across Texts

Do you think Encyclopedia Brown should sign up for a forensics class at Potterville Middle School?

Writing Across Texts Explain why you answered the question about Encyclopedia Brown as you did.

Who Knows?

by Fatou Ndiaye Sow

Who knows
How many stars
Are in the roof of the sky?
How many fishes
In the deep seas?
How many people
In the whole wide world?
Who knows
Where, every evening
The sun flees to?
Where the moon lights up?
Where dawn starts,
Where the endless horizon ends,
Who knows?... Who knows?

Poetry

by Eleanor Farjeon

What is Poetry? Who knows?
Not a rose, but the scent of the rose;
Not the sky, but the light in the sky;
Not the fly, but the gleam of the fly;
Not the sea, but the sound of the sea;
Not myself, but what makes me
See, hear, and feel something that prose
Cannot: and what it is, who knows?

The Seed

by Aileen Fisher

How does it know,
this little seed,
if it is to grow
to a flower or weed,
if it is to be
a vine or shoot,
or grow to a tree
with a long deep root?
A seed is so small,
where do you suppose
it stores up all
of the things it knows?

Carolyn's Cat

by Constance Kling Levy

She's a house cat
pampered like a child,
cuddled and petted
and very well fed,
a stranger
to the wild
outside.
(She's the kind of cat
you'd invite to tea.)

Her life, it seems,
is peaceful and good
with only her house
for a neighborhood:
the plump pillows,
the soft chairs,
the smooth wood.

But I saw her one night
posed perfectly still,
like a china cat,
on the windowsill,
meeting, with moonlike
      eyes,
the full moon's glow.

And I think
there are things
about Carolyn's cat
that even Carolyn
doesn't know.

WRAP-UP

MYSTERIOUS MOMENTS

connect to **DRAMA**

Work with a partner or a small group to brainstorm ideas for a mystery you could write together. Make a story map with notes about the characters, setting, and main events of the plot. Then write a script for a five-minute mystery. Practice your mystery play and present it to the class.

STORY MAP

Characters
- Grandmother
- pet kangaroo
- 10-year-old boy

Setting
- New York City
- now

Events
- Beginning: An old woman meets a kangaroo in Central Park
- Middle:
- End:

IS THERE AN EXPLANATION FOR EVERYTHING?

SEEK AND YOU WILL FIND

connect to
SCIENCE

Much of what scientists know today came about as a result of asking questions about the world around them and searching for answers. Make a chart. On it write one question you still have about each selection in this unit. Then write where you might look for an answer.

Titles	Question	Where to Look
The Houdini Box		
Encantado		
The King in the Kitchen		
Seeker of Knowledge		

CURIOUS BEGINNINGS

connect to
WRITING

The King in the Kitchen takes a humorous look at how glue might have been invented. Make up a funny account of another curious event in this unit. Write a limerick or another type of poem to explain the event.

UNIT 5

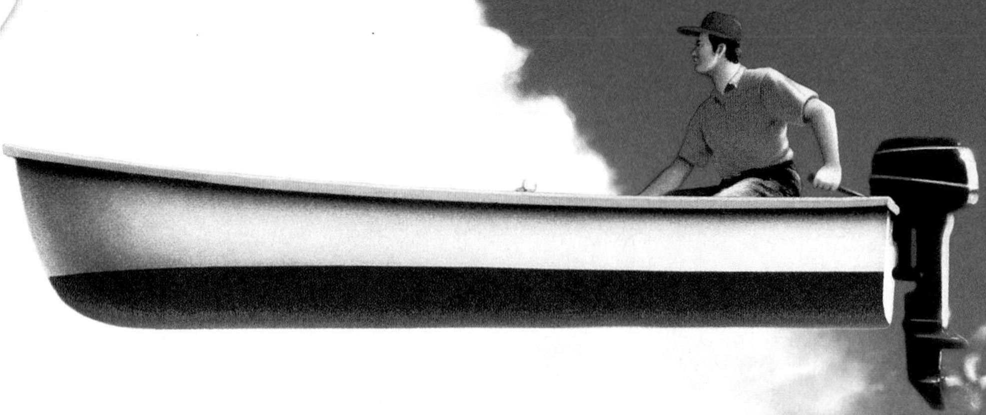

ADVENTURES BY LAND, AIR, AND WATER

WHAT MAKES AN ADVENTURE?

Read It ONLINE
sfsuccessnet.com

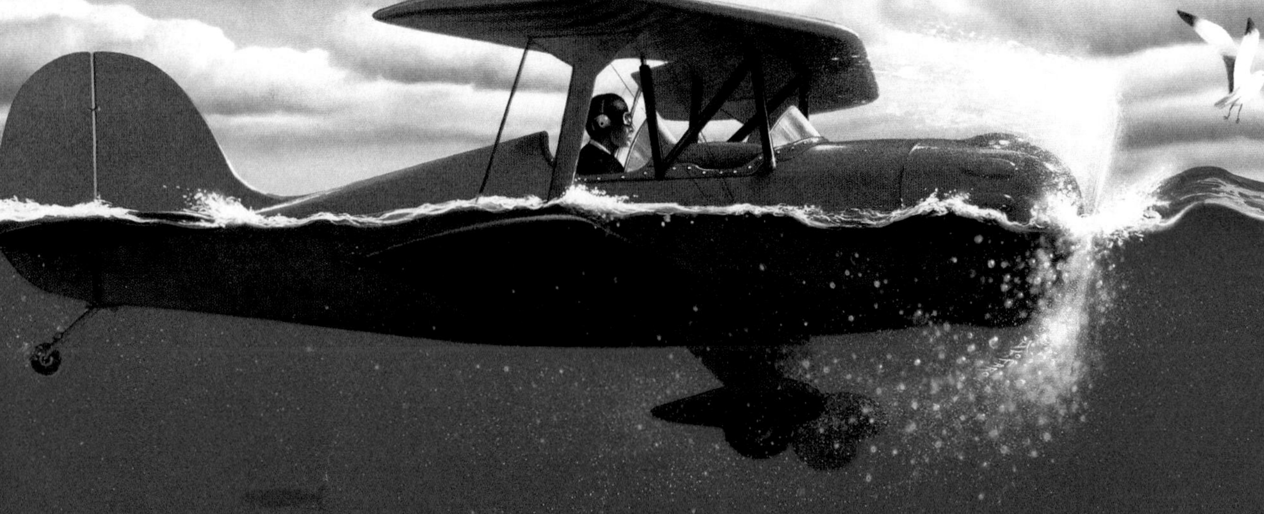

Skill
Author's Purpose

Strategy
Predict

Author's Purpose

- An author might have more than one reason for writing. Four common reasons are to persuade, to inform, to express ideas or feelings, and to entertain.

- *How* you read can depend on *what* you're reading. For example, you might read a funny story faster than a news article.

Before		After
Predicted Author's Purpose	Reason(s) for This Prediction	Author's Actual Purpose(s)

Strategy: Predict

Good readers think about the author's purpose. Before you read an article or story, look it over to predict the author's purpose so you have an idea of how to read the piece. While you read, use the author's purpose to predict what he or she may write next. Hint: Illustrations and diagrams are clues to the author's purpose.

1. Look over "A Life at Sea." Make a graphic organizer like the one above and fill in the first two empty boxes. After reading, fill in the last box.

2. Write about what you think the author's purpose was and whether or not she achieved that purpose.

A Life at Sea

Picture a graceful clipper ship out on the ocean. The wind billows its sails as it glides smoothly over the waves. For the crew, life on board must be relaxed and easy, right?

Picture yourself as a cabin boy. You signed on because you wanted adventure. Well, you might find adventure, and you might even become a captain yourself one day. The skills of sailing are called *seamanship.* On board the ship, you might learn which rope knots you need and how to tie them. Perhaps you would learn how to measure the ship's rate of speed and the depth of the water. You certainly would learn to tell where you are and what weather is coming your way.

Still, you are a cabin boy, which means you have many chores. You have to swab (scrub) the deck, polish the brass, waterproof the rigging with tar, catch rainwater in a barrel, clean dirty living areas on the ship, carry coal for the stove, and— well, you get the picture. At night, you crawl into a hammock, fall asleep to the sound of the ship's bell marking the time, and dream of faraway places.

Strategy What do you predict this article will be about? What makes you think that? What might the author's purpose be? How should you read this?

Skill Which author's purpose relates to writing about the beauty of life at sea? Watch for another possible purpose as you read.

Skill Why do you think the author told you about some of the things you could learn on a clipper ship? Did you read more slowly or reread any parts of this section?

Strategy How did predicting the author's purpose help you understand the article better?

Words to Know

cargo

bow

stern

dignified

navigation

celestial

conducted

quivered

Try the strategy. Then, if you need more help, use your glossary or a dictionary.

Vocabulary Strategy
for Homonyms and Homographs

Context Clues When you are reading, you may find a familiar word used in a new way. It may be a homonym or homograph. Homonyms are spelled and pronounced the same, but they are words with different meanings and histories. Homographs are spelled the same but are pronounced differently and have different meanings. You can use the context to figure out the meaning of a homonym or homograph.

1. Think about the different meanings homonyms and homographs can have. For example, a *jar* is a glass container, but if you *jar* someone, you shake him or her. *Wind* (with the short *i* sound) means "a current of air," but *wind* (with the long *i* sound) means "to coil around something."

2. Read the words and sentences around the unknown word. Are there any clues that can help you tell which homonym or homograph is being used?

3. Put that meaning into the sentence and see if it makes sense.

As you read "Adventure on the Sea," use the context to help you decide which homonym or homograph the author is using.

ADVENTURE ON THE SEA

In the 1800s, sailors set sail for adventure every time they left port. A trade ship might be loaded with cargo to be sold on the far side of the world. The captain and crew might be gone for months, even years.

The ship itself was interesting to look at. Often a fancy carving of a beautiful woman set off the bow, or front part of the ship. In many cases, she was the only female on board. From the bow to the stern, or rear part of the ship, sailors worked hard. They climbed quickly up and down masts and sails. They repaired sails and cleaned the ship.

The captain, a dignified figure, might stand on the upper decks to watch the work and give orders. He knew all the methods of navigation. He could use instruments or steer a course using the celestial bodies, or stars. The captain was the powerful commander of the ship. He conducted all the ship's business and had to be obeyed without question. When the ship quivered and rolled in a terrible storm, the crew depended on his steady guidance.

Write

Pretend you are a sailor bound for India in 1850. Write a letter home about your life on board the ship. Use words from the Words to Know list.

Genre

Historical fiction is based on real events in history, but it is a story to which the author has added details from his or her imagination. As you read this story about a family's life at sea, think about which details are historical and which are from the author's imagination.

SAILING HOME

A Story of a Childhood at Sea

told by Gloria Rand • illustrated by Ted Rand

Could a ship be a good place to call "home"?

Ours was a wonderful childhood, a childhood spent at sea. My sister Dagmar, my brother, Albert, and I, Matilda, grew up aboard the *John Ena,* a four-masted sailing bark that carried cargo all over the world.

Our father was the ship's captain; the ship was our home. Only when the cargo was coal, which is highly inflammable, did we have to live ashore.

The *John Ena* had bedrooms, a bathroom, and a main saloon that was a combination living room with a pink marble fireplace and a dining room with a big round table. There was a kitchen called the galley and a storage room full of everything we needed.

Unlike most homes, ours didn't stay put. At night, the ship kept moving, so every morning we woke up far away from where we'd gone to sleep.

It often seemed as if we lived on a farm, not a ship. Roosters crowed, hens clucked, and ducks quacked. Mother raised them all in neat pens below deck, so we'd have fresh meat and eggs to add to the ship's food supply. Dagmar and I collected the eggs.

We all took turns caring for our pets as we traveled around the world. There was Minnie the cat and a dog named Murphy. We had a mongoose, a monkey, a pig, and even a kangaroo.

The day the kangaroo accidentally jumped overboard we screamed for help. The crew quickly lowered a life boat and rescued it.

Our pet pig wasn't so lucky. She fell into a pot of hot tar the men were using to repair the ship's deck. Piggy died. We had a real funeral for her and a dignified burial at sea.

Instead of a backyard or a playground we had a great wooden deck where we played tag, hide-and-seek, and catch, always with beanbags, because balls bounced overboard. We swung on rope swings and, after our baby sister Ena was born, we took turns wheeling her around the deck in a baby buggy.

When the winds were blowing hard and the sea was full of big waves, we played inside. Our favorite game was sliding across the main saloon floor in cardboard boxes, crashing into one another as the ship rolled from side to side.

"Time to calm down," Mother would say softly when we got rowdy. "Let's read for a while."

Mother taught us how to read and count. She was a good teacher. Father was a good teacher, too.

"Name that planet," he'd say, pointing to a bright steady light in the dark night sky. Before long we could tell planets from stars, and even understood about celestial navigation. As a special treat Father gave us our own set of signaling flags, and we learned to send messages. From the stern of the ship we sent messages to Father at the bow, and he signaled messages back to us.

There were no radios then, and when we were out at sea we seldom saw another ship. If a ship did pass close enough for us to see each other clearly, Father, or one of the crew, exchanged greetings and information, using signaling flags.

Real school began when Miss Shipman, a governess, came aboard as our teacher. Albert didn't like her at all. Dagmar said she looked mean, but I thought she was nice.

With Miss Shipman in charge, we went to school at the dining table six days a week, mornings and afternoons, with only an hour off for lunch and no recesses.

Miss Shipman was good at teaching us history, science, mathematics, and languages. But teaching us geography was impossible for her. We'd seen so much of the world, we knew more than she did. We'd tell her about family picnics in Japan and all about palaces and cathedrals we had visited in Europe. Miss Shipman was impressed, but not with Albert.

Albert didn't like school. He played hooky a lot. He'd sneak off to mend sails with the ship's carpenter, or help the crew scrub down the deck with flat stones called holy stones. Sometimes Albert crawled up and hid in a little cubbyhole by the masthead. Miss Shipman would tattle to Father, and Father would bring Albert back to school.

I liked to get away, too, and be alone up in the rigging, high above the deck. I liked to feel the wind, smell the salty air, and watch the rolling ocean for as far as I could see. But I never got to stay up there for long. As soon as one of the crew spotted me, I'd hear a loud shout, "Get down, Matilda, you little spider!"

The crew watched us all the time to make sure we didn't get into serious trouble. They watched us even when they were working, scrubbing sails, laying them out to dry, polishing brass cleats and handles, and mending ropes.

The carpenter made toys for us, the sailmaker taught us how to tie nautical knots, and the cook baked us special treats. We had the whole crew for friends.

Even though our life was different from other children's, we didn't miss out on anything. We had marshmallow roasts at the fireplace, taffy pulls in the galley, and footraces out on deck. Mother always brought along Christmas and birthday presents, and decorations for every holiday.

Only once, when I was ten, we almost didn't have Christmas.

That year, as we crossed the China Sea, the weather turned wild. We had just started to put up red and green garlands and ropes of sparkling tinsel when Father rushed in.

"Here, grab this end, and tie up that chair," Father ordered as he unwound a big coil of heavy line.

We all knew what to do. Like experts we tied the piano and all the furniture to the railing that ran along the walls of the main saloon and to big hooks the carpenter was screwing into the floor. Mother put little things, lamps, knickknacks, and our candy dish into a heavy sea chest. Everything had to be tied up or put away, otherwise, when the ship pitched and rolled, there would have been stuff crashing and flying all over the place.

It wasn't long before we were in the middle of a terrible storm that stayed with us for days. The sky was black. There were huge bolts of lightning, and thunder roared so loud you could hardly think.

No matter how bad the storm became, Miss Shipman made us go to school. The seas got so rough it wasn't safe to sit at the dining table, so we all sat on the floor while Miss Shipman conducted class. We slid back and forth across the floor as the ship rode the waves. It was like riding a roller coaster.

After school we pressed our faces against the portholes and cheered as tons of water smashed against the glass. When Mother saw what we were doing she pulled us back.

"I don't want you to get hurt," she said. "Those waves could shatter the glass."

Two of the crew did get hurt when a gigantic wave swept them down the length of the ship. Father dashed out and pulled them to safety. Mother sewed up their bad cuts with ordinary needle and thread. One of the sailors cried.

The storm got worse and worse. Lifeboats were torn loose and smashed into pieces by gigantic waves, and the sails were ripped to shreds by screaming winds. But lucky for us we didn't get seasick. We never did. Father decided the safest place for all of us to be was on the floor of the ship's chart room. That's when we began to get scared. Father tried to get us to think about something else, like having a Christmas party.

"When we get through this storm," he promised, "we're going to have a grand holiday celebration. It will be the most wonderful party we've ever had. Let's start planning it now."

At that moment the ship rolled onto her side, and didn't roll back. We all clung together.

"Mary," he said as he kissed our mother, "the ship has broached, and I think we're about to sink."

"Yes, dear," said Mother, looking Father right in the eye and smiling the bravest smile you'd ever hope to see.

Neither of them showed any panic or fear, and that made us children feel brave, too. Father kissed each of us and told us we were great sailors.

It seemed our family stayed hugging together forever, then the *John Ena* quivered a strange quiver and slowly righted herself!

Gradually, the storm ended, and the sea became calm.

"Time to get our celebration ready," said Father. He had never sounded so happy.

With all of us helping, everything was soon put back where it belonged.

"Girls, hang all this ribbon and tinsel up everywhere. And Albert, you're in charge of decorating the wooden Christmas tree, the one the carpenter made for us." Mother was excited.

"Don't look, I'm about to bring out the presents. Your father has a surprise for you, too, don't you, dear?"

We all laughed because we knew what Father's surprise always was at Christmas. He became Santa.

That night we dressed up in our party clothes. The crew sang "My Bonnie Lies Over the Ocean." They sang the best they had ever sung. The cook filled the table with delicious treats, and we played the gramophone and clapped and cheered watching Father dance with Mother. They were such good dancers.

As promised, it was the best Christmas ever. We were safe, right where we loved to be. We were at home, home on the sea.

This story is based on a real family's life aboard a four-masted sailing bark, the *John Ena*, one of many sailing ships that carried cargo all over the world in the 1800s. Named for an important Chinese-Hawaiian merchant, the magnificent *John Ena* was 312 feet 9 inches long, and 48 feet wide. She carried coal, lumber, sugar, barley, wheat, and general cargo to ports around the world.

She made forty-four voyages between 1896 and 1910 under the command of Captain Mads Albert Madsen, some only a few weeks long, others nearly five months. On most of these voyages, Captain Madsen was accompanied by his wife Anna Marie and their children, Matilda, Albert, Dagmar, and Ena. Two of the children, Albert and Dagmar, were born aboard.

"When do we sail?" the children would ask their parents whenever the *John Ena* was in port. "When are we going back out to sea?"

Out at sea was where they most wanted to be. On the few occasions when these young sailors lived ashore they described school as a

Pictures from a life at sea

From left to right: the *John Ena* under full sail; Captain Mads Albert Madsen; Anna Marie Madsen; Dagmar, Albert, and Matilda on deck; baby Ena in a wicker carriage with diapers drying in the wind behind her.

nightmare, even though they did well, and easily made friends with other children.

Their life aboard ship was luxurious, as family life was on many tall ships. Linen tablecloths and napkins were standard at their table. Food was served on heavy white ironstone ware, decorated with a deep blue band and inscribed with the *John Ena* insignia. Furnishings were plush and would have been acceptable in any mansion ashore.

When faster, more efficient steamships took over trade and passenger routes, Captain Madsen became a qualified steamship captain. Quarters aboard these ships did not offer the same spacious accommodations for family living as had the large sailing ships. The Madsens settled in Honolulu, Hawaii.

Their walk down the *John Ena*'s gangplank for the last time was heartbreaking for each member of the Madsen family. The captain was the last to leave. With baby Ena in his arms and tears in his eyes, he turned as he stepped onto the dock and saluted his ship. Then he saluted his crew.

"Aloha, Captain, good luck." The crew was heartbroken, too.

Reader Response

Open for Discussion Suppose you were with the Madsens for five months at sea. Describe your best adventure, your worst adventure, or your scariest adventure.

1. Why does the author tell the Madsens' true story as if Matilda were telling it?

2. Figuring out the author's purpose helps you adjust the way you read. Did you read *Sailing Home* quickly or slowly? Why?

3. Did you predict that the Madsens would survive the storm at sea? Explain what you thought would happen and why.

4. The children tell of learning about *celestial navigation*. *Celestial navigation* is an open compound. Figure out the meaning of each part of the compound and then tell what the compound means.

Test Practice

Look Back and Write Describe the adventure of the kangaroo and the pet pig. Based on what you read on page 523, tell what happened to them.

GLORIA AND TED RAND

Read more books by Gloria and Ted Rand.

Sailing Home is the fifth book about sailing that Gloria Rand has written and her husband, Ted Rand, has illustrated. Gloria and Ted Rand live with their two children on St. Mercer Island off the coast of Washington state. So it's not surprising that they have made books together about the sea that surrounds them. The Rands also spend a lot of time hiking in the forest near their home.

Ted Rand has been an award-winning illustrator of children's books for many years. Gloria Rand began writing children's books in 1989 at the suggestion of her husband. "I like to write and I'm a natural exaggerator, which doesn't hurt," she says. "I research carefully with each new manuscript, no matter what the subject. It frees me from worrying that I'm going to pass on misinformation to readers. I also try to keep my writing simple and clear."

The Cabin Key

Fighting for the Forest

Social Studies
in Reading

Narrative Nonfiction

Genre

- **Narrative nonfiction can be a record of the true experiences of a person or several people.**

- **In narrative nonfiction the author might describe how the subject or subjects felt as well as what they saw and did.**

Text Features

- **Photographs give a glimpse of the man who made the voyage.**

- **A caption expands on information in the text.**

Link to Social Studies

Research another adventurer who has traveled across an ocean for discovery or pleasure. Share what you learn with the class.

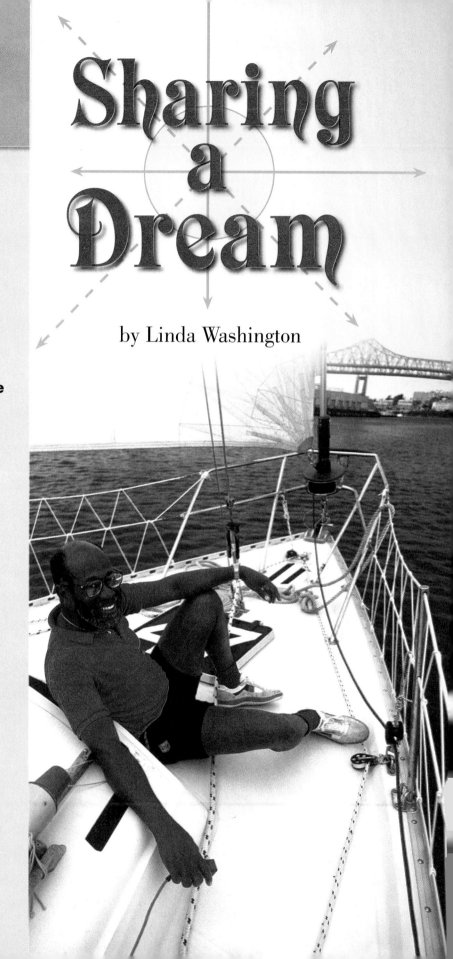

Sharing a Dream

by Linda Washington

What's your idea of an adventure? For William Pinkney (Captain Bill), it meant sailing around the world alone. He wanted to be the first African American sailor to make this 27,000-mile voyage. But he also wanted the trip to be educational, not only for himself, but for thousands of schoolchildren in his hometown of Chicago, Illinois.

Captain Bill describes his voyage.

Captain Bill left Boston Harbor on August 5, 1990, in a 47-foot sailboat named *Commitment*. He planned to sail around the five southern capes of the world: the Cape of Good Hope (South Africa); Cape Leeuwin (Australia); South West Cape (Tasmania); Stewart Island Cape (New Zealand); and Cape Horn (South America). Only three other Americans had made this trip.

Thanks to support from sponsors in business and other groups who wanted to help, students were able to use classroom computers to follow Mr. Pinkney's day-to-day progress and to ask him questions and get answers. He, in turn, asked students to help him with math problems dealing with time, distance, and wind speed. When Captain Bill stopped in ports along the way, he introduced children to the languages and customs of the people he met there.

All was not perfect on this nearly two-year journey. Captain Bill faced storms, sickness, loneliness, and exhaustion. But four months after rounding Cape Horn, he sailed back into Boston Harbor. He had made his dream come true.

Reading Across Texts

Compare and contrast the journeys of the Madsen family and William Pinkney.

Writing Across Texts Write two ways in which the journeys were alike and two ways in which they were different.

Author's Purpose The graphics help you decide that this text informs.

Comprehension

Skill
Compare
and Contrast

Strategy
Visualize

Compare and Contrast

- To compare means to tell how two or more things are alike. To contrast means to tell how two or more things are different.

- Authors may use clue words such as *like*, *as*, and *same* to show comparisons. They may use clue words such as *but*, *unlike*, and *different* to show contrasts.

Similarities	Differences

Strategy: Visualize

Active readers transform the words on the page into mental images. Visualizing likenesses and differences between two people or things that are being compared is especially helpful. As you read, picture in your mind new information that is coming to you from the text.

1. Read "Archaeology: Dig It." Make a graphic organizer like the one above to show similarities and differences in how people live today and how they lived long ago.

2. Visualize yourself living in the distant past. On a graphic organizer, compare your life as it would have been then with how it is now. Write a paragraph comparing the two.

ARCHAEOLOGY: DIG IT

Archaeology is the study of things left behind by people who lived in the past. Some archaeologists study people who left behind not only things, but also written records. Others study people who had no written language.

Skill What does one type of archaeologist do that the other does not? Tell how the two types are alike and different.

With the passing of time, ancient places often are covered over with layers of earth. The archaeologist has to dig down to find the things people left behind. These things give clues to how those people lived.

Strategy Visualize a place where an archaeologist is digging. How does your mental picture of the past compare with an everyday scene from your own life?

People of all times and places have certain things in common. For example, we all need to eat, and we all need a place to live. So archaeologists look for everyday things such as dishes, cooking pots, arrowheads, and hunting knives. They also hope to find things people built, such as houses and roads. Archaeologists study all of these things to try to understand how people lived in the past.

Skill Compare and contrast the way many people live today with how people lived long ago.

Of course, the way we live today is often different from how people lived long ago. Most of us don't hunt our food. We don't make our own cooking pots or dishes. But we do live in homes and travel on roads, and we do keep written records. We will leave behind these records for other people to read in the future. We will leave behind many other things as well. All of these things will help people understand how we lived.

Strategy What will people in the future discover about the way we lived? Visualize things they might find that will tell them about us.

LOST CITY
The Discovery of Machu Picchu

Words to Know

curiosity

thickets

torrent

ruins

glorious

terraced

granite

Remember

Try the strategy. Then, if you need more help, use your glossary or a dictionary.

Vocabulary Strategy
for Greek and Latin Roots

Word Structure Many English words have Latin or Greek roots. For example, the Latin word terra means "earth, land." Part of it appears in words such as terrain (surface of the ground) and territory (an area of land). The Latin word gloria means "praise"; part of it appears in words such as glorify, meaning "to praise." You may be able to use Latin and Greek roots to help you figure out the meaning of an unknown word.

1. Look at the unknown word. Try to identify a Greek or Latin root.

2. What is the meaning of the Greek or Latin root? How does it affect the meaning of the unknown word?

3. Try the meaning in the sentence. Does it make sense?

As you read "Looking for the Past," look for words with Greek or Latin roots to help you figure out the meanings of the words.

Looking for the Past

Some scientists study the past. They look at objects and buildings from past civilizations. They have curiosity about people who lived long ago. How did they live? What did they eat? What did they do every day? Did they read and write? Thanks to these scientists, we have learned a great deal about long-ago people.

These scientists have ventured into places that few others would go. They have cut their way through jungles with thickets full of dangerous animals. They have climbed steep mountains and slipped on rocks. They have crossed mountain rivers that fall in a raging torrent. They have found ruins of places people built long ago. These may look like rocks to us, but they are glorious to these scientists.

Imagine the little team of scientists as they discover terraced fields on the side of a mountain. These show that people long ago were clever farmers. Think of the scientists as they look at beautiful temples made of granite or marble. These show that people long ago had beliefs. Watch as the scientists carefully uncover clay pots and carvings. These show that people long ago were artistic and loved beauty.

Write

Look at the pictures in the next selection, *Lost City*. Pick one to write about. Use as many words from the Words to Know list as you can.

LOST
The Discovery of Machu Picchu

BY TED LEWIN

Genre

Narrative nonfiction can tell the story of a real event such as the discovery of a lost city. The details of the event are presented in sequence so that readers can understand the cause-and-effect relationships. Look for these relationships as you read.

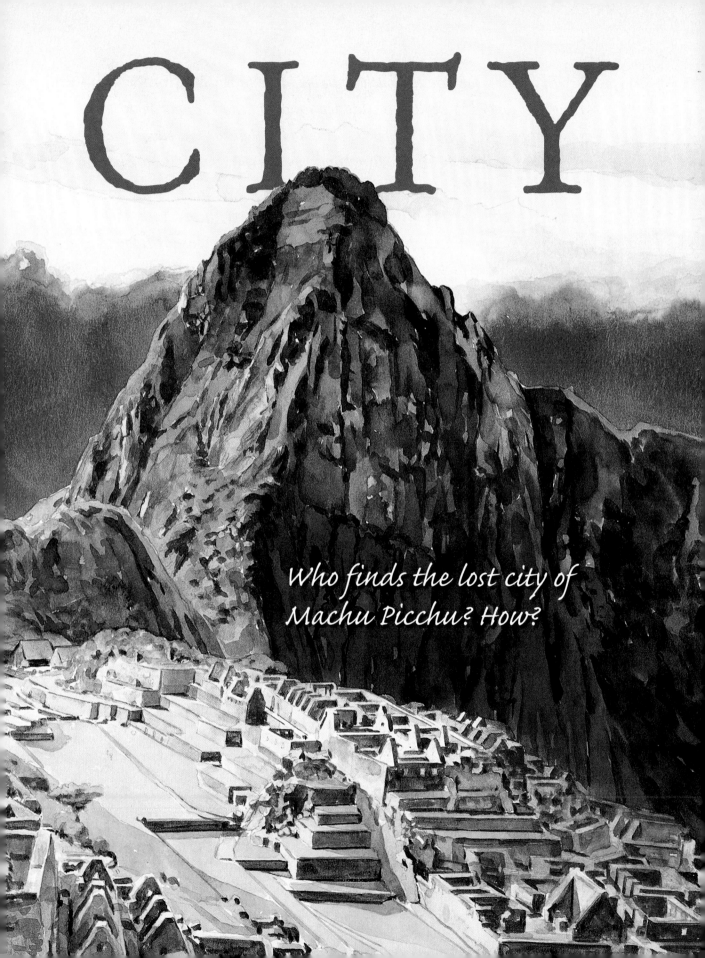

CITY

Who finds the lost city of Machu Picchu? How?

In his first journey to South America, Yale professor Hiram Bingham longed to explore the hidden lands that lay beyond the snowcapped peaks of the Andes. Legend had it that the lost city of the Inca, Vilcapampa, lay there. Bingham was determined to discover it. So in 1910, the Yale Peruvian Expedition was organized. Finally, in July 1911, Bingham and his fellow adventurers arrived in Cusco, the first capital city of the Inca. What lay ahead for them was far from what they had expected. And more amazing. Our story begins high in the mountains of Peru. . . .

The boy looked out at the cloud-covered peaks all around him. Already his papa was working in the terraced fields. But last night he had dreamed of a tall stranger carrying a small black box. He could not get the dream out of his mind.

Suddenly, the clouds burned off and the mountains were bathed in glorious light. The dream foretold of something wonderful, he was sure.

Sixty miles south, in Cusco, Hiram Bingham gazed thoughtfully at the old Incan stone wall. He had come to Peru in search of Vilcapampa, the lost city of the Inca. But right here was the most beautiful stonework he had ever seen—huge stones cut so perfectly that not even a razor blade could be slipped between them.

The Inca had no iron tools to carve them, no wheel or draft animals to move them. The wall had withstood time and earthquakes. How had the Inca built it?

It was a mystery.

He walked through the cobbled streets of the old capital. The Spanish had come to this city, conquered the Inca, taken their gold, and built churches over their temples. Suddenly, he stopped. Before him was the famous Temple of the Sun. He placed his hands on the sun-warmed stones so beautifully carved, as if they had grown together.

Hidden in the mountains, the lost city would be built of stones like these. Would it hold gold and fabulous riches like the Spanish had found in Cusco?

More than ever he was determined to find that city.

The next day Bingham began his search. He would look for ruins—that might be the key.

He and his party, accompanied by military escort Sergeant Carrasco, left by mule train for the sacred valley of the Urubamba River.

They came to the sleepy old village of Ollantaytambo, long ago an important city. Its ancient stone terraces stepped up into the clouds.

"Are there any ruins nearby?" Bingham asked. He went door to door. He sat for hours in the cantina. "Are there any ruins near here?" he asked anyone who came in. "Do you know of the lost city of Vilcapampa?" No one knew of it.

Traveling north, the adventurers came upon a remote and wild canyon. Granite cliffs rose thousands of feet above the roaring rapids of the Urubamba River. In the distance were snowcapped mountains over three miles high. Bingham's

determination to find the lost city grew with each turn of the increasingly wild trail.

Meanwhile, high on one of these granite ridges, the boy tried to help his papa on the terraces. But he couldn't shake the dream from his mind. Who was this stranger with the black box? When would he come? What was in the black box? Anxiously, he searched the mountains for a sign.

Far below in the valley, Bingham's party camped on a sandy beach alongside the thundering rapids of the Urubamba. Days had gone by. He was tired and discouraged. No one knew of any ruins.

But now the travelers aroused the curiosity of a local farmer named Arteaga.

"Are there ruins nearby?" Bingham asked when Arteaga ventured into camp.

This time, through the interpreter, the farmer said, "Yes. There are very good ruins on top of the mountain called Machu Picchu."

The farmer pointed straight up.

547

"Can you take us there?" Bingham asked.

"No," said Arteaga. "It is a very hard climb and there are many snakes." Bingham offered him coins. Arteaga nodded–he would show them the way.

Arteaga led them down the river trail. Suddenly, he plunged into the jungle. Bingham and the sergeant followed Arteaga through dense undergrowth down to the very edge of the river to a flimsy bridge made of slim logs. What was he getting himself into!

Sergeant Carrasco and Arteaga took off their shoes and crossed easily, gripping with their bare feet. Bingham was terrified–he crept across the bridge on hands and knees. One slip and he would be dashed to pieces in the roaring torrent below.

They climbed the bank into dense jungle. Now the slopes were slippery and the heat terrible. Arteaga had warned them of the fer-de-lance, a very venomous snake. Bingham's eyes searched the jungle.

Up and up they climbed. The wide river was now but a silver thread, far below. Arteaga could think of nothing but the fer-de-lance;

548

Sergeant Carrasco thought about his good, sturdy shoes; Bingham thought of nothing but the lost city. They cut their way through tangled thickets. Up and up they climbed.

Had an hour passed? Two? Three? Now they crept on all fours. They slipped and slid. In some places, they held on by their fingertips.

Finally, thirsty and exhausted, they broke through the jungle into sunlight. Above them stood a little Quechua boy beside a stone hut. What could he be doing at the top of this mountain?

"Ama llulla, ama quella, ama su'a" (Don't lie, don't be lazy, don't steal), the boy called out in the traditional Quechua greeting.

It was the tall stranger from his dream. Carrying the black box!

The boy's whole family crowded around to greet the exhausted travelers, then brought gourds of cool water and boiled sweet potatoes.

Bingham, still gasping for breath, asked, "Where are the ruins?" The boy said, *"Amuy, amuy!"* (Come, come!)

Bingham and the sergeant left Arteaga behind and followed at the boy's urging. *"Amuy, amuy!"* he kept saying.

At first they saw only stone terraces like the ones they had seen at Ollantaytambo. They looked as if they had been recently cleared of jungle and the vegetation burned off in order to plant crops.

But there were no ruins. Just more jungle beyond. Bingham had climbed this mountain and found—no lost city.

"*Amuy, amuy!*" Still, the boy beckoned him into the jungle beyond. Weary and discouraged, Bingham followed. At first all he saw were bamboo thickets and more tangled vines. Then he looked closer. Through the vines, he saw—stones. Inca stones. Then walls, beautiful stone walls! They were covered with mosses. And trees.

"*Jaway, jaway!*" (See, see!) the boy whispered, pointing ahead to a curved stone wall. Bingham pushed his way to it and placed his hands on the fine granite stones. A sun temple. More beautiful even than the one in Cusco.

They came to a grand stone staircase. Where could this lead? What else was here?

"*Jaway, jaway,*" the boy called.

At the top of the staircase was a clearing. A small vegetable garden, and then . . . a temple built of enormous stones. Grander than any Bingham had ever seen. It stole his breath away.

Something was going on here, he could sense it.

Something just beyond his eyes. What was it?

He followed the boy to another temple. As magnificent. This one had three windows. But now he looked across the countryside. He looked past the thickets, past the vines. He began to see the outlines of stone streets and stone cottages. He began to see the outlines of a city!

"Here, boy," he said as he opened the black box that he had been carrying, extended the bellows and focused his camera.

The first picture would be of the boy. The boy who had led him to Vilcapampa, lost city of the Inca.

But about this Bingham was wrong. When the vines were removed and the tales told, he had discovered not Vilcapampa, but a place even more amazing.

He had stumbled on Machu Picchu, a city lost in time, a city lost in the clouds.

AUTHOR'S NOTE

To research this book on the discovery of Machu Picchu, I first read Hiram Bingham's journal. In it he tells how a little Quechua boy led him to the site in the jungle. Then I traveled to Peru and followed in Hiram's footsteps as closely as I could.

I traveled to Ollantaytambo, as Hiram did, climbed the ancient terraces there, and sat in a little cantina, maybe the very one in which Hiram sat. I walked part of the rugged Inca trail to Pisac, and finally arrived at the Sun Gate above Machu Picchu.

I also journeyed through the sacred valley of the Urubamba River to Machu Picchu, and spent a week exploring and photographing the site and its surrounding cloud forest. And from the high pastures, I witnessed the magical sunset that I tried to capture on the jacket painting.

But the day the story began to come alive in my mind was the day I saw a young Quechua boy who raced our bus 2,500 feet down the mountain from Machu Picchu to the valley below—and won. As he stood, dripping with perspiration and chest heaving with exertion, I thought that Hiram's young guide must have looked just like this boy.

The most exciting part of working on the paintings was re-creating the way Machu Picchu must have looked when Hiram Bingham discovered it, hidden by five hundred years of jungle growth.

—Ted Lewin

Reader Response

Open for Discussion Be a "you-are-there" reporter. Tell about Hiram Bingham's search for the lost city as if you were there. Use the illustrations to help make your report exciting.

1. The illustrations in this selection are big and bold, and cover two pages. Why do you think Ted Lewin used this illustration style?

2. In what ways was Hiram Bingham like the stranger in the boy's dream?

3. The author describes the moment Hiram Bingham first sees Machu Picchu. Visualize as you reread that part of the selection. Describe what you see, hear, smell, and feel.

4. *Snowcapped peaks, sleepy old village,* and *sun-warmed stones* are phrases that describe what Hiram Bingham saw. Make a web. Write *Machu Picchu* in the center. Around it, write descriptive phrases you find in the selection. Include words from the Words to Know list.

Test Practice

Look Back and Write What is the mystery of the Incan stone walls? Look back at page 545 and then write what the mystery is.

TED LEWIN

Read more books by Ted Lewin.

Ted Lewin loves to travel. He writes and illustrates books about his trips. For *Lost City,* he hiked the jungle trail to Machu Picchu in Peru. He has also photographed gorillas in Uganda and rhinos in Nepal. He has watched a tiger from an elephant's back in India. And he has been much too close to grizzly bears, rattlesnakes, and bison.

When he travels, Mr. Lewin uses a journal, a sketch book, photographs, and recordings to help him remember what he sees. His wife, Betsy, comes with him. She is also an artist, and they sometimes write books together.

Mr. Lewin grew up in Buffalo, New York, where he says he had "two brothers, one sister, two parents, a lion, an iguana, a chimpanzee, and an assortment of more conventional pets." The lion stayed only a short time—his mother donated it to the Buffalo Zoo.

Gorilla Walk by Ted and Betsy Lewin

Elephant Quest by Ted and Betsy Lewin

Personal Essay

Genre

- A personal essay is written to inform and/or entertain a reader.

- A personal essay is an account of an individual's experience and is written in the first person.

- A personal essay introduces a reader to an author's personality and preferences.

Text Features

- Photographs capture the beauty of Machu Picchu and allow the reader to explore the land and its people.

- A map gives information about Peru and the distance people travel when they make the journey from Cusco to Machu Picchu.

Link to Social Studies

Do research to learn about the Inca way of life. Share an interesting finding with your class.

Riding the Rails to Machu Picchu

by Katacha Díaz

High atop one of the Andes Mountains in Peru is one of the greatest human-made wonders of the world—Machu Picchu, the lost city of the Incas. Every year about 400,000 people from around the world make the journey to see this amazing site. Several years ago I was one of them.

Anyone who visits Machu Picchu begins in the city of Cusco. Cusco itself is historic. Founded in the twelfth century by the Incas, it was conquered by an army from Spain in 1533.

There are three ways to get to Machu Picchu from Cusco. You can hike the old Inca Trail, a hard four-day journey. Guides will take you. Tents, food supplies, and anything other than your backpack will be carried by llamas. You can whisk from Cusco to Machu Picchu by helicopter. On this 25-minute trip you will quickly see glorious scenery. Finally, you can take a daily three-hour train ride. I am adventuresome. However, I didn't feel like making the hike! I chose the third way. Journey with me in your mind as I experience Machu Picchu!

Compare & Contrast   Compare and contrast the routes to Machu Picchu.

557

As the sun rises over Cusco's red tile rooftops, the train climbs through a series of steep switchback turns, out of the city and into the hillside.

We see tiny villages. People wave at the passing train. We see farmers atop the tin roofs of their cottages or in their fields, spreading corn for the sun to dry. Women and children tend animals nearby. We pass llamas and sheep grazing on grasses and wildflowers. Snaking its way through the Sacred Valley beside the train tracks is the fast-flowing Urubamba River. All around us are the beautiful mountains of the Andes.

Three hours after leaving Cusco, we reach the end of the rails, the train station called Puentes Ruinas. Looking up the mountain from the valley, I can see no evidence that Machu Picchu even exists. To get from the train station to the ruins, visitors can hike up a steep footpath or board buses that will take them to the entrance.

The town of Cusco

From the entrance of the ruins, I follow a narrow dirt path and am stunned by what I see. I stop to feast my eyes on the stone city. Nearby a small lizard suns itself on an ancient rock. A large hummingbird sips nectar from a wildflower.

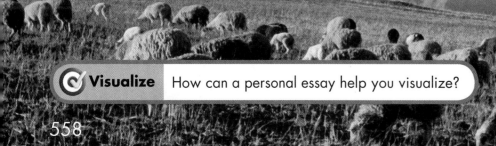

Visualize How can a personal essay help you visualize?

In my mind's eye, I picture Inca women filling ceramic jugs with water from one of the sixteen stone basins. I imagine Inca farmers harvesting crops from the terraces that look like giant steppingstones climbing the steep hillsides.

I walk up narrow flights of stone stairs to the highest point, the Intihuatana. I photograph the stunning sculpture called the Hitching Post of the Sun.

I climb steep steps and cross agricultural terraces to the Watchman's Hut. There I have a view of the entire city. It is spectacular and breathtaking!

View from the Watchman's Hut

In the middle of the afternoon, I must catch the train back to Cusco. I don't want to leave this amazing place. On the train, as I listen to Peruvian flute music, I think about my visit to mysterious Machu Picchu, lost city of the Incas. I remember the morning mist weaving its way through the steep hillsides of jungle. I dream of Inca cities that have not yet been discovered.

There are more adventures to be experienced!

The Hitching Post of the Sun
Below: A shepherd tends his flock.

Reading Across Texts
The two selections cover very different time periods. What are they?

Writing Across Texts Tell in which period you would have liked to visit Machu Picchu and why.

559

Comprehension

Skill
Sequence

Strategy
Story Structure

Sequence

- Sequence means the order in which things happen.

- Look for clue words that signal sequence, such as *first, next, then,* and *last.*

- Pay attention to dates and times the author gives you.

- Notice that some events happen simultaneously, or at the same time.

Strategy: Story Structure

Good readers use the structure of an article or story to help them understand what they are reading. Almost all fictional stories are arranged by sequence of events. Sometimes chronological (time) order is important in nonfiction. Look for references to dates and times as well as signal words. Make a time line to keep track of what happens. Study any illustrations that help you understand the sequence.

1. Read "The Mystery of Amelia Earhart." Make a time line to track the events in Earhart's journey.

2. Make a time line for an incident in which the order of events was important. Then write about the incident.

The Mystery of Amelia Earhart

Amelia Earhart wanted to be the first woman to fly around the world. She and her guide, Fred Noonan, planned to fly east from Florida, with many stops around the globe, before returning to the United States.

Strategy Biographies and books about historical events are almost always written in sequence. What do you think you will read about in the next paragraph?

Now they were in New Guinea with 29,000 miles behind them. There were 7,000 miles to go. First, they would fly to tiny Howland Island in the Pacific Ocean. Next, they would fly to Hawaii. Last, they would land in California.

Skill What clue words show the sequence of events in this paragraph?

Amelia and Fred took off from New Guinea on July 2, 1937. Howland is about 2,500 miles away. It would take them about 20 hours to get there. Meanwhile, the U.S. Coast Guard cutter *Itasca* was at Howland waiting for them. But the weather was bad, and so were the radio signals. The next morning, the *Itasca* got a radio transmission from Amelia: "We must be on you but cannot see you . . . gas is running low."

Skill The word *meanwhile* signals that two events are happening at the same time. What two events are happening here?

An hour later, she reported where she was. That was the last time she was heard from. The plane had disappeared.

President Roosevelt ordered a full search, but no trace of Amelia, Fred, or the airplane was ever found. What happened to them remains a mystery.

Strategy Why does sequence work well as the structure for this article?

Words to Know

| daring |
| elegant |
| outspoken |
| aviator |
| brisk |
| cockpit |
| solo |

Remember

Try the strategy. Then, if you need more help, use your glossary or a dictionary.

Vocabulary Strategy
for Unfamiliar Words

Context Clues Sometimes you can use context clues—the words and sentences around an unknown word—to help you figure out the meaning of the word.

1. Read the words and sentences around the unknown word. The author may give you a definition of the word.

2. If not, say what the sentence means in your own words.

3. Predict a meaning for the unknown word.

4. Try that meaning in the sentence. Does it make sense?

As you read "Amelia Earhart," use the context to help you figure out the meanings of vocabulary words.

AMELIA EARHART

Amelia Earhart was always daring. Even as a child, she bravely did things that were considered more suitable for boys than girls. But she wanted to change that kind of thinking. Society might declare that a woman should be elegant and passive, but Amelia said, in her outspoken way, "Women must try to do things as men have tried." That is what Amelia did as an aviator. On a brisk spring day in 1932, alone in the cockpit of her small plane, she set out from Newfoundland, Canada, and flew to Ireland. She was the first woman to fly solo across the Atlantic Ocean. She was also the first woman to fly solo from coast to coast and the first person to fly solo from Hawaii to California. As her final record, she wanted to be the first woman to fly around the world. In 1937, Amelia and her navigator, Fred Noonan, set out from Florida, flying east. They disappeared over the Pacific Ocean and were never found.

Write

Imagine you are Amelia Earhart flying alone across the Atlantic Ocean. Write a journal entry about your trip. Use words from the Words to Know list.

AMELIA AND

Genre

ELEANOR
GO FOR A RIDE

BY Pam Muñoz Ryan
pictures by Brian Selznick

WHY DO AMELIA AND ELEANOR GO FOR A RIDE, AND WHERE DOES IT TAKE THEM?

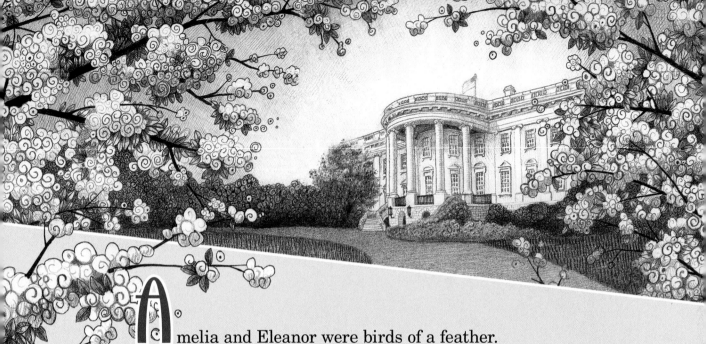

melia and Eleanor were birds of a feather.

Eleanor was outspoken and determined.

So was Amelia.

Amelia was daring and liked to try things other women wouldn't even consider.

Eleanor was the very same.

So when Eleanor discovered that her friend Amelia was coming to town to give a speech, she naturally said, "Bring your husband and come to dinner at my house! You can even sleep over."

It wasn't unusual for two friends to get together. But Eleanor was Eleanor Roosevelt, the First Lady of the United States, who lived in the White House with her husband, President Franklin Roosevelt.

Amelia was Amelia Earhart, the celebrated aviator who had been the first female pilot to fly solo across the Atlantic Ocean. And when two of the most famous and adventurous women in the world got together, something exciting was bound to happen.

In a guest room at the White House, Amelia and her husband, G. P., dressed for dinner. Amelia pulled on the long white evening gloves that were so different from the ones she sometimes wore while flying.

Many people didn't understand why a woman would
want to risk her life in a plane. But Amelia had said it more
than once: "It's for the fun of it." Besides, she loved the feeling
of independence she had when she was in the cockpit.

She carefully folded a gift for Eleanor—a silk scarf that
matched her own. The powder blue with streaks of indigo
reminded Amelia of morning sky.

Meanwhile, Eleanor dressed for dinner, too. Her brother,
Hall, would be escorting her this evening because the President
had a meeting to attend. But Eleanor was used to that.

She pulled on the long white evening gloves that were
so different from the ones she sometimes wore while driving.
Then she peeked out the window at the brand-new car that had
just been delivered that afternoon. She couldn't wait to drive it.

Many people thought it was too bold and dangerous for
a woman to drive a car, especially the First Lady of the
United States. But Eleanor always gave the same answer:
"It's practical, that's all." Besides, she loved the feeling of
independence she had when she was behind the wheel.

It was a brisk and cloudless April evening. The guests
had gathered in the Red Room, and the table looked elegant,
as even small dinner parties at the White House can be.

Eleanor and Hall greeted Amelia and G. P., as well as
several reporters and a photographer.

Amelia gave Eleanor the scarf.

"I love it!" Eleanor exclaimed. "It's just like yours."

Dinner started with George Washington's crab chowder.

"This is delicious," said Amelia. "But if soup at the White
House has such a fancy name, what will dessert be called?"

Perhaps Abraham Lincoln's peach cobbler? Or maybe
Thomas Jefferson's custard? They laughed as everyone took
turns guessing.

By the time they got to the roast duck, the conversation
had turned to flying.

"Mrs. Roosevelt just received her student pilot's license," said one of the reporters.

Amelia wasn't surprised. She had been the one to encourage Eleanor. She knew her friend could do anything she set her mind to.

"I'll teach you myself," offered Amelia.

"I accept! Tell us, Amelia, what's it like to fly at night in the dark?"

Everyone at the table leaned closer to hear. Very few people in the whole world had ever flown at night, and Amelia was one of them. Amelia's eyes sparkled. "The stars glitter all about and seem close enough to touch."

"At higher elevations, the clouds below shine white with dark islands where the night sea shows through. I've seen the planet Venus setting on the horizon, and I've circled cities of twinkling lights."

"And the capital city at night?" asked Eleanor.

"There's no describing it," said Amelia. "You just have to experience it on a clear night, when you can see forever. Why, we should go tonight! We could fly the loop to Baltimore and back in no time!"

The Secret Service men protested. "This hasn't been approved!"

"Nonsense!" said Eleanor. "If Amelia Earhart can fly solo across the Atlantic Ocean, I can certainly take a short flight to Baltimore and back!"

Before dessert could be served, Amelia had called Eastern Air Transport and arranged a flight.

Within the hour, Amelia and Eleanor boarded the Curtis Condor twin-motor airplane. For a moment, both women looked up at the mysterious night sky. Then, without changing her gloves, Amelia slipped into the cockpit and took the wheel.

The plane rolled down the runway, faster and faster.
Lights from the airstrip flashed in front of them. And they
lifted into the dark.

"How amusing it is to see a girl in a white evening
dress and high-heeled shoes flying a plane!" Eleanor said.

Amelia laughed as she made a wide sweep over
Washington, D.C., and turned off all the lights in the plane.

Out the window, the Potomac River glistened with
moonshine. The capitol dome reflected a soft golden halo. And
the enormous, light-drenched monuments looked like tiny
miniatures.

Soon the peaceful countryside gave way to shadowy
woodlands. The Chesapeake Bay became a meandering outline
on the horizon. And even though they knew it wasn't so, it
seemed as if the plane crawled slowly through starstruck space.

Eleanor marveled, "It's like sitting on top of the world!"

When it was time to land, Amelia carefully took the plane down. A group of reporters had gathered, anxious to ask questions.

"Mrs. Roosevelt, did you feel safe knowing a girl was flying that ship?"

"Just as safe!" said Eleanor.

"Did you fly the plane, Mrs. Roosevelt?" asked one reporter.

"What part did you like best?" said another.

"I enjoyed it so much, and no, I didn't actually fly the plane. Not yet. But someday I intend to. I was thrilled by the city lights, the brilliance of the blinking pinpoints below."

Amelia smiled. She knew just how Eleanor felt.

As the Secret Service agents drove them slowly back to the White House, Amelia and Eleanor agreed that there was nothing quite as exciting as flying. What could compare? Well, they admitted, maybe the closest thing would be driving in a fast car on a straightaway road with a stiff breeze blowing against your face.

Arms linked, they walked up the steps to the White House. Eleanor whispered something to Amelia, and then they hesitated, letting the rest of the group walk ahead of them.

"Are you coming inside, Mrs. Roosevelt?" someone asked.

But by then, they had wrapped their silk scarves around their necks and were hurrying toward Eleanor's new car.

Without changing her gloves, Eleanor quickly slipped into the driver's seat and took her turn at the wheel. With the wind in their hair and the brisk air stinging their cheeks, they flew down the road.

And after they had taken a ride about the city streets
of Washington, D.C., they finally headed back to the White
House . . .

. . . for dessert! Eleanor Roosevelt's pink clouds on angel
food cake.

Eleanor Roosevelt's Pink Clouds on Angel Food Cake

Angel Food Cake

1 cup cake flour (sift before measuring)
1 1/4 cups egg whites (10 or 12)
1 1/2 teaspoons cream of tartar
1 1/2 cups sugar
1 teaspoon almond flavoring
1/4 teaspoon salt

Sift flour at least twice. Beat egg whites with beater until foamy; add cream of tartar and 1 cup of sugar gradually. Continue beating until egg whites stand up in peaks. Add almond flavoring. Sift remaining 1/2 cup of sugar with salt and flour, and very carefully fold into egg whites. Bake in tube pan in 375 degree oven for 30 to 35 minutes.

Whipped Cream and Strawberries (Pink Clouds)

1 pint strawberries
1/2 pint heavy cream, whipped
1/2 cup sugar

Crush berries with sugar. Let stand 30 minutes. Carefully fold berries into whipped cream. Spoon on top of angel food cake.

Amelia and Eleanor look out the window of the Eastern Air Transport plane during their night flight on April 20, 1933.

Reader Response

Open for Discussion QUIET WHITE HOUSE DINNER. That is the headline you had planned to write. Now, as a star reporter, you'd better revise your story. Why? How?

1. Read page 571 slowly, starting with "Out the window...." How does the author help you see the view of Washington, D.C.?

2. Describe the sequence of events that leads up to Amelia and Eleanor's flight over Washington, D.C.

3. Did the story end as you expected it to end? Why or why not?

4. Write the names *Amelia* and *Eleanor* at the top of a two-column chart. List adjectives the author uses to describe them. Use words from the Words to Know list and the story.

Look Back and Write How did Amelia Earhart become famous? Look back at page 566 for information to help you write your answer.

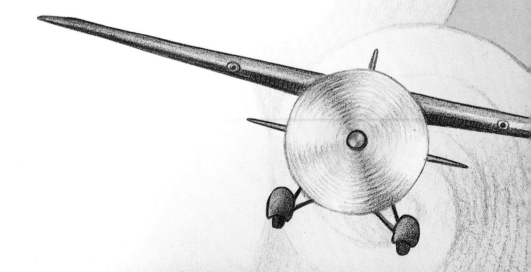

Read more books by Pam Muñoz Ryan and Brian Selznick.

Pam Muñoz Ryan has always admired Amelia Earhart and Eleanor Roosevelt. "When I read something about their meeting, I couldn't wait to write a book about it. I sat in a library and finally found the old newspaper articles. Later, Brian Selznick found a photograph from that very evening. It actually happened!"

Brian Selznick, an award-winning illustrator, was living in Washington, D.C., when he did the pictures for the book. "I was thrilled to be living in the city where Amelia and Eleanor went on their journey. I took the subway to the National Air and Space Museum to see one of the planes Amelia owned and to find pictures of other planes she flew. I walked to the White House, and I got to stand in the actual room where they ate. For the picture of them driving, all I had to do was walk out my door and draw the street."

Pam Muñoz Ryan and Brian Selznick have worked together on several books and are good friends.

How Do You Raise a Raisin?
by Pam Muñoz Ryan

The Meanest Doll in the World
by Ann Martin, illustrated by Brian Selznick

577

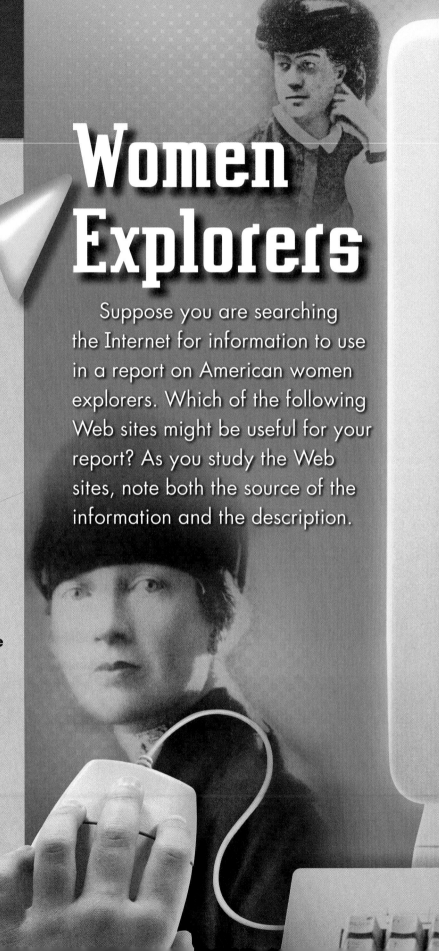

Evaluating Online Sources

Genre

- You can find information fast on the Internet. Only some of it will be useful and reliable (information that you can trust).

- When evaluating a Web site, think carefully, and remember what you know about statements of fact and opinion.

Text Features

- The addresses of useful and reliable Web sites often end in *.gov, .edu,* or *.org.* Web sites that end in *.com* may also be useful and reliable.

- The source of the Web site (the end of the address) and the description of the Web site can help you decide whether or not the site is useful and reliable.

Link to Social Studies

Research the achievements of a woman explorer. Share your findings.

Women Explorers

Suppose you are searching the Internet for information to use in a report on American women explorers. Which of the following Web sites might be useful for your report? As you study the Web sites, note both the source of the information and the description.

Take It to the NET™
ONLINE
578
more activities sfsuccessnet.com

When you place your cursor on this link, you see that it is a .edu Web site. The letters *edu* are short for *education*. A .edu site is usually a school and is often reliable. After you read the description, though, you realize that the site is not useful. *Explorers* must be the nickname of a sports team.

File Edit View Favorites Tools Help

http://www.url.here

Search *Engine*

american women explorers

Search

Glenview University Athletics
Athletics. Go Glenview **Explorers**.
Glenview University Athletics.

Resources—A Regional Museum's Women in Science
Women Explorers in Africa: Christina Dodwell, Delia Akeley, Mary Kingsley.

An Online Encyclopedia—First Ladies in the Field
First Ladies in the Field: **American Women Explorers.** Columbus, Magellan, Lewis and Clark, Hiram Bingham. Their stories are well known. But what about the ladies?

Women in
Explorers
Sacagawe

This is a .org Web site. The letters *org* are short for *organization*. A .org site may or may not be reliable. After you read the description, you decide that it is not useful because you are looking for information on American explorers.

This is a .com Web site. The letters *com* are short for *commercial*. A .com site usually sells something or contains ads. It may or may not be reliable. Both the source and the description tell you that this site should be useful.

✓ **Text Structure**   For text like this, you decide what part to read first.

You click on the online encyclopedia link to connect to the Web site. The following information appears on your screen.

Edit   View   Favorites   Tools   Help

http://www.url.here

First Ladies in the Field: Women Explorers

Columbus, Magellan, Lewis and Clark, Hiram Bingham— their stories are well known. But what about the ladies? Here are some extraordinary women adventurers.

1. In 1869, **Alexandrine Pieternella Françoise Tinné** became the first Dutch woman to cross the Sahara Desert.

2. American **Louise Arner Boyd** spent many years exploring the Arctic. In 1955, at age 68, Boyd became the first woman to fly over the North Pole.

3. Austrian **Ida Reyer Pfeiffer** traveled around the world ... Voyage Round the World.

Looking through the list, you decide to research **Louise Arner Boyd.** You type "Louise Arner Boyd" into the SEARCH window of a search engine and you get these results.

Sites about Louise Arner Boyd and other Female Explorers

An educational Web site — Louise Arner Boyd

Barbara Rhodes writes about Louise Arner Boyd

An online reference source — Louise Arner Boyd

Female Explorers Homepage

You click on the link Barbara Rhodes writes about Louise Arner Boyd and a new window opens with the following information.

File   Edit   View   Favorites   Tools   Help

http://

You take notes on Louise Arner Boyd for your report. Then you search for information on other American women explorers and evaluate the sources you find. As you learn about these women, you take notes and finish your report.

LOUISE ARNER BOYD

by Barbara Rhodes

Louise Boyd was born in 1887 into a rich San Raphael, California, family. She made her first trip to the Arctic in 1924. Boyd first became known in the Arctic in 1928, when she searched for the missing explorer Roald Amundsen. Boyd received a medal from the king of Norway for her efforts.

In the 1930s and 1940s, Boyd made five trips to the Arctic. During some of those trips, she worked for the United States military.

In 1955, at age 67, she chartered a DC-4 aircraft to fly her over the North Pole. The 16-hour flight flew nonstop to the Pole and back. She became the first woman to go to the North Geographic Pole. Boyd died in 1972 at age 85.

Reading Across Texts

Both this article and *Amelia and Eleanor* describe adventurous women. Think about what these women were like. Make a list of words that describe them.

Writing Across Texts Use your list to write a job description for an adventurer.

 Sequence   When evaluating a Web site, what should you do first?

Comprehension

Skill
Main Idea
and Details

Strategy
Text Structure

Main Idea
and Details

- A topic is what a piece of writing is about.

- The main idea is the most important idea about the topic. Think about the overall idea of a paragraph, section, or article.

- Supporting details give small pieces of information about the main idea.

Main Idea

Supporting Detail	Supporting Detail	Supporting Detail

Strategy: Text Structure

Good readers use the text structure, or the way text is organized, to help them understand what they read. For example, a nonfiction article may compare and contrast two things, put events in sequence, or be a series of clear main ideas. When you preview, look for text features such as titles, heads, and underlined words to help you know what to expect.

1. Read "Glaciers and Icebergs." Make a graphic organizer like the one above for each paragraph.

2. Use your graphic organizers to help you write a summary of "Glaciers and Icebergs."

Glaciers and Icebergs

Glaciers and icebergs are both made of ice and are both very large.

Glaciers Glaciers are huge pieces of ice that are on land. They are found in areas where there is steady snowfall. Glaciers form when more snow falls than melts away over the years. The leftover snow slowly recrystallizes to form ice.

Types of Glaciers There are two types of glaciers. Mountain glaciers move down the sides of mountains. Ice sheets, on the other hand, form on level ground and spread out in all directions. The continent of Antarctica is covered by a huge ice sheet.

Icebergs Some glaciers or ice sheets go all the way to the seashore. As the ice reaches the shore, a part of it may break off and fall into the sea. This huge piece of ice, now floating in the ocean, is called an iceberg. About 10,000 icebergs each year come from the glaciers that cover Greenland.

Skill The main idea of a paragraph tells the most important idea. Which sentences could be taken out and still leave an important idea?

Strategy Which text structure is used in this paragraph? How can you tell?
A. sequence
B. compare and contrast
C. problem and solution

Skill Is the last sentence of this paragraph a main idea or a supporting detail? How can you tell?

Strategy How did the text headings help you understand this article?

Words to Know

forbidding

continent

anticipation

depart

heaves

icebergs

convergence

Remember

Try the strategy. Then, if you need more help, use your glossary or a dictionary.

Vocabulary Strategy
for Greek and Latin Roots

Word Structure Many English words have Latin or Greek parts. For example, the Latin prefix *com-* (or *con-*) means "with" or "together." It appears in words such as *companion* and *connect.* You can think, "What will go with something or be together?" The Latin prefix *de-* means "away from" and appears in words such as *defrost.* You can often think, "What is going away from something or is the opposite of something?" You can often use these prefixes to help you figure out the meaning of an unknown word.

1. Look at the unknown word. Does it have a Latin or Greek prefix that you know?

2. What is the meaning of the Greek or Latin prefix? How does it affect the meaning of the unknown word?

3. Try the meaning in the sentence. Does it make sense?

As you read "The Hunger to Know," look for words with Latin or Greek parts to help you figure out the meanings of the words.

THE HUNGER TO KNOW

There is something in us that yearns to explore new places. Often these places are dangerous, even forbidding. That doesn't stop us from going there, though. In fact, risk may be part of what calls to us.

Five hundred years ago, the continent of North America lay waiting. Explorers from Europe sailed the Atlantic. Filled with anticipation, they couldn't wait to depart. These adventurers had no idea whether they would find treasure or be killed by monsters. They were ready for the new, the strange, the unexpected.

Today men and women still wonder, plan, and go. They travel to the ocean floor. There they see fantastic forms of life. They view wild mountains and canyons formed when the stuff of Earth heaves and twists. They sail through fields of icebergs to the frozen poles. They blast into space, leaving the only home humans have ever known.

What drives people so? It may be the convergence of two needs: the hunger to know and the desire to be the first. Whatever makes it so, we gain from it. As long as we keep seeking and learning, our world keeps growing.

Write

Imagine you are going to explore the South Pole. Describe your journey. Use as many words from the Words to Know list as you can.

Antarctic Journal

Four Months at the Bottom of the World

by Jennifer Owings Dewey

What would you expect to see and do at the "bottom of the world"?

587

November 12th

Depart from home in the early morning, to be gone four months to Antarctica, a part of the planet as remote as the moon in its own way.

The woman sitting next to me on the shuttle is headed for San Antonio, Texas. She has more luggage than I do.

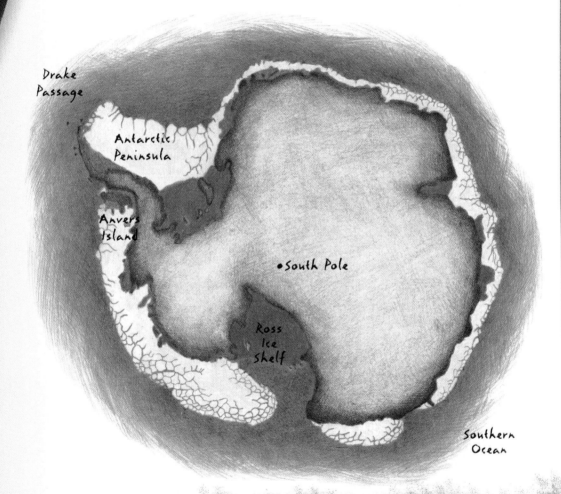

For millions of years Antarctica, the fifth largest continent, has been in the grip of an ice age. It is the windiest, coldest, most forbidding region on Earth, and I am heading straight for it.

"Good-bye, America," I whisper as the airplane heaves off the ground with a shuddering roar. "See you later."

Drake Passage

Antarctic Peninsula

Anvers Island

• South Pole

Ross Ice Shelf

Southern Ocean

November 17th

We flew from Miami to Santiago, Chile. Early the next morning we boarded a plane bound for Punta Arenas, a town at the southern tip of Chile.

We landed and were driven to a hangarlike building, where we received our Antarctic clothing issue, on loan for the length of our stay, to be returned when we head back.

Our next stop was the pier where the *Polar Duke,* our ship, was tied up.

I was shown to my cabin— a space so tiny, I wished I were an elf. A desk and chair are bolted to the floor. The bedding is a well-padded sleeping bag.

We're off this morning. Clear skies, cool breeze, and no chop. The ship heaves and rolls like the smallish, sturdy seaworthy vessel it is.

I make a nest in one of the boats tied on deck, a cozy spot to spend hours drawing or just looking. I resist going below to sleep or eat. There is too much to take in—rolling seas, salt spray, broad-winged seabirds soaring inches above the wave tops.

The sun never sets. It lowers and rolls lazily along the northern horizon before rising again. I shiver with anticipation when we leave the calm waters of the Beagle Channel and enter Drake Passage.

sooty
albatross

Two days pass and we cross the Antarctic Convergence. Along this invisible line warm northern water meets cold southern water. The layering of warm and cold, and the upwelling that results, creates ideal conditions for an abundance of life in the seas.

From the convergence on, we are *in* Antarctica.

A day later the ship's motor stops humming. From the bridge I look out over the bow. A group of whales breaks the surface of the sea, spy hopping, heads pointing straight up out of the water. They slap their flukes and roll playfully.

"Humpbacks," one of the crew says. "Whales have the right of way in these waters. We stop when we see them, turn the engines off, and let them pass before we start up again."

It's good to know an ocean exists where whales have the right of way over ships.

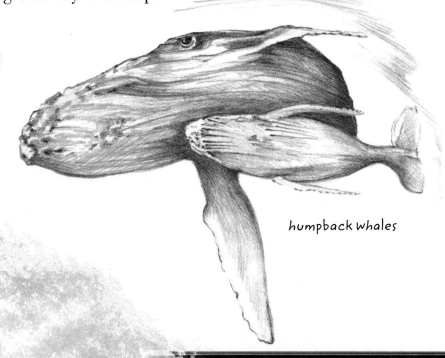

humpback whales

November 18th
Palmer Station

Palmer Station

Dear T.,
   Palmer Station is a group of insulated
metal buildings, housing fifty people comfortably. The
station was built on Anvers Island. You don't know you're
on an island because permanent ice fills the gap between
Anvers and the mainland.
   We learn the rules the first night: no travel alone,
except to climb the glacier behind Palmer, flagged
with poles to show the safest way up. We sign out when
leaving, giving a departure hour and an estimated time
of return. We are given walkie-talkies and check with
"base" every hour. If we're half an hour off schedule,
someone comes looking, unless a storm blows in. If
it's too dangerous for anyone to come after us, we are
expected to wait out the bad weather.
   The sunscreen they pass out is "the only kind strong
enough." We are ordered never to forget to use it.
   Tomorrow we learn about the zodiacs, small
rubber boats with outboard motors. I'm excited
about what comes next, and sleepy.
   Much love,
   Mom

dressed for
fieldwork

view looking away
from Palmer

typical room,
not mine!

592

November 27th
Litchfield Island

In fair weather I go to Litchfield Island and spend the day, sometimes the night. Litchfield is three miles from Palmer by zodiac, a protected island visited by two or three people a year. Before going to Litchfield, I'm shown how to walk on open ground in Antarctica. An inch of moss takes one hundred years to grow. The careless scuff of a boot heel could rip out two hundred years of growth in seconds.

I pack my food and extra clothes in a waterproof sea bag. A daypack holds pencils, pens, and paper for drawing and writing. There is no fresh water on the island. I carry two one-gallon canteens.

gray gull chick

Each island has an emergency cache of food and supplies, marked with a flag, available if a person gets stranded during a storm.

Alone after being dropped on the island, I hear birds call, the whine of the wind, the waves pounding gravel shores, and no human sounds except my breathing.

Twilight falls and I crawl into my tent, alert and unable to sleep for a long time, listening to the sounds of the Antarctic night.

The emergency cache on Litchfield contained a tarp, blankets, rope, candles, matches, anchovy paste, crackers, and chocolate.

593

December 15th
Visiting Old Palmer

gentoo parent
feeding chicks

Dear B.,

I am in a tiny office behind the kitchen. Supper is over. I came to find quiet time and write you. It's strange to write at night by the light of the sun.

Today I went with a penguin scientist to Old Palmer, twenty minutes by zodiac from New Palmer. Not used for years, the base is empty of life except for a small colony of gentoo penguins. A few of the birds have built stone nests on top of abandoned oil drums and other debris left behind. The chicks have orange spots on their bills and are identical to the parents, only smaller. They sit half squashed under a parent's white belly, black-billed faces poking out, eyes blinking. A sunny day, thirty-two degrees, dangerously hot for the chicks. I've seen some keel over dead on days like this, their blubber-rich bodies unable to tolerate temperatures above freezing. A parent penguin suffering heat stroke will not abandon a nest. It will fall dead in a heap first.

traveling by zodiac

gentoos on nests

orca

young Adélie

orca

We had a scary encounter on the way back from Old Palmer. A pair of orcas was in Arthur Harbor. They swam near the surface, sleek backs glistening.

These enormous predators sometimes take bites out of boats, mistaking a zodiac for a seal or a penguin. We slowed the engine and held back.

A small group of Adélies was porpoising in the water. In a quick stroke one orca grabbed a penguin in its huge mouth and whirled the helpless bird in the air. Teeth gripped penguin flesh, penguin wings flailed. The skin of the penguin flew away and landed with a plop on the sea. The bird was stripped of its hide as easily as we remove a sweater.

The second orca took a penguin before the pair surged out of the harbor, leaving a swirling wake behind.

We sped back to Palmer, aware that what we'd seen was a reminder that we are in a wilderness where a delicate balance exists between predator and prey.

I'm tired, although I have the BIG EYE. This is when we can't sleep because it's never dark. We get silly and wide-eyed, peculiar in our behavior, until a friend says, "Time for bed," and sees that we get there.

Love and hugs,

J.

December 20th
Palmer Station

I have learned that the largest animal on Earth, the hundred-ton blue whale, eats only one of the smallest animals on Earth: krill (*Euphausia supurba*). There are more krill in the seas than there are stars in the visible universe.

blue whales

Krill is one link in a simple food chain. Penguins, seals, and whales eat krill. In turn the tiny shrimplike krill eat phytoplankton, one-celled plants that bloom in the sea in spring and summer.

My new friend, Carl, an oceanographer, said, "We ought to try eating krill since so many animals thrive on it."

In the bio lab we scooped krill into a jar.

We got a small fry pan, then melted butter and cooked up the krill.

Someone said, "Add garlic."

Somebody said, "How about pepper and salt?"

These were added. When the mixture looked ready, we ate it.

"Tastes like butter," one person said.

"More like garlic," another said.

"Tastes like butter *and* garlic," Carl said.

"Krill don't have their own taste," I concluded.

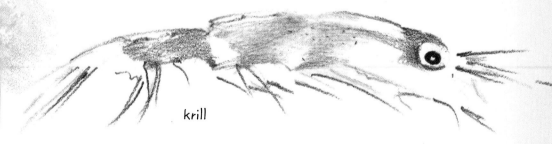

krill

December 21st
Palmer Station

A storm has raged for three days. A blast of wind smacked the main window with such force, we thought a bomb had gone off. The storm rose in intensity in minutes. Looking out the big window, we see a solid wall of sleet and blowing snow.

A friend and I checked the wind-speed monitor a few hours ago. It was clocking eighty knots. We decided to sneak outside and see what eighty-knot winds feel like. It's against the rules to leave the protection of the station in such high winds. Nobody saw us leave.

We were barely able to force the door open against the gale. Head down, face stung with driven sleet, I leaned with all my weight on the wind and did not fall over.

Fearing I'd be blown away, I pressed my mittened hands on the side of the building.

We crawled on hands and knees, lashed by pellets of frozen rain. In five minutes we were back inside.

Thinking of the penguins and their chicks on Litchfield, I can't help wondering how many will die of exposure to the cold and wet.

after the storm

597

Christmas Eve, December 24th
Palmer Station

It was three in the morning, bright outside, and I couldn't sleep. I crept downstairs, signed out, and took the flagged trail up the glacier.

Dressed in a watchman's cap, three layers under my parka, and Sorel boots, I climbed in a stillness broken only by the noise of snow crunching under my soles. Greenish-purple clouds covered the sky from edge to edge. The sea was the color of pewter.

Near the top I heard a cracking sound, a slap magnified a million times in my ear. Another followed, then another. Echoes of sound, aftershocks, sizzled in the air. The sky began to glow with an eerie luminescence, as if someone in the heavens had switched on a neon light in place of the sun.

front of glacier

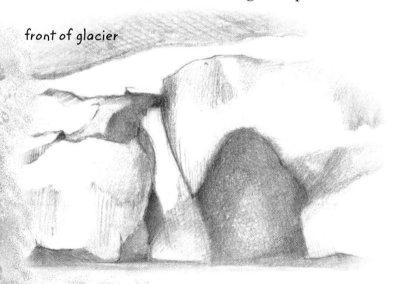

I felt myself dropping straight down. A crack had appeared under me, a crevasse in the glacier. Summer softening of the ice had thrown the pole settings off.

I'm alive because the crack was narrow. I fell to my shoulders, my boot soles too wide to fit through the bottom of the crack. I stared below into a blue-green hole cut with facets like a diamond.

After a few deep breaths, I began to scramble out. Terrified the crack would keep growing. I moved slowly. It was an hour before I was on firm ice.

young tern

The color of the sky shifted to blue-gray with streaks of yellow along the western horizon. To my horror, I saw a pattern of cracks zig-zagging, like fractured window glass, across the glacier surface.

I checked my watch. I'd been gone three hours. I don't know why, but I didn't want anyone rescuing me. I decided to crawl down the glacier on hands and knees.

I felt my way inch by inch, rubbing the surface of the snow with my palms before making a move.

Back before the hour someone would have come looking for me, I told the station manager what happened. Trained in glaciology, he went up the glacier to reset the flags.

I have a new weariness tonight, born of having been frightened out of my wits while watching one of the most beautiful skies I'll ever see.

February 16th
On the *Polar Duke*

I am along on a trip of the *Polar Duke,* north of Palmer in Gerlache Strait. The crew and scientists trawl for krill using fine-mesh nets dropped off the stern.

Coming back we see icebergs drifting south out of the Weddell Sea. The bergs originate hundreds of miles away and ride ocean currents.

We sail close, but not too close, for beneath the waves is where the bulk of an iceberg is.

Weddell seal under the ice

Seawater splashes up on iceberg shores shaped by years of wave action. Sunlight strikes gleaming ramparts that shine with rainbow colors. Erosion works at the ice, creating caves and hollows, coves, and inlets.

Penguins and seals hitch rides on icebergs. Gulls and other seabirds rest on high points.

One iceberg collides in slow motion with another. The smaller one topples, rolls, and heaves like a dying rhinoceros, emerald seawater mixed with spray drenching its surfaces.

I yearn to ride an iceberg like a penguin or a gull, touching its frozen sides, drifting slowly on the waves. I draw them, but I can't capture their splendor.

March 12th
Winging Home

penguin egg

Before leaving, I collected (with permission) a sterile penguin egg that would never hatch. I made room for it in my suitcase by giving a lot of my clothes away.

The airline lost my bag in Miami. I told the airline people that I had to have it back, pleading, begging. "It has a penguin egg in it," I said. They glanced at each other and eyed me funny.

Fortunately for me, and them, they found the bag.

The egg reminds me of my trip to the place where penguins raise downy chicks, krill swarm in numbers greater than stars in the sky, whales have rights, and icebergs drift in graceful arcs across Southern Ocean swells. At home, I'll look out at the desert landscape and remember the Antarctic desert, the last great wilderness on Earth.

Reader Response

Open for Discussion If you had the opportunity, would you go on an Antarctic journey? Come up with three reasons why you would or wouldn't want to go.

1. The author tries to tell her experiences in Antarctica so that readers feel as if they are there with her. Did you feel as if you were with her on her journey? Why or why not?

2. The author describes Antarctica as the "most forbidding region on Earth." What details does she provide to support this idea?

3. Think about text structure. In what way is the passage on pages 598–599 told? Why do you think the author chose this method? Would another text structure be more effective? Explain.

4. Imagine that you are on your way to Antarctica aboard the *Polar Duke.* Write about something you see as you approach the continent. Use words from the Words to Know list and the selection.

Look Back and Write The author and her friends thought they had discovered a new food for humans. Read page 596 again. What was this food and why did they think it would be good to eat? What did they think after they tasted it?

Meet the Author and Illustrator
Jennifer Owings Dewey

Read more books about Antarctica.

Jennifer Owings Dewey loves to study and write about animals and nature. She says, "I enjoy traveling to remote or wild places to do research." For *Antarctic Journal,* she traveled to Antarctica. During her four months there, she drew the animals and landscape, took photographs, and wrote in her journal. Friends and family saved the letters she wrote home. All these went into her book.

Ms. Dewey lives in Santa Fe, New Mexico. She has written more than twenty nonfiction books for children. She says, "I like writing about extreme environments—cold and hot, dry and wet." She also writes about the amazing variety of animals on Earth. "Writing about the world we live in prevents running out of ideas," she says.

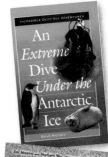

An Extreme Dive Under the Antarctic Ice by Brad Matsen

Antarctic Ice by Jim Mastro and Norbert Wu

Swimming Towards Ice

by Claire Daniel

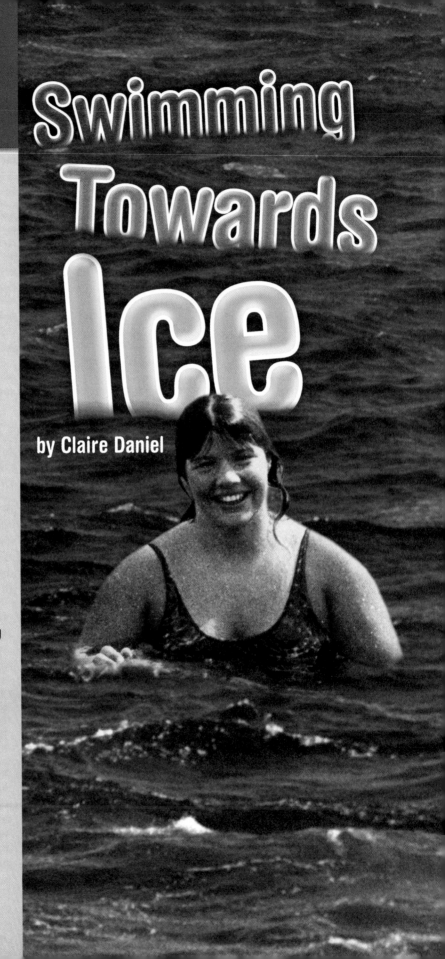

Narrative Nonfiction

Genre

- Narrative nonfiction can record an important event in a person's life.

- Narrative nonfiction often includes researched facts about a person and why he or she is noteworthy.

Text Features

- Two opening paragraphs introduce the reader to Lynne Cox.

- Subheads mark passages in her life and establish her goals.

- A table gives information about her record-breaking swims.

Link to Social Studies

Learn about the International Swimming Hall of Fame, of which Lynne Cox is a member. Are there other open-water swimmers who are members?

604

Unlike the usual visitor to Antarctica, who is bundled from head to toe, Lynne Cox approached the continent a bit differently. Dressed in only a swimsuit, swim cap, and goggles, she lowered herself from a boat into the freezing 32°F water and swam more than a mile to Antarctica's shore.

Lynne Cox is among the best cold-water, long-distance swimmers in the world. But she wasn't born that way.

Lynne Cox makes a test swim in the chilly waters (33°F) north of Antarctica.

A Swimmer Is Born

When Lynne was 14 years old, she became bored with swimming laps in a pool. Encouraged by her coach, she entered a series of rough water swims near her home in California. She loved the cold water, the chopping of the waves, the quiet of the ocean, and the feeling of freedom. Lynne Cox became hooked on long-distance, cold-water swimming.

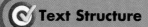 **Text Structure**   Notice how the text moves from past to present.

Preparing for the Icy Plunge

To prepare for her swim to Antarctica, Lynne trained hard for two years. Each day, for an hour, she worked out in a gym, using weights and other equipment to strengthen her muscles. Five- to six-mile walks were also part of her daily training, and

for one hour each day, she swam as hard and as fast as she could in a pool.

Lynne also borrowed ideas from sea animals that survive in cold water. She added 12 pounds of body fat to help keep her body temperature from falling in the icy water. And she grew her hair long to trap warm air inside her swim cap.

A Swimmer's Hope

For most of her life, Lynne Cox has braved the elements to swim in the world's major bodies of water. Often she has been the first woman to do so. While it is always her hope to have successful swims, it is also Lynne's wish to bring people of the world together to show how closely they live to each other and to work for peace and understanding.

Now in her forties, Lynne looks forward to her next swimming challenge. While she won't say where it will be, she has said that it will be "[in] an area I've never seen, some place that captures my imagination, something that's never been tried before." To be sure, it will be amazing.

Lynne Cox's Record-Breaking Swims

Year	Age	Location	Swimming Distance*	Time	Sea Temperature (Fahrenheit)
1971	14	First crossing of Catalina Channel (CA)	27 miles	12 hours 36 minutes	65°– 70°
1972	15	English Channel	27 miles	9 hours 57 minutes	55°– 60°
1973	16	English Channel	27 miles	9 hours 36 minutes	55°– 60°
1976	19	Strait of Magellan (Chile)	3.0 miles	1 hour 2 minutes	44°
1987	30	Bering Strait (between the former Soviet Union and the United States)	5.0 miles	2 hours 6 minutes	38°– 42°
2002	45	Swim to Antarctica	1.2 miles	25 minutes	32°

*This number reflects the miles Lynne swam, not the actual distance between two points.

Reading Across Texts

How were the adventures of Jennifer Owings Dewey and Lynne Cox alike? How were they different?

Writing Across Texts Tell which adventurer you might like to accompany on a future trip and why.

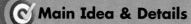 **Main Idea & Details** What are the most important ideas in this text?

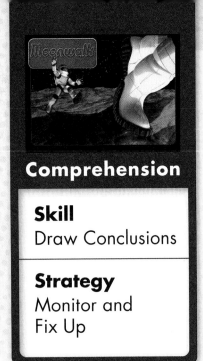

Comprehension

Skill
Draw Conclusions

Strategy
Monitor and
Fix Up

 # Draw Conclusions

- The small pieces of information in a piece of writing are called the facts and details.

- When you put these facts and details together to form a logical, well thought-out opinion, you are drawing a conclusion. It is also called making an inference.

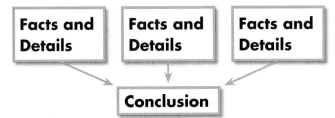

| Facts and Details | Facts and Details | Facts and Details |

Conclusion

Strategy: Monitor and Fix Up

Good readers think about how they're doing as they read. Sometimes they realize they no longer understand what they are reading and can't draw logical conclusions. If you think you don't understand the text, it's a good idea to reread it slowly. You might also read on to look for an explanation.

 **Write**

1. Read "The Man in the Moon." Make a graphic organizer like the one above to draw a conclusion about what it would be like to be on the moon.

2. Write a letter home from the moon, telling what the moon looks like up close.

The Man in the Moon

When we look up and see (with the help of our imaginations) a face in the moon, the question is not *who* we see, but *what* we see. For when we gaze at the moon, we are seeing craters, mountains, deep narrow valleys, and wide open plains.

The moon is a dry and airless place made up of rocks and dust. But when the telescope was first invented–about 400 years ago–people had no way of knowing that there was no water on the moon. So when they looked through the telescope and saw the open plains, they assumed they were looking at bodies of water. They named these places *mares* (MAH-rees), which is Latin for "seas."

Today, we know there is no water on the moon, but the names have stuck. That is why these dry and dusty places have such lovely names as *Bay of Rainbows, Lake of Dreams,* and *Sea of Tranquility.*

Will you travel to the moon someday? Maybe. And maybe you'll come back and say, "It's a nice place to visit, but I wouldn't want to live there!"

Skill Draw a conclusion from the first sentence. Is this piece going to be science or fantasy? (It's a little tricky!)

Strategy How does reading on to the next sentence help you to keep or change your conclusion?

Skill If you read these names without your knowledge of the moon, what conclusion might you draw?

Strategy Is there anything about the article you don't understand? Rereading those parts can help.

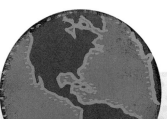

Words to Know

runt

taunted

summoning

loomed

rille

trench

trudged

staggered

Remember

Try the strategy. Then,
if you need more help,
use your glossary or
a dictionary.

Vocabulary Strategy
for Synonyms

Context Clues Sometimes when you are reading,
you see a word you don't know. The author may
give you a synonym for the word. A synonym is a
word that has the same or almost the same meaning
as another word. Look for a synonym. It can help
you understand the meaning of the word you
don't know.

1. Look at the sentence in which the unknown word
appears. The author may give a synonym in the
same sentence.

2. Look at the sentences around the sentence
with the unknown word. The author may use a
synonym there.

3. Try the synonym in place of the word in the
sentence. Does it make sense?

As you read "Gone to the Moon," look for
synonyms to help you understand the meanings of
the vocabulary words.

Gone to the Moon

People have long dreamed of going to the moon. Maybe this is because the moon circles so close by. No other thing in space is closer to Earth. How could we not conquer this small thing, this runt?

When the machine age arrived, the moon still taunted us. "I'm so close," it teased. "Why don't you come on up?" In 1969, three people did. Summoning all our knowledge and technology, we sent them into space and guided them to the moon. They had to call on all their bravery to blast off into the unknown.

Imagine how their hearts raced as the moon loomed before them. Imagine their awe as two of them stepped where no person had ever set foot. They saw craters and a rille, a narrow valley that looks like a trench.

With every step, they leaped rather than trudged. (On Earth, because of gravity, we plod along.) It was easy to pick up moon rocks under whose weight they would have staggered and stumbled on Earth.

Was it worth it to go to the moon? Yes!

Imagine you made a trip to the moon. Write a journal entry describing a walk on the moon. Use words from the Words to Know list.

611

Moonwalk

by Ben Bova   illustrated by Peter Bollinger

What could happen during a walk on the moon?

"Bet you can't jump over that rille, Runt," Vern challenged.

Gerry Kandel hated it when his older brother called him Runt.

"Watch me, Runt," Vern taunted. "I'll show you how to do it."

Inside his hard-shell moonsuit, with its big backpack and astronaut-type helmet, Gerry watched as Vern got a running start, kicking up lazy puffs of dust with each step. He sailed over the crooked crack in the ground, floating like a cloud until he touched down on the other side.

The boys were out on the floor of the giant crater Alphonsus. Their father had brought them along with him to the half-buried shelter fifteen miles from the main base. Dad had left them at the shelter and gone off with the tractor to inspect the new telescope that was being built still farther out on the crater floor.

Dad had told them to stay inside the shelter until he came back. But Vern wanted to go outside for a moonwalk. Now he was jumping over gullies in the bare, dark ground.

"Come on, Runt," Vern called from the other side of the rille. "Let's see you do it!"

Gerry glanced at the thermometer on the wrist of his moonsuit. It was 214 degrees below zero. Yet he was sweating inside his suit.

"What's the matter? You scared?"

Even though it was nighttime, it wasn't really dark. A big, blue and white Earth hung in the starry sky, shining beautifully. Gerry could see the rough uneven ground, the rocks and boulders scattered everywhere on the moon's surface.

And the rille. A wide, meandering crack in the ground.
"Well?" Vern demanded.

In the moon's light gravity, Gerry weighed only about thirty pounds, even with his bulky moonsuit.

"OK," he said into his microphone. "Here I come."

He took four running steps, then soared over the rille. It felt like flying. He stumbled when he landed, though. Vern grabbed him and kept him from falling.

"Not bad for a runt, Runt," Vern said laughing. "Now let's find a really big one."

"We shouldn't be doing this," Gerry said. "Dad told us to stay inside the shelter. If he finds out. . . ."

"Who's going to tell him?" Vern demanded.

"Um . . . nobody, I guess."

"That's right. We'll be back in the shelter by the time Dad gets back. And you'll keep your mouth shut. Right?"

"Right," Gerry said reluctantly.

He followed Vern along the rille they had just crossed, their boots kicking up dust that settled slowly in the low gravity.

They trudged along for nearly an hour, leaving boot prints in the dust. Off on the other side of the crater, sunlight was bathing the top of the ringwall mountains with harsh, brilliant light. It would soon be daytime.

"Hey, there's one," Vern called out, pointing with a gloved hand at a broad gully up ahead. It was much wider than the one they'd jumped across. It looked deep, too, like a trench.

"Bet you can't jump over that one, Runt."

Gerry peered at the rille. "It's pretty wide," he said.

"Scared?"

Gerry was, but he didn't want to admit it. He shook his head inside his helmet, then realized that Vern couldn't see it.

"Well? Want me to go first?"

Summoning up his courage, Gerry said, "Naw, I'll try it."

Gerry backed up several paces, then started running. In the light gravity, every step was a leap. The edge of the rille loomed up like the rim of the Grand Canyon. Gerry jumped as hard as he could.

He soared, sailing up and over the yawning trench, and landed almost perfectly. He hardly staggered.

Turning to look back across the rille at Vern, he called, "Nothing to it! Piece of cake!"

"OK," Vern answered. "Here I come."

Vern started running, each stride a long hop across the uneven ground. With his last step, though, he stumbled on a small rock. When he took off for the jump across, Gerry saw that he wasn't going to make it.

"Watch out!" he yelled uselessly.

Vern soared, arms and legs flailing, and landed hard—just short of the rille's rim. Gerry heard him go "Oof!" as he hit the side of the rift and tumbled down, out of sight.

Gerry rushed to the edge of the gully and saw his brother halfway down the rille, lying motionless.

"Vern! You OK?"

No answer. He's hurt, Gerry thought. Maybe he's dead!

Gerry scrambled down into the gully. Vern was lying on his back, one leg bent under him, arms sprawled.

"Vern!" he called again as he slid and scraped down the side of the rille.

Vern moved one hand, then waved feebly. He's alive, Gerry thought. He's conscious.

He dropped to his knees at his brother's side. "Are you OK? Can you get up?"

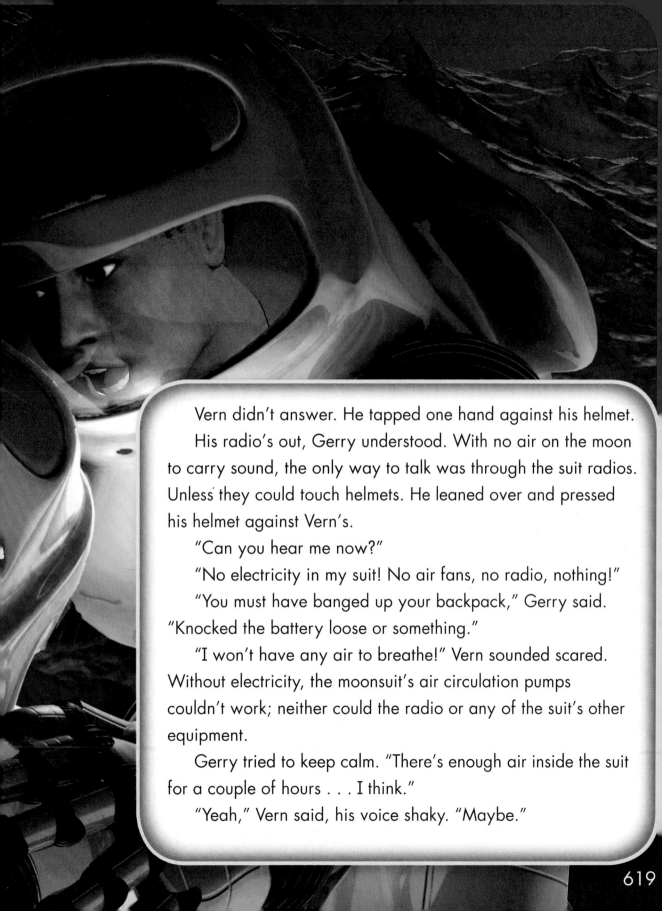

Vern didn't answer. He tapped one hand against his helmet.

His radio's out, Gerry understood. With no air on the moon to carry sound, the only way to talk was through the suit radios. Unless they could touch helmets. He leaned over and pressed his helmet against Vern's.

"Can you hear me now?"

"No electricity in my suit! No air fans, no radio, nothing!"

"You must have banged up your backpack," Gerry said. "Knocked the battery loose or something."

"I won't have any air to breathe!" Vern sounded scared. Without electricity, the moonsuit's air circulation pumps couldn't work; neither could the radio or any of the suit's other equipment.

Gerry tried to keep calm. "There's enough air inside the suit for a couple of hours . . . I think."

"Yeah," Vern said, his voice shaky. "Maybe."

"Come on, get up."

Vern started to push himself to his feet. "Oow!" he cried, sinking back to the dusty ground again.

"What's the matter?"

"My knee! It must be broken!"

Gerry shook his head inside his helmet. "Maybe sprained or dislocated. I don't think you could break it in the suit."

"I can't stand on it!"

"OK, OK. Lean on me. I'll help you."

Grunting, staggering, the two boys scrabbled their way across the bottom of the rille and back to the surface, Vern leaning on Gerry's shoulder. Even on the moon, he felt heavy.

"Oh my gosh," Vern said. "The sun."

Gerry saw that daylight had crept across the floor of the crater and was almost upon them. He knew that, without electricity, Vern's cooling system and heat radiator wouldn't work. Once they were in sunlight, the temperature would soar to 250 degrees.

"I'm gonna boil inside my suit!" Vern shouted.

Keeping his helmet pressed against his brother's, Gerry said, "Come on, let's get back to the shelter."

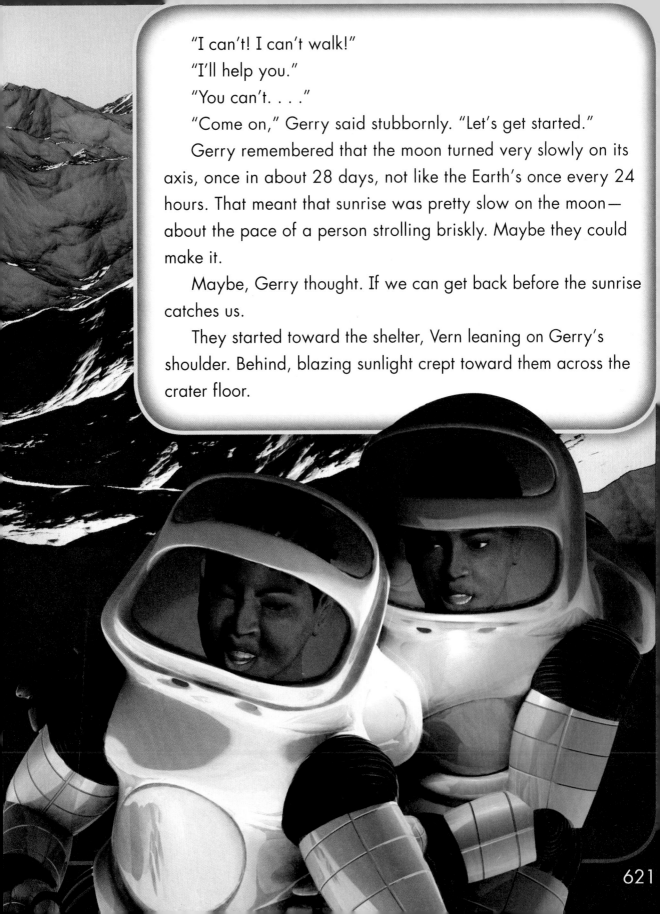

"I can't! I can't walk!"

"I'll help you."

"You can't. . . ."

"Come on," Gerry said stubbornly. "Let's get started."

Gerry remembered that the moon turned very slowly on its axis, once in about 28 days, not like the Earth's once every 24 hours. That meant that sunrise was pretty slow on the moon — about the pace of a person strolling briskly. Maybe they could make it.

Maybe, Gerry thought. If we can get back before the sunrise catches us.

They started toward the shelter, Vern leaning on Gerry's shoulder. Behind, blazing sunlight crept toward them across the crater floor.

621

As long as we stay in the night we'll be OK, Gerry told himself. If we can get back to the shelter before Vern's air runs out.

They trudged along for what seemed like hours. The sky was spangled with thousands of stars; they seemed like hard, solemn eyes watching the two boys.

"We can make it," Gerry kept muttering. "We can make it."

But with every step Vern seemed to get heavier. The line of daylight was catching up with them. Gerry could almost feel the sun's blazing heat roasting him.

Vern coughed. "Hard . . . to breathe," he gasped.

"We're almost there." Gerry could see the rounded hump of dirt that covered the shelter.

"Can't. . . ." Vern collapsed. Gerry staggered under the full weight of his brother's unconscious body.

Blinking sweat from his eyes, trying hard not to cry, grunting, puffing hard, Gerry dragged Vern to the shelter. The tractor was nowhere in sight. Dad's not back yet, he realized, not knowing if he should be glad or sorry.

As he pulled his brother into the airlock, he saw the tractor coming slowly over the horizon, kicking up a lazy roostertail of dust.

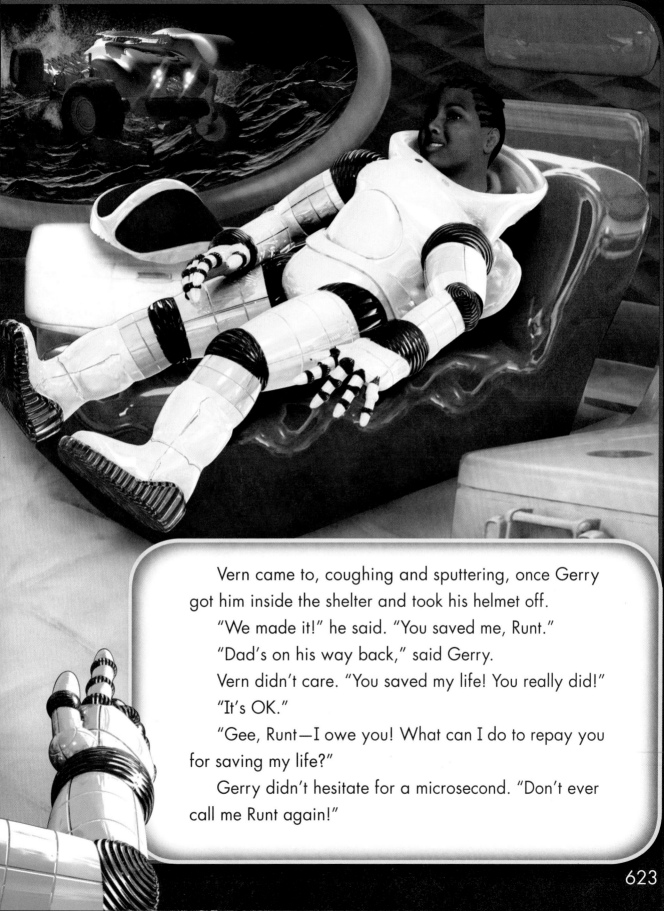

Vern came to, coughing and sputtering, once Gerry got him inside the shelter and took his helmet off.

"We made it!" he said. "You saved me, Runt."

"Dad's on his way back," said Gerry.

Vern didn't care. "You saved my life! You really did!"

"It's OK."

"Gee, Runt—I owe you! What can I do to repay you for saving my life?"

Gerry didn't hesitate for a microsecond. "Don't ever call me Runt again!"

Reader Response

Open for Discussion The time has come for Gerry and Vern to tell their father what really happened that night on the moon. Tell what they said and how they said it.

1. Ben Bova's science fiction stories contain a careful mix of the familiar and the unfamiliar. What seemed familiar to you as you read "Moonwalk"? What seemed unfamiliar?

2. What conclusions did you draw about the relationship between Gerry and Vern after reading the first line of the story?

3. What is a *rille?* How did you figure out what it is?

4. There were several heart-stopping moments in this story. Tell about one. Use words from the Words to Know list and the story.

Test Practice

Look Back and Write If you were going on a moon adventure, you would have to know the temperature change from night (page 614) to day (page 620). Compute the difference and tell why it is important.

Meet the Author

Ben Bova

Read more science fiction books.

The Wonderful Flight to the Mushroom Planet by Eleanor Cameron

The Forgotten Door by Alexander Key

Ben Bova has been writing science fiction for more than fifty years. He combines an understanding of science with the ability to tell great stories. His popular "Grand Tour" series of books for older readers tells of humans who explore and colonize the solar system in the future.

As a scientist, Mr. Bova has worked on major research projects. (For example, he helped prepare *Apollo 11* for flight.) He calls upon the latest in scientific knowledge to write his books about the future. In the past, he predicted the first U.S. trip to the moon, virtual reality, video games, and possible life on Mars. Now, he predicts that we will one day enjoy tours in space and the discovery of extraterrestrial life. We'll see— he's been right so far!

Expository Nonfiction

Genre

- **Expository nonfiction gives information about topics the reader might never be able to experience directly.**

- **Expository nonfiction might give serious thoughts and opinions as well as factual information.**

Text Features

- **Small inset photos add interest to the article.**

- **A chart gives facts about astronauts on the moon.**

Link to Science

Name some activities, other than jumping, whose effect when done on the moon would be different from what it is on Earth.

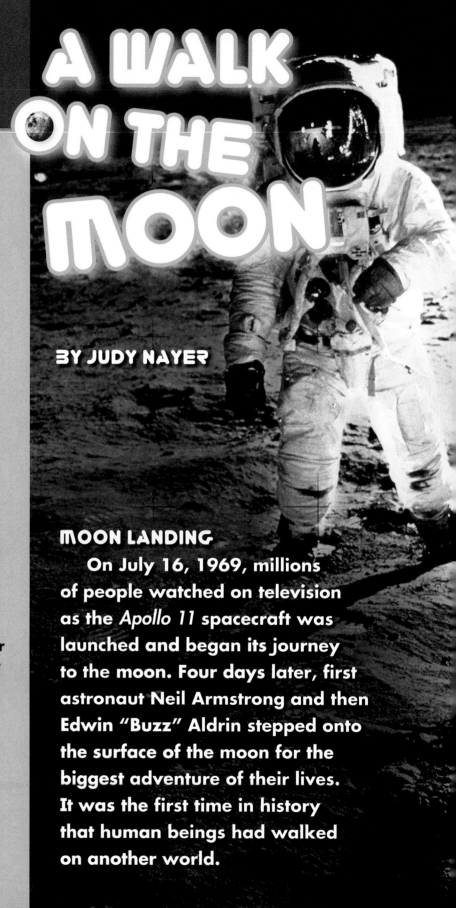

A WALK ON THE MOON

BY JUDY NAYER

MOON LANDING

On July 16, 1969, millions of people watched on television as the *Apollo 11* spacecraft was launched and began its journey to the moon. Four days later, first astronaut Neil Armstrong and then Edwin "Buzz" Aldrin stepped onto the surface of the moon for the biggest adventure of their lives. It was the first time in history that human beings had walked on another world.

MOON SUITING

The astronauts could not have walked on the moon without wearing special spacesuits. The moon has no air, so a backpack supplies oxygen for the astronaut to breathe. The spacesuit's many layers protect the astronaut from extreme temperatures—+250°F in the sun and -250°F in the shade—and cool water pumped through tubes inside the suit keeps the astronaut's body temperature constant. The suit and helmet protect the astronaut from the sun's harmful rays and from flying particles hurtling through space. There is also a headset and a microphone in the helmet so that astronauts can talk to one another.

MOON WALKING

What was it like for Neil Armstrong and Buzz Aldrin to walk on the moon? The moon's lower gravity had a big effect. Gravity is the force that pulls things toward the center of the Earth and keeps them from floating away. The Earth's metallic core has a lot to do with gravity. The moon is only one quarter the size of the Earth, and it has only a tiny metallic core, about 15 times smaller than the Earth's. The result is that the moon has only one-sixth the gravity of Earth. The moon's weaker gravity means that the astronauts feel lighter—and they can float!

When the astronauts walked on the moon, each step was a leap that threw off clouds of fine dust. In order to land in the right place, they had to think a few steps ahead instead of just putting one foot in front of the other. They also had to be careful not to lose their balance.

✓ Draw Conclusions   Link facts with experiences to draw conclusions.

The astronauts experimented with different ways of moving on the moon. When Aldrin tried running, he made giant strides and felt as though he was running in slow motion! The astronauts found that the easiest way to get around was to hop on two feet and bound like a kangaroo. They also discovered that they could effortlessly jump several feet off the ground and float gently down!

MOON SIGHTINGS

What did Armstrong and Aldrin see on the moon? With no atmosphere to protect it, objects that hit the moon make a deep impact. Most of the moon's surface is covered with thousands of craters caused by rocks from space crashing into it. The craters range in size from small holes to basins more than a hundred miles across. The smoother areas on the moon are called maria, or "seas," which are not really seas but large, dark plains. Armstrong and Aldrin touched down at the Sea of Tranquility.

MOON COLLECTING

Besides walking around, what did the astronauts do on the moon? Armstrong and Aldrin's moonwalk lasted two and a half hours. During this time, they collected 48 pounds of rock and soil, took photographs, and planted an American flag. They also set up experiments to find out more about the moon.

THE APOLLO MISSIONS

Between 1969 and 1972, the Apollo space program landed twelve astronauts on the surface of the moon in six separate missions. In all, they spent 300 hours on the moon's surface, including 80 hours outside the landing craft.

MANNED MOON MISSIONS

Mission*	Date	Landing Site on Moon	Astronauts Who Walked on the Moon
Apollo 11	July 1969	Sea of Tranquility	Neil A. Armstrong Edwin E. "Buzz" Aldrin, Jr.
Apollo 12	November 1969	Ocean of Storms	Charles P. "Pete" Conrad Alan L. Bean
Apollo 14	February 1971	Fra Mauro crater region	Alan B. Shepard, Jr. Edgar D. Mitchell
Apollo 15	July 1971	Hadley Rille-Apennine mountain region	David Scott James Irwin
Apollo 16	April 1972	Descartes highlands	John W. Young Charles W. Duke
Apollo 17	December 1972	Between the Taurus mountains and Littrow crater	Eugene A. Cernan Harrison H. Schmitt

* In April 1970, the *Apollo 13* mission was abandoned after an
explosion in the spacecraft.

Reading Across Texts

How do you know that "Moonwalk" is science fiction?
What leads you to think that "A Walk on the Moon" is nonfiction?

Writing Across Texts Tell whether you would rather read science
fiction or nonfiction about scientific topics and why.

 **Monitor & Fix Up** Charts, with their many facts, must be examined carefully.

The Best Paths
by Kristine O'Connell George

The best paths
are whispers
in the grass,
a bent twig,
a token, a hint,
easily missed.

The best paths
hide themselves
until the right
someone
comes along.

The best paths
lead you
to where
you didn't know
you wanted to go.

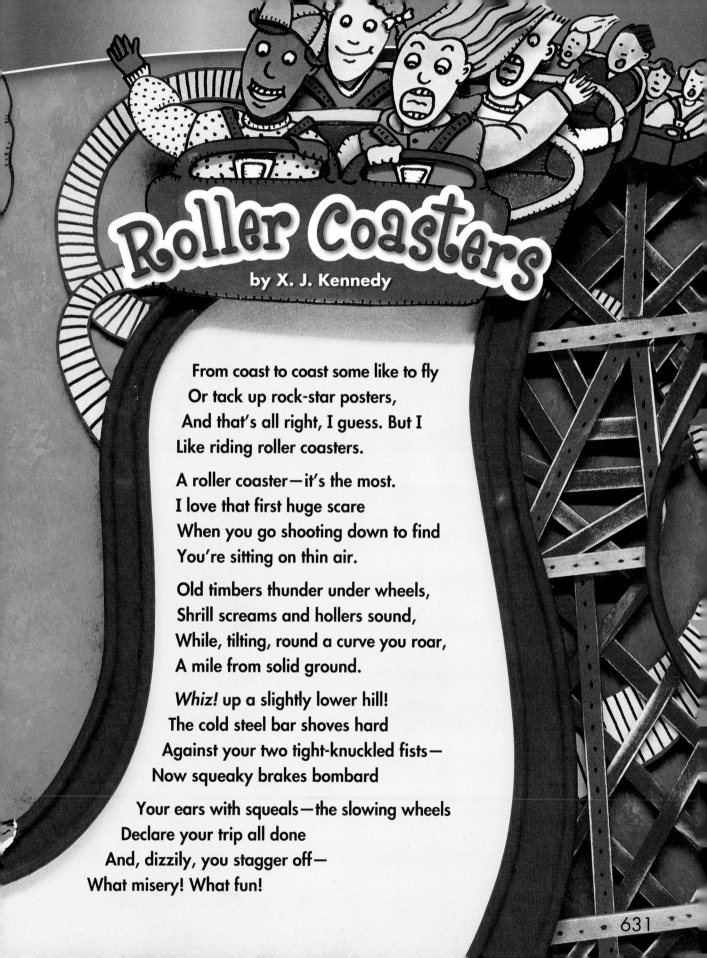

Roller Coasters

by X. J. Kennedy

From coast to coast some like to fly
Or tack up rock-star posters,
And that's all right, I guess. But I
Like riding roller coasters.

A roller coaster—it's the most.
I love that first huge scare
When you go shooting down to find
You're sitting on thin air.

Old timbers thunder under wheels,
Shrill screams and hollers sound,
While, tilting, round a curve you roar,
A mile from solid ground.

Whiz! up a slightly lower hill!
The cold steel bar shoves hard
Against your two tight-knuckled fists—
Now squeaky brakes bombard

Your ears with squeals—the slowing wheels
Declare your trip all done
And, dizzily, you stagger off—
What misery! What fun!

THE DOOR

by Miroslav Holub

Go and open the door.
    Maybe outside there's
    a tree, or a wood,
    a garden,
    or a magic city.

Go and open the door.
    Maybe a dog's rummaging.
    Maybe you'll see a face,
or an eye,
or the picture
            of a picture.

Go and open the door.
    If there's a fog
    it will clear.

Go and open the door.
Even if there's only
the darkness ticking,
even if there's only
the hollow wind,
even if
nothing
is there,
go and open the door.

At least
there'll be
a draft.

633

WRAP-UP

A DAY IN THE LIFE

connect to **WRITING**

Suppose you are traveling with one of the people you read about in this unit. Write two or three postcards home that tell about an adventure you had with this person.

Dear Mom and Dad,
What a great place
Antarctica is! Today
we traveled by zodiac
to Litchfield Island.
We saw...

ANTARCTICA
OCT 7
6-PM

WHAT MAKES AN ADVENTURE?

YOU ON THE MAP

connect to
SOCIAL STUDIES

South America
Amazon River— We will hire a river guide to help us find pink dolphins.
Machu Picchu— We will hike the Inca trail to the ruins.
Pacific Ocean
Atlantic Ocean

Suppose you could explore anywhere in the world—or even out of it! Draw a map of the places you would go. Put in captions about what might happen in each place.

AHEAD OF THEIR TIME

connect to
SOCIAL STUDIES

Eleanor Roosevelt and Amelia Earhart were women ahead of their time. Pick another real person you know about who was ahead of his or her own time. Imagine that you could interview this person about his or her adventures. With a partner, write the questions you might ask and the answers this person might give.

Reaching
for
Goals

Read It
ONLINE
sfsuccessnet.com

What does it take to achieve our
goals and dreams?

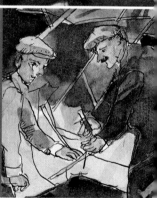

Cause and Effect

- The *effect* is what happens. The *cause* is why it happens.

- Clue words such as *because, so, therefore,* and *as a result* can signal causes and effects.

- Sometimes one effect becomes the cause of another effect, which causes another, and so on. This is called a chain of events.

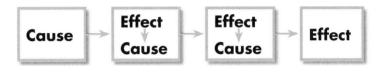

Strategy: Answer Questions

Good readers can answer questions about what they read. Sometimes the answer to a question will be in one place in the text. Sometimes it will be in several places. Sometimes you must combine what you read with what you already know. As you read, look for causes and effects. Answer the questions "What happened?" and "Why did it happen?"

1. Read "Rosa Parks Started Something Big." Make a graphic organizer like the one above to show the chain of events.

2. Why is Cleveland Avenue now called Rosa Parks Boulevard? Use information from your graphic organizer plus what you know about naming streets to write an answer to that question.

Rosa Parks
Started Something Big

Rosa Parks was a tired woman. She had worked hard all day. To ride home, she took a seat on the Cleveland Avenue bus in Montgomery, Alabama.

On that evening of December 1, 1955, segregation was the law. That meant white people could ride in the front of the bus, but black people had to ride in back. Black people could sit in the middle rows, the first rows of the section for black people—as long as no white people wanted those seats. •

An African American, Rosa Parks was settled in the first row of the section for black people when a white man demanded her seat. She refused to get up. •

Because she refused, the bus driver called the police. Rosa Parks was arrested. Black people throughout the city protested by refusing to ride the buses. This action, called a boycott, was organized by a minister named Martin Luther King, Jr. After more than a year, the law was changed. Segregation on the buses was no longer allowed. •

Because of Martin Luther King's work, he became widely known. He went on to lead the struggle for African Americans' rights throughout the country.

Cleveland Avenue is now called Rosa Parks Boulevard. •

Strategy What effect did segregation have on the city buses? Look for the answer in one spot.

Skill Rosa's action was the cause of a chain of events. Look for the first effect it had. The word *because* is a clue word.

Skill What was the final effect in the chain of events that started with Rosa's action?

Strategy Why did Martin Luther King become a well-known leader? Where did you find the answer to this question?

MY BROTHER
MARTIN

Words to Know

generations

pulpit

minister

shielding

avoided

numerous

ancestors

Remember

Try the strategy. Then,
if you need more help,
use your glossary or
a dictionary.

Vocabulary Strategy
for Endings

Word Structure Sometimes the ending *-ed* or *-ing*
is added to a verb or the ending *-s* is added to a
noun. If a word with one of these endings seems
hard to you, try this strategy.

1. Cover the ending and identify the base form
of the verb or noun.

2. Do you know this word? If you do, think
about its meaning. Picture the action the
verb describes.

3. If you do not, check the words around the word.
Try to find clues that can help you figure out
the meaning.

4. Check to see if the meaning makes sense in
the sentence.

As you read "Out of Slavery," look for words that
end with *-s, -ed,* or *-ing.* Use the endings and the
way the words are used to help you figure out
their meanings.

OUT OF SLAVERY

Slavery caused great hardship and sorrow in the United States. Africans were forced to come here as slaves. For generations, the slaves lived without freedom, and many white masters were cruel to them. All along, some white people said it was wrong to keep slaves. Over the years, more and more believed and said this. Often these voices came from the pulpit. It took a courageous minister to speak out and work for change. Slowly, the number of people who wanted to free all slaves grew.

Some very brave white and free black people helped slaves escape to freedom. They found ways of shielding the runaway slaves. For example, they hid them in safe houses to sleep and gave them food and clothes. Slaves who had run away avoided being seen by staying off roads and traveling at night.

Neither of these ways ended slavery. That took a long, terrible war in which numerous people died. Today African Americans remember their ancestors and are proud and thankful for the sacrifices they made.

Write ✏️

Think about one of your ancestors, such as a great-grandparent. (You have them, even if you know little about them!) Write about what makes you proud of your ancestor. Use words from the Words to Know list.

A **biography** is the story of a real person's life as told by someone else. In this biography, a sister shares childhood memories of her younger brother. Why do you think she chose to tell about these experiences?

MY BROTHER MARTIN

A Sister Remembers Growing Up with the Rev. Dr. Martin Luther King Jr.

by Christine King Farris
illustrated by Chris Soentpiet

What was it like to grow up with the Rev. Dr. Martin Luther King Jr.?

Gather around and listen as I share the childhood memories of my brother, the Reverend Dr. Martin Luther King Jr. I am his older sister, and I've known him longer than anyone else. I knew him long before the speeches he gave and the marches he led and the prizes he won. I even knew him before he first dreamed the dream that would change the world.

We were born in the same room, my brother Martin and I. I was an early baby, born sooner than expected. Mother Dear and Daddy placed me in the chifforobe drawer that stood in the corner of their upstairs bedroom. I got a crib a few days afterward. A year and a half later, Martin spent his first night in that hand-me-down crib in the very same room.

The house where we were born belonged to Mother Dear's parents, our grandparents, the Reverend and Mrs. A. D. Williams. We lived there with them and our Aunt Ida, our grandmother's sister. And not long after my brother Martin—who we called M. L. because he and Daddy had the same name—our baby brother was born. His name was Alfred Daniel, but we called him A. D., after our grandfather.

They called me Christine, and like three peas in one pod, we grew together. Our days and rooms were filled with adventure stories and Tinkertoys, with dolls and Monopoly and Chinese checkers.

And although Daddy, who was an important minister, and Mother Dear, who was known far and wide as a musician, often had work that took them away from home, our grandmother was always there to take care of us. I remember days sitting at her feet, as she and Aunt Ida filled us with grand memories of their childhood and read to us about all the wonderful places in the world.

And of course, my brothers and I had each other. We three stuck together like the pages in a brand-new book. And being normal young children, we were almost *always* up to something.

Our best prank involved a fur piece that belonged to our grandmother. It looked almost alive, with its tiny feet and little head and gleaming glass eyes. So, every once in a while, in the waning light of evening, we'd tie that fur piece to a stick, and, hiding behind the hedge in front of our house, we would dangle it in front of unsuspecting passersby. Boy! You could hear the screams of fright all across the neighborhood!

Then there was the time Mother Dear decided that her children should all learn to play piano. I didn't mind too much, but M. L. and A. D. preferred being outside to being stuck inside with our piano teacher, Mr. Mann, who would rap your knuckles with a ruler just for playing the wrong notes. Well, one morning, M. L. and A. D. decided to loosen the legs on the piano bench so we wouldn't have to practice. We didn't tell Mr. Mann, and when he sat . . . *CRASH!* down he went.

But mostly we were good, obedient children, and M. L. did learn to play a few songs on the piano. He even went off to sing with our mother a time or two. Given his love for singing and music, I'm sure he could have become as good a musician as our mother had his life not called him down a different path.

But that's just what his life did.

My brothers and I grew up a long time ago. Back in a time when certain places in our country had unfair laws that said it was right to keep black people separate because our skin was darker and our ancestors had been captured in far-off Africa and brought to America as slaves.

Atlanta, Georgia, the city in which we were growing up, had those laws. Because of those laws, my family rarely went to the picture shows or visited Grant Park with its famous Cyclorama. In fact, to this very day I don't recall ever seeing my father on a streetcar. Because of those laws, and the indignity that went with them, Daddy preferred keeping M. L., A. D., and me close to home, where we'd be protected.

We lived in a neighborhood in Atlanta that's now called Sweet Auburn. It was named for Auburn Avenue, the street that ran in front of our house. On our side of the street stood two-story frame houses similar to the one we lived in. Across it crouched a line of one-story row houses and a store owned by a white family.

When we were young all the children along Auburn Avenue played together, even the two boys whose parents owned the store.

And since our house was a favorite gathering place, those boys played with us in our backyard . . .

. . . and ran with M. L. and A. D. to the firehouse on the corner where they watched the engines and the firemen.

The thought of *not* playing with those kids because they were different, because they were white and we were black, never entered our minds.

Well, one day, M. L. and A. D. went to get their playmates from across the street just as they had done a hundred times before. But they came home alone. The boys had told my brothers that they couldn't play together anymore because A. D. and M. L. were Negroes.

And that was it. Shortly afterward the family sold the store and moved away. We never saw or heard from them again.

Looking back, I realize that it was only a matter of time before the generations of cruelty and injustice that Daddy and Mother Dear and Mama and Aunt Ida had been shielding us from finally broke through. But back then it was a crushing blow that seemed to come out of nowhere.

"Why do white people treat colored people so mean?" M. L. asked Mother Dear afterward. And with me and M. L. and A. D. standing in front of her trying our best to understand, Mother Dear gave the reason behind it all.

Her words explained the streetcars our family avoided and the WHITES ONLY sign that kept us off the elevator at City Hall. Her words told why there were parks and museums that black people could not visit and why some restaurants refused to serve us and why hotels wouldn't give us rooms and why theaters would only allow us to watch their picture shows from the balcony.

But her words also gave us hope.

She answered simply, "Because they just don't understand that everyone is the same, but someday, it will be better."

And my brother M. L. looked up into our mother's face and said the words I remember to this day.

He said, "Mother Dear, one day I'm going to turn this world upside down."

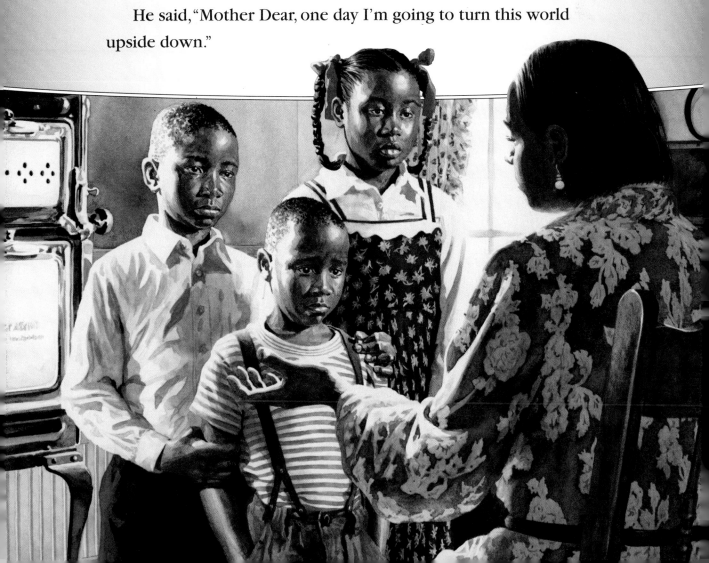

In the coming years there would be other reminders of the cruel system called segregation that sought to keep black people down. But it was Daddy who showed M. L. and A. D. and me how to speak out against hatred and bigotry and stand up for what's right.

Daddy was the minister at Ebenezer Baptist Church. And after losing our playmates, when M. L., A. D., and I heard our father speak from his pulpit, his words held new meaning.

And Daddy practiced what he preached. He always stood up for himself when confronted with hatred and bigotry, and each day he shared his encounters at the dinner table.

When a shoe salesman told Daddy and M. L. that he'd only serve them in the back of the store because they were black, Daddy took M. L. somewhere else to buy new shoes.

Another time, a police officer pulled Daddy over and called him "boy." Daddy pointed to M. L. sitting next to him in the car and said, "This is a boy. I am a man, and until you call me one, I will not listen to you."

These stories were as nourishing as the food that was set before us.

Years would pass, and many new lessons would be learned. There would be numerous speeches and marches and prizes. But my brother never forgot the example of our father, or the promise he had made to our mother on the day his friends turned him away.

And when he was much older, my brother M. L. dreamed a dream ...

. . . that turned the world upside down.

Reader Response

Open for Discussion How did Martin Luther King Jr. become a hero? What did you find out about his early life that must have prepared him to become a hero?

1. The three King children were like "peas in a pod" and "pages in a brand new book." What does the author mean? Why does she make these comparisons?

2. Why did M. L. promise his mother that he would turn the world upside down one day?

3. How were the author's family and other African Americans made to feel during this time? Give three examples from the selection.

4. The words *ancestors* and *generations* are words that tell about family. List some other family words that the author uses in the selection.

Look Back and Write M. L.'s father "practiced what he preached." Look back at pages 652–653 to find one example of this. Then write what that example meant to the King family.

Test Practice

655

Read more books about Martin Luther King Jr. and the Civil Rights Movement.

Meet the Author
CHRISTINE KING FARRIS

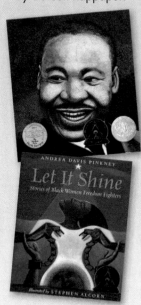

Martin's Big Words
by Doreen Rappaport

Let It Shine
by Andrea Davis Pinkney

Christine King Farris was close in age to her brother Martin Luther King Jr. The two of them played together a lot as they were growing up. Ms. Farris's main goal in writing *My Brother Martin* was to let children know that her brother was an ordinary child. Many youngsters seem to think he "came from outer space," she says.

Ms. Farris thinks her brother can be a role model for all children. "I want children to understand as they are growing up that they, too, can become great individuals." Even as a child, her brother seems to have known that. "It all goes back to what Martin said to my mother. He said, 'You know, Mother dear, one day I'm going to turn this world upside down.' And that is exactly what he did."

Ms. Farris has two Masters degrees and is an Associate Professor of Education at Spelman College in Atlanta, Georgia.

**See more art by
Chris Soentpiet
in these books.**

Chris Soentpiet, a native Korean, got a hard start in life. When he was only six, his mother died. A year later, his father was killed in a car accident. He and his older sister were adopted by the Soentpiets, an American family who lived in Hawaii. Since his new family spoke no Korean, Chris had to learn English quickly.

Now in his thirties, Mr. Soentpiet has illustrated almost twenty award-winning children's books. He felt honored to be asked to illustrate *My Brother Martin.* Mr. Soentpiet says, "It was exciting to work with the sister of Dr. King. When I was young, in school we celebrated his birthday every year. Dr. King was and still is one of my heroes. Mrs. Christine King Farris and her family played such an important part in Dr. King's childhood. I hope this book will tell boys and girls that Dr. King was just like them when he was their age."

Peacebound Trains
by Haemi Balgassi

Around Town
by Chris Soentpiet

Poetry

Genre

- People write poetry to express thoughts and feelings.

- Some poetry has rhyme. Some poetry is simply an arrangement of words in verse form.

- The lines of a poem may be grouped into stanzas, or verses.

- The poet may bend the rules of capitalization and punctuation to fit his or her purpose.

Link to Writing

Find out how to write haiku. Then choose a topic, and give it a try. Share your haiku with the class.

Hopes and Dreams of Young People

by Cristina Beecham (9 years old)

Just a small seedling
Can make a big difference
Could you be that seed?

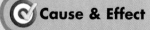

Cause & Effect   How can hopes and dreams make a difference?

When You Hope, Wish, and Trust

by Ek Ongkar K. Khalsa (10 years old)

There was something that kept
   me on a path,
like a strong steady rope,
but what really kept me there,
was nothing more than hope.

You cannot let yourself fail,
when you hope, wish and trust,
when you give up your dream,
it's like letting your wish rust.

Like Martin Luther King Jr.,
he made his dream come true,
so I know if you don't give up,
your dream will come to you.

Sometimes the words we speak,
became real and near,
so when we hope,
wish and trust,
our dreams will
really appear.

My Life Is A Buried Treasure

by Dawn Withrow (9 years old)

My life is
a buried treasure
to me. I want
to find it.
I dig all day.
It is very hard
to find it
all by myself.

Reading Across Texts

Which of the three poems do you think would
most appeal to Reverend Martin Luther King Jr.?

Writing Across Texts Explain your choice.

Comprehension

Skill
Fact and Opinion

Strategy
Text Structure

 Skill

Fact and Opinion

- Statements of fact can be proved true or false. Statements of opinion are judgments, beliefs, or ways of thinking about something.

- Evaluate statements of opinion by using the text, your prior knowledge, and logic. Based on what you know or have read, ask: Is the statement of opinion valid—is it supported well? Or is it faulty, having little or no support?

Statement of Fact or Opinion	How to Check Statement of Fact/ Support for Statement of Opinion	Valid or Faulty?

 Strategy

Strategy: Text Structure

Good readers look over the text before they read. Much nonfiction text follows a time sequence. Even writing this way, an author sometimes gives a statement of opinion and then makes supporting statements. Sometimes statements of fact are given first, followed by the author's opinion.

1. Read "Are You Ready for Some Football?" Make a graphic organizer like the one above to analyze the statements of fact and opinion.

2. Based on your graphic organizer and the article, write a brief paragraph that supports this statement: *Sports fans have grown to love football.*

ARE YOU READY FOR SOME FOOTBALL?

WHEN DID THE GAME BEGIN?

American football wasn't invented all at once. Rather, it evolved at colleges in the late 1800s from two other games: soccer and rugby. Football was like soccer in that you could move the ball toward a goal by kicking it. Football was like rugby in that you could run with the ball and tackle other players.

PLAY NICE!

By 1900, football had become pretty rough! For one thing, a team could have as many as 25 or 30 players on the field at one time. That's a lot of people to be running, blocking, and tackling. Often the "game" was more like a brawl! To make matters worse, players did not wear pads or helmets. Not a good idea! Finally, President Theodore Roosevelt said that the sport must have rules for safety.

FOOTBALL TODAY

Over the years, the game of football has continued to change. New rules have been added, and while college football is still popular, sports fans have also grown to love professional football. In fact, do you know what the most watched American TV sports event is? The Super Bowl! It is also the best American sports event.

Strategy Headings break up the article. How does this heading hint that it is about the way football used to be played?

Skill Even in an informational text, there can be statements of opinion. Ask: Will this statement be supported by facts or logic? Will it be valid or faulty?

Strategy Did the author write the article in a way that makes it easy to tell where statements of fact and statements of opinion are?

Skill Is this last statement one of fact or opinion? Can it be proved true or false? Is it supported?

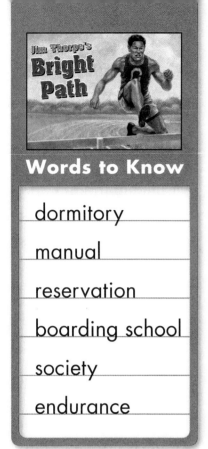

Jim Thorpe's
Bright Path

Words to Know

dormitory

manual

reservation

boarding school

society

endurance

Vocabulary Strategy
for Multiple-Meaning Words

Dictionary/Glossary Sometimes when you read, you may come across a word whose meaning you know, but that meaning doesn't make sense in the sentence. It may be a word with more than one meaning. You can use a dictionary or glossary to help you find the right meaning.

1. Try the meaning you know. Does it make sense in the sentence?

2. If it doesn't make sense, try to think of another meaning for the word. Does that meaning make sense?

3. If it doesn't make sense either, look up the word in a dictionary or glossary to see what other meanings it can have. Try one of those meanings in the sentence.

As you read "Dreaming of Home," look for words that can have more than one meaning. Use a dictionary or glossary to find meanings to try in the sentence. Which meaning makes sense?

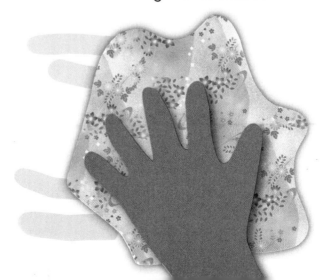

DREAMING OF HOME

Annie gazed out the window of the dormitory and longed to go outside. She knew that being outside would make her feel less homesick. But the students were required to do three hours of manual labor every day.

Annie's task was to wash the windows. While her hands were busy, her mind was back home on the reservation. There, she was talking to her mother and playing games with her sisters. Here, she lived in the dormitory with a hundred other girls. There, she was riding her pony and listening to her grandfather tell stories. Here, she sat in a classroom reciting English verbs.

Annie did not want to go away to boarding school, but that was the policy for Indian children in 1895. The school was supposed to teach them how to live in white society. Annie thought about what her father had said to her: "Akikta, remember the meaning of your name. You have determination. This experience will teach you patience and endurance."

Write

How would you feel if you had to leave home and go to school somewhere far away? Write about your thoughts and feelings. Use words from the Words to Know list.

Jim Thorpe's Bright Path

by Joseph Bruchac
illustrated by S. D. Nelson

Genre

A **biography** is the story of a real person's life as told by someone else. As you read this biography, think about why the author chose to write about this athlete.

Where will Jim Thorpe's bright path lead him?

They say Jim Thorpe's story began in May of 1887 in a small log cabin on the North Canadian River. There in the Indian Territory that became the state of Oklahoma, Charlotte Vieux Thorpe, a Pottowatomie woman, gave birth to twin boys. Her husband, Hiram, a mixed-blood Indian of the Sac and Fox nation, stood close by on that spring day.

The sun was in Hiram Thorpe's heart as he looked down at the sons he named Charles and James. Jim's mother gave him another name.

"Wa-tho-huck," she said, thinking of how the light shone on the road to their cabin. "Bright Path."

As good as that name was, neither of them knew just how far that path would lead their son.

Like most twins, Jim and Charlie were close, even though they were not exactly the same. Charlie had darker skin and brown hair, while Jim's skin was light and his hair dark black. When they raced or wrestled, Jim was always a little ahead of Charlie, his best friend. Whenever Jim got too far ahead, he would stop and wait.

"Come on, Charlie," he would say with a grin.

Then, when his brother caught up, they would be off again.

Summer or winter, Jim and Charlie's favorite place was outdoors. They roamed the prairies, swam, and played together. By the time they were three, Pa Thorpe had taught his boys to ride a horse. He showed them how to shoot a bow, set a trap, and hunt. Jim took to it all like a catfish takes to a creek. Although small, he was quick and tough. He was so fast and had so much endurance that he could run down a rabbit on foot. When it came to the old ways, those skills that made the men of the Sac and Fox great providers for their families, Jim was a great learner. By the time the twins were six, Pa Thorpe said Jim knew more about the woods than many men.

Their sixth year also brought a big change for Jim and Charlie. The Indian Agency that oversaw the reservation said that when Sac and Fox children reached age six, they had to go to the Agency Boarding School. Indian boarding schools did not provide the same education offered to whites. In addition the boarding schools were designed to cut them off from everything that made them Indians—their language, their traditions, even their families.

Jim's father had become one of the few Sac and Fox men who could read and write English. He'd seen uneducated Indians cheated out of everything by dishonest men who tricked the Indians into signing papers they could not read.

"My sons," he said to Jim and Charlie, "you need white man's knowledge to survive."

It was no surprise that Jim hated school. He had to wear awful clothes—a heavy wool suit, a felt cap, tight shoes, a shirt and necktie that strangled him. He also got smacked hard across his knuckles with a wooden ruler whenever he spoke a word of Sac. He missed Ma's cooking and Pa's stories about their clan ancestor, Chief Black Hawk, the famous warrior who had fought the whites to defend his people. Worst of all, school kept Jim inside all day and locked him up all night in a cold dormitory away from the forest and prairies. It made him feel like a fox caught in an iron trap. Jim didn't care about what school might do for him or his people. He just wanted to get away from it.

Charlie was better at his studies than Jim. He didn't seem to mind the military discipline or being stuck at a desk. Solving an arithmetic problem was a challenge to Charlie the way winning a race was to Jim. Now it was Charlie who was waiting for his brother to catch up.

"Come on, Jim," Charlie said. "Don't give up. You can do it."

So, Jim tried to master basic arithmetic, reading, and writing. Then, in his third year of school, something happened that broke his heart.

Sickness often struck the crowded, unheated dormitories of the Indian boarding schools. Sanitation was poor, and there were no real doctors to tend the sick. Epidemics of influenza swept through like prairie fires. Even common childhood diseases such as measles and whooping cough could be fatal to the Indian children jammed together in those schools.

Charlie was one of those who became sick. He caught pneumonia and died. Jim felt as if the sunlight had gone from his life. His twin brother had been his best friend.

Jim's mother tried to comfort her son, but he was inconsolable. He would never hear Charlie's encouraging voice again. The thought of going back to school without his brother tore at Jim's heart.

"Let me work around the farm, Pa," Jim begged.

His father, though, was sure he knew what was best.

"Son," he said, "you have to get an education. Charlie would have wanted you to keep learning."

Jim tried to listen to his father, but when he returned to school and saw the empty cot where Charlie had slept, it was too much for him. As soon as the teacher's back was turned, Jim ran the twenty-three miles back home, straight as an arrow.

Pa Thorpe had no choice but to send his stubborn son even farther away. So young Jim, at age eleven, was sent to Haskell Institute in Lawrence, Kansas, almost three hundred miles away.

Haskell was stricter than the Agency Boarding School. There children from more than eighty tribes were dressed in military uniforms and were awakened before dawn with a bugle call. Manual training was mixed with classroom studies to teach them trades useful to white society. Hard work was the rule, and the students of Haskell did it all—growing corn, making bread, building wagons, and sewing their own uniforms.

Jim did better at Haskell. He worked in the engineering shop. Learning how things were made was more interesting than being cooped up in a classroom.

Plus Haskell had something the Agency Boarding School didn't have—football. For the first time in his life, Jim saw a football game. The cheers of the crowd and the athleticism of the players wakened something deep inside Jim, the same emotions that had been stirred by Pa's stories of Black Hawk and the other warriors who had fought for their people. Jim knew right away that football was something he wanted to play.

671

But Jim was too small for the sport. He was less than five feet tall and weighed just one hundred pounds. He joined the track team instead and became one of the fastest runners. Meanwhile, he watched every football game he could. Jim also met Chauncy Archiquette, Haskell's best football player, who taught him about the game. Chauncy even helped Jim make a little football out of scrap leather stuffed with rags. With that football Jim organized games with other boys too small for the school team.

Near the end of his second year at Haskell, Jim got word that his father had been shot in a hunting accident and was dying. Jim's only thought was that he had to get home. He ran off and headed south. It took him two weeks to reach their farm. To his surprise, Pa was there, recovered from his wound and waiting.

"We knew you were coming home," his father said, embracing him.

Jim never went back to Haskell. Shortly after he returned home, his mother died of a sudden illness. Jim grieved over the loss of his mother, and Pa Thorpe finally agreed that his son did not have to go back to boarding school.

Jim's father believed his son still needed education, so Jim began attending school nearby in Garden Grove. At Garden Grove, students were learning about a new thing called electricity. Electricity could make it seem as if the sun were still shining, even at night. The thought of that appealed to Jim. Electrical sunlight could be brought to Indian homes too. Pa Thorpe had always told Jim that education would give him the ability to help his people. Maybe becoming an electrician was the bright path he was supposed to follow.

One day a recruiter from the Carlisle Indian School in Pennsylvania came to Garden Grove. Carlisle was always looking for Indian students who were good athletes, and the recruiter had heard of Jim's success as a runner at Haskell.

"Would you like to be a Carlisle man?" the recruiter asked.

"Can I study electricity there?" Jim said.

"Of course," the recruiter replied, even though Carlisle offered no such course.

Something else also attracted Jim to Carlisle—sports. Carlisle was one of the most well-known of the Indian boarding schools. Everyone knew about the school and its amazing record of winning sports teams. The Carlisle Indians even beat teams from the big, famous colleges. At Carlisle, Jim thought, he could play football.

Pa Thorpe urged Jim to seize the opportunity. Somehow he knew Carlisle would be the first step on a trail that would lead his son to greatness.

"Son," he said, "you are an Indian. I want you to show other races what an Indian can do."

Soon after Jim arrived at Carlisle, he received bad news. His father had been bitten by a snake while working in his fields and had died of blood poisoning. The man who had fought so hard to force his son to get an education was gone.

Already a quiet person, Jim retreated further into silence after his father's death. But he did not desert Carlisle. Perhaps, Jim felt the best way to remember his father was to live the dream Pa Thorpe had for him. It was now up to Jim to push himself.

The Carlisle system of sending new students off campus for work experience helped. Jim ended up at a farm in New Jersey. The farm labor reminded him of the many hours he had spent working by Pa's side in Oklahoma. Jim worked so hard and with such quiet confidence that everyone saw him as a man they could like and trust. To his delight, Jim was made foreman, head of all the workers.

When Jim came back to Carlisle in the fall, he was no longer a boy. He had grown taller, stronger, more self-assured. He was ready to play football, but he knew it would not be easy. Carlisle's famous coach Pop Warner would only allow the best to join his track squad or his football team as one of his "Athletic Boys."

One day Jim's big chance came. He was on his way to play a game of scrub football with some of his friends who were too small for the school team. As Jim crossed the field, he saw a group of varsity athletes practicing the high jump.

Jim asked if he could have a try, even though he was wearing overalls and an old pair of work shoes. The Athletic Boys snickered as they reset the bar for him. They placed it higher than anyone at Carlisle had ever jumped. Even in his work clothes, Jim cleared the bar on his first jump. No one could believe it. People stood around with their mouths wide open, staring. Jim just grinned and walked off to play football with his friends.

The next day Jim was told to report to the office of Coach Warner. Everyone knew Pop Warner was a great coach, but he was also a man with a bad temper. Jim wondered if Pop was going to yell at him for interrupting track practice.

"Do you know what you've done?" Pop Warner growled.

"Nothing bad, I hope," Jim said.

"Bad?" Pop Warner said. His face broke into a smile. "Boy, you've just broken the school record. Go down to the clubhouse and exchange those overalls for a track outfit. You're on my track team now."

Before long Jim Thorpe was Carlisle's best track athlete. He competed in the high jump, hurdles, and dashes, winning or placing in all of them. Still, Jim wanted to play football. Reluctantly Pop Warner told him he could give it a try.

Pop Warner didn't like the idea of his slender high jumper being injured in a football game, so he decided to discourage Jim by beginning his first practice with a tackling drill. Jim, the newcomer, had to take the ball and try to run from one end to the other, through the whole varsity team.

"Is that all?" Jim said. He looked at the football in his hands. It was the first time he'd ever held a real football, but he believed in himself. Then he took off down the field like a deer. He was past half the team before the players even saw him coming. At the other end Jim looked back. Behind him was the whole Carlisle team, the players holding nothing in their hands but air.

There was a grin on Jim's face when he handed Coach Warner the ball.

"Doggone it," Pop Warner said. "You're supposed to give the first team tackling practice, not run through them." Pop Warner slammed the ball back into Jim's belly. "Do it again."

Jim's jaw was set as he ran the Carlisle gauntlet a second time. He was carrying not just a football, but the hopes and dreams of his family, his people, and all the Indians who had been told they could never compete with the white man. Tacklers bounced off Jim as he lowered his shoulders. No one stopped him. The sun shone around him as he stood in the end zone.

For years Jim had fought against his education. He had run away from it so many times. This time Jim used all he had learned from his mother's wisdom, his brother's encouragement, and his father's fierce determination that his son show what an Indian could do. From now on Jim Thorpe would run forward, toward the finish line, toward the goal. He didn't know how far he would go, but he believed in his journey. His education had put his feet on the bright path.

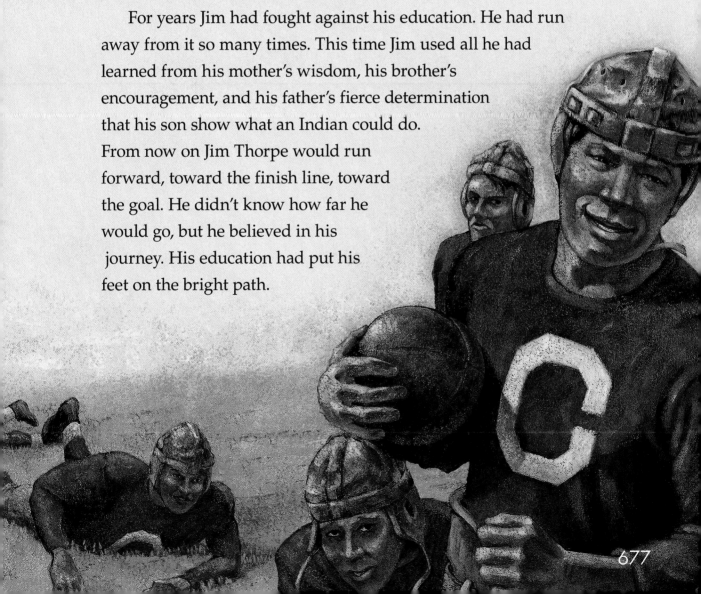

Important Dates in Jim Thorpe's Life and Legacy

1887* James Francis Thorpe and twin brother, Charles, born on Sac and Fox Indian Reservation along North Canadian River in Oklahoma, May 28

Jim, left, and Charlie, age 3

1893 Enters Agency Boarding School with Charlie

1896 Charlie dies of pneumonia

1898 Arrives at Haskell Institute in Lawrence, Kansas

1902* Charlotte Thorpe (mother) dies; begins attending school in Garden Grove, Oklahoma

1904 Enters United States Indian Industrial School in Carlisle, Pennsylvania; Hiram Thorpe (father) dies

*Date cited obtained from Thorpe family or most reliable sources

1907–1912 Plays college football

1909–1910 Plays minor league baseball

1911, 1912 Named First Team All American Halfback at Carlisle

1912 Wins gold medals in Pentathlon and Decathlon at Summer Olympic Games in Stockholm, Sweden

Original Olympic gold medals

1913 Stripped of Olympic medals and name removed from record books for playing minor league professional baseball

678

1982 International Olympic Committee restores Thorpe's name to record books

1983 Duplicate Olympic gold medals given to Thorpe family; inducted into U.S. Olympic Hall of Fame

1998 U.S. Postal Service issues Jim Thorpe commemorative stamp as part of its Celebrate the Century program

1913–1919 Plays major league baseball

1915–1929 Plays professional football

1917 Becomes a United States citizen

1920 Elected first president of American Professional Football Association (now National Football League)

1922 Forms Oorang Indians, an all-Indian professional football team

1929 Retires from professional football at age forty-two

1953 Dies March 28; buried in Mauch Park, Pennsylvania, which later is renamed Jim Thorpe, Pennsylvania

1963 Inducted into Pro Football Hall of Fame as part of original class

Thorpe statue in Pro Football Hall of Fame

Reader Response

Open for Discussion Suppose you could spend one day with young Jim Thorpe to get to know him in person. Which day would you choose? What would you expect to see and do?

1. Biographers usually write about grown-ups. Instead, this biographer wrote about the early life of Jim Thorpe, before he became famous. Why? What is good about this idea?

2. Look back at page 673. Find three facts and one opinion. How can you tell the difference between the facts and the opinion?

3. Take another look at the illustrations in this selection. How do they show the text structure? What is the text structure?

4. Jim Thorpe attended three boarding schools as a young man. Choose one and write about it. Use words from the Words to Know list and the selection.

Look Back and Write King Gustav of Sweden once said that Jim Thorpe was the greatest athlete in the world. Why do you think he said this? Look back at pages 675–679 to find examples of Jim Thorpe's athletic greatness.

The Arrow over the Door

Joseph Bruchac, who is of Abenaki Indian descent, grew up admiring Jim Thorpe. He says, "Jim Thorpe struck me as a true American hero. The fact that part of my own heritage was American Indian made Jim even more special to me."

Mr. Bruchac learned more about Jim Thorpe from a friend. "One of my dearest friends was a Pueblo/ Apache elder named Swift Eagle. For many years, Swift Eagle told me stories about Jim Thorpe, who had been a personal friend of his when both of them were living in California and working in the movies. It made me feel even closer to Jim and his story." He adds, "I think that all of us, whatever our backgrounds, can find inspiration from our unique heritages."

A Boy Called Slow: The True Story of Sitting Bull

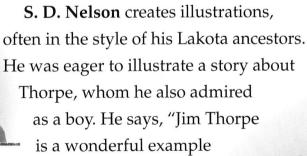

S. D. Nelson creates illustrations, often in the style of his Lakota ancestors. He was eager to illustrate a story about Thorpe, whom he also admired as a boy. He says, "Jim Thorpe is a wonderful example of someone who struggled against many difficulties in order to make his dream come true. I hope young people today will be inspired by his true life story."

Expository Nonfiction

Genre

- Expository nonfiction can tell about events in history.
- Usually expository nonfiction includes photographs that illustrate information in the text.

Text Features

- The author gives information about the *who, what, when, where,* and *how* of Special Olympics.
- The photographs give the reader a quick look at some of the sports and athletes.

Link to Social Studies

Research some of the athletes in Special Olympics. Find information such as where they are from, where they train, and what their goals are. Share what you learn with the class.

Special

Athletes from all over the world have made their dreams come true at the Special Olympics World Games. The Games are a place for mentally disabled athletes to compete in twenty-six different sports.

How did the Special Olympics Games get started? In 1962, a woman named Eunice Kennedy Shriver had an idea. She wanted to start a sports day camp for mentally disabled children. Her sister Rosemary was mentally disabled. She wanted to help mentally disabled children like her sister succeed

Eunice Kennedy Shriver

IRELA

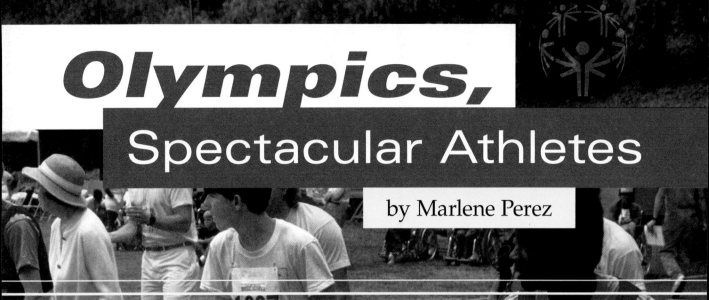

Olympics,
Spectacular Athletes

by Marlene Perez

as athletes. Mrs. Shriver was part of a famous family. Her brother was U.S. President John F. Kennedy.

Thirty-five mentally disabled boys and girls attended the first camp at the Shriver home in Maryland. It was called Camp Shriver. The camp grew and soon became what is now known as Special Olympics.

In 1968, the first International Special Olympics Games were held in Chicago. Eunice Kennedy Shriver opened the Games with a quote from Roman gladiators. She said, "Let me win. But if I cannot win, let me be brave in the attempt." This quote became the motto of Special Olympics. A thousand athletes took part in the first Games and the number has grown ever since.

Athletes compete at local Special Olympics events. The athletes who do well move on to the next level. Finally, the top athletes go to the World Games.

Fact & Opinion   Will you find many opinions in a factual article?

LAND   HUNGARY   683 FINLAND

The current leader of Special Olympics is Chairman Timothy Shriver. He says that Special Olympics athletes are the true leaders. In his words, "They have taught me what it is to lead without fear, to succeed without ego, and to approach challenges with a positive attitude."

The Special Olympics Summer and Winter Games are each held every four years. The 2005 Special Olympics World Winter Games were held in Nagano, Japan. The Winter Games featured contests in several sports, including figure skating, hockey, skiing, and snowboarding.

In 2007, Special Olympics will hold its Summer Games in Shanghai, China. The Summer Games will have contests in twenty different sports, including basketball, judo, tennis, and volleyball.

approach challenges

with a positive attitude

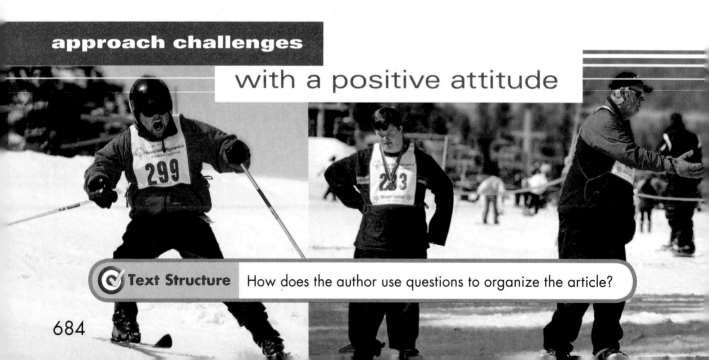

Text Structure How does the author use questions to organize the article?

Alisa Harding

Who are some of the athletes of Special Olympics?

The athletes are people like Alisa Harding. Harding, from Michigan, competed in the snowshoe competition at the 2005 Winter Games. She has an impressive collection of medals from past Special Olympics Games.

Dane Waites ran in the half marathon and the 10,000-meter event in the 2003 Summer Games. His small town in Australia raised money to get him to the Games.

Special Olympics athletes often find new challenges after experiencing Special Olympics. Special Olympics athlete Kester Edwards was in a fashion shoot with a professional tennis player. Paula Sage, a Special Olympics athlete from Great Britain, had a starring role in a major motion picture.

Special Olympics provide a way for mentally disabled athletes to achieve their dreams, as athletes and beyond.

Reading Across Texts

How did Jim Thorpe and Special Olympics athlete Dane Waites achieve their goals?

Writing Across Texts List some of the accomplishments of Jim Thorpe and Special Olympics athletes.

Character and Theme

- What the characters in a story do and say gives clues about what they are like.

- The theme is the underlying meaning of a story. "Crime doesn't pay" is one example.

- The author may state the theme directly, but more often, the reader has to think about the story in order to figure out the theme.

- A reader must have proof from the story to support a theme statement.

Character	Goal	Plot Events	Theme

Strategy: Summarize

As you read a story, summarize the characters' goals and how they try to reach them. Ask yourself, "What are the characters like as they try to reach their goals? Do they succeed?" Summarizing will help you figure out the theme of the story.

1. Read "Dare to Dream." Use the graphic organizer above to jot down notes about the characters' goals and what they do to reach them. Summarize your notes.

2. Record on the graphic organizer the theme of the story and what support you have for this theme. Write a paragraph giving your support for the theme.

Dare to Dream

Everyone in town said that Rico was one of the best young baseball players in the Dominican Republic. That was saying a lot, since so many great players in the major leagues have come from this Caribbean nation. Carlos was sure that one day his big brother would play for a major league team in the United States.

Carlos loved his older brother very much, and not just because he was a great baseball player. Though Rico was eighteen and Carlos was ten, they were best buddies. Carlos went to every one of Rico's games. But today there was no game–there was something much more important. Rico was trying out for one of the baseball training camps that are run by major league teams from the States.

Would Rico be chosen? Would all of his dedication and hard work pay off? Carlos knew that the training camps were the next step in Rico's journey. The best players from these camps would be sent to the States to play in the minor leagues there. And the best minor league players would go on to the major leagues.

The very next day, Carlos was the first to hear the happy news from Rico. He was going to training camp! Dreams *can* come true, thought Carlos–especially if you help them along with lots of hard work.

Skill The title of a story may help you figure out its theme. Keep the title in mind as you read the story.

Strategy What important things have you learned about the characters so far? Use two sentences to summarize what you know at this point.

Strategy Summarize Rico's goals in one or two sentences. Which goal is he trying to reach now? Which goals does he want to reach sometime in the future?

Skill What is the theme, or underlying meaning, of this story? What proof from the story supports your theme statement?

How
Tia Lola
Came to
Visit
Stay

Words to Know

colonel

quaint

resemblance

affords

lurking

glint

palettes

Remember

Try the strategy. Then, if you need more help, use your glossary or a dictionary.

Vocabulary Strategy
for Unfamiliar Words

Context Clues Sometimes you can use context clues—the words and sentences around an unknown word—to help you figure out the meaning of the word.

1. Read the words and sentences around the unknown word. The author may put a definition of the word in parentheses or between commas or dashes.

2. If not, say what the sentence means in your own words.

3. Predict a meaning for the unknown word.

4. Try that meaning in the sentence. Does it make sense?

As you read "An Officer and an Artist," use the context to help you figure out the meanings of the vocabulary words.

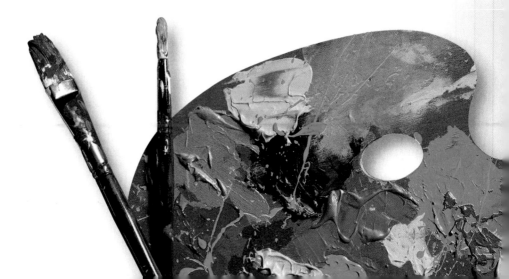

An Officer and *an Artist*

My great-uncle Bob is an artist who has never sold a painting. In fact, he had a career that has nothing to do with art. He was a colonel (an officer in the army). He doesn't look like an artist. He doesn't wear a quaint beret or paint-stained clothes. His face has no resemblance to a wild-eyed dreamer such as the Dutch painter Van Gogh. No, Colonel Bob stands at attention, and he does everything precisely.

Ever since he retired from the army, Colonel Bob spends hours every day painting. Having been an officer affords, or gives, him the income to now pursue his dream.

You may see him lurking and waiting, as though to surprise an enemy, for the right light. He knows just when the sun should produce a glint, or shine, on a pond or a barn roof. He takes many pictures of a scene. Then he draws it on canvas and begins to paint. Nothing is just green, blue, or yellow. One flower contains enough colors to fill two palettes. Colonel Bob says he sees everything with different eyes now.

Write

Write a description of an interesting person you know. Use some words from the Words to Know list.

How Tía Lola Came to Visit Stay

by Julia Alvarez
illustrated by Macky Pamintuan

Realistic fiction is made up, but the characters and events are so lifelike that the story seems as if it must be true. As you read, think about what makes this story seem as if it could happen in real life.

What makes Tía Lola such a welcome houseguest?

Miguel and Juanita have moved to a rented farmhouse in Vermont with their mother, Mami. Their father, an artist, has stayed in New York. Tía Lola, Mami's aunt from the Dominican Republic, has come to visit. But some of the ideas she has brought along are a little "different" and not always to the liking of Miguel or the family's landlord, Colonel Charlebois.

The long, sweet, sunny days of summer come one after another after another. Each one is like a piece of fancy candy in a gold-and-blue wrapper.

Most nights, now that school is out, Tía Lola tells stories, sometimes until very late. The uncle who fell in love with a *ciguapa* and never married. The beautiful cousin who never cut her hair and carried it around in a wheelbarrow. The grandfather whose eyes turned blue when he saw his first grandchild.

Some nights, for a break, they explore the old house. In the attic, behind their own boxes, they find dusty trunks full of yellowing letters and photographs. Miguel discovers several faded photos of a group of boys all lined up in old-fashioned baseball uniforms. Except for the funny caps and knickers and knee socks, the boys in the photos could be any of the boys on Miguel's team. One photo of a boy with a baseball glove in his hand is inscribed, *Charlebois, '34.*

Miguel tries to imagine the grouchy old man at Rudy's Restaurant as the young boy with the friendly smile in the photograph.

But he can't see even a faint resemblance.

Since the team doesn't have a good place for daily practice, Miguel's mother suggests they use the back pasture behind the house. "But let me write Colonel Charlebois first, just in case."

Their landlord lives in a big white house in the center of town. He has already written them once this summer, complaining about "the unseemly shape of the vegetation," after Tía Lola trimmed the hedges in front of the house in the shapes of pineapples and parrots and palm trees.

"Can't you just call him and ask him, Mami?" Miguel asks. After all, the team is impatient to get started with practice. A letter will take several days to be answered.

"You try calling him," Miguel's mother says, holding out the phone. Miguel dials the number his mother reads from a card tacked on the kitchen bulletin board. The phone rings once, twice. A machine clicks on, and a cranky old voice speaks up: "This is Colonel Charles Charlebois. I can't be bothered coming to the phone every time it rings. If you have a message, you can write me at 27 Main Street, Middlebury, Vermont 05753."

"Let's write that letter, shall we?" Mami says, taking the phone back from Miguel.

Two days later, Colonel Charlebois's answer is in their mailbox. It has not been postmarked. He must have driven out and delivered it himself.

"I would be honored to have the team practice in my back pasture," he replies in a shaky hand as if he'd written the letter while riding in a car over a bumpy road.

"Honored!" Miguel's mother says, lifting her eyebrows. She translates the letter for Tía Lola, who merely nods as if she'd known all along that Colonel Charlebois is really a nice man.

And so every day Miguel's friends come over, and the team plays ball in the back field where only six months ago, Miguel (or maybe it was the *ciguapas?*) wrote a great big welcome to Tía Lola. Twice a week, Rudy drops by to coach. They play all afternoon, and afterward, when they are hot and sweaty, Tía Lola invites them inside for cool, refreshing smoothies, which she calls *frío-fríos.* As they slurp and lick, she practices her English by telling them wonderful stories about Dominican baseball players like Sammy Sosa and the Alou brothers and Juan Marichal and Pedro and Ramón Martínez. The way she tells the stories, it's as if she knows these players personally. Miguel and his friends are enthralled.

After a couple of weeks of practice, the team votes to make Miguel the captain. José, who is visiting from New York, substitutes for whoever is missing that day. Tía Lola is named manager.

"*¿Y qué hace el manager?*" Tía Lola wants to know what a manager does.

695

"A manager makes us *frío-fríos*," Captain Miguel says.

Every day, after practice, there are *frío-fríos* in a tall pitcher in the icebox.

It is a happy summer–

Until Tía Lola decides to paint the house purple.

Miguel and his friends have been playing ball in the back field–their view of the house shielded by the ample trees. As they walk back from practice, they look up.

"Holy cow!" Miguel cries out.

The front porch is the color of a bright bruise. Miguel can't help thinking of the deep, rich purple whose name he recently learned from his father in New York. "Dioxazine," he mutters to himself. The rest of the house is still the same color as almost every other house in town. "Regulation white," Papi calls it whenever he comes up to visit and drives through town.

In her high heels and a dress with flowers whose petals match the color of the porch stands Tía Lola, painting broad purple strokes.

For a brief second, Miguel feels a flash of that old embarrassment he used to feel about his crazy aunt.

"Awesome," his friend Dean is saying.

"Cool!" Sam agrees.

"*¡Qué* cool!" José echoes.

They wave at Tía Lola, who waves back.

"*¡Frío-fríos!*" she calls out. Today she has chosen grape flavor in honor of the new color of the house.

By the time Miguel's mother comes home from work, he and his friends look like they have helped Tía Lola paint the house: their mouths are purple smudges. When they open their mouths to say hello, their tongues are a pinkish purple.

696

"Okay, what is going on?" Mami asks, glancing from Miguel to Tía Lola. She looks as if she is about to cry, something she has not done in a long time.

Tía Lola speaks up. Don't the colors remind her of the island? *"La casita de tu niñez."* The house where Mami spent her childhood.

Miguel can see his mother's face softening. Her eyes have a faraway look. Suddenly, Mami is shaking her head and trying not to laugh. "Colonel Charlebois is going to throw a fit. Actually, he's going to throw us out."

"El coronel, no hay problema," Tía Lola says, pointing to herself and Miguel and his friends. Miguel's mother looks from face to face as if she doesn't understand. Miguel and his friends nod as if they understand exactly what Tía Lola is up to.

The next afternoon, when Miguel's friends come inside from practice, Tía Lola takes their measurements. She has bought fabric with the money the team has collected and is making them their uniforms.

When it is Miguel's turn, he stands next to the mark that his mother made on the door frame back in January. He is already an inch taller!

"Tía Lola, what are you up to?" the team keeps asking. "Are we going to lose our playing field if Colonel Charlebois takes back his house?"

"No hay problema," Tía Lola keeps saying. Her mouth curls up like a fish hook that has caught a big smile.

"Are you going to work magic on him?" Miguel asks his aunt that night.

"The magic of understanding," Tía Lola says, winking. She can look into a face and see straight to the heart.

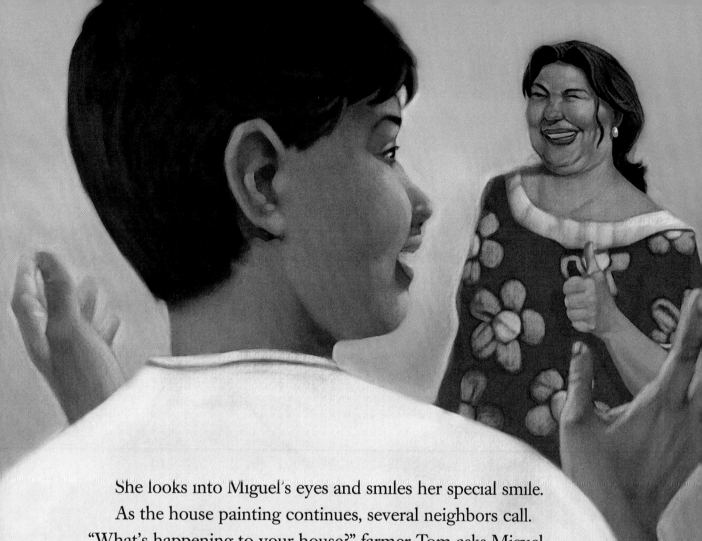

She looks into Miguel's eyes and smiles her special smile.

As the house painting continues, several neighbors call. "What's happening to your house?" farmer Tom asks Miguel. "I don't believe I've ever seen a purple house. Is that a New York style or something?"

Their farming neighbors think of New York as a foreign country. Whenever Miguel and his family do something odd, Tom and Becky believe it is due to their having come from "the city."

"I've never seen a purple house in my life," Miguel admits.

"Neither have I," José adds, "and I live in the city!"

"I've seen one!" Juanita speaks up, showing off.

"Where?" Miguel challenges.

"In my imagination." She grins.

Miguel has been trying to imitate Tía Lola, looking for the best in people. He stares straight into Juanita's eyes, but all he can see is his smart-alecky little sister.

One afternoon, soon after José has returned to the city, Miguel is coming down the stairs to join his teammates in the back field. He pauses at the landing. The large window affords a view of the surrounding farms and the quaint New England town beyond.

A silver car Miguel doesn't recognize is coming down the dirt road to their house. Just before arriving at the farmhouse, it turns in to an old logging road at the back of the property. Behind a clump of ash trees, the car stops and the door opens.

Later, as he stands to bat, Miguel can make out a glint of silver among the trees. Who could it be? he wonders. He thinks of telling his mother about the stranger, but decides against it.

She would probably think an escaped convict was lurking in the woods and not allow the team to practice in the back field anymore.

The next afternoon, Miguel watches from behind the curtain as the same silver car he saw in the woods yesterday comes slowly up the drive. His friends have already left after their baseball practice, and his mother is not home from work yet. He can hear Tía Lola's sewing machine humming away upstairs.

"Who is it?" Juanita is standing beside him, holding on to her brother's arm. All her smart-alecky confidence is gone.

"I think it's him–Colonel Charlebois," Miguel whispers. Now that the car is so close, he can make out the old man behind the wheel. The hood has a striking ornament: a little silver batter, crouched, ready to swing. "I'm going to pretend no one is home," Miguel adds.

But Colonel Charlebois doesn't come up to the door. He sits in his car, gazing up at the purple-and-white house for a few minutes, and then he drives away. Later that day, a letter appears in the mailbox. "Unless the house is back to its original white by the end of the month, you are welcome to move out."

"*Welcome* to move out?" Miguel repeats. He wrote *¡BIENVENIDA!* to his Tía Lola when she moved in. It doesn't sound right to *welcome* someone to move out.

"We've got three weeks to paint the house back or move," their mother says in a teary voice at dinner. "I'm disappointed, too," she admits to Tía Lola. After all, she really loves the new color. That flaking white paint made the place look so blah and run-down. "But still, I don't want to have to move again," Mami sighs.

Tía Lola pats her niece's hand. There is something else they can try first.

"What's that?" her niece asks.

They can invite *el coronel* over on Saturday.

"But that's the day of our big game," Miguel reminds his aunt. They'll be playing against another local team from the next county over.

Tía Lola winks. She knows. *"Pero tengo un plan."* She has a plan. Miguel should tell his friends to come a little early so they can change.

"Change what?" Miguel's mother asks. "Change the color of the house?"

Tía Lola shakes her head. Change a hard heart. She'll need more grape juice from the store.

The day dawns sunny and warm. The cloudless sky stretches on and on and on, endlessly blue with the glint of an airplane, like a needle sewing a tiny tear in it. Every tree seems filled to capacity with dark green rustling leaves. On the neighboring farms, the corn is as tall as the boys who play baseball in the fallow field nearby. Tía Lola's garden looks like one of Papi's palettes. But now, after living in the country for seven months, Miguel has his own new names for colors: zucchini green, squash yellow, chili-pepper red, raspberry crimson. The eggplants are as purple as the newly painted house. It is the full of summer. In a few weeks, up in the mountains, the maples will begin to turn.

Miguel's friends and their parents arrive early. The boys head upstairs behind Tía Lola and Rudy. Their parents stay downstairs, drinking grape smoothies and talking about how their gardens are doing. At last, the silver car rolls into the driveway.

Slowly, Colonel Charlebois climbs out. He stands, a cane in one hand, looking up at the house. One quarter of the house is purple. The other three-quarters is still white. Which color will the whole house end up being?

Miguel looks down at the old man from an upstairs window. Suddenly, he feels a sense of panic. What if Tía Lola's plan doesn't work? He doesn't want to move from the house that has finally become a home to him.

He feels his aunt's hand on his shoulder. *"No hay problema, Miguelito,"* she reassures him as if she can read his thoughts even without looking into his eyes.

Colonel Charlebois is still staring up at the house when the front door opens. Out file nine boys in purple-and-white striped uniforms and purple baseball caps. They look as if the house itself has sprouted them! Miguel leads the way, a baseball in his hand. Behind them, Tía Lola and Rudy each hold the corner of a pennant that reads: CHARLIE'S BOYS.

Colonel Charlebois gazes at each boy. It is difficult to tell what is going through his mind. Suddenly, he drops his cane on the front lawn and calls out, "Let's play ball!" He stands, wobbly and waiting and smiling. Miguel looks into the old man's eyes and sees a boy, legs apart, body bent forward, a gloved hand held out in front of him.

He lifts his arm and throws the ball at that young boy—and the old man catches it.

Reader Response

Open for Discussion Think about the setting of the story. Close your eyes and imagine the old farmhouse, its beautiful garden, and the Vermont countryside. How would you describe this setting? What kind of mood does it create?

1. Describe Tía Lola as the author portrays her in the story. Think about her actions, appearance, and thoughts.

2. A story's theme is its underlying meaning or message. What do you think the theme of *How Tía Lola Came to ~~Visit~~ Stay* is? Use details from the story to support your answer.

3. If you were to summarize the story, would you include the fact that Tía Lola makes smoothies for the baseball team? Why or why not?

4. Make a web. In the center write *Colonel Charlebois*. Around the center, write words used to describe the Colonel in the beginning of the story. Then add words of your own that describe him at the end.

Test Practice

Look Back and Write Miguel finds something that helps him learn about Colonel Charlebois's past. Look back at page 692 and write about what Miguel finds.

Meet the Author
Julia Alvarez

Read more books about children who are new to the United States.

Julia Alvarez wrote *How Tía Lola Came to Visit Stay* for her nephew when he was ten. He kept asking when he was going to get to read one of her books. Ms. Alvarez decided to write a story about an aunt like the ones she had in the Dominican Republic. She says Tía Lola is "a kind of Mary Poppins with a Spanish accent."

Julia Alvarez grew up in the Dominican Republic, a beautiful tropical island. When she was ten, her family moved to the United States. It was difficult starting over in a New York City school. Ms. Alvarez says, "Not understanding the language, I had to pay close attention to each word—great training for a writer."

Ms. Alvarez became a teacher. Her first novel, *How the Garcia Girls Lost Their Accents,* was successful, and she was able to start writing full-time. She now lives on a farm in Vermont and writes novels, essays, and poetry.

In the Year of the Boar and Jackie Robinson
by Bette Lord

The Magic Shell
by Nicholasa Mohr

Social Studies
in Reading

The Difficult Art of Hitting

by Sadaharu Oh and David Falkner

Autobiography

Genre

- An autobiography is the story of a person's life written by the person who lived it.

- Autobiographies are written in the first person, using *I*, *me*, and *my*.

- People write autobiographies to share their achievements, thoughts, and feelings.

Text Features

- A brief introduction gives the reader some background information about Sadaharu Oh.

- The use of quotations gives the reader the feeling of being there during the brief encounter.

Link to Social Studies

Research Sadaharu Oh's baseball career. Make a time line of his career in Japanese baseball.

Sadaharu Oh was fourteen when this event took place. He would go on to become Japan's greatest home-run hitter, hitting a record 868 home runs in the Japanese Professional Baseball League. At the time of this event, however, Mr. Oh was still struggling to master the difficult art of hitting.

It was toward dusk. We were playing a practice game in Sumida Park in Asakusa. There was a good chill in the air. Winter was coming. You could feel it, but it didn't matter. I was pitching for our side; we were winning 5–0. Then, suddenly, there was a commotion on the field. One of the players recognized a man walking a dog nearby. The man was Hiroshi Arakawa, an outfielder for the Mainichi Orions, one

Text Structure What structure is used for autobiography?

of Japan's major league teams. We tried to continue with the game, but it was almost impossible. We watched the man following the dog—the dog pulling forward on the end of a taut leash—as they came closer and closer to our field. When he reached the area where we were playing, Arakawa-san stood behind the backstop at home plate and watched the action. All of us—players on both sides—became so keyed up! I felt my body fill with fighting spirit. I pitched as powerfully as I could. At bat, I swung from the heels, trying to send the ball clear across the river. Between innings, as I was about to leave the bench for the mound, my life changed. Arakawa-san left the backstop area and threaded his way between the players, who seemed to step aside before him in awe. He was making his way toward me! I felt myself freeze in place. I couldn't believe what was about to happen. He wanted to speak to me! He nodded to me and smiled, very gently. I very stiffly bowed to him.

"How come you pitch left-handed and bat right-handed?"

Sounds gurgled in my throat, but I had no words. I so badly wanted to make the best impression. I nodded my head, wanting to show that I accepted what he said—whatever he said.

"You know, you're probably wasting your talent that way. You look left-handed. Why don't you try to bat left-handed next time you come up?"

"Y– . . . yes, yes I will, of course, I will," I finally blurted out, so ashamed of myself that I raced back out to the field at top speed. I expected Arakawa-san then to leave the area, to go on with his evening's stroll. But, no, he took a seat on a bleacher bench behind the plate!

It seemed like a year before my next turn at bat, and all the while I felt Arakawa-san's eyes on me. The game, the cold, the time of day, everything seemed to drop away. There was only this need to live within the cocoon of Arakawa-san's words. Finally, it was my turn to bat again. For the first time in my life I stepped to the plate to bat from the left side. I swung the bat back and forth. It felt easy, natural, as though I had done it always. I seemed now to come to my senses. I could feel everyone on the field watching me, as though in envy because a major league ballplayer had spoken only to me. I felt like a star! I knew I would hit! Nothing was going to stop me. If a building had fallen from the sky, I'm not sure I would have paid any attention to it, even if it had fallen on my head. I waited for the pitch I wanted. My bat met the ball squarely. For a moment, I watched the blur of the ball as it streaked out over the infield. Then I put my head down and ran. I looked up again at second base. I had lined a clean double to the fence in right-center field. I looked toward the bleacher bench behind the plate. Arakawa-san was still there. He gave me a big nod of approval. My body filled with gooseflesh.

When the inning was over, he came up to me again.

"See that," he said, "that was a really nice hit."

"Thank you! Thank you!"

"No reason to thank me. How old are you?"

I responded crisply, "I'm in the second year."

"Ah, good," he said, "then you'll be thinking of university next year. You might think of Waseda University. I went there. It has an excellent baseball program, and you will have a chance to develop your talents to the fullest."

I stood rigidly at attention.

"I am in the second year of *junior* high school," I said.

"Oh, I see. I thought . . . well, never mind what I thought. Perhaps you'll go to Waseda High School, then."

"Yes. Yes."

"You're a very good player, you know."

He smiled. We shook hands, and I bowed to him deeply. Then,

with his dog, he turned and walked away. It seemed like only a few feet between where we were standing and the darkness surrounding the field. I tried to call to him. But I couldn't. Just like that, he was lost in the shadows as surely as if he had evaporated.

Reading Across Texts

How did Colonel Charlebois and Mr. Arakawa each contribute to baseball?

Writing Across Texts Pretend you are Miguel or Sadaharu Oh. Write a letter to either the Colonel or Mr. Arakawa thanking him for his support.

Summarize What main ideas would summarize this article?

711

Skill
Generalize

Strategy
Ask Questions

Generalize

- A generalization is a special kind of conclusion. It is a statement that applies to many examples that have something in common.

- Generalizations are called valid if they are well supported and faulty if they are not.

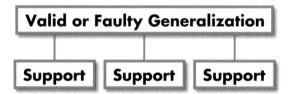

Strategy: Ask Questions

Active readers ask themselves questions before, during, and after they read. Some good questions to ask yourself are: What generalizations is the author making? Are there any facts in the text to back them up? Is there anything I already know that supports the generalization? What other generalizations can I make from what I've read?

1. Read "Necessity Is the Mother of Invention." Make a graphic organizer like the one above to help you recognize and evaluate generalizations.

2. Ask what generalizations the author is making about inventors. Complete the chart with information from the article or from what you already know. Write about whether the generalizations are well supported or poorly supported.

Necessity Is the Mother of Invention

Where would we be without inventions? They make our lives easier. Cars, computers, electric lights, refrigeration—each of these things meets a need in our lives. That's where an inventor begins—with a need.

An inventor is always asking, "What is the problem here? Is there a better way to do this?" Then the inventor asks, "What do I already know about this?" and "What do I have to work with?"

Once the inventor decides what he or she wants to do, the idea is improved through trial and error. The inventor knows that the first time an idea is tested it may not work, but that doesn't mean it's time to give up! Instead, the inventor asks, "Why didn't this work? What can I do differently?" Then it's time to apply the old saying, "If at first you don't succeed, try, try, again."

Sometimes the answer to a problem comes to the inventor in a sudden burst of insight. Sometimes the answer comes about almost by accident, and the inventor is surprised.

However the solution comes about, it is the result of hard work. As Thomas Edison, one of the greatest inventors of all time, once said, "Genius is 1 percent inspiration and 99 percent perspiration."

Skill This old saying—like most old sayings—is a generalization. Which generalization means the same thing as the title?
a) Don't act without thinking.
b) A problem "gives birth" to creative thinking.
c) Think again.

Strategy You could ask here: What does this statement mean? Will the author explain it?

Strategy What question might you ask here?

Skill Edison's statement is a generalization. It may be exaggerated but has a valid idea behind it. What proof is there to support the idea?

Words to Know

| hangars |
| glider |
| drag |
| flex |
| cradle |
| rudder |
| stalled |

Remember

Try the strategy. Then, if you need more help, use your glossary or a dictionary.

Vocabulary Strategy
for Unfamiliar Words

Context Clues Sometimes you can use context clues—the words and sentences around an unknown word—to help you figure out the meaning of the word.

1. Read the words and sentences around the unknown word. The author may give you a definition of the word.

2. If not, say what the sentence means in your own words.

3. Predict a meaning for the unknown word.

4. Try that meaning in the sentence. Does it make sense?

As you read "A Different Way to Fly," use the context to help you figure out the meanings of the vocabulary words.

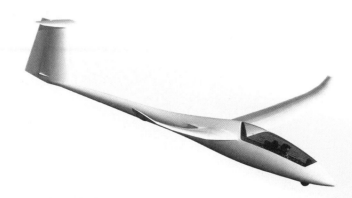

A Different Way to Fly

Here at Mojave Airport, the hangars have an unusual kind of aircraft in them. Let's take a look at one. A glider is like an airplane—without an engine. It relies on air currents to keep it aloft.

Like an airplane, a glider has wings, a body, and a tail. All three parts are designed to be smooth and streamlined to help the glider move through the air with little **drag**, or air resistance.

A glider has long, narrow wings. The wings produce lift, which is the upward force that makes all planes fly. And like airplanes, the wings are fixed. They do not move; they do not **flex**, or bend. A glider's body is very narrow. Wedged into a tight **cradle**, the pilot has to lie back while flying! The tail of the glider has a **rudder**, which the pilot moves to the right or the left when making a turn.

When a plane loses lift and begins to fall, it has **stalled**. An airplane pilot can increase engine power to stop the stall. But a glider pilot has to locate an air current that is rising faster than the glider is falling!

Write

Write a description of a glider. Tell what you think it would be like to fly in a glider. Use words from the Words to Know list.

TO FLY

THE STORY OF THE
WRIGHT BROTHERS

by Wendie C. Old   illustrated by Robert Andrew Parker

CAN TWO BROTHERS DO WHAT NO ONE HAS DONE BEFORE?

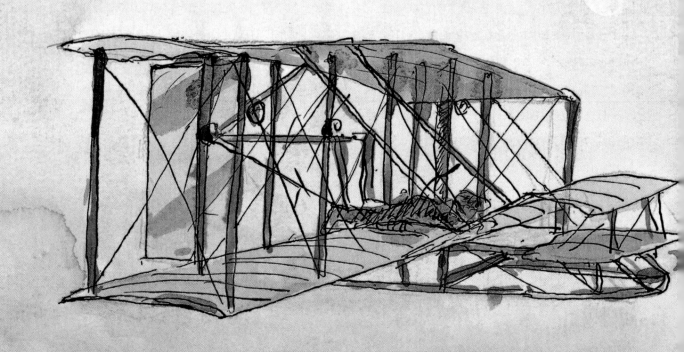

DREAMS OF FLYING

People had always known it wasn't possible for humans to fly like birds. But that didn't stop them from dreaming about it.

Orville Wright was one of those dreamers. Many a night he lay in his bed in Dayton, Ohio, imagining what it would be like to swoop through the sky. Sometimes in school, when he was supposed to be doing math or working on penmanship, he would be thinking about flying.

In 1878, his father brought home a toy called a Pénaud helicopter. It was made of cork, bamboo, and thin paper. When its long rubber band was wound up and then let go, the helicopter jumped out of its holder and flew almost fifty feet.

Could a person fly that way? Orville and his older brother, Wilbur, tried making more helicopters. They tried making them larger.

Miss Ida Palmer, Orville's second grade teacher, caught him fiddling with pieces of wood at his desk instead of doing classwork.

Orville explained that he was making a flying machine. If it worked, he planned to build a much larger one and fly with his eleven-year-old brother.

But the boys' larger machine wouldn't fly. They had not yet learned that a machine twice as big required eight times the amount of energy to move it. For a man-sized machine, they certainly needed something stronger than a rubber band.

So they put the idea of a flying machine away. For a time.

KITES

Wilbur and Orville Wright had two older brothers, Reuchlin and Lorin. Their sister, Katharine, was the baby of the family.

Their father and mother, Bishop Milton Wright and Susan Wright, encouraged their five children to do their own thinking. They wanted them to explore many ideas and come to their own conclusions. They even let their children take time off from school if they felt the children would learn something from the experience.

On the other hand, if the children wanted money to spend on hobbies or experiments, they had to earn it themselves. Some of their projects, like the circus the brothers put on, were successful. Others, such as the attempt to make chewing gum out of hunks of tar, were not.

One of Orville's best money-making ideas was to build kites to sell to his friends.

At first, Orville had very little money to buy supplies, so he cut the wooden ribs for the kites very, very thin. This way he could get more ribs from each piece of wood. These thin ribs bent in the wind, creating a kite with a curved surface. Orville's kites flew better than flat kites with thicker, stronger ribs.

This flying experiment was a success. Orville built the best kites in Dayton, Ohio. And he also made an important discovery that he would use later—curved wings fly better than flat ones.

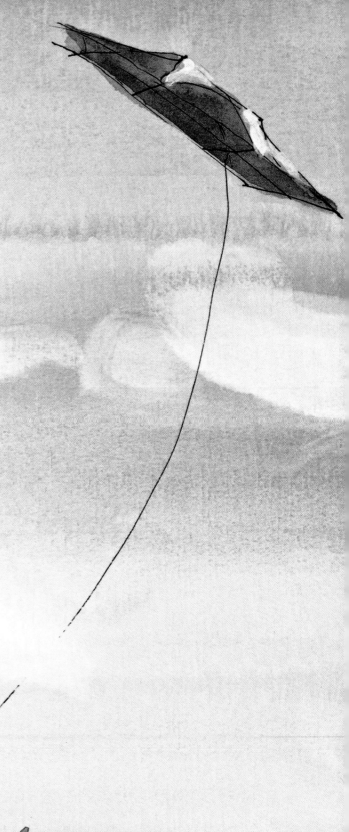

WORKING TOGETHER

In time, Orville and Wilbur's older brothers moved out into the working world and got married. But Orville and Wilbur continued to live at home. Neither of them ever married.

Wilbur finished all but the last few weeks of high school. He never graduated. He spent the next three years taking care of their sick mother. Susan Wright died of tuberculosis on July 4, 1889. After she died, their sister, Katharine, kept house for the boys and their father.

During high school, Orville had started a printing business. When their mother died, Wilbur joined him. Their newspaper advertisements read: **WRIGHT BROS.: JOB PRINTERS AT 7 HAWTHORN STREET.**

This was the first time the word "Wright Brothers" appeared in print.

During his last year in high school, Orville only took one course—Latin. The rest of the time he worked in the print shop. The two brothers printed posters, business cards, and several newspapers.

Orville never graduated from high school either. Katharine, however, graduated from both high school and college. She became a teacher.

Soon a new interest took the boys' time away from the print shop—bicycles.

They both enjoyed fixing bicycles, too—so much so that they opened a bicycle shop in 1893 and moved the printing business upstairs.

KITES BECOME GLIDERS

In 1896, Orville almost died from typhoid. The well near their bicycle shop had become polluted, and Orville became sick from drinking the water. Wilbur immediately moved the shop to another location.

While Orville lay in bed recovering, his brother read to him. Mostly, Wilbur read about the German glider expert Otto Lilienthal, who had recently crashed and died.

Gliders! Now, that was one way to fly. As Orville grew stronger, the brothers searched libraries for more information about flight.

Finally, in early 1899, the Smithsonian Institution sent them information about American flight experts.

Wilbur wrote letters to many of them. The most successful seemed to be Octave Chanute and Samuel Pierpont Langley.

Langley, head of the Smithsonian Institution in Washington, D.C., used a steam-driven motor on his fourteen-foot-long unmanned model airplanes. He called them Aerodromes. Aerodrome #5 actually flew more than a half a mile before it ran out of steam and crashed.

Chanute was to become the Wright brothers' greatest supporter. He was experimenting near Chicago with gliders that had two or more

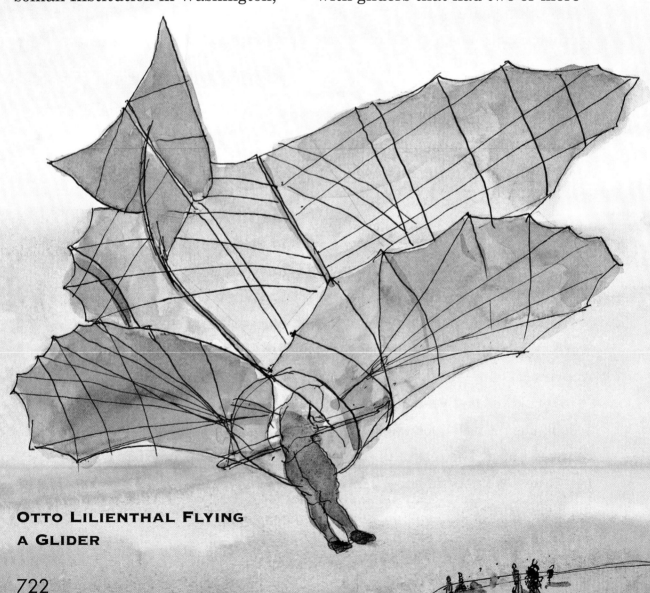

OTTO LILIENTHAL FLYING A GLIDER

wings. One of his gliders had twelve wings. A person hanging on to a glider attempts to guide it by swinging his legs back and forth. The glider is held in the air by wind. Gradually, it falls to the ground.

Neither Langley nor Chanute could completely control the flight of his flying machine.

CONTROL

From their reading and discussions, Wilbur and Orville thought they had identified the problem of flight: control. How could a person *control* his flight once he was in the air? Gliders flew in a straight line. They could not be steered. But birds swooped and turned. People should be able to do that, too.

The brothers watched birds fly. Birds circle in the air by curving one wing up while the tip of the other curves down. How could a person make a flying machine do this? Orville and Wilbur chewed on this idea.

One day Wilbur sold a bicycle inner tube to a customer. The inner tube came in a long rectangular box.

While he was talking to the customer, Wilbur began twisting the box. One hand twisted down while the other hand twisted up. All at once he realized what he was doing. The twisted box looked like a pair of bird's wings circling in the air.

He ran to show Orville. If they could make the wings of a two-winged glider flex like this, they could control its flight!

Orville and Wilbur built a double-winged kite to test the idea. It measured five feet from wingtip to wingtip.

In August 1899, Wilbur took the kite to a nearby lot. Wires stretched from his hands to each of the wings. These controlled the warping, or twisting, of the wings. The kite rolled to the right and to the left in the air. The neighborhood boys cheered and yelled, falling to the ground to avoid being hit when the kite dove too low. It worked! Flight could be controlled.

A larger kite should be able to carry a man. All the Wright brothers had to do was build it.

VACATIONS AT THE OUTER BANKS

Wilbur wrote to the U.S. Weather Bureau asking where winds blew strong and steady. The spot closest to Dayton was on the Outer Banks of North Carolina. For the next three years the brothers built gliders of various shapes and tested them on the Atlantic seashore near the village of Kitty Hawk.

THE FLYER

During the winter of 1902–03, Orville and Wilbur built a motor and propellers for their aircraft. They were so confident that it would fly that they called it the Flyer.

Other people thought that propellers should have flat blades with sharp angles and a sharp front edge to cut through the air.

By experimenting in the wind tunnel*, the brothers discovered that a propeller is actually like a rotating wing. Therefore, it has to be curved like a scoop and have rounded front edges. This is how propellers are made even today.

They mounted the propellers, one on each side, behind the wings to push the Flyer along. Since they were bicycle men, they used bicycle chain to connect each propeller to the motor.

None of the early automobile companies had an engine available that was as strong and as lightweight as the brothers needed. Wilbur and Orville had to design and build one themselves, which they did with the help of their bicycle mechanic, Charlie Taylor. It was made from cast aluminum, a lightweight metal.

Now all they had to do was see if it would fly.

*THE WIND TUNNEL WAS A SIX-FOOT-LONG RECTANGULAR BOX WITH A FAN ATTACHED TO ONE END AND A GLASS TOP THROUGH WHICH THE BROTHERS COULD OBSERVE THE MOVEMENT OF AIR AROUND DIFFERENT WING SHAPES.

TIGHTENING THE CHAIN

THE OUTER BANKS: 1903

In the fall of 1903, Orville and Wilbur shipped the pieces of their new Flyer to Kill Devil Hills on the Outer Banks to test it.

Instead of living in a tent, they built two wooden hangars near the sand dunes. One was for the old 1902 glider, which they used for flight practice. In the other one they assembled the Flyer. Their beds hung overhead.

The kitchen area was at the back of one hangar.

This time they covered both the top *and* bottom of each wing with cloth. This created a smooth surface that reduced wind resistance and drag. The engine was mounted on the lower wing, to the right of the pilot.

The pilot controlled the wing warping and the tail rudder with his hips, which were wedged into a wooden cradle. When he wiggled his hips, wires from the cradle moved the wings and tail.

The front elevator* wings were operated by a hand control.

The engine was either on or off. There was no way to make it go faster or slower. Once the pilot turned the engine off, the aircraft became a glider, and the brothers knew they could control it as a glider.

Like all their gliders, the Flyer had no wheels. Instead, there were two skids underneath it. These skids were supposed to act like the runners of a sled, sliding along the sand during landing.

The fall of 1903 was cold and stormy. The bad weather delayed the first flight. Also, things on the Flyer kept breaking or coming loose.

While Orville took a broken propeller shaft home to Dayton to be fixed, another inventor was also attempting a manned flight.

Near Washington D.C., Samuel P. Langley from the Smithsonian twice sent his Great Aerodrome off a houseboat in the Potomac River. His second and last attempt was on December 8, 1903. Again, just as it did the first time, the Great Aerodrome slid off the houseboat directly into the river. It could not fly. The pilot, Charles Manly, had to be rescued from the icy water.

Langley had failed, despite receiving huge amounts of government money. Could the Wright brothers succeed using only bicycle parts and a homemade engine?

*THE ELEVATOR WAS A FLAT PIECE OF THE TAIL THAT THE WRIGHT BROTHERS HAD MOVED FROM THE REAR TO THE FRONT. IT CONTROLLED MOVEMENT UP AND DOWN.

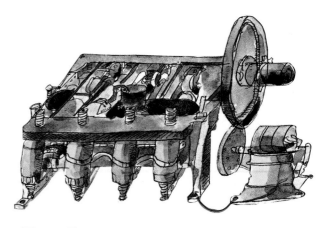

THE ENGINE

THE FIRST ATTEMPT

On Monday, December 14, Orville and Wilbur Wright called the nearby Kill Devil Hills Lifesaver Corps for help. These surfmen helped to drag the Flyer partway up Big Kill Devil Hill, the largest sand dune. Because the wind was blowing at only five miles per hour, it was not strong enough to lift a glider, let alone a heavy flying machine. Gravity would help get the Flyer into the air.

The Flyer was placed at the top of a sixty-foot-long wooden rail that had been pegged into the sand. This rail would guide the Flyer until it lifted up off the ground.

No one knew who would be the first pilot to fly.

Wilbur won the coin toss.

Once he was on the Flyer, Wilbur discovered that the wind was coming from the side and the track was not straight.

He gave the signal to go, anyway.

Orville and some of the surfmen had to help the Flyer stay on the track as it sped down the hill. As soon as the Flyer lifted from the track, Wilbur turned the elevator wings up to make it go higher.

This was the wrong move. It slowed the Flyer too much. After rising only fifteen feet into the air, the Flyer stalled and slid toward the ground. The left wingtip caught in the sand. The front rudder dug deep into the sand. A few sticks in the rudder broke, plus several supports and braces.

Wilbur lay there, stunned. Finally, he managed to switch the engine off. This had not been a successful flight.

THE FIRST HEAVIER-THAN-AIR MANNED FLIGHT

It took two days to repair the Flyer. The brothers were ready to go again on December 16. The men set up the rail to take off on level ground, but the wind died.

December 17 dawned freezing cold, but clear. The puddles around camp from the most recent storm had frozen. A brisk wind was blowing—between twenty and twenty-five miles per hour. This was almost too strong to be safe. But Orville and Wilbur wanted to be home for Christmas, and so they decided to try to fly anyway. This time, Orville was the pilot.

The brothers put up a red flag to summon the surfmen. Willie Dough, Adam Etheridge, and John Daniels responded. Two unexpected helpers also arrived— W. C. Brinkley, a lumber merchant from Manteo, and a boy named Johnny Moore from the nearby village of Nags Head.

The track was laid out on the flat sand. Each brother cranked a propeller. While the motor putt-putted away, the brothers stood talking a little way down the beach.

John Daniels later remembered, "After a while they shook hands, and we couldn't help notice how they held on to each other's hand, sort o' like they hated to let go; like two folks parting who weren't sure they'd ever see each other again."

At 10:35 a.m Orville gave the signal. The Flyer began to move. Daniels snapped a picture as the Flyer rose into the air, with Wilbur running alongside it. It's probably one of the most famous photographs ever taken.

Wilbur had asked the surfmen to cheer when the airplane took off, but Orville did not hear them. The Flyer jerked up and down, up and down. The elevator was over-responding to Orville's corrections. One hundred and twenty feet away a skid caught in the sand. It cracked. The Flyer dragged to a halt.

The first controlled heavier-than-air manned flight had lasted twelve seconds. The Flyer had taken off from level ground, moved through the air under its own power, and landed on a place that was level with its takeoff point. They had done it!

Everyone huddled by the kitchen stove in the hangar to keep warm while the cracked skid was repaired. At 11:20 a.m it was Wilbur's turn to fly. He flew 175 feet in fifteen seconds. Then Orville flew 200 feet in the same amount of time.

Exactly at noon, the fourth flight took off. Wilbur bobbed up and down for 300 feet. Then he managed to smooth out his flight path, flying for 500 more feet before the Flyer began bobbling again and swooped to the ground. In fifty-nine seconds Wilbur had flown a total of 852 feet.

The Age of Aviation had begun.

Reader Response

Open for Discussion Two boys experiment with a toy helicopter. Two men fly a heavier-than-air craft. Tell what happened between those two scenes.

1. The Wright brothers had a goal early in their lives. How does the author present that goal, even on the first page of the selection?

2. Is it valid to generalize that all early attempts to fly were unsuccessful? Explain your answer.

3. As you read the selection, what questions did you want to ask the author? Were any of them answered as you kept reading?

4. Write a newspaper account telling of the day Wilbur Wright flew 852 feet. Use words from the Words to Know list and the selection.

Look Back and Write How did the Wright brothers invent a new kind of propeller? Look back at page 724 for information to write your answer.

Meet the Author

Wendie Old

Read other books about flight.

Wendie Old's life is filled with books. For over thirty years, she has been a children's librarian near Baltimore, Maryland. She has also written many biographies and picture books for children.

To honor the one-hundredth anniversary of the flight at Kitty Hawk, Ms. Old decided to write about the Wright brothers. This was fun, she says, because "I LOVE flying and have always been interested in the first flight." For research, Ms. Old visited the Wright brothers' hometown of Dayton, Ohio. "I always go visit the places people lived and worked, " she says, "so that I can describe them in my books." She also read all the books she could find on the topic.

Ms. Old sees the Wright brothers' lives as proof that anyone can fulfill big dreams. As she points out, "The problems of flight were solved, not by people with huge amounts of money from the government, but by small-town bicycle repairmen."

The Wright Brothers and Other Pioneers of Flight
by Ole Steen Hansen

Sky Pioneer
by Corinne Szabo

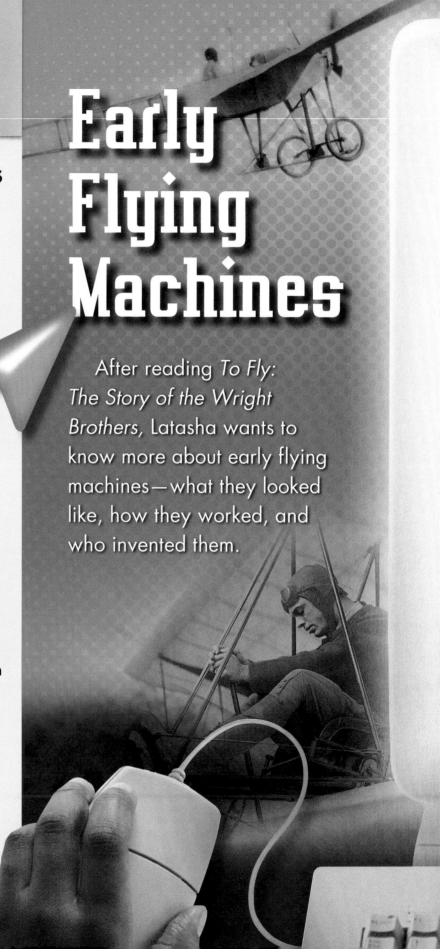

Reading Online

Online Directories

Genre

- Internet Web sites called online directories list links to many Web sites.

- Online directories are organized to help you find information quickly and easily.

- You can use an online directory to learn about a topic.

Text Features

- The home page of an online directory shows you how the directory is organized.

- You can search for information by clicking on a link or series of links. Or sometimes there is a SEARCH window into which you can type keywords.

Link to Science

Do research to find out why early attempts at flight failed. Report your findings.

Early Flying Machines

After reading *To Fly: The Story of the Wright Brothers,* Latasha wants to know more about early flying machines—what they looked like, how they worked, and who invented them.

Take It to the NET™
ONLINE
more activities sfsuccessnet.com

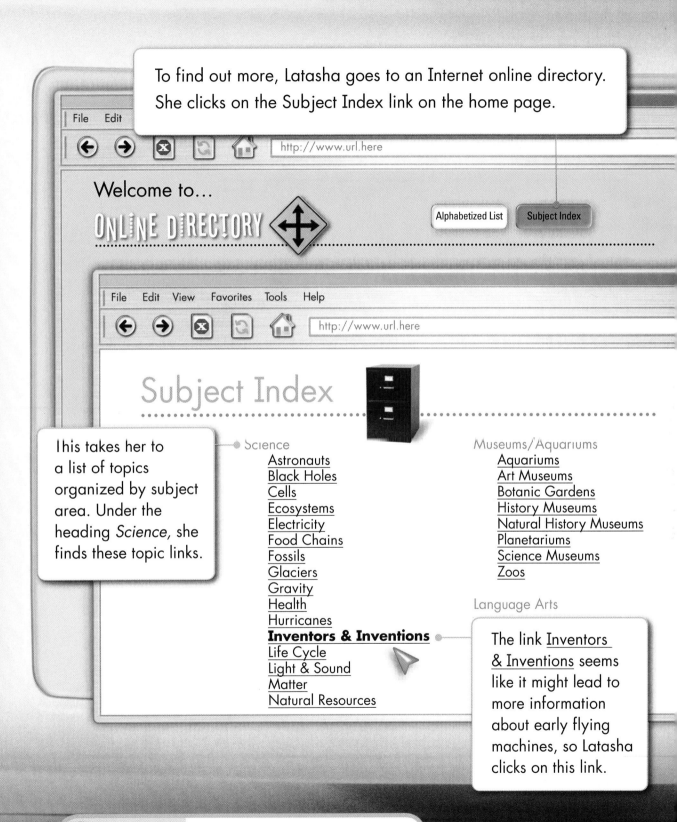

To find out more, Latasha goes to an Internet online directory. She clicks on the Subject Index link on the home page.

http://www.url.here

Welcome to...

ONLINE DIRECTORY

Alphabetized List   Subject Index

File   Edit   View   Favorites   Tools   Help

http://www.url.here

Subject Index

This takes her to a list of topics organized by subject area. Under the heading *Science,* she finds these topic links.

Science

Astronauts
Black Holes
Cells
Ecosystems
Electricity
Food Chains
Fossils
Glaciers
Gravity
Health
Hurricanes
Inventors & Inventions
Life Cycle
Light & Sound
Matter
Natural Resources

Museums/Aquariums

Aquariums
Art Museums
Botanic Gardens
History Museums
Natural History Museums
Planetariums
Science Museums
Zoos

Language Arts

The link Inventors & Inventions seems like it might lead to more information about early flying machines, so Latasha clicks on this link.

Generalize   How is an online directory useful?

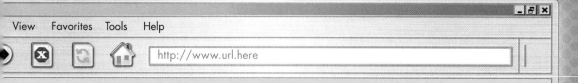

Inventors & Inventions

American Inventors
Alexander Graham Bell
George Washington Carver
John Deere
George Eastman

Nikola Tesla
George Westinghouse
Eli Whitney
Wright Brothers
Linus Yale, Jr.
Vladimir K. Zworykin

The link takes her to a list of links specific to inventing. Latasha decides to click on the Wright Brothers link.

She finds herself at a Web site about flight, on a page about the Wright brothers. On the left side of the page is a menu. She sees a link called Flights of fancy. Thinking that this might be a link to information about early, fanciful flying machines, Latasha opens this link.

http://www.url.here

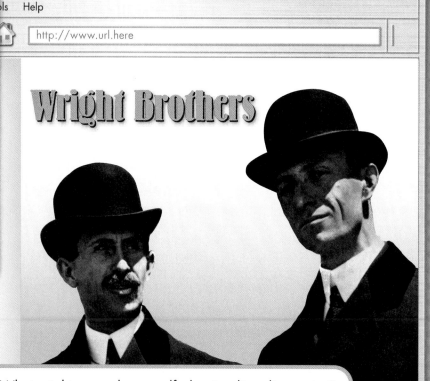

Wright Brothers

History of Flight
Flights of fancy
Flying chariot

  **Ask Questions**   What might you ask yourself about online directories?

Aerial steam carriage
Phillips's flyer

That Web page shows four early flying machines. Latasha decides to find out more about the one called Ader's Eole.

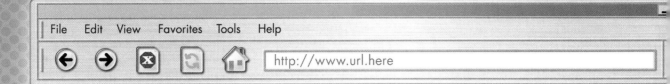

Ader's Eole

Clement Ader's Eole was the first piloted airplane to take off under its own power, for a brief uncontrolled hop in 1890.

The Eole had a light but powerful 20 hp steam engine and batlike wings. Unfortunately it had little flight control and no forward vision for the pilot.

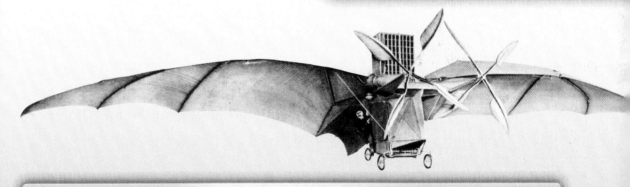

Reading Across Texts

Both *To Fly* and this article give information about early flying machines. How were these machines alike and different? Look back at the selections to make notes.

Writing Across Texts Use your notes to compare and contrast two of the flying machines.

Comprehension

Skill
Graphic Sources

Strategy
Monitor
and Fix Up

Graphic Sources

- Graphic sources, or graphic aids, show information in a visual way. Maps, charts, tables, diagrams, and pictures are some examples of graphic sources.

- Looking at graphic sources before you read will help you see what the text is about.

- Do not skip graphic sources. Look at them as you read to help yourself understand the text.

Strategy: Monitor and Fix Up

Good readers check in with themselves to make sure they understand what they are reading. One good way to do this is to use any graphic sources that come with the text. Don't just glance at the graphic; really study it to be sure you understand what it has to tell you. If you don't understand it, try rereading the part of the text that explains it.

1. Read "The Other Side of the Moon." Study the graphic sources as you carefully read the text.

2. Write an explanation in your own words about why we cannot see the back of the moon.

The Other Side of the Moon

There is a side of the moon—called the far side—that no one standing on the Earth has ever seen. Astronauts have gone behind the moon to see the other side, and they have brought back pictures. However, no one simply looking up at the sky has ever seen the back of the moon.

Why?

The answer lies in the way the moon moves. The moon orbits the Earth, but it also turns once on its axis in the same amount of time. This is called synchronous rotation.

Study the diagram below.

Imagine you went to the moon and painted a crater red to serve as a marker. Then imagine you came back to Earth and looked up at the moon night after night. If the moon did not rotate, your marker would seem to move across the moon and even disappear for a while as the moon orbited the Earth. The fact that your red crater stays in sight means that the moon rotates and thus shows us only one side.

Skill When there are graphic sources with an article, part of your preview should be to notice them and decide that this is nonfiction and should be read carefully.

Strategy Do you understand what this paragraph is saying? Take a moment to remember the times you have looked up at the moon.

Skill You took a quick look at the diagram before you started to read. This is the time to look at it carefully, because the author intends to tell you more about it.

Strategy Did you understand this paragraph and the diagram? If not, what can you do to help yourself understand it?

Words to Know

astronauts

hatch

lunar

capsule

module

horizon

quarantine

Remember

Try the strategy. Then, if you need more help, use your glossary or a dictionary.

Vocabulary Strategy
for Homonyms

Context Clues When you are reading, you may come to a familiar word used in a new way. The word may be a homonym. Homonyms are words that are spelled the same but have different meanings because they have come to us from different languages. You can use the context—the words and sentences around the word—to figure out which meaning is being used.

1. Think about the meanings the homonym can have. For example, *riddle* can mean "to make holes in." A *riddle* is also a question or problem with a tricky answer.

2. Reread the words and sentences around the homonym.

3. Look for clues that suggest which meaning is being used.

4. Try that meaning in the sentence in place of the homonym. Does the meaning make sense?

As you read "Travelers in Space," look for homonyms. Use the context to figure out the meanings of the homonyms.

TRAVELERS in SPACE

Astronauts are space workers. Since the 1960s, they have blasted off into space. Astronauts explore the unknown, which is exciting. But much of their time is spent working hard.

They may repair a space station or satellite. To do this, they suit up, open the hatch, and float out into space. When they finish the job, they float back into the spacecraft through this small door. Astronauts also do lots of experiments and make calculations related to their flight.

Early in the space program, there were many lunar flights. The astronauts took off in a huge spaceship. Part of it fell away after they got into orbit. Then they rode in a capsule, or small space vehicle. By the time they landed on the moon, the astronauts were riding in a module. This tiny spacecraft fit into the larger ship and could fly on its own.

Just think. They stood on the moon's surface and saw the Earth rise on the horizon! However, when they got back to Earth, the astronauts were in quarantine. They had to stay away from everyone to be sure they had not brought back any diseases.

Write

Pretend you are traveling in space. Describe your spaceship and what you can see. Use words from the Words to Know list.

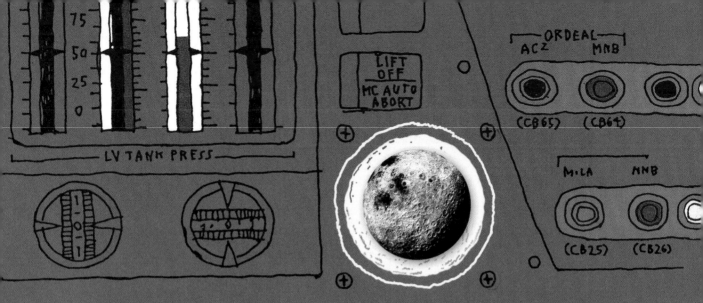

The Man Who Went to the Far Side of the Moon

The Story of Apollo 11 Astronaut Michael Collins

by Bea Uusma Schyffert

Narrative nonfiction can be an account of a historical event. As you read this selection about the historic *Apollo 11* space flight, imagine what it would have been like to have been part of the mission.

Is the **moon** anything like the **Earth?**

COLLINS

On July 16, 1969, the United States launched the *Saturn 5* rocket into space. Aboard this spacecraft, the largest rocket ever built, were three men: astronauts Michael Collins, Buzz Aldrin, and Neil Armstrong. Their mission: to be the first to land on the moon. One of these men would not land on the moon, however. That man, Michael Collins, would circle the moon in the command module while Buzz Aldrin and Neil Armstrong landed the lunar module, *Eagle,* and explored the moon's surface.

It is July 20, 1969. A Sunday. It's four minutes to ten in the morning. It is –250°F (–180°C) in the shade and +250°F (+120°C) in the sun at the Sea of Tranquility, where Neil and Buzz have landed the *Eagle.* They are 242,000 miles (390,000 kilometers) from Launch Pad 39A at Kennedy Space Center in Florida.

In the earliest versions of the checklists, Buzz Aldrin would be the first man to step down onto the moon. But the lunar module hatch opens inward to the right, and Buzz, who stood right behind it, had difficulty climbing out. When the astronauts tried to switch places during practice, they damaged the cramped cabin. A few months before the launch, it was decided that Neil should go first. He crawls backward through a tiny hatch near the floor. As he looks toward the horizon, he can see that they have landed on a sphere: the horizon is a little bent since the moon is so small. His arms are covered with goosebumps. There is no air. No sound. No life. No footprints.

Wait: now there is one.

Neil Armstrong is the first man on the moon.

...I'M GOING TO STEP OFF THE LM NOW...

When you stand on the moon, you can cover the entire Earth with your hand.

242,000 miles (390,000 kilometers) from home, trapped inside a small vessel, two men are taking snapshots of each other.

Neil Armstrong's picture of Buzz Aldrin

Buzz Aldrin's picture of Neil Armstrong

745

Neil and Buzz stay on the moon for 21 hours and 36 minutes, but only a little more than 2 hours of that time is spent outside the lunar module. They perform three minor experiments and load two aluminum suitcases with 48 pounds (22 kilograms) of moon dust and rocks.

The three minor experiments:
  To measure solar particles
  To measure the exact distance to Earth
  To measure moonquakes and meteoritic impact

The major experiment:
  To land on the moon

When they have climbed back into the lunar module and shut the hatch, they take their helmets off. They look at each other because they both sense a strong smell. Neil thinks it smells like wet ashes. Buzz says it smells like spent gunpowder. It is the moon. The moon has a smell.

you down,

OK, we copy eagle

Six hundred million people in 47 countries are watching the blurred TV transmission of the lunar landing. There is one person who has no chance of catching Neil and Buzz on TV. He is traveling at a height of 70 miles (110 kilometers) above the far side of the moon. All he can see is darkness and stars outside his window.

In case something unexpected should happen, the astronauts never bounce farther than 200 feet (60 meters) from the landing site.

Michael Collins has 28 hours to go, alone in the capsule. He has trained for so long. He has traveled so far. He is so close now and still he can't land on the moon. They did not choose him.

He was going for 99 percent of the trip and that was good enough for him, he has replied when people have asked. But he knew he didn't have the best seat on *Columbia.*

He thinks to himself that he never really got to know the astronauts who are now on the moon. Neil and Buzz trained together for many months in the lunar module simulator. Michael trained by himself in the capsule.

Once every two hours *Columbia* passes over the landing site. Michael Collins tries to locate the *Eagle.* He can't see it. He only sees crater after crater, cast with sharp shadows from the sun.

apollo 11, this is houston, we're three minutes away from loss of signal over

Every other hour, all radio communication with Earth is lost as the spacecraft skims over the far side of the moon. When Neil and Buzz are on the moon's surface, Michael Collins has to do three people's jobs. He has to make 850 computer commands. He has been taught just *how* to push the buttons—hard, right in the center, and to hold them pushed for a little over a second. They must be pushed in the right order, one after the other: VERB-88-ENTER. VERB-87-ENTER. If he loses track on the far side of the moon, there is no one to ask.

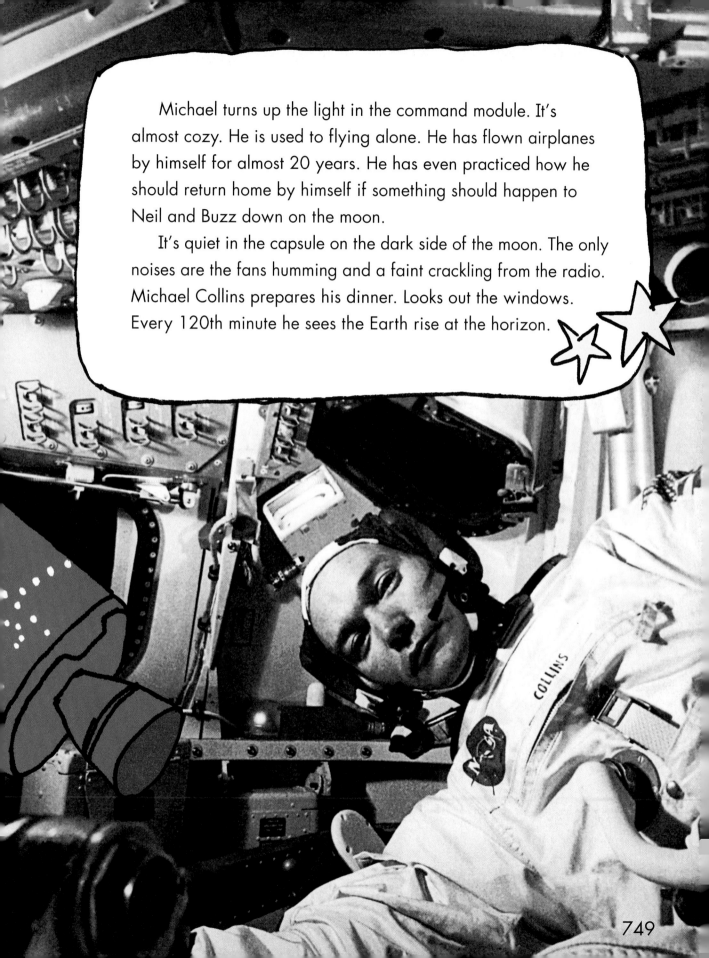

Michael turns up the light in the command module. It's almost cozy. He is used to flying alone. He has flown airplanes by himself for almost 20 years. He has even practiced how he should return home by himself if something should happen to Neil and Buzz down on the moon.

It's quiet in the capsule on the dark side of the moon. The only noises are the fans humming and a faint crackling from the radio. Michael Collins prepares his dinner. Looks out the windows. Every 120th minute he sees the Earth rise at the horizon.

MICHAEL COLLINS'S FOOD PACK ON THE FOURTH DAY OF THE TRIP

BREAKFAST:

FROSTED FLAKES
(FREEZE-DRIED)

4 PEANUT CUBES
(BITE-SIZED)

COCOA (POWDER)

ORANGE AND
GRAPEFRUIT DRINK
(POWDER)

CANADIAN BACON
AND APPLESAUCE
(FREEZE-DRIED)

LUNCH:

SHRIMP COCKTAIL
(FREEZE-DRIED)

HAM AND POTATOES
(WET-PACK)

FRUIT COCKTAIL
(FREEZE-DRIED)

4 DATE FRUITCAKE
CUBES (BITE-SIZED)

GRAPEFRUIT DRINK
(POWDER)

DINNER:

BEEF STEW
(SPOON-BOWL)

4 COCONUT CUBES
(BITE-SIZED)

BANANA PUDDING
(POWDER)

GRAPE PUNCH (POWDER)

ALL THE FOOD IS VACUUM PACKED AND MARKED WITH LABELS, SINCE IT IS DIFFICULT
TO TELL WHAT EACH ITEM IS SUPPOSED TO BE. THE TRICKY THING ABOUT EATING
IN WEIGHTLESSNESS IS MOVING THE FOOD FROM THE PACKAGE TO THE MOUTH,
WITHOUT LETTING IT FLOAT AWAY. THE ASTRONAUTS EAT:

FREEZE-DRIED AND POWDERED FOOD:

THEY INJECT COLD OR
HOT WATER INTO THE
PACKAGE WITH A
SPECIAL WATER GUN,
SQUEEZE THE PACKAGE
FOR ABOUT THREE
MINUTES, THEN CUT
OFF A CORNER AND
SQUEEZE THE PASTE
INTO THEIR MOUTHS.

WET-PACKED FOOD:

THEY SUCK THE READY-
MIXED WET-PACK FOOD,
COLD, STRAIGHT OUT OF
THE PACKAGE.

SPOON-BOWL FOOD:

THEY INJECT COLD
OR HOT WATER WITH
THE WATER GUN AND
SQUEEZE THE PACKAGE A
LITTLE BEFORE THEY OPEN
THE TOP. SPOON-BOWL
FOOD IS EATEN WITH A
SPOON. IT IS SO STICKY
THAT IT EITHER STAYS IN
THE PACKAGE OR CLINGS
TO THE SPOON.

It is July 24, 1969. A Thursday. Ever since they left the moon, the astronauts have been eager to get back home. After 8 days, 3 hours, and 18 minutes in *Columbia* without washing, the entire body itches. It is hard to breathe in the spacecraft now. It smells like wet dogs and rotten swamp. Michael Collins has flown *Columbia* during reentry into the Earth's atmosphere. For 14 minutes, the astronauts have been pushed down into their seats. They have weighed seven times their weight on Earth. Now the capsule has splashed down in the ocean near Hawaii.

No one knows if the astronauts have been exposed to dangerous lunar germs that could potentially wipe out the human race. Because of this they are sent straight to a quarantine facility: a silver-colored mobile home. Inside, the astronauts write reports about their trip. Michael beats Neil in cards. As they sit there, bored as can be, they begin to understand just what they have experienced. During the trip itself they were so focused on their job that they didn't have time to think about what they have actually done. Everyone on Earth gathered together because of the moon landing. But the astronauts themselves have been far, far away.

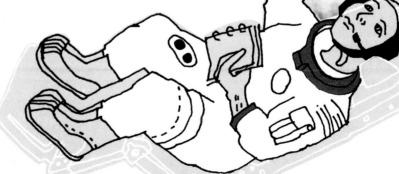

apollo 11, this is houston do you copy?

As they watch a taped recording of the moon landing, Buzz suddenly turns to Neil and says: "Neil, we missed the whole thing!"

In the past, Michael Collins never really cared about the machines he has flown, but this time it's different. On the second night of quarantine, he climbs back into *Columbia* and takes a seat. Then he leans over and scribbles a message in ballpoint pen on the capsule wall, in the tiniest handwriting imaginable:

Spacecraft 107—alias Apollo 11—alias Columbia
The best ship to come down the line
God bless her
Michael Collins, CMP

To find out if the astronauts are carrying deadly germs, mice are let into the quarantine trailer. The mice have grown up in a germ-free laboratory. After 17 days the astronauts are let out. For the first time in a month they breathe fresh air. If the mice had died, Michael Collins, Buzz Aldrin, and Neil Armstrong might still be quarantined.

This picture of *Apollo 16* astronaut Charlie Duke and his family, Dottie, Charles Jr., and Thomas, has been lying in the exact same place on the moon since 1972. ▼

LEFT ON THE MOON

SINCE *APOLLO 11*, THERE HAVE BEEN FIVE OTHER LUNAR MODULES ON THE MOON. THE LAST ONE LANDED IN 1972. EVERYTHING THE ASTRONAUTS LEFT BEHIND STAYS EXACTLY LIKE IT WAS WHEN IT WAS FIRST PUT THERE. THERE IS NO RUST. THERE IS NO WEAR AND TEAR. IN THE GRAY MOON DUST LIE THE TRACES OF SIX APOLLO MISSIONS:

2 GOLF BALLS HIT BY ASTRONAUT ALAN SHEPARD *(APOLLO 14)*	6 LUNAR MODULES	A SCULPTURE OF A FALLEN ASTRONAUT, IN MEMORY OF ALL THOSE WHO HAVE DIED IN THE EFFORTS TO REACH THE MOON
	3 MOON BUGGIES (FROM *APOLLO 15, 16,* AND *17*)	
TO SAVE ON WEIGHT, THE ASTRONAUTS LEFT EVERYTHING THEY DIDN'T NEED BEFORE TAKING OFF IN THE LUNAR MODULE:	MEMENTOS AND HONORARY OBJECTS:	ONE RED BIBLE
	PLAQUES	6 AMERICAN FLAGS
SCIENTIFIC EXPERIMENTS	MEDALLIONS	UNVERIFIED:
	ASTRONAUT BADGES	LAS BRISAS HOTEL IN ACAPULCO, MEXICO, INSISTS THAT THE *APOLLO 11* ASTRONAUTS PLACED A PINK FLAG FROM THE HOTEL ON THE MOON IN GRATITUDE FOR THEIR COMPLIMENTARY STAY.
TV CAMERAS AND CABLES	CRUCIFIXES	
	A GOLD OLIVE BRANCH	
HASSELBLAD CAMERAS	A COMPUTER DISC THE SIZE OF A SILVER DOLLAR WITH PEACEFUL GREETINGS FROM PRESIDENTS AND PRIME MINISTERS OF 73 COUNTRIES	
EMPTY FOOD PACKAGES		
PARTS OF THE SPACESUITS: BACKPACK, BOOTS		

OVER FOUR HUNDRED SIXTY THOUSAND PEOPLE WORKED ON THE APOLLO PROJECT. THEY GOT 12 ASTRONAUTS TO THE MOON. ALTOGETHER, THE APOLLO ASTRONAUTS BROUGHT 840 POUNDS (380 KILOGRAMS) OF MOON MATERIAL BACK TO EARTH. ON THE MOON THERE ARE FOOTPRINTS FROM 12 PEOPLE, TRACES THAT WILL NEVER BE SWEPT AWAY BY ANY WIND.

When Michael Collins returned from the moon, he made a decision to never travel again. He wanted to spend the rest of his life fishing, bringing up his children, taking care of his dogs, and sitting on the porch with his wife.

Sometimes, when he's talking to other people, the thought strikes him: *I have been to places and done things that no one can ever imagine. I will never be able to explain what it was like. I carry it inside, like a treasure.*

At night, Michael Collins tends to the roses in his garden at the back of his house. The soil smells good. The wind feels warm and humid against his face. He looks up at the yellow disk in the sky and thinks to himself: *I have been there. It was beautiful, but compared to Earth it was nothing.*

He never wants to go back to the moon.

URSA

44

URSA MAJOR

We're lucky to have
this planet. I know.

Reader Response

Open for Discussion He didn't get the best seat on *Columbia.* He didn't get to walk on the moon. But Michael Collins *did* get a biography. Tell why.

1. Look back at the author's description of the moon landing on page 744. How does she make it suspenseful?

2. The selection contains many graphic sources. Which one best helps you understand events in the selection? Why?

3. Why did Michael Collins never return to the moon? Reread page 754. How does he feel about the moon compared to the Earth?

4. Create a crossword puzzle using words from the Words to Know list and the selection. Write the clues (definitions) first. Then give the puzzle to a classmate to solve.

Look Back and Write Alone in the spacecraft, Michael Collins had many responsibilities. What did he have to do? Reread page 748 and then write your answer.

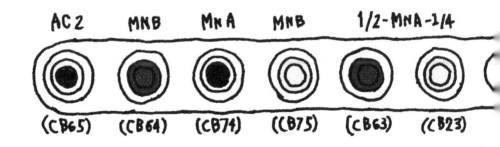

Meet the Author and Illustrator

Bea Uusma Schyffert

Read more books about the Apollo moon landing.

Growing up in Sweden, Bea Uusma Schyffert didn't hear much about space travel. After spending time in the United States, however, she says she became "a space geek." She remembers, "I just had to learn everything there is about the Apollo program. The more I learned, the more questions I had."

Until recently, Ms. Schyffert illustrated books. With her strong interest in the Apollo missions, she was eager to both write and illustrate a book about Michael Collins. To uncover quirky facts about his mission, such as strange smells and foods, Ms. Schyffert visited NASA and "asked their space historians all kinds of odd questions."

For her next project, Ms. Schyffert will write a book about a Swedish polar expedition. She is going to the North Pole as part of her research! She lives with her husband and two sons in Stockholm, Sweden, and New York City.

Flying to the Moon: An Astronaut's Story
by Michael Collins

Apollo 11: First Moon Landing
by Michael D. Cole

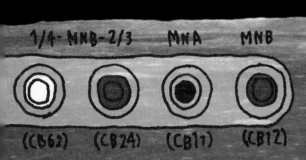

1/4 - MNB - 2/3   MNA   MNB

(CB62)   (CB24)   (CB17)   (CB12)

Textbook

Genre

- Textbooks are used in classrooms to teach facts about a subject and to help students understand those facts.

- Textbooks must be factual and are considered an authority on the information they provide.

Text Features

- Titles, heads, and subheads often serve as clear guides to what a lesson is about.

- Textbooks often include charts, tables, and graphs that organize information in a visual way.

Link to Science

Research the planets on which space probes have landed. Which one seems most hospitable for human colonization? Report your findings.

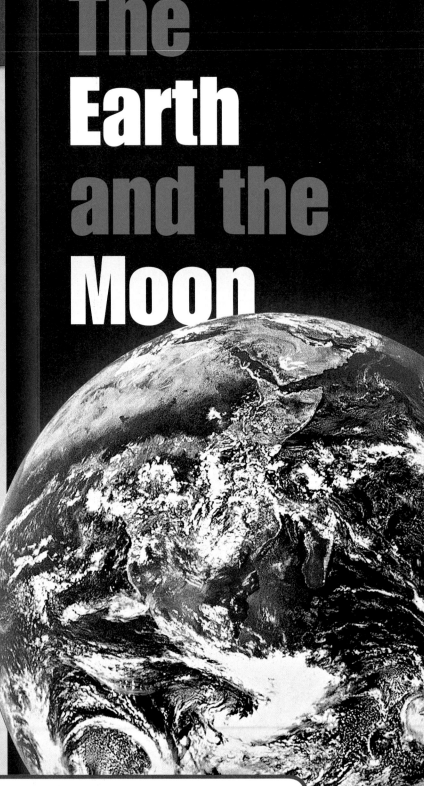

The Earth and the Moon

 Graphic Sources Study graphic sources carefully—don't skip over them.

Earth

Earth, our home, is the third planet from the sun. It is also the solar system's largest rocky planet. Earth is the only planet that has liquid water on its surface. In fact, most of Earth's surface is covered with water.

Earth is wrapped in a layer of gas that is about 150 kilometers (93 mi) thick. This layer of gas, or atmosphere, makes life possible on Earth. It filters out some of the sun's harmful rays. It also contains nitrogen, oxygen, carbon dioxide, and water vapor. Plants and animals on Earth use these gases. Earth is the only planet in the solar system known to support life.

Earth Facts

Distance from sun
149,600,000 km (93,000,000 mi)

Diameter
12,756 km (7,926 mi)

Length of day as measured in Earth time
24 hours

Length of year as measured in Earth time
365.25 days

Average surface temperature
15°C (59°F)

Moons
1

This article is from *Scott Foresman Science,*
Grade 4.

The Moon

Moons are satellites of planets. A satellite is an object that orbits another object in space. Just as planets revolve around the sun because of gravity, moons revolve around planets. The force of gravity between a planet and its moon keeps the moons in their orbits.

Earth has one large moon. The moon is about one-fourth the size of Earth. The moon has no atmosphere. It has many craters that formed when meteorites crashed onto its surface.

Exploring the Moon

Space exploration started in 1957 when the former Soviet Union launched *Sputnik*, the first artificial satellite. The Soviet Union sent the first space probes to the moon in 1959. These spacecraft did not carry people.

In 1961, Yuri Gagarin, a Soviet cosmonaut, became the first person to travel in space. On his journey on *Vostok I*, he circled the Earth in less than 2 hours. In 1969, Americans Neil Armstrong and Buzz Aldrin were the first people to step onto the powdery soil that covers the moon's surface. The moon has no atmosphere to create wind or rain, so their footprints will remain for years to come.

Reading Across Texts

Which astronaut would you prefer to have been: Michael Collins, Buzz Aldrin, or Neil Armstrong? Why?

Writing Across Texts Pretend you are the astronaut you chose. Write a few sentences about your adventure that you would like others to know.

 Monitor & Fix Up You may need to slow your rate as you read many facts.

UNIT 6

Poetry

Dream Dust

by Langston Hughes

Gather out of star-dust
    Earth-dust,
    Cloud-dust,
    Storm-dust,
And splinters of hail,
One handful of dream-dust
    Not for sale.

Martin Luther King

by Myra Cohn Livingston

Got me a special place
For Martin Luther King.
His picture on the wall
Makes me sing.

I look at it for a long time
And think of some
Real good ways
We will overcome.

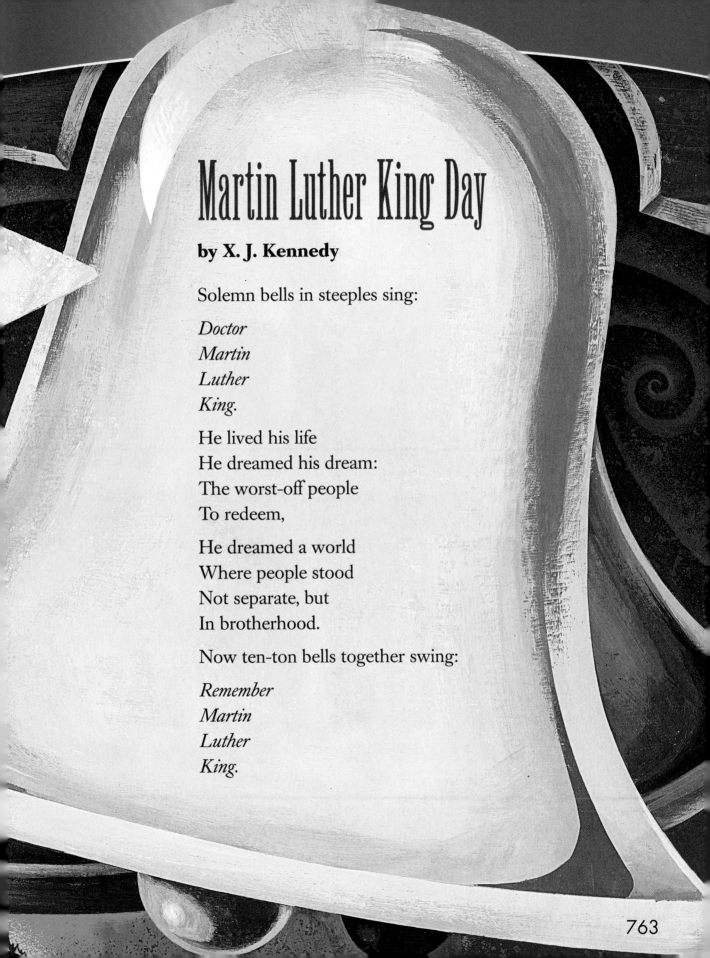

Martin Luther King Day

by X. J. Kennedy

Solemn bells in steeples sing:

Doctor
Martin
Luther
King.

He lived his life
He dreamed his dream:
The worst-off people
To redeem,

He dreamed a world
Where people stood
Not separate, but
In brotherhood.

Now ten-ton bells together swing:

Remember
Martin
Luther
King.

Fall Football

by Gary Soto

Autumn swung down from the tree,
Leaf by leaf.

Me, I put away my baseball glove.
I picked up the football

And ran after a pass I tossed in the air,
Not far but far enough to make me a hero–
I tripped myself to build up grass stains on my knees
And rolled on the lawn
While my cat, the one fan, watched from the sidelines.

The score remained 7–0, then went up to 14–0.
The game ended when the first porch light on the block
    snapped on.

The interview from the press followed:
"Me, tell me about the game."

I wiped my forehead. I massaged my shoulder,
Sore from all the passes I had to catch on my own.

"It was a personal challenge," I said, exhausted.
"It's always hard when I play against myself."

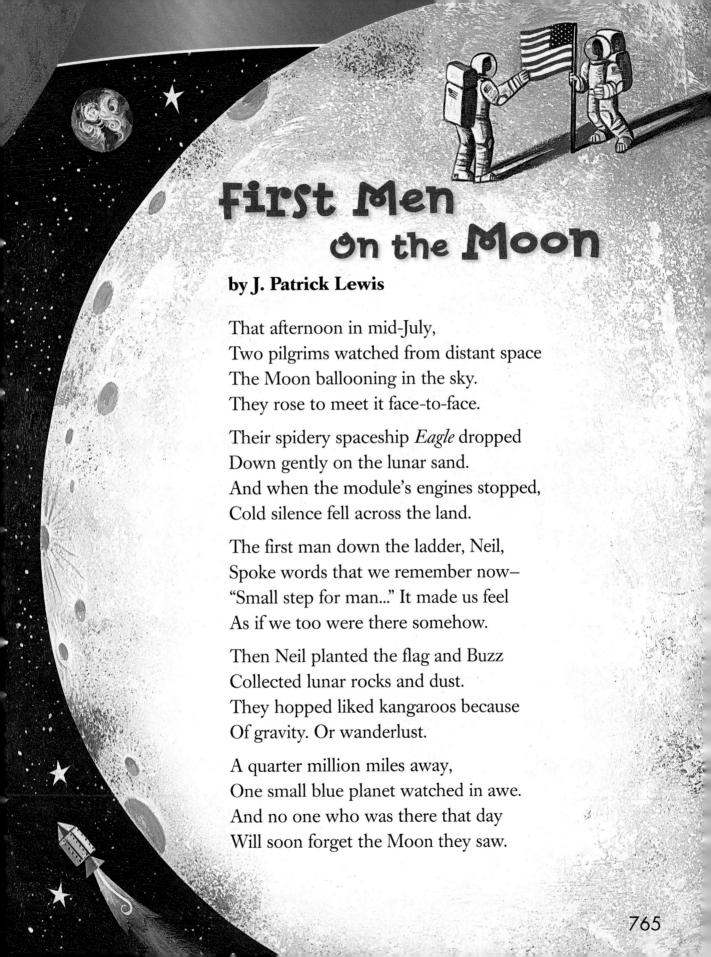

First Men on the Moon

by J. Patrick Lewis

That afternoon in mid-July,
Two pilgrims watched from distant space
The Moon ballooning in the sky.
They rose to meet it face-to-face.

Their spidery spaceship *Eagle* dropped
Down gently on the lunar sand.
And when the module's engines stopped,
Cold silence fell across the land.

The first man down the ladder, Neil,
Spoke words that we remember now–
"Small step for man..." It made us feel
As if we too were there somehow.

Then Neil planted the flag and Buzz
Collected lunar rocks and dust.
They hopped liked kangaroos because
Of gravity. Or wanderlust.

A quarter million miles away,
One small blue planet watched in awe.
And no one who was there that day
Will soon forget the Moon they saw.

The Lessons They Teach

Think about the lesson you could learn from the real people you read about in this unit or others like them. Choose one of these people. Write about the lesson others can learn from how this person tried to achieve his or her goals and dreams.

What does it take to achieve our goals and dreams?

Reach

connect to
SOCIAL STUDIES

Think of a goal or dream achieved by one of the people you read about in this unit. Make a paper cube with the words *who, what, when, where,* and *how.* Take turns in a group tossing the cube. Use the word on the cube to ask a question about this person and his or her goal or dream. Let others in the group answer the question.

Path to a Goal

connect to
SOCIAL STUDIES

Talk with a partner about different goals you both have. Choose one. Then think about several steps that could help you achieve your goal and obstacles that might get in your way. Use these ideas to make up a game. Write the goal, steps, and obstacles on a game board. Make up rules, and then play the game.

Strategies

100%

GREAT JOB!

Answering Questions Well

Different Kinds of Questions

As a student, you must answer many questions.

- Your teacher asks you questions.
- Your textbooks contain questions.
- Practice books and workbooks contain questions.
- The tests you must take are full of questions.

Some tests have one kind of question. Other tests have more than one kind of question.

You might find multiple-choice or fill-in-the-blank questions. You might be asked to write your answers. If you write, your answers might have to be short or long.

To help you answer questions and take tests, read the pages that follow. You will learn strategies to help you read questions and find the answers. You can also use these strategies when you take tests. Some pages ask you to try to find the answers yourself. Write your answers on a separate sheet of paper.

Remember, you can develop the skills you need to do well.

A Lifelong Skill

The skills you are learning will help you do well on tests while you are in school. They will also help you after you finish school.

Throughout your life, you will have to answer questions that come from many sources. You may need to answer questions on a job. You will need to understand what you are being asked and answer the best you can.

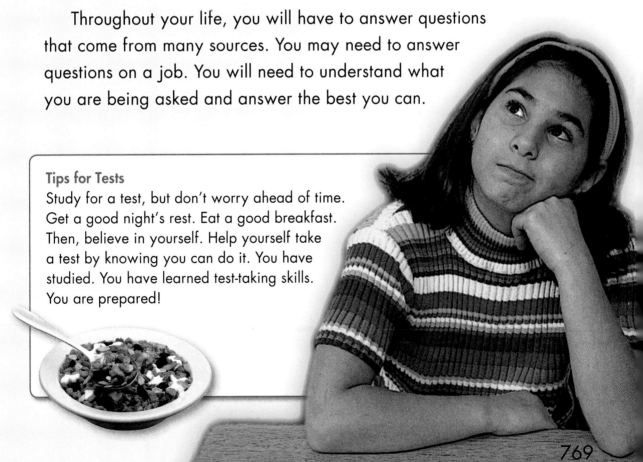

Tips for Tests
Study for a test, but don't worry ahead of time. Get a good night's rest. Eat a good breakfast. Then, believe in yourself. Help yourself take a test by knowing you can do it. You have studied. You have learned test-taking skills. You are prepared!

Understand the Question

Key Words

Before you can answer a question in a book or on a test, you must understand it. One way is to find key words. These tips will help you.

Read the question slowly. Ask yourself, "Who or what is this question about?" The words that tell who or what the question is about are **key words.**

Look for other key words in the question. Often the first word of the question is another key word. The first word might be *who, what, where, when,* or *how.*

Read the sentence and the sample question. Notice the key words.

> Look for **key words** in the question. The question often uses words that are clues to the answer.

> David Thompson, a fur trader, crossed the Rocky Mountains in 1807.

1 When did David Thompson cross the Rocky Mountains?

Turn the question into a statement. Use the key words in a sentence that begins "I need to find out. . . ." After you read a question that begins with *when,* you might think to yourself, "I need to find out *when* David Thompson crossed the Rocky Mountains." Then look back at the text. The answer must be "in 1807."

Here is a sample text.

Some ants build their nests under stones. The stones absorb the sun's heat during the day, and the heated stones then keep the ant nest warm during the night.

Here is a sample question about the text. See how one student makes sure she understands the question.

Test Question

1 Where do some ants build their nests?

I've read the question. What is it about? Well, it's talking about ants and where they build their nests. **Ants** and **nests** must be key words.

Okay, I'm going to read the question again. There's the key word **where,** and there's the key word **build.** I need to find out where some ants build their nests. The answer must be "under stones."

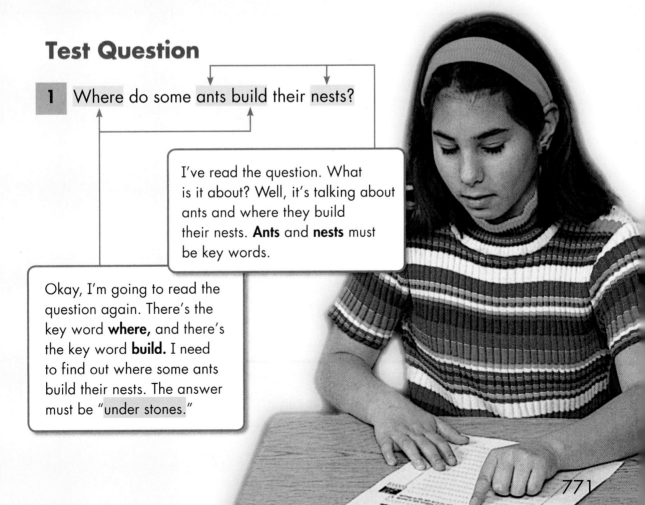

Here are strategies that will help you anytime you answer questions. Think about each one. Which have you tried before? Which are new to you?

In the Book

Sometimes the answer to a question is **in the book.** You can find these answers right there in the text.

Right There

- The answer is RIGHT THERE in one spot in the text.

- The answer is usually easy to find.

- You can put your finger on the answer.

Think and Search

- The answer IS in the text, but NOT in one spot.

- You need to SEARCH for the answer in different parts of the text.

- You need to THINK about how to put the information together.

In My Head

Sometimes the answers to questions are **in your head.**
The answers are NOT right there in the text.

Author and Me

- The answer is NOT written in the text.

- The AUTHOR gives you clues about the answer.

- You also must use what YOU already know.

- You put all this together to find the best answer.

On My Own

- The answer is NOT in the text at all.

- You must think about what you already know.

- You need to use your background knowledge to answer the question.

I Can Find the Answer

In the Book

Right There

When you answer questions, sometimes you can find the answer RIGHT THERE in the text. You can find the answer in one sentence.

Read this selection and the test question. Notice that the answer to the question is RIGHT THERE in the text. You can find the answer in one sentence and put your finger on it. The answer is highlighted for you.

> Notice that the answer appears in just one sentence. The answer is **right there.**

Swamps are large areas of wet, muddy land that are usually found in warm climates. **Deepwater swamps** are often **found** near rivers. The flooding of the river keeps the soil in the swamps moist. Tall trees grow in deepwater swamps. Shallow-water swamps, on the other hand, are often found in lowlands. Here the soil is very wet or flooded during most of the year. Short trees, bushes, and flowers grow in shallow-water swamps.

1 Where are **deepwater swamps** often **found?**

- (A) in lowlands
- (B) near lakes
- (C) near rivers
- (D) in unusual climates

When you read a question in a book or for a test, decide what the key words are. Then look for the key words in the text. The key words in this question are marked for you in bold type. Find the answer near the key words in the text.

Try It!

Now you choose the correct answers. Read this selection and the questions. Look for key words in the questions and in the text. Find the answers RIGHT THERE in the text.

Immigrants are people who come to a new country to live. Between 1880 and 1920, twenty-three million immigrants arrived in the United States. Most of them were very poor. They hoped their life in America would be better. The first stop for most of the immigrants was Ellis Island, near New York City. There doctors examined them. Those who did not pass the medical examinations could be sent back to their own countries. For this reason, Ellis Island was sometimes called "Heartbreak Island."

Look for key words in the question. Then look for them in the text.

Remember: Sometimes you can find the answers to test questions **right there** in one place in the text. Test questions that start with these words often have the answers right there: *who, what, where, when.*

1 When did millions of immigrants arrive in the United States?

(A) in 1880
(B) between 1880 and 1920
(C) in 1920
(D) between 1880 and 1910

2 Where did most of the immigrants stop first?

(F) western New York
(G) New England
(H) Long Island
(J) Ellis Island

I Can Find the Answer

In the Book

Think and Search

Sometimes the answer to a question is in the text, but it is not in just one sentence. You may need to SEARCH for the answer in two or more places in the text. Then you need to THINK how to put the information together for your answer.

Read this selection and study the chart. Then read the question. Think about the key words in bold type. Put together the information from the selection and the chart. The answer is highlighted for you.

Type of Warning	Wind Speed
Small Boat Warning	25 to 38 m.p.h.
Gale Warning	39 to 54 m.p.h.
Storm Warning	55 to 73 m.p.h.
Hurricane Warning	above 74 m.p.h.

The information needed to answer the test question is in two places.

The weather report in this small seaside town often includes storm warnings. **Most** warnings are for people in **small boats** and include the **wind speed.** It is not very often that a weather report includes a warning of hurricane wind speeds.

1 Which **wind speed** is reported **most** on the weather news?

(A) 25–38 m.p.h.
(B) 39–54 m.p.h.
(C) 55–73 m.p.h.
(D) above 74 m.p.h.

The key words in the question are **most** and **wind speed.** The text says that "most" warnings are for people in small boats and include "wind speed." The chart tells you the "wind speed" needed to warn people in boats. Put together, the information points to answer A.

Try It!

Now you decide the correct answers. Read this selection and the test questions. Remember that you may have to SEARCH in more than one place to find the answers. Then THINK about how the information fits together.

A caterpillar is hatched from a gypsy moth egg in late April. The caterpillar begins eating leaves right away. After the caterpillar has reached its full size, it spins a cocoon around itself. It stays in the cocoon for up to eighteen days, beginning in late June. Then, an adult moth emerges in mid-July. Shortly after the adult female leaves her cocoon, she lays a batch of eggs. There may be up to 500 eggs in one batch. The moth dies soon after, in late July.

Decide what the key words are in each question. Search for words that signal "how old" and "how long," such as the names of months.

Remember: Sometimes you need to put together information from different places in the selection.

1 How old is the caterpillar when it begins to stay in its cocoon?

(A) one month
(B) two months
(C) three months
(D) eighteen days

2 About how long does a gypsy moth live after leaving its cocoon?

(F) two weeks
(G) three weeks
(H) one month
(J) two months

I Can Find the Answer

In My Head

Author and Me

Sometimes your reading does not give you every part of the answer to a question. You have to find the answer by putting together what the author tells you and what you already know. YOU and the AUTHOR work together.

Read this text and the question. Notice how the author gives you some of the information you need to answer the question. In the text, Scott sees an animal and tells what it looks like. Dad sees what the animal is ready to do. Put this information together with what you already know.

> Dad sat down in the lawn chair. "A quiet day in the yard," he thought. He started to relax. Mrs. Todd stopped by. Her little son Scott stayed in the yard. He pointed to an animal under the tree. "Look at that funny black cat," Scott said. "It has a white stripe on its back." Dad's hair stood on end. The animal was getting ready to spray its awful smell. "That's no cat!" Dad shouted.

1 What is the animal Scott describes?

(A) chipmunk
(B) raccoon
(C) skunk
(D) groundhog

Notice that the author does not tell you what the animal is, but you know from the text. You know that a skunk is black with a white stripe and sprays an awful smell. YOU and the AUTHOR worked together to answer the question.

Try It!

Now you decide the correct answers. Read the text and the questions. Think about what the AUTHOR tells you and what YOU know.

Outside, thunder sounded. There was a bright streak of lightning. Then the lights in the house blinked and went out. "Don't get upset," Rachel told herself. She was home alone. She knew her mother had an "emergency" drawer in the kitchen. She inched her way there and opened the drawer. Her hand touched a long, tubelike object. One end was glass. Rachel pushed a button. At last she could see. Five minutes later the lights came back on.

Read carefully. Think about what the author tells you.

Remember this about working with the author: Information from the author + information from me = the correct answer.

1 Which word best describes Rachel?

- (A) pleased
- (B) calm
- (C) eager
- (D) upset

2 What does Rachel find at last to help her in the dark?

- (F) a lantern
- (G) a light bulb
- (H) a light switch
- (J) a flashlight

I Can Find the Answer

In My Head

On My Own

Sometimes the answer to a question is *not* in the selection. You have to think about it. You have to think about what you already know. For this kind of question, you can answer ON YOUR OWN.

Sometimes a test will ask you to write about a topic. Your answer should give details that tell what you know about the topic.

Read this selection and the test directions. Then read how one student wrote an answer.

> The key words are highlighted. They tell the *topic* to write about.

The life of Dr. Albert Schweitzer is an example of bravery and kindness. In 1913, Dr. Schweitzer had a hospital built in Africa. He helped save the lives of many who were suffering from diseases. He never thought twice about putting himself in danger.

Directions: Write about the bravery of a person. The person can be someone you know or someone you have heard of. The person could also be someone in history, such as George Washington. Tell why you think the person was brave.

> A plane crashed in a field near my house. Later my parents found out that the pilot was very brave. He flew the plane over the field so it would not crash on our house. He died, but he kept a lot of people from getting killed.

Notice that the student did not find the answer in the text. The student had to use personal ideas and experiences to write the answer.

780

Try It!

Read the text below. Notice that you do not need the text to write your answer. Remember that sometimes you need to write an answer ON YOUR OWN.

Fuzzball, my new kitten, checked out her new environment carefully. First she found her food and water bowls. Next she scooted through the cat door to the porch and her litter box. After that, she headed for her wicker basket. She gently padded around the cushion. Then she curled up and started purring. Her new home passed inspection.

Read the directions carefully. Find key words that tell you what topic to write about.

Directions: Maybe you have a pet at home. If you don't have a pet, you may have a favorite animal. Write about your pet or your favorite animal. Tell what your pet does or why you like the animal. Write your answer on a separate sheet of paper.

Remember: Think before you write. Give clear details about your topic.

In the Book	In My Head
Right There	Author and Me
Think and Search	On My Own

Directions: Read this selection. Then answer the questions that follow.

The Everglades National Park in Florida was established in 1947 to protect the animals and plants that live in the Everglades. The park presently covers almost 1,500,000 acres.

The flat forests of the Everglades are flooded for many months each year. The floodwaters create large swamps with plants and trees that grow in the hot tropical climate. Many visitors each day follow the miles and miles of paths that wind through the lush landscape.

Yellowstone National Park is quite different but no less beautiful. Established in 1872, it was the first national park in the United States. Spreading across Wyoming, Idaho, and Montana, the park covers 2,219,823 acres.

The park's impressive landscape includes snow-covered mountains, forests, meadows, and sparkling freshwater rivers. There are almost one thousand miles of hiking trails and many campsites where visitors can stay.

Write the correct letter of each answer. **Use a separate sheet of paper.**

1 Which would you *not* find in the Everglades?

(A) forests

(B) skating ponds

(C) swamps

(D) hiking paths

2 Why was Everglades National Park established?

(F) to create hiking trails and campsites

(G) to hold back the floodwaters

(H) to raise tropical plants and trees

(J) to protect the animals and plants that live there

3 When was Yellowstone National Park established?

(A) 1947

(B) 1972

(C) 1872

(D) 1847

4 How many states does Yellowstone National Park spread across?

(F) 3

(G) 2

(H) 1

(J) 5

5 How alike in size are the two national parks?

(A) Yellowstone is about twice as big.

(B) They are about the same size.

(C) Yellowstone is a little bigger.

(D) Yellowstone is not as big.

6 Write about a time you visited a park or a place you thought was beautiful. Tell what the place was like and what you did while you were there.

Glossary

How to Use This Glossary

This glossary can help you understand and pronounce some of the words in this book. The entries in this glossary are in alphabetical order. There are guide words at the top of each page to show you the first and last words on the page. A pronunciation key is at the bottom of every other page. Remember, if you can't find the word you are looking for, ask for help or check a dictionary.

The entry word is in dark type. It shows how the word is spelled and how the word is divided into syllables.

The pronunciation is in parentheses. It also shows which syllables are stressed.

Part-of-speech labels show the function or functions of an entry word and any listed form of that word.

an·ces·tor (an′ses′tər), *NOUN.* person from whom you are descended, such as your great-grandparents: *Their ancestors had come to the United States in 1812.* ❏ *PLURAL* **an·ces·tors.**

Sometimes, irregular and other special forms will be shown to help you use the word correctly.

The definition and example sentence show you what the word means and how it is used.

Aa

a·board (ə bôrd′), *ADVERB.* on board; in or on a ship, train, bus, airplane, etc.: *"All aboard!" shouted the conductor, and everyone rushed for the train.*

a·bun·dance (ə bun′dəns), *NOUN.* quantity that is a lot more than enough: *There is an abundance of apples this year.*

af·ford (ə fôrd′), *VERB.* to give as an effect or a result; provide; yield: *Reading a good book affords real pleasure.* ❏ *VERB* **af·ford·ed, af·ford·ing.**

al·ti·tude (al′tə tüd), *NOUN.* a high place: *At some altitudes, snow never melts.*

a·maze (ə māz′), *VERB.* to surprise greatly; strike with sudden wonder; astound: *He was amazed at how different the strand of hair looked under a microscope.* ❏ *VERB* **a·mazed, a·maz·ing.**

am·phib·i·an (am fib′ē ən), *NOUN.* any of many cold-blooded animals with backbones and moist, scaleless skins. Their young usually have gills and live in water until they develop lungs for living on land. Frogs, toads, newts, and salamanders are amphibians. ❏ *PLURAL* **am·phib·i·ans.**

an·ces·tor (an′ses′tər), *NOUN.* person from whom you are descended, such as your great-grandparents: *Their ancestors had come to the United States in 1812.* ❏ *PLURAL* **an·ces·tors.**

an·cient (ān′shənt), *ADJECTIVE*. of times long past: *In Egypt, we saw the ruins of an ancient temple built 6000 years ago.* (*Ancient* comes from the Latin word *ante* meaning "before.")

an·tic·i·pa·tion (an tis′ə pā′shən), *NOUN*. act of anticipating; looking forward to; expectation: *In anticipation of a cold winter, they cut extra firewood.*

ap·pear (ə pir′), *VERB*. to be seen; come in sight: *One by one, the stars appear.* ❑ *VERB* **ap·peared, ap·pear·ing.**

a·quar·i·um (ə kwâr′ē əm), **1.** *NOUN*. tank or glass bowl in which fish or other water animals and water plants are kept in water. **2.** *NOUN*. building used for showing collections of live fish, water animals, and water plants.

as·tro·naut (as′trə nȯt), *NOUN*. pilot or member of the crew of a spacecraft. ❑ *PLURAL* **as·tro·nauts.**

astronaut

at·las (at′ləs), *NOUN*. book of maps.

a·vi·a·tion (ā′vē ā′shən), *NOUN*. science or art of operating and navigating aircraft.

a·vi·a·tor (av′ē ā′tər), *NOUN*. person who flies an aircraft; pilot.

a·void (ə void′), *VERB*. to keep away from; keep out of the way of: *We avoided driving through large cities on our trip.* ❑ *VERB* **a·void·ed, a·void·ing.**

awk·ward (ȯk′wərd), *ADJECTIVE*. not easily managed: *This is an awkward corner to turn.*

Bb

back·board (bak′bôrd′), *NOUN*. in basketball, the flat, elevated surface of glass, plastic, or wood, on which the basket is mounted. Bank shots are bounced off the backboard.

bar·gain (bär′gən), *NOUN*. agreement to trade or exchange; deal: *You can't back out on our bargain.*

a in hat	ō in open	sh in she
ā in age	ȯ in all	th in thin
â in care	ô in order	ᴛʜ in then
ä in far	oi in oil	zh in measure
e in let	ou in out	ə = a in about
ē in equal	u in cup	ə = e in taken
ėr in term	u̇ in put	ə = i in pencil
i in it	ü in rule	ə = o in lemon
ī in ice	ch in child	ə = u in circus
o in hot	ng in long	

bawl (bȯl), *VERB.* to shout or cry out in a noisy way: *a lost calf bawling for its mother.* ❑ *VERB* **bawled, bawl·ing.**

be·wil·der (bi wil′dər), *VERB.* to confuse completely; puzzle: *bewildered by the confusing instructions.* ❑ *VERB* **be·wil·dered, be·wil·der·ing.**

bi·ol·o·gist (bī ol′ə jist), *NOUN.* a scientist who studies living things, including their origins, structures, activities, and distribution.

bluff¹ (bluf), *NOUN.* a high, steep slope or cliff.

bluff¹

bluff² (bluf), *VERB.* to fool or mislead, especially by pretending confidence: *She bluffed the robbers by convincing them that the police were on the way.*

board·ing school (bôr′ding skül), *NOUN.* school with buildings where the pupils live during the school term.

bow¹ (bou), *VERB.* to bend the head or body in greeting, respect, worship, or obedience: *The people bowed before the queen.* ❑ *VERB* **bowed, bow·ing.**

bow² (bō), **1.** *NOUN.* weapon for shooting arrows. A bow usually consists of a strip of flexible wood bent by a string. **2.** *NOUN.* a looped knot: *The gift had a bow on top.*

bow³ (bou), *NOUN.* the forward part of a ship, boat, or aircraft.

bril·liant (bril′yənt), *ADJECTIVE.* shining brightly; sparkling: *brilliant sunshine.*

brisk (brisk), *ADJECTIVE.* keen; sharp: *A brisk wind was blowing from the north.*

bus·tle (bus′əl), *VERB.* to be noisily busy and in a hurry: *The children were bustling to get ready for the party.* ❑ *VERB* **bus·tled, bus·tling.**

Cc

can·o·py (kan′ə pē), *NOUN.* the uppermost layer of branches in forest trees.

ca·pa·ble (kā′pə bəl), *ADJECTIVE.* having fitness, power, or ability; able; efficient; competent: *He was such a capable student that everyone had great hopes for his future.*

cap·sule (kap′səl), *NOUN.* the enclosed front section of a rocket made to carry instruments, astronauts, etc., into space. In flight, the capsule can separate from the rest of the rocket and go into orbit or be directed back to Earth.

car·go (kär′gō), *NOUN.* load of goods carried by a ship, plane, or truck: *The freighter had docked to unload a cargo of wheat.*

ce·les·tial (sə les′chəl), *ADJECTIVE.* of the sky or outer space: *The sun, moon, planets, and stars are celestial bodies.*

chant (chant), *VERB.* to call over and over again: *The football fans chanted, "Go, team, go!"* ❑ *VERB* **chant·ed, chant·ing.**

cho·rus (kôr′əs), *NOUN.* anything spoken or sung all at the same time: *The children greeted the teacher with a chorus of "Good morning."*

cock·pit (kok′pit′), *NOUN.* the place where the pilot sits in an airplane.

colo·nel (kėr′nl), *NOUN.* a military rank below general.

con·duct (kon′dukt *for noun;* kən dukt′ *for verb*), **1.** *NOUN.* way of acting; behavior thought of as good or bad: *Her conduct was admirable.* **2.** *VERB.* to direct; manage: *The teacher conducted our efforts.* ❑ *VERB* **con·duct·ed, con·duct·ing.**

con·fide (kən fid′), *VERB.* to tell as a secret: *He confided his troubles to his brother.* ❑ *VERB* **con·fid·ed, con·fid·ing.**

con·front (kən frunt′), *VERB.* to face boldly; oppose: *Once she confronted her problems, she was able to solve them easily.* ❑ *VERB* **con·front·ed, con·front·ing.**

con·scious (kon′shəs), *ADJECTIVE.* aware of what you are doing; awake: *About five minutes after fainting, he became conscious again.*

con·sist (kən sist′), *VERB.* to be made up; be formed: *A week consists of seven days.* ❑ *VERB* **con·sist·ed, con·sist·ing.**

Con·sti·tu·tion (kon′stə tü′shən), *NOUN.* the written set of fundamental principles by which the United States is governed.

con·sult (kən sult′), *VERB.* to seek information or advice from; refer to: *You can consult travelers, books, or maps for help in planning a trip abroad.* ❑ *VERB* **con·sult·ed, con·sult·ing.**

conduct
(def. 2)

a	in hat	ō	in open	sh	in she
ā	in age	ȯ	in all	th	in thin
â	in care	ô	in order	ᴛʜ	in then
ä	in far	oi	in oil	zh	in measure
e	in let	ou	in out	ə	= a in about
ē	in equal	u	in cup	ə	= e in taken
ėr	in term	u̇	in put	ə	= i in pencil
i	in it	ü	in rule	ə	= o in lemon
ī	in ice	ch	in child	ə	= u in circus
o	in hot	ng	in long		

con·ti·nent (kon′tə nənt), *NOUN.* one of the seven great masses of land on the Earth. The continents are North America, South America, Europe, Africa, Asia, Australia, and Antarctica. (*Continent* comes from two Latin words, *com* meaning "in" or "together" and *tenere* meaning "to hold.")

con·trap·tion (kən trap′shən), *NOUN.* device or gadget.

con·ver·gence (kən vėr′jəns), *NOUN.* act or process of meeting at a point. (*Convergence* comes from two Latin words, *com* meaning "in" or "together" and *vergere* meaning "incline.")

cord (kôrd), *NOUN.* measure of quantity for cut wood, equal to 128 cubic feet. A pile of wood 4 feet wide, 4 feet high, and 8 feet long is a cord.

cow·ard (kou′ərd), *NOUN.* person who lacks courage or is easily made afraid; person who runs from danger, trouble, etc.

coy·o·te (kī ō′tē or kī′ōt), *NOUN.* a small, wolflike mammal living in many parts of North America. It is noted for loud howling at night.

cra·dle (krā′dl), *NOUN.* a frame to support weight.

crime (krīm), *NOUN.* activity of criminals; violation of law: *Police forces combat crime.*

crum·ble (krum′bəl), *VERB.* to fall to pieces; decay: *The old wall was crumbling away at the edges.* ❏ *VERB* **crum·bled, crum·bling.**

cur·i·os·i·ty (kyùr′ē os′ə tē), *NOUN.* an eager desire to know: *She satisfied her curiosity about animals by visiting the zoo every week.* (*Curiosity* comes from the Latin word *cure* meaning "care.")

Dd

dan·gle (dang′gəl), *VERB.* to hang and swing loosely. ❏ *VERB* **dan·gled, dan·gling.**

dangle

dap·pled (dap′əld), *ADJECTIVE.* marked with spots; spotted.

dar·ing (dâr′ing), *ADJECTIVE.* bold; fearless; courageous: *Performing on a trapeze high above a crowd is a daring act.*

de·ci·pher (di sī′fər), **1.** *VERB.* to make out the meaning of something that is puzzling or not clear: *I can't decipher this poor handwriting.* **2.** *VERB.* to change something in cipher or code to ordinary language; decode. ❑ *VERB* **de·ci·phered, de·ci·pher·ing.**

de·part (di pärt′), *VERB.* to go away; leave: *Your flight departs at 6:15.* ❑ *VERB* **de·part·ed, de·part·ing.** (*Depart* comes from the Latin word *departire* meaning "to divide.")

de·pot (dē′ pō), *NOUN.* a railroad or bus station.

depot

des·ti·na·tion (des′tə nā′shən), *NOUN.* place to which someone or something is going or is being sent.

de·struc·tion (di struk′shən), *NOUN.* great damage; ruin: *The storm left destruction behind it.*

dig·ni·fied (dig′nə fid), *ADJECTIVE.* having dignity; noble; stately: *The queen has a dignified manner.*

dis·may (dis mā′), *NOUN.* sudden, helpless fear of what is about to happen or what has happened: *I was filled with dismay when the basement began to flood.*

dock (dok), *NOUN.* platform built on the shore or out from the shore; wharf; pier. Ships load and unload beside a dock. ❑ *PLURAL* **docks.**

dol·phin (dol′fən), *NOUN.* any of the numerous sea mammals related to the whale, but smaller. Dolphins have beaklike snouts and remarkable intelligence. ❑ *PLURAL* **dol·phins.**

dor·mi·to·ry (dôr′mə tôr′ē), *NOUN.* a building with many rooms in which people sleep. Many colleges have dormitories for students whose homes are elsewhere.

drab (drab), *ADJECTIVE.* not attractive; dull; monotonous: *the drab houses of the smoky, dingy mining town.*

a in hat	ō in open	sh in she
ā in age	ȯ in all	th in thin
â in care	ô in order	ᴛʜ in then
ä in far	oi in oil	zh in measure
e in let	ou in out	ə = a in about
ē in equal	u in cup	ə = e in taken
ėr in term	u̇ in put	ə = i in pencil
i in it	ü in rule	ə = o in lemon
ī in ice	ch in child	ə = u in circus
o in hot	ng in long	

draft (draft), **1.** *NOUN.* current of air: *I caught cold by sitting in a draft.* **2.** *NOUN.* a rough copy: *She made two drafts of her book report before she handed in the final form.*

drag (drag), **1.** *NOUN.* the force acting on an object in motion, in a direction opposite to the object's motion. It is produced by friction. **2.** *VERB.* to pull or move along heavily or slowly; pull or draw along the ground: *We dragged the heavy crates out of the garage. I dragged along on my sprained ankle.* ❑ *VERB* **dragged, drag·ging.**

drib·ble (drib′əl), *VERB.* to move a ball along by bouncing it or giving it short kicks: *dribble a basketball or soccer ball.* ❑ *VERB* **drib·bled, drib·bling.**

dude (düd), **1.** *NOUN.* in the western parts of the United States and Canada, person raised in the city, especially an easterner who vacations on a ranch. **2.** *NOUN.* guy; fellow (slang). ❑ *PLURAL* **dudes.**

duke (dük), *NOUN.* nobleman of the highest title, ranking just below a prince.

dun·geon (dun′jən), *NOUN.* a dark underground room or cell to keep prisoners in.

dunk (dungk), *VERB.* to shoot a basketball by leaping, so that the hands are above the rim, and throwing the ball down through the netting. ❑ *VERB* **dunked, dunk·ing.**

dwell (dwel), *VERB.* to make your home; live: *He dwells in the city.* ❑ *VERB* **dwelled, dwell·ing.**

Ee

el·e·gant (el′ə gənt), *ADJECTIVE.* having or showing good taste; gracefully and richly refined; beautifully luxurious: *The palace had elegant furnishings.*

em·bar·rass·ment (em bar′əs mənt), *NOUN.* shame; an uneasy feeling: *He blushed in embarrassment at such a silly mistake.*

en·chant (en chant′), *VERB.* to delight greatly; charm: *The music enchanted us all.* ❑ *VERB* **en·chant·ed, en·chant·ing.** ❑ *ADJECTIVE* **en·chant·ing.**

en·coun·ter (en koun′tər), *NOUN.* an unexpected meeting: *The explorers had a surprising encounter with a polar bear.*

encounter

en·dur·ance (en dúr′əns), *NOUN.* power to last and to withstand hard wear: *It takes great endurance to run a marathon.*

endurance

en·grave (en grāv′), *VERB.* to cut deeply in; carve in; carve in an artistic way: *The jeweler engraved my initials on the back of the watch.* ❑ *VERB* **en·graved, en·grav·ing.**

es·cape (e skāp′), *VERB.* to get out and away; get free: *The bird escaped from its cage.* ❑ *VERB* **es·caped, es·cap·ing.**

es·cort (e skôrt′), *VERB.* to go with another to give protection, show honor, provide companionship, etc. ❑ *VERB* **es·cort·ed, es·cort·ing.**

etch (ech), **1.** *VERB.* to engrave a drawing or design on a metal plate, glass, etc. **2.** *VERB.* to impress deeply: *Her face was etched in my memory.* ❑ *VERB* **etched, etch·ing.**

ex·e·cute (ek′sə kyüt), *VERB.* to carry out; do: *He executed her instructions.* ❑ *VERB* **ex·e·cut·ed, ex·e·cut·ing.**

ex·hale (eks hāl′), *VERB.* to breathe out: *We exhale air from our lungs.* ❑ *VERB* **ex·haled, ex·hal·ing.**

ex·hib·it (eg zib′it), *NOUN.* display or public showing: *The village art exhibit drew 10,000 visitors.*

ex·ile (eg′zīl or ek′sīl), *VERB.* to be forced to leave your country or home, often by law as a punishment; banish: *Napoleon was exiled to Elba.* ❑ *VERB* **ex·iled, ex·il·ing.**

ex·pect (ek spekt′), *VERB.* to think something will probably happen: *They expected the hurricane to change directions.* ❑ *VERB* **ex·pect·ed, ex·pect·ing.**

ex·po·sure (ek spō′zhər), *NOUN.* condition of being without protection; condition of being uncovered.

a in hat	ō in open	sh in she
ā in age	ȯ in all	th in thin
â in care	ô in order	ᴛʜ in then
ä in far	oi in oil	zh in measure
e in let	ou in out	ə = a in about
ē in equal	u in cup	ə = e in taken
ėr in term	ü in put	ə = i in pencil
i in it	ü in rule	ə = o in lemon
ī in ice	ch in child	ə = u in circus
o in hot	ng in long	

Ff

fas·ci·nate (fas′n āt), *VERB.* to interest greatly; attract very strongly; charm: *She was fascinated by the designs and colors in African art.* ❑ *VERB* **fas·ci·nat·ed, fas·ci·nat·ing.**

fa·vor (fā′vər), *NOUN.* act of kindness: *Will you do me a favor?*

fee·bly (fē′blē), *ADVERB.* weakly; without strength: *She walked feebly when she was first recovering from the flu.*

flex (fleks), *VERB.* to bend: *She flexed her stiff arm slowly.* ❑ *VERB* **flexed, flex·ing.**

flex·i·ble (flek′sə bəl), **1.** *ADJECTIVE.* easily bent; not stiff; bending without breaking: *Leather, rubber, and wire are flexible.*
2. *ADJECTIVE.* able to change easily to fit different conditions: *My mother works from our home, and her hours are very flexible.*

flexible (def. 1)

for·bid·ding (fər bid′ing), *ADJECTIVE.* causing fear or dislike; looking dangerous or unpleasant: *The coast was rocky and forbidding.*

fore·cast (fôr′kast′), *NOUN.* statement of what is coming; prediction: *What is the weather forecast today?* ❑ *PLURAL* **fore·casts.**

for·ma·tion (fôr mā′shən), *NOUN.* series of layers or deposits of the same kind of rock or mineral. ❑ *PLURAL* **for·ma·tions.**

foul (foul), *VERB.* to make an unfair play against. ❑ *VERB* **fouled, foul·ing.**

fra·grant (frā′grənt), *ADJECTIVE.* having or giving off a pleasing odor; sweet-smelling: *fragrant roses.*

friend·less (frend′les), *ADJECTIVE.* to be without people who know and like you.

frost (fròst), **1.** *NOUN.* a freezing condition; temperature below the point at which water freezes: *Frost came early last winter.*
2. *NOUN.* moisture frozen on or in a surface; feathery crystals of ice formed when water vapor in the air condenses at a temperature below freezing: *On cold fall mornings, there is frost on the grass.*

frus·tra·tion (fru strā′shən), *NOUN.* a feeling of anger and helplessness, caused by bad luck, failure, or defeat.

fur·i·ous·ly (fyùr′ē əs lē), *ADVERB.* with unrestrained energy, speed, etc.

Gg

gash (gash), *NOUN.* a long, deep cut or wound.

gen·e·ra·tion (jen′ə rā′shən), **1.** *NOUN.* all people born about the same time. Your parents and their siblings and cousins belong to one generation; you and your siblings and cousins belong to the next generation. **2.** *NOUN.* about thirty years, or the time from the birth of one generation to the birth of the next generation. There are three generations in a century. ❑ *PLURAL* **gen·e·ra·tions.**

gen·ius (jē′nyəs), *NOUN.* person having very great natural power of mind: *Shakespeare was a genius.*

gla·cier (glā′shər), *NOUN.* a great mass of ice moving very slowly down a mountain, along a valley, or over a land area. Glaciers are formed from snow on high ground wherever winter snowfall exceeds summer melting for many years.

gleam (glēm), *VERB.* to flash or beam with light: *The car's headlights gleamed through the rain.* ❑ *VERB* **gleamed, gleam·ing.**

glid·er (glī′dər), *NOUN.* aircraft without an engine. Rising air currents keep it up in the air.

glider

glimpse (glimps), **1.** *NOUN.* a short, quick view or look: *I caught a glimpse of the falls as our train went by.* **2.** *NOUN.* a short, faint appearance: *There was a glimpse of truth in what they said.* ❑ *PLURAL* **glimp·ses.**

glint (glint), *NOUN.* a gleam; flash: *The glint in her eye showed that she was angry.*

glo·ri·ous (glôr′ē əs), *ADJECTIVE.* magnificent; splendid: *a glorious day.* (*Glorious* comes from the Latin word *gloria* meaning "praise.")

grand (grand), *ADJECTIVE.* excellent; very good: *We had a grand time at the party last night.*

gran·ite (gran′it), *ADJECTIVE.* made from a very hard gray or pink rock that is formed when lava cools slowly underground: *a granite countertop.*

griz·zly (griz′lē), **1.** *ADJECTIVE.* grayish; gray. **2.** *NOUN.* grizzly bear; a large, gray or brownish gray bear of western North America.

a in hat	ō in open	sh in she
ā in age	ȯ in all	th in thin
â in care	ô in order	ᴛʜ in then
ä in far	oi in oil	zh in measure
e in let	ou in out	ə = a in about
ē in equal	u in cup	ə = e in taken
ėr in term	u̇ in put	ə = i in pencil
i in it	ü in rule	ə = o in lemon
ī in ice	ch in child	ə = u in circus
o in hot	ng in long	

Hh

hang·ar (hang′ər), *NOUN.* building for storing aircraft. ❑ *PLURAL* **hang·ars.**

hatch¹ (hach), **1.** *VERB.* to come out of an egg: *One of the chickens hatched today.* **2.** *VERB.* to keep an egg or eggs warm until the young come out: *The heat of the sun hatches turtles' eggs.*

hatch² (hach), *NOUN.* a trapdoor covering an opening in an aircraft's or ship's deck.

heave (hēv), **1.** *VERB.* to lift with force or effort: *The heavy cargo plane heaved off the runway.* **2.** *VERB.* to rise and fall alternately: *The waves heaved in the storm.* ❑ *VERB* **heaved, heav·ing.**

her·mit (hėr′mit), *NOUN.* person who goes away from others and lives alone.

hi·er·o·glyph (hī′ər ə glif), *NOUN.* picture, character, or symbol standing for a word, idea, or sound. The ancient Egyptians used hieroglyphics instead of an alphabet like ours. ❑ *PLURAL* **hi·er·o·glyphs.**

home·land (hōm′land′), *NOUN.* country that is your home; your native land.

hoop (hủp *or* hüp), *NOUN.* ring; round, flat band: *a hoop for embroidery, a basketball hoop.*

ho·ri·zon (hə rī′zn), *NOUN.* line where the Earth and sky seem to meet; skyline. You cannot see beyond the horizon.

howl·ing (hou′ling), *ADJECTIVE.* very great: *a howling success.*

hum·ble (hum′bəl), *ADJECTIVE.* not proud; modest: *to be humble in spite of success.*

hyp·no·tize (hip′nə tīz), *VERB.* to put someone into a state resembling deep sleep, but more active, in which the person acts according to the suggestions of the person who brought about the condition. ❑ *VERB* **hyp·no·tized, hyp·no·tiz·ing.**

Ii

ice·berg (īs′bėrg′), *NOUN.* a large mass of ice, detached from a glacier and floating in the sea. About 90 percent of its mass is below the surface of the water. ❑ *PLURAL* **ice·bergs.**

iceberg

im·mense (i mens′), *ADJECTIVE*. very large; huge; vast: *An ocean is an immense body of water.*

im·pact (im′pakt), *NOUN*. action of striking one thing against another; collision: *The impact of the heavy stone against the windowpane shattered the glass.*

im·pres·sive (im pres′iv), *ADJECTIVE*. able to have a strong effect on the mind or feelings; able to influence deeply.

in·con·sol·a·ble (in′kən sō′lə bəl), *ADJECTIVE*. not able to be comforted; brokenhearted: *The girl was inconsolable because her kitten was lost.*

in·fer·i·or (in fir′ē ər), *ADJECTIVE*. not very good; below most others; low in quality: *an inferior grade of coffee.*

in·jus·tice (in jus′tis), *NOUN*. lack of justice, fairness, lawfulness: *We were angry at the injustice of the new rule.*

in·land (in′lənd), *ADVERB*. in or toward the interior: *He traveled inland from New York to Chicago.*

Jj

jer·sey (jėr′zē), *NOUN*. shirt that is pulled over the head, made of soft, knitted cloth: *Members of the hockey team wear red jerseys.*

Ll

la·goon (lə gün′), *NOUN*. pond or small lake, especially one connected with a larger body of water.

land·lord (land′lôrd′), *NOUN*. person who owns buildings or land that is rented to others.

las·so (la sü′), *VERB*. to catch with a long rope with a loop on one end. ❑ *VERB* **las·soed, las·so·ing.**

lei·sure·ly (lē′zhər lē), *ADVERB*. without hurry; taking plenty of time: *He walked leisurely across the bridge.*

link (lingk), *NOUN*. anything that joins or connects, as a loop of a chain does: *a link between his love of art and his career.*

liz·ard (liz′ərd), *NOUN*. any of many reptiles with long bodies and tails, movable eyelids, and usually four legs. Some lizards have no legs and look much like snakes. Iguanas, chameleons, and horned toads are lizards. ❑ *PLURAL* **liz·ards.**

a in hat	ō in open	sh in she
ā in age	ȯ in all	th in thin
â in care	ô in order	ᴛʜ in then
ä in far	oi in oil	zh in measure
e in let	ou in out	ə = a in about
ē in equal	u in cup	ə = e in taken
ėr in term	ū in put	ə = i in pencil
i in it	ü in rule	ə = o in lemon
ī in ice	ch in child	ə = u in circus
o in hot	ng in long	

long (lông), **1.** *ADJECTIVE.* measuring a great distance from end to end: *A year is a long time.* **2.** *VERB.* to wish very much; desire greatly: *long to see a good friend.* ❑ *VERB* **longed, long·ing.**

loom (lüm), *VERB.* to appear dimly or vaguely as a large, threatening shape: *A large iceberg loomed through the thick fog.* ❑ *VERB* **loomed, loom·ing.**

lull (lul), *VERB.* to soothe with sounds or caresses; cause to sleep: *The soft music lulled me to sleep.* ❑ *VERB* **lulled, lull·ing.**

lum·ber·jack (lum′bər jak′), *NOUN.* person whose work is cutting down trees and sending the logs to the sawmill; woodsman; logger.

lu·nar (lü′nər), *ADJECTIVE.* of, like, or about the moon: *a lunar landscape.*

lurk (lėrk), *VERB.* to move about in a secret and sly manner: *Several people were seen lurking near the house before it was robbed.* ❑ *VERB* **lurked, lurk·ing.**

Mm

ma·gi·cian (mə jish′ən), *NOUN.* person who entertains by art or skill of creating illusions, especially a sleight of hand: *The magician pulled not one, but three rabbits out of his hat!*

maj·es·ty (maj′ə stē), *NOUN.* title used in speaking to or of a king, queen, emperor, empress, etc.: *Your Majesty, His Majesty, Her Majesty.*

man·u·al (man′yü əl), **1.** *ADJECTIVE.* done with the hands: *Digging a trench with a shovel is manual labor.* **2.** *NOUN.* a small book that helps its readers understand and use something; handbook: *A manual came with my pocket calculator.*

mar·vel (mär′vəl), *VERB.* to be filled with wonder; be astonished: *She marveled at the beautiful sunset.* ❑ *VERB* **mar·veled, mar·vel·ing.**

mas·sive (mas′iv), *ADJECTIVE.* big and heavy; bulky: *a massive boulder.*

me·chan·i·cal (mə kan′ə kəl), *ADJECTIVE.* like a machine; automatic; without expression: *The performance was very mechanical.*

me·mo·ri·al (mə môr′ē əl), *ADJECTIVE.* helping people to remember some person, thing, or event: *memorial services.*

memorial

me·squite (me skēt′), *ADJECTIVE*. any of several trees or bushes common in the southwestern United States and Mexico, which often grow in dense clumps or thickets. Mesquite pods furnish a valuable food for cattle. The wood is used in grilling food.

mi·grate (mī′grāt), *VERB*. to go from one region to another with the change in the seasons: *Most birds migrate to warmer countries in the winter.* ❑ *VERB* **mi·grat·ed, mi·grat·ing.**

migrate

min·i·a·ture (min′ē ə chùr *or* min′ə chər), *NOUN*. anything represented on a small scale: *In the museum, there is a miniature of the famous ship.* ❑ *PLURAL* **min·i·a·tures.**

min·is·ter (min′ə stər), *NOUN*. member of the clergy; spiritual guide; pastor.

mir·a·cle (mir′ə kəl), *NOUN*. a wonderful happening that is contrary to, or independent of, the known laws of nature: *His family considered his complete recovery from the accident to be a miracle.*

mod·ule (moj′ül), *NOUN*. a self-contained unit or system within a larger system, often designed for a particular function: *The lunar module circled the moon.*

mon·u·ment (mon′yə mənt), *NOUN*. something set up to honor a person or an event. A monument may be a building, pillar, arch, statue, tomb, or stone.

monument

mu·tu·al (myü′chü əl), *ADJECTIVE*. done, said, felt, etc., by each toward the other; both given and received: *They had mutual affection for each other.*

a in hat	ō in open	sh in she
ā in age	ò in all	th in thin
â in care	ô in order	ŦH in then
ä in far	oi in oil	zh in measure
e in let	ou in out	ə = a in about
ē in equal	u in cup	ə = e in taken
ėr in term	ù in put	ə = i in pencil
i in it	ü in rule	ə = o in lemon
ī in ice	ch in child	ə = u in circus
o in hot	ng in long	

Nn

nat·ur·al·ist (nach′ər ə list), *NOUN.* person who makes a study of living things.

nau·ti·cal (nȯ′tə kəl), *ADJECTIVE.* of or about ships, sailors, or navigation.

nav·i·ga·tion (nav′ə gā′shən), *NOUN.* skill or process of finding a ship's or aircraft's position and course.

no·ble (nō′bəl), *ADJECTIVE.* high and great by birth, rank, or title; showing greatness of mind; good: *a noble person.*

nour·ish·ing (nėr′ish ing), **1.** *ADJECTIVE.* keeping well-fed and healthy; producing health and growth: *a nourishing diet.* **2.** *ADJECTIVE.* supporting, encouraging.

nu·mer·ous (nü′mər əs), *ADJECTIVE.* very many: *The child asked numerous questions.*

Oo

oath (ōth), *NOUN.* a solemn promise: *The oath bound him to secrecy.*

of·fend (ə fend′), *VERB.* to hurt the feelings of someone; make angry; displease; pain: *My friend was offended by my laughter.* ❏ *VERB* **of·fend·ed, of·fend·ing.**

out·spo·ken (out′spō′kən), *ADJECTIVE.* not reserved; frank: *an outspoken person.*

Pp

pal·ette (pal′it), **1.** *NOUN.* a thin board, usually oval or oblong, with a thumb hole at one end, used by painters to lay and mix colors on. **2.** *NOUN.* set of colors used by a painter. ❏ *PLURAL* **pal·ettes.**

pan·to·mime (pan′tə mīm), *VERB.* to express by gestures: *They pantomimed being hungry by pointing to their mouths and their stomachs.* ❏ *VERB* **pan·to·mimed, pan·to·mim·ing.**

pantomime

par·lor (pär′lər), **1.** *NOUN.* formerly, a room for receiving or entertaining guests; sitting room. **2.** *NOUN.* room or set of rooms used for various business purposes; shop: *a beauty parlor, an ice cream parlor.*

pay·roll (pā′rōl′), *NOUN.* list of persons to be paid and the amount that each one is to receive.

peas·ant (pez′nt), *NOUN.* farmer of the working class in Europe, Asia, and Latin America.

pe·cul·iar (pi kyü′lyər), *ADJECTIVE.* strange; odd; unusual: *It was peculiar that the fish market had no fish last Friday.*

plush (plush), *ADJECTIVE.* luxurious; expensive; stylish: *a plush office.*

pol·i·tics (pol′ə tiks), *NOUN SINGULAR OR PLURAL.* the work of government; management of public business: *Our senior senator has been engaged in politics for many years.*

pol·len (pol′ən), *NOUN.* a fine, yellowish powder released from the anthers of flowers. Grains of pollen carried by insects, wind, etc., to the pistils of flowers fertilize the flowers.

pol·li·nate (pol′ə nāt), *VERB.* to carry pollen from anthers to pistils; bring pollen to. Flowers are pollinated by bees, bats, birds, wind, etc. ❑ *VERB* **pol·li·nat·ed, pol·li·nat·ing.**

por·ridge (pôr′ij), *NOUN.* food made of oatmeal or other grain boiled in water or milk until it thickens.

pos·i·tive (poz′ə tiv), *ADJECTIVE.* permitting no question; without doubt; sure: *We have positive evidence that the Earth moves around the sun.*

po·ten·tial (pə ten′shəl), *NOUN.* something possible: *a potential for danger.*

prair·ie (prâr′ē), **1.** *NOUN.* a large area of level or rolling land with grass but few or no trees, especially such an area making up much of central North America. **2.** *NOUN.* (regional) a wide, open space.

pre·serve (pri zėrv′), *VERB.* to keep from harm or change; keep safe; protect: *Good nutrition helps preserve your health.* ❑ *VERB* **pre·served, pre·serv·ing.**

preserve— fly preserved in amber

pride·ful (prīd′ fəl), *ADJECTIVE.* haughty; having too high an opinion of oneself.

a	in hat	ō	in open	sh	in she
ā	in age	ȯ	in all	th	in thin
â	in care	ô	in order	₮н	in then
ä	in far	oi	in oil	zh	in measure
e	in let	ou	in out	ə	= a in about
ē	in equal	u	in cup	ə	= e in taken
ėr	in term	ů	in put	ə	= i in pencil
i	in it	ü	in rule	ə	= o in lemon
ī	in ice	ch	in child	ə	= u in circus
o	in hot	ng	in long		

pri·or·i·ty (prī ôr′ə tē), *NOUN.* something given attention before anything else: *The young couple's first priority was to find a pleasant house.*

pro·mote (prə mōt′), *VERB.* to raise in rank, condition, or importance: *Pupils who pass the test will be promoted to the next higher grade.* ❏ *VERB* **pro·mot·ed, pro·mot·ing.**

pul·pit (púl′pit), *NOUN.* platform or raised structure in a church from which the minister preaches.

pulse (puls), **1.** *NOUN.* the regular beating of the arteries caused by the rush of blood into them after each contraction of the heart. By feeling a person's pulse in the artery of the wrist, you can count the number of times the heart beats each minute. **2.** *NOUN.* any regular, measured beat: *the pulse in music.* ❏ *PLURAL* **pul·ses.**

Qq

quaint (kwānt), *ADJECTIVE.* strange or odd in an interesting, pleasing, or amusing way: *Many old photographs seem quaint to us today.*

quar·an·tine (kwôr′ən tēn′ *or* kwär′ən tēn′), *NOUN.* detention, isolation, and other measures taken to prevent the spread of an infectious disease.

quiv·er (kwiv′ər), *VERB.* to shake; shiver; tremble: *The dog quivered with excitement.* ❏ *VERB* **quiv·ered, quiv·er·ing.**

Rr

re·call (ri kȯl′), *VERB.* to call back to mind; remember: *I can recall stories told to me when I was a small child.* ❏ *VERB* **re·called, re·call·ing.**

re·cruit·er (ri krüt′ər), *NOUN.* a person who gets new members, who gets people to join or come: *The college recruiter attended our football game to watch our quarterback.*

ref·er·ence (ref′ər əns), *ADJECTIVE.* used for information or help: *The reference librarian can find the article that you need.*

reign (rān), **1.** *VERB.* to rule: *A king reigns over his kingdom.* **2.** *VERB.* to exist everywhere; prevail: *On a still night, silence reigns.* ❏ *VERB* **reigned, reign·ing.**

re·mote (ri mōt′), *ADJECTIVE.* out of the way; secluded.

rep·tile (rep′tīl), *NOUN.* any of many cold-blooded animals with backbones and lungs, usually covered with horny plates or scales. Snakes, lizards, turtles, alligators, and crocodiles are reptiles. Dinosaurs were reptiles. ❏ *PLURAL* **rep·tiles.**

re·seat (rē sēt′), *VERB.* to sit again. ❏ *VERB* **re·seat·ed, re·seat·ing.**

re·sem·blance (ri zem′bləns), *NOUN.* similar appearance; likeness: *Twins often show great resemblance.*

res·er·va·tion (rez′ər vā′shən), **1.** *NOUN.* arrangement to have a room, a seat, etc., held in advance for your use later on: *make a reservation for a room in a hotel.* **2.** *NOUN.* land set aside by the government for a special purpose: *an Indian reservation.*

res·er·voir (rez′ər vwär), *NOUN.* place where water is collected and stored for use: *This reservoir supplies the entire city.*

re·sist·ance (ri zis′təns), *NOUN.* thing or act that resists; opposing force; opposition: *Air resistance makes a feather fall more slowly than a pin.*

re·spon·si·bil·i·ty (ri spon′sə bil′ə tē), *NOUN.* the act or fact of taking care of someone or something; obligation: *We agreed to share responsibility for planning the party.*

rift (rift), *NOUN.* a split; break; crack: *The sun shone through a rift in the clouds.*

rille (ril), *NOUN.* a long, narrow valley on the surface of the moon.

rim (rim), *NOUN.* an edge, border, or margin on or around anything: *the rim of a wheel, the rim of a glass.*

riv·er·bed (riv′ər bed′), *NOUN.* channel in which a river flows or used to flow.

round·up (round′up′), *NOUN.* act of driving or bringing cattle together from long distances.

rud·der (rud′ər), *NOUN.* a flat piece of wood or metal hinged vertically to the rear end of an aircraft and used to steer it.

rug·ged (rug′id), *ADJECTIVE.* covered with rough edges; rough and uneven: *rugged ground.*

rugged

ruin (rü′ən), *NOUN.* often ruins, *PL.* what is left after a building, wall, etc., has fallen to pieces: *the ruins of an ancient city.* (*Ruin* comes from the Latin word *ruina* meaning "a collapse.")

a in hat	ō in open	sh in she
ā in age	ȯ in all	th in thin
â in care	ô in order	ᴛʜ in then
ä in far	oi in oil	zh in measure
e in let	ou in out	ə = a in about
ē in equal	u in cup	ə = e in taken
ėr in term	ú in put	ə = i in pencil
i in it	ü in rule	ə = o in lemon
ī in ice	ch in child	ə = u in circus
o in hot	ng in long	

rum·ble (rum′bəl), *VERB.* to make a deep, heavy, continuous sound: *Thunder was rumbling in the distance.* ❏ *VERB* **rum·bled, rum·bling.**

runt (runt), *NOUN.* animal, person, or plant that is smaller than the usual size. If used about a person, *runt* is sometimes considered offensive.

Ss

sal·a·man·der (sal′ə man′dər), *NOUN.* any of numerous animals shaped like lizards, but related to frogs and toads. Salamanders have moist, smooth skin and live in water or in damp places. ❏ *PLURAL* **sal·a·man·ders.**

sas·sy (sas′ē), *ADJECTIVE.* lively; spirited: *a sassy attitude.*

scan (skan), *VERB.* to glance at; look over hastily. ❏ *VERB* **scanned, scan·ning.**

scent (sent), *NOUN.* a smell: *The scent of roses filled the air.*

schol·ar (skol′ər), *NOUN.* a learned person; person having much knowledge: *The professor was a famous scholar.* ❏ *PLURAL* **schol·ars.** (*Scholar* comes from the Greek word *schol* meaning "discussion.")

sculp·ture (skulp′chər), **1.** *NOUN.* the art of making figures by carving, modeling, casting, etc. Sculpture includes the cutting of statues from blocks of marble, stone, or wood, casting in bronze, and modeling in clay or wax. **2.** *NOUN.* sculptured work; piece of such work. ❏ *PLURAL* **sculp·tures.**

sculpture (def. 2)

sea·coast (sē′kōst′), *NOUN.* land along the ocean or sea; seaboard: *the seacoast of Maine.*

seek·er (sēk′ər), *NOUN.* one who tries to find; one who searches: *That judge is a seeker of truth.*

se·lect (si lekt′), *VERB.* to pick out; choose: *Select the book you want.* ❏ *VERB* **se·lect·ed, se·lect·ing.**

shat·ter (shat′ər), *VERB.* to break into pieces suddenly: *A stone shattered the window.* ❏ *VERB* **shat·tered, shat·ter·ing.**

shield (shēld), *VERB.* to protect; defend: *They shielded me from unjust punishment.* ❏ *VERB* **shield·ed, shield·ing.**

shim·mer (shim′ər), *VERB.* to gleam or shine faintly: *Both the sea and the sand shimmered in the moonlight.* ❏ *VERB* **shim·mered, shim·mer·ing.** ❏ *ADJECTIVE* **shim·mer·ing.**

shriek (shrēk), *VERB.* to make a loud, sharp, shrill sound. People sometimes shriek because of terror, anger, pain, or amusement. ❏ *VERB* **shrieked, shriek·ing.**

sil·hou·ette (sil′ü et′), *NOUN.* a dark image outlined against a lighter background: *Silhouettes of skyscrapers could be seen against the moonlit sky.*

silhouette

slith·er (sliҭн′ər), *VERB.* to go with a sliding motion: *The snake slithered into the weeds.* ❏ *VERB* **slith·ered, slith·er·ing.**

slope (slōp), *NOUN.* any line, surface, land, etc., that goes up or down at an angle: *If you roll a ball up a slope, it will roll down again.* ❏ *PLURAL* **slopes.**

so·ci·e·ty (sə sī′ə tē), **1.** *NOUN.* the people of any particular time or place: *twentieth-century society, American society.* **2.** *NOUN.* company; companionship: *I enjoy their society.*

sol·emn·ly (sol′əm lē), *ADVERB.* seriously; earnestly; with dignity.

so·lo (sō′lō), **1.** *ADJECTIVE.* without a partner, teacher, etc.; alone: *The flying student made her first solo flight.* **2.** *ADVERB.* on one's own, alone: *to fly solo.*

spe·cies (spē′shēz), *NOUN.* a set of related living things that all have certain characteristics. Spearmint is a species of mint.

spec·i·men (spes′ə mən), *NOUN.* one of a group or class taken to show what the others are like; sample: *He collects specimens of all kinds of rocks and minerals.*

speech·less (spēch′lis), *ADJECTIVE.* not able to talk: *He was speechless with wonder.*

a in hat	ō in open	sh in she
ā in age	ȯ in all	th in thin
â in care	ô in order	ҭн in then
ä in far	oi in oil	zh in measure
e in let	ou in out	ə = a in about
ē in equal	u in cup	ə = e in taken
ėr in term	u̇ in put	ə = i in pencil
i in it	ü in rule	ə = o in lemon
ī in ice	ch in child	ə = u in circus
o in hot	ng in long	

spell·bound (spel′bound′), *ADJECTIVE.* too interested to move; fascinated: *The children were spellbound by the circus performance.*

sphere (sfir), *NOUN.* ball or globe. The sun, moon, Earth, and stars are spheres.

splen·dor (splen′dər), *NOUN.* magnificent show; glory.

spur (spėr), *NOUN.* a metal point or pointed wheel, worn on a rider's boot heel for urging a horse on. ❑ *PLURAL* **spurs.**

stag·ger (stag′ər), *VERB.* to become unsteady; waver: *The troops staggered because of their exhaustion.* ❑ *VERB* **stag·gered, stag·ger·ing.**

stall (stȯl), *VERB.* to stop or bring to a standstill, usually against your wish: *The engine stalled.* ❑ *VERB* **stalled, stall·ing.**

steam·ship (stēm′ship′), *NOUN.* ship moved by engines that work by the action of steam under pressure.

stern¹ (stėrn), *ADJECTIVE.* harshly firm; hard; strict: *a stern parent.*

stern² (stėrn), *NOUN.* the rear part of a ship or boat.

still (stil), **1.** *ADJECTIVE.* staying in the same position or at rest; without motion; motionless: *to stand or lie still. The lake is still today.* **2.** *VERB.* to make or become calm or quiet: *The father stilled the crying baby.* ❑ *VERB* **stilled, stil·ling.**

stump (stump), *VERB.* to puzzle: *The riddle stumped me.* ❑ *VERB* **stumped, stump·ing.**

sub·merge (səb mėrj′), *VERB.* to put under water; cover with water: *A big wave momentarily submerged us.* ❑ *VERB* **sub·merged, sub·merg·ing.**

sum·mon (sum′ən), *VERB.* to stir to action; rouse: *We were summoning our courage before entering the deserted house.* ❑ *VERB* **sum·moned, sum·mon·ing.**

sur·face (sėr′fis), **1.** *NOUN.* the top of the ground or soil, or of a body of water or other liquid: *The stone sank beneath the surface of the water.* **2.** *NOUN.* the outward appearance: *He seems rough, but you will find him very kind below the surface.* **3.** *VERB.* to rise to the surface: *The submarine surfaced.*

surge (sėrj), *NOUN.* a swelling motion; sweep or rush, especially of waves: *Our boat was upset by a surge.*

sus·pi·cious·ly (sə spish′əs lē), *ADVERB.* without trust; doubtfully.

swat (swät), *VERB.* to hit sharply or violently: *swat a fly.* ❑ *VERB* **swat·ted, swat·ting.**

Tt

taunt (tȯnt), *VERB.* to jeer at; mock; reproach: *My classmates taunted me for being the teacher's pet.* ❑ *VERB* **taunt·ed, taunt·ing.**

teem (tēm), *VERB.* to be full of; abound; swarm: *The swamp teemed with mosquitoes.* ❏ *VERB* **teemed, teem·ing.**

tem·ple (tem′pəl), *NOUN.* building used for the service or worship of God or gods. ❏ *PLURAL* **tem·ples.** (*Temple* comes from the Latin word *templum* meaning "temple.")

ter·race (ter′is), *VERB.* to form into flat, level land with steep sides; terraces are often made in hilly areas to create more space for farming. ❏ *VERB* **ter·raced, ter·rac·ing.** (*Terrace* comes from the Latin word *terra* meaning "earth, land.")

terrace

ter·ror (ter′ər), *NOUN.* great fear: *The dog has a terror of thunder.*

thick·et (thik′it), *NOUN.* bushes or small trees growing close together: *We crawled into the thicket and hid.* ❏ *PLURAL* **thick·ets.**

tim·id (tim′id), *ADJECTIVE.* easily frightened; shy: *The timid child was afraid of the dark.*

tor·rent (tôr′ənt), *NOUN.* a violent, rushing stream of water: *The mountain torrent dashed over the rock.* (*Torrent* comes from the Latin word *torrentum* meaning "boiling.")

torrent

tow·er·ing (tou′ər ing), **1.** *ADJECTIVE.* very high: *a towering mountain peak.* **2.** *ADJECTIVE.* very great: *Developing a polio vaccine was a towering achievement.*

a in hat	ō in open	sh in she
ā in age	ȯ in all	th in thin
â in care	ô in order	ŦH in then
ä in far	oi in oil	zh in measure
e in let	ou in out	ə = a in about
ē in equal	u in cup	ə = e in taken
èr in term	u̇ in put	ə = i in pencil
i in it	ü in rule	ə = o in lemon
ī in ice	ch in child	ə = u in circus
o in hot	ng in long	

trans·late (tran slāt′ or tranz lāt′), *VERB.* to change from one language into another: *translate a book from French into English.* ❏ *VERB* **trans·lat·ed, trans·lat·ing.** (*Translate* comes from the Latin word *trans*, which means "across, through, or behind.")

trans·mis·sion (tran smish′ən or tranz mish′ən), *NOUN.* passage of electromagnetic waves from a transmitter to a receiver: *When transmission is good, even foreign radio stations can be heard.*

treas·ur·y (trezh′ər ē), *NOUN.* money owned; funds: *We voted to pay for the party out of the club treasury.*

trench (trench), *NOUN.* any ditch; deep furrow: *to dig a trench for a pipe.*

tri·umph (trī′umf), *NOUN.* victory; success: *The exploration of outer space is a great triumph of modern science.*

trop·i·cal (trop′ə kəl), *ADJECTIVE.* of or like the regions 23.45 degrees north and south of the equator where the sun can shine directly overhead: *tropical heat.*

tropical

trudge (truj), *VERB.* to walk wearily or with effort. *We trudged up the hill.* ❏ *VERB* **trudged, trudg·ing.**

twang (twang), *VERB.* to make or cause to make a sharp, ringing sound: *The banjos twanged.* ❏ *VERB* **twanged, twang·ing.**

Uu

un·be·liev·a·ble (un′bi lē′və bəl), *ADJECTIVE.* incredible; hard to think of as true or real: *an unbelievable lie.*

un·cov·er (un kuv′ər), *VERB.* to make known; reveal; expose: *The reporter uncovered a scandal.* ❏ *VERB* **un·cov·ered, un·cov·er·ing.**

un·ex·plain·a·ble (un ek splān′ə bəl), *ADJECTIVE.* not able to be explained; mysterious.

Vv

vain (vān), *ADJECTIVE.* having too much pride in your looks, ability, etc.: *a good-looking but vain person.*

van·ish (van′ish), *VERB.* to disappear, especially suddenly: *The sun vanished behind a cloud.* ❏ *VERB* **van·ished, van·ish·ing.**

ve·hi·cle (vē′ə kəl), *NOUN.* device for carrying people or things, such as a car, bus, airplane, etc. Cars and trucks are motor vehicles. Rockets are space vehicles.

ven·ture (ven′chər), *VERB.* to dare to come or go: *We ventured out on the thin ice and almost fell through.* ❑ *VERB* **ven·tured, ven·tur·ing.**

Ww

wharf (wôrf), *NOUN.* platform built on the shore or out from the shore, beside which ships can load and unload. ❑ *PLURAL* **wharves.**

wil·der·ness (wil′dər nis), *NOUN.* a wild, uncultivated region with few or no people living in it.

wilderness

with·stand (wiŦH stand′), *VERB.* to stand against; hold out against; resist; endure: *These heavy shoes will withstand much hard wear.* ❑ *VERB* **with·stood, with·stand·ing.**

won·drous (wun′drəs), *ADJECTIVE.* wonderful; marvelous, remarkable.

wreck·age (rek′ij), *NOUN.* what is left behind after the destruction of a motor vehicle, ship, building, train, or aircraft: *The hurricane left behind much wreckage.*

Yy

yearn (yėrn), *VERB.* to feel a longing or desire; desire earnestly: *I yearned for home.* ❑ *VERB* **yearned, yearn·ing.**

a in hat	ō in open	sh in she
ā in age	ȯ in all	th in thin
â in care	ô in order	ŦH in then
ä in far	oi in oil	zh in measure
e in let	ou in out	ə = a in about
ē in equal	u in cup	ə = e in taken
ėr in term	u̇ in put	ə = i in pencil
i in it	ü in rule	ə = o in lemon
ī in ice	ch in child	ə = u in circus
o in hot	ng in long	

English/Spanish
Selection Vocabulary List

Unit 1

Because of Winn-Dixie

English	Spanish
grand	estupendo
memorial	conmemorativa
peculiar	peculiar
positive	segura
prideful	demasiado orgullosa
recalls	recuerda
selecting	seleccionando

Lewis and Clark and Me

English	Spanish
docks	puerto
migrating	emigrando
scan	escudriñar
scent	aroma
wharf	embarcadero
yearned	anhelaba

Grandfather's Journey

English	Spanish
amazed	maravillaban
bewildered	desconcertaban
homeland	tierra natal
longed	deseaba
sculptures	esculturas
still	calmar
towering	imponentes

The Horned Toad Prince

English	Spanish
bargain	pacto
favors	favores
lassoed	enlazó
offended	ofendida
prairie	pradera
riverbed	lecho
shrieked	chilló

Letters Home from Yosemite

English	Spanish
glacier	glaciar
impressive	impresionante
naturalist	naturalista
preserve	preservar
slopes	laderas
species	especies
wilderness	zona silvestre

Unit 2

What Jo Did

English	Spanish
fouled	hizo una falta
hoop	aro
jersey	camiseta
marveled	se maravillaban
rim	canasta
speechless	estupefactos
swatted	le dio
unbelievable	increíble

Coyote School News

English	Spanish
bawling	berreando
coyote	coyote
dudes	dandis
roundup	rodeo
spurs	espuelas

Grace and the Time Machine

English	Spanish
aboard	a bordo
atlas	atlas
awkward	incómodo
capable	capaces
chant	cantan
mechanical	mecánicas
miracle	milagro
reseats	vuelve a sentarse
vehicle	vehículo

Marven of the Great North Woods

English	Spanish
cord	pila de leña
dismay	consternación
grizzly	pardo
immense	enormes
payroll	nómina

So You Want to Be President?

English	Spanish
Constitution	Constitución
howling	rotundo
humble	humildes
politics	política
responsibility	responsabilidad
solemnly	solemnemente
vain	vano

Unit 3

The Stranger

English	Spanish
draft	corriente de aire
etched	grabadas
fascinated	fascinaba
frost	escarcha
parlor	salón
terror	terror
timid	tímido

Adelina's Whales

English	Spanish
biologist	bióloga
bluff	despeñadero
lagoon	laguna
massive	inmensas
rumbling	retumbante
tropical	tropical

How Night Came from the Sea

English	Spanish
brilliant	brillante
chorus	coro
coward	cobarde
gleamed	relucía
shimmering	centelleante

Eye of the Storm

English	Spanish
destruction	destrucción
expected	esperaba
forecasts	pronósticos
inland	tierra adentro
shatter	hace añicos
surge	oleada

The Great Kapok Tree

English	Spanish
canopy	copas (de los árboles)
dangle	colgar
dappled	salpicada
fragrant	fragante
pollen	polen
pollinate	polimizar
slithered	se deslizó
wondrous	maravilloso

Unit 4

The Houdini Box

English	Spanish
appeared	apareció
bustling	bulliciosa
crumbled	se desintegró
escape	escapar
magician	mago
monument	monumento
vanished	desapareció

Encantado: Pink Dolphin of the Amazon

English	Spanish
aquarium	acuario
dolphins	delfines
enchanted	encantado
flexible	flexibles
glimpses	vistazos fugaces
pulses	impulsos
surface	superficie

The King in the Kitchen

English	Spanish
duke	duque
dungeon	mazmorra
furiously	furiosamente
genius	genio
majesty	majestad
noble	noble
peasant	campesino
porridge	gachas de avena

Seeker of Knowledge

English	Spanish
ancient	antiguo
link	conexión
scholars	eruditos
seeker	buscador
temple	templo
translate	traducir
triumph	triunfo
uncover	descubrir

Encyclopedia Brown and the Case of the Slippery Salamander

English	Spanish
amphibians	anfibios
crime	crimen
exhibit	exposición
lizards	lagartos
reference	referencia
reptiles	reptiles
salamanders	salamandras
stumped	perplejo

Unit 5

Sailing Home: A Story of a Childhood at Sea

English	Spanish
bow	proa
cargo	carga
celestial	celestial
conducted	condujo
dignified	digno
navigation	navegación
quivered	estremeció
stern	popa

Lost City: The Discovery of Machu Picchu

English	Spanish
curiosity	curiosidad
glorious	gloriosa
granite	granito
ruins	ruinas
terraced	en terrazas
thickets	matorrales
torrent	torrente

Amelia and Eleanor Go for a Ride

English	Spanish
aviator	aviadora
brisk	fresco
cockpit	cabina
daring	valiente
elegant	elegante
outspoken	franca
solo	sola

Antarctic Journal

English	Spanish
anticipation	anticipación
continent	continente
convergence	convergencia
depart	salir
forbidding	inhóspita
heaves	sube
icebergs	icebergs

Moonwalk

English	Spanish
loomed	surgía
rille	valle lunar
runt	pequeño
staggered	se tambaleó
summoning	armándose
taunted	burló
trench	zanja
trudged	caminaron fatigosamente

Unit 6

My Brother Martin

English	Spanish
ancestors	ancestros
avoided	evitaba
generations	generaciones
minister	ministro
numerous	numerosos
pulpit	púlpito
shielding	protegiéndonos

Jim Thorpe's Bright Path

English	Spanish
boarding school	internado
dormitory	dormitorio
endurance	resistencia
manual	manual
reservation	reserva
society	sociedad

How Tía Lola Came to ~~Visit~~ Stay

English	Spanish
affords	ofrece
colonel	coronel
glint	destello
lurking	acechando
palettes	paletas
quaint	pintoresco
resemblance	semejanza

To Fly: The Story of the Wright Brothers

English	Spanish
cradle	soporte
drag	arrastrar
flex	doblar
glider	planeador
hangars	hangars
rudder	timón
stalled	entró en pérdida

The Man Who Went to the Far Side of the Moon

English	Spanish
astronauts	astronautas
capsule	cápsula
hatch	escotilla
horizon	horizonte
lunar	lunar
module	módulo
quarantine	cuarentena

Acknowledgments

Text

22: *Because of Winn-Dixie.* Copyright © 2000 by Kate DiCamillo; Cover Illustration Copyright © 2000 by Chris Sheban. Reprinted by permission of Candlewick Press, Inc., Cambridge, MA; **36:** "Fast Facts: Black Bears" by Kathy Kranking as appeared in *Ranger Rick,* August 1995. © Kathy Kranking. Reprinted with permission of the author; **44:** Text excerpt and selected illustrations from *Lewis and Clark and Me, A Dog's Tale* by Laurie Myers, illustrated by Michael Dooling. Text © 2002 by Laurie Myers, illustrations © 2002 by Michael Dooling. Reprinted by permission of Henry Holt and Company, LLC; **70:** From *Grandfather's Journey* by Allen Say. Copyright © 1993 by Allen Say. Reprinted by permission of Houghton Mifflin Company. All rights reserved; **92:** From *The Horned Toad Prince* by Jackie Mims Hopkins. Illustrated by Michael Austin. Text © 2000 by Jackie Mims Hopkins. Illustrations © 2000 by Michael Austin. Reprinted by permission of Peachtree Publishers; **108:** "Horned Lizards and Harvesting Ants," from *Journey into the Desert* by John Brown, copyright © 2002 by John Brown. Reprinted by permission of Oxford University Press, Inc.; **116:** From *Letters Home from Yosemite* by Lisa Halvorsen, Blackbirch Press. © 2000, Blackbirch Press. Reprinted by permission of The Gale Group; **130:** "This Land Is Your Land." Words and Music by Woody Guthrie. TRO - Copyright 1956 (Renewed), 1958 (Renewed), 1970 (Renewed), 1972 (Renewed), Ludlow Music, Inc., New York, NY. Used by permission; **134:** "We're All in the Telephone Book" from *The Collected Poems of Langston Hughes* by Langston Hughes, Alfred A. Knopf, 1994; **135:** "Speak Up" from *Good Luck Gold And Other Poems* by Janet S. Wong. Copyright © 1994 by Janet S. Wong. Reprinted with permission of Margaret K. McElderry Books, an imprint of Simon & Schuster Children's Publishing Division. All rights reserved; **136:** "City I Love" by Lee Bennett Hopkins from *Home to Me: Poems Across America* by Lee Bennett Hopkins, Orchard Books, 2002; **137:** "Midwest Town" by Ruth De Long Peterson, The Saturday Evening Post Society, *Saturday Evening Post,* Nov. 13, 1954; **146:** "What Jo Did," from *Tall Tales: Six Amazing Basketball Dreams* by Charles R. Smith Jr., copyright © 2000 by Charles R. Smith Jr. Used by permission of Dutton Children's Books, A Division of Penguin Young Readers Group, A Member of The Penguin Group (USA) Inc., 345 Hudson Street, New York, NY 10014. All rights reserved; **158:** "Fast Break," from *Rimshots: Basketball Pix, Rolls and Rhythms* by Charles R. Smith Jr., copyright © 1999 by Charles R. Smith Jr. Used by permission of Dutton Children's Books, A Division of Penguin Young Readers Group, A Member of Penguin Group (USA) Inc., 345 Hudson Street, New York, NY 10014. All rights reserved; **160:** "Allow Me to Introduce Myself," from *Short Takes: Fast Break Basketball Poetry* by Charles R. Smith Jr., copyright © 2001 by Charles R. Smith Jr. Used by permission of Dutton Children's Books, A Division of Penguin Young Readers Group, A Member of Penguin Group (USA) Inc., 345 Hudson Street, New York, NY 10014. All rights reserved; **166:** Text and illustrations from *Coyote School News* by Joan Sandin. Copyright © 2003 by Joan Sandin. Reprinted by permission of Henry Holt and Company, LLC; **192:** Adaptation of "Grace and the Time Machine" from *Starring Grace* by Mary Hoffman, Phyllis Fogelman Books, 2000; **210:** "What's There to Do?"

formerly titled "Help an Elderly Neighbor with Yard Work" and "Put on an Outdoor Arts-and-Crafts Show" from *101 Outdoor Adventures* by Samantha Beres, copyright © 2002 by Dutton Children's Books. Used by permission of Dutton Children's Books, A Division of Penguin Young Readers Group, A Member of Penguin Group (USA) Inc., 345 Hudson Street, New York, NY 10014. All rights reserved; **216:** From *Marven of the Great North Woods* by Kathryn Lasky Knight, illustrated by Kevin Hawkes. Text copyright © 1997 by Kathryn Lasky Knight. Illustrations copyright © 1997 by Kevin Hawkes. Reprinted by permission of Harcourt, Inc.; **239:** Adaptation of "Cook Shanty & Bunkhouse" from the Paul Bunyan Logging Camp Web site, paulbunyancamp.org. Reprinted by permission of the Paul Bunyan Logging Camp Museum, Eau Claire, WI; **244:** From *So You Want to Be President?* by Judith St. George, illustrations by David Small, copyright © 2000 by Judith St. George, text, copyright © 2000 by David Small, illustrations. Used by permission of Philomel Books, A Division of Penguin Young Readers Group, A Member of Penguin Group (USA) Inc., 345 Hudson Street, New York, NY 10014. All rights reserved; **260:** "His Hands" by Nikki Grimes from *My Man Blue* by Nikki Grimes, Dial Books for Young Readers, 1999; **261:** "Homework" by Russell Hoban from *Egg Thoughts and Other Frances Songs.* Copyright © 1964 by Russell Hoban. Reprinted by permission of David Higham Associates Ltd.; **262:** "Lem Lonnigan's Leaf Machine" by Andrea Perry from *Here's What You Do When You Can't Find Your Shoe* by Andrea Perry, Atheneum Books for Young Readers, 2003; **272:** From *The Stranger* by Chris Van Allsburg. Copyright © 1986 by Chris Van Allsburg. Reprinted by permission of Houghton Mifflin Company. All rights reserved; **296:** From *Adelina's Whales* by Richard Sobol, copyright © 2003 by Richard Sobol. Used by permission of Dutton Children's Books, A Division of Penguin Young Readers Group, A Member of Penguin Group (USA) Inc., 345 Hudson Street, New York, NY 10014. All rights reserved; **318:** *How Night Came from the Sea* retold by Mary-Joan Gerson, illustrations by Carla Golembe. Text copyright © 1994 by Mary-Joan Gerson. Illustrations copyright © 1994 by Carla Golembe. Reprinted by permission of Goodman Associates Literary Agents as authorized agent for Mary-Joan Gerson and Carla Golembe; **334:** "The Ant and the Bear" from *Spirit of the Cedar People: More Stories and Paintings of Chief Lelooska* edited by Christine Normandin, A DK Ink Book, 1998; **342:** From *Eye of the Storm* by Stephen Kramer, photographs by Warren Faidley, copyright © 1997 by Stephen Kramer, text. Used by permission of G. P. Putnam's Sons, A Division of Penguin Young Readers Group, A Member of Penguin Group (USA) Inc., 345 Hudson Street, New York, NY 10014. All rights reserved; **364:** From *The Great Kapok Tree: A Tale of the Amazon Rain Forest,* copyright © 1990 by Lynne Cherry, reprinted by permission of Harcourt, Inc.; **380:** From *Living in a World of Green* by Tanya Lee Stone. Copyright © 2001 Blackbirch Press, Inc. Used by permission of Thomson Learning; **384:** "Autumn" by Charlotte Zolotow from *River Winding* by Charlotte Zolotow, HarperCollins Publishers, 1970; **385:** "Winter Solstice" by Marilyn Singer from *Footprints on the Roof: Poems About the Earth* by Marilyn Singer, Alfred A. Knopf, Inc., 2002; **386:** "Early Spring" from *Navajo: Visions and Voices Across the Mesa* by Shonto Begay. Copyright © 1995 by Shonto Begay.

Dallas Poems by Myra Cohn Livingston. Copyright © 1980 by Myra Cohn Livingston. Used by permission of Marian Reiner; **763:** "Martin Luther King Day" from *The Kite That Braved Old Orchard Beach* by X. J. Kennedy, Margaret K. McElderry Books, 1991; **764:** "Fall Football" by Gary Soto from *Fearless Fernie: Hanging out with Fernie and Me* by Gary Soto, G. P. Putnam's Sons, 2002; **765:** "First Men on the Moon" by J. Patrick Lewis. © J. Patrick Lewis, 1998. Reprinted by permission of the author.

Illustrations

Cover: Tim Jessell; **21:** Barry Gott; **22–33, 216–231:** © Kevin Hawkes; **37, 120, 259, 298, 312, 558, 612–623:** Peter Bollinger; **44–57:** Michael Dooling; **58–59:** © Dave Stevenson; **70–81:** Allen Say; **89–91:** Laura Ovresat; **92–105, 107:** Michael Austin; **130–133:** Robert Crawford; **134–137:** Patrick Corrigan; **166–183:** Joan Sandin; **186–187:** Sachiko Yoshikawa; **192–207, 208–209:** Matt Faulkner; **210–211:** Stephen Kroninger; **214–215:** © Erika Le Barre; **260–263:** Lee White; **272–285:** Chris Van Allsburg; **318–331:** Carla Golembe; **334–337:** Chief LeLooska; **360–361:** Richard Downs; **364–377:** Lynne Cherry; **396–409, 564–575:** Brian Selznick; **412–415:** Vitali Konstantinov; **441–443:** Christine Benjamin; **462–463:** Matthew Trueman; **464–465:** Amy Vangsgard; **470–481:** James Rumford; **492–500, 501–503:** © Brett Helquist; **508–511, 609:** © Joel Nakamura; **517:** © Dan Andreasen; **520–531:** Ted Rand; **542–553:** Ted Lewin; **586–601:** Jennifer Owings Dewey; **642–654:** Chris Soentpiet; **658–659:** Stephen Daigle; **662–663:** Gwen Connelly; **664–677:** S. D. Nelson; **690–705:** Macky Pamintuan; **708–711:** SuLing Wang; **742–756:** Bea Uusma Schyffert; **762–765:** Rafael Lopez

Photographs

Every effort has been made to secure permission and provide appropriate credit for photographic material. The publisher deeply regrets any omission and pledges to correct errors called to its attention in subsequent editions.

Unless otherwise acknowledged, all photographs are the property of Scott Foresman, a division of Pearson Education.

Photo locators denoted as follows: Top (T), Center (C), Bottom (B), Left (L), Right (R), Background (Bkgd).

16: © Laurance B Aiuppy/Getty Images; **37:** © Norbert Rosing/NGS Image Collection; **39:** © Joe McDonald; **41:** © Royalty-Free/Corbis; **42:** Getty Images; **43:** Bettmann/ Corbis; **58:** Getty Images; **60:** Getty Images; **69:** Joseph Sohm/Corbis; **84:** © Michael Haynes, Photo/Mira; **86:** (R) © Michael Haynes, (L) © The Newark Museum/Art Resource, NY; **87:** © Andreas Von Einsiedel/DK Images; **113:** Getty Images; **114:** © Royalty-Free/Corbis; **115:** (TL) © Royalty-Free/Corbis, (TR) Corbis; **116:** Getty Images; **118:** Getty Images; **119:** Corel; **120:** Corel; **121:** (C) Digital Vision, (CR) Corel; **123:** (CR) © Royalty-Free/Corbis, (BR) Corel; **125:** Getty Images; **126:** © Royalty-Free/Corbis; **127:** Corel; **138:** © Laurance B Aiuppy/Getty Images; **139:** Getty Images; **140:** © Paul King/ Getty Images; **143:** Getty Images; **145:** © Royalty-Free/ Corbis; **164:** Getty Images; **217:** © ThinkStock/SuperStock;

258: Getty Images; **259:** (C)Corbis, (BC, CL) Getty Images, (TR) © David Muench/Corbis, (TL) © Royalty-Free/Corbis; **264:** © Paul King/Getty Images; **266:** © Stewart Cohen/Getty Images; **267:** Getty Images; **269:** Getty Images; **271:** Getty Images; **292:** © Royalty-Free/Corbis; **294:** © ThinkStock/ SuperStock; **295:** Chase Swift/Corbis, (T) Brand X Pictures; **314:** © Natalie Fobes/Corbis; **315:** (CR) © Flip Nicklin/ Minden Pictures, (BL) © Gunter Marx Photography/Corbis, (BC) AlaskaStock, (T) Getty Images; **316:** (TR) © Royalty-Free/Corbis, (CR) © Natalie Fobes/Corbis; **317:** (TR) © Joel W. Rogers/Corbis, (C) © Jeffrey L. Rotman/Corbis; **337:** Getty Images; **342:** (B) Getty Images, (BC) Warren Faidley/ Weatherstock; **343:** Getty Images; **344:** Warren Faidley/ Weatherstock; **345:** Warren Faidley/Weatherstock; **347:** (TR) Warren Faidley/Weatherstock, (TL) Getty Images; **348:** Warren Faidley/Weatherstock; **349:** Getty Images; **356:** Corbis; **358:** Getty Images; **382:** (TR) Brand X Pictures, (BR) Digital Vision; **383:** Corel; **384:** © Tom Brakefield/Corbis; **385:** Corel; **388:** © Stewart Cohen/Getty Images; **389:** Getty Images; **395:** Bettmann/Corbis; **396:** Comstock Production Department/© Comstock Inc.; **397:** (TR) Dave King/© DK Images, (T) © Royalty-Free/Corbis, (BR) Myrleen Ferguson/ PhotoEdit; **410:** Todd Pusser/Nature Picture Library; **412:** Wolfgang Kaehler/Corbis; **413:** Getty Images; **414:** Getty Images; **418:** Brand X Pictures; **419:** (C) Andre Baertschi, (TR) Brand X Pictures, (CL) © Royalty-Free/Corbis; **420:** (BL) Bob Krist/Corbis, (TL) © Royalty-Free/Corbis; **421:** (TR) © Royalty-Free/Corbis, (BR) Getty Images; **422** (TC), **423** (BC), **425, 426, 427, 428** (BR), **430** (B), **431, 432, 433** (T): © 2002 by Dianne Taylor-Snow; **423:** Getty Images; **424:** Dr. Morley Read/Photo Researchers, Inc.; **425:** (CC) Andy Crawford/© DK Images, (CR) Getty Images, (BR) Getty Images; **426:** William Grenfell/Visuals Unlimited; **456:** Getty Images; **459:** Getty Images; **472:** Gianni Dagli Orti/Corbis; **474:** © Royalty-Free/Corbis; **475:** Archivo Iconografico, S.A./Corbis; **484:** © Royalty-Free/Corbis; **486:** (CL) © Ralph A. Clevenger/ Corbis, (CR, CC, BC, BR, BL) Getty Images, (TC) © Lisa Henderling/Images, Inc.; **487:** (TL, TC, TCL, TCR, CR, BL) Getty Images, (CL) © Rubberball Productions; **504:** © Becky Shink/*Lansing State Journal;* **505:** © Royalty-Free/Corbis; **506:** (CL) © Becky Shink/*Lansing State Journal*, (BC) Getty Images; **507:** Getty Images; **536:** © Harry Benson; **537:** © Kevin Horan/Time Life Pictures/Getty Images; **539:** © Lowell Georgia/Corbis; **541:** Getty Images; **604:** Corbis; **605:** © Gabriella Motto; **606:** (TL) © Gabriella Motto, (BR) AP/Wide World Photos; **607:** Corbis; **626:** Getty Images; **627:** Getty Images; **628:** Getty Images; **629:** Getty Images; **648:** Getty Images; **649:** Getty Images; **678:** (TC) © Joseph Sohm; ChromoSohm Inc/Corbis, (BL) © Reuters/Corbis; **679:** © Stephane Cardinale/Corbis; **680:** (TR) © Kathleen Kliskey-Geraghty/Index Stock Imagery, (BL, B) © Jonathan Nourok/ PhotoEdit; **711:** Getty Images; **755:** Getty Images; **756:** Getty Images; **757:** Getty Images; **767:** Getty Images

Glossary

The contents of this glossary have been adapted from *Thorndike Barnhart Intermediate Dictionary.* Copyright © 1997, Pearson Education, Inc.